The RoutledgeFalmer Reader in Gender and Education

Gender is an important lens through which we can interpret the role of education in society and the ways in which it contributes to social change in late modernity. This brings together classic pieces of gender theory, as well as examples of the sophistication of contemporary gender theory and research methodologies in the field of education.

Leading international gender researchers address current debates about gender, power, identity and culture and concerns about boys' and girls' schooling. They explore gender achievement patterns, the boys' education debate, and gender relationships in the curriculum, the classroom and youth cultures.

The Reader is divided into five sections which reflect contemporary concerns about Gender and Education:

- Gender and educational theory
- Difference and power
- Identity work
- Knowledge and pedagogy
- Reflexivity and risk.

As experts in feminist and masculinity research, the editors have designed an important Reader which shows how complex, fluid masculinities and femininities are negotiated in relation to sexuality, ethnicity and new transitions to work and citizenship. The analysis of the gender dimensions of the curriculum, teaching and alternative pedagogies also provide important insights for practitioners wishing to promote gender equality.

Undergraduates, postgraduates and academics interested in gender studies and women's studies, as well as educational practitioners concerned with gender equality, will find this a stimulating and important resource.

Madeleine Arnot is Fellow of Jesus College and Professor of Sociology of Education at the University of Cambridge, UK.

Mairtin Mac an Ghaill is Professor of Sociology at the University of Birmingham, UK.

Readers in education

The RoutledgeFalmer Reader in
Gender & Education
*Edited by Madeleine Arnot and
Mairtin Mac an Ghaill*

The RoutledgeFalmer Reader in
Higher Education
Edited by Malcolm Tight

The RoutledgeFalmer Reader in
History of Education
Edited by Gary McCulloch

The RoutledgeFalmer Reader in
Inclusive Education
*Edited by Keith Topping and
Sheelagh Maloney*

The RoutledgeFalmer Reader in
Language and Literacy
Edited by Teresa Grainger

The RoutledgeFalmer Reader in
Multicultural Education
*Edited by Gloria Ladson-Billings and
David Gillborn*

The RoutledgeFalmer Reader in
Philosophy of Education
Edited by Wilfred Carr

The RoutledgeFalmer Reader in
Psychology of Education
*Edited by Harry Daniels and
Anne Edwards*

The RoutledgeFalmer Reader in
Science Education
Edited by John Gilbert

The RoutledgeFalmer Reader in
Sociology of Education
Edited by Stephen J. Ball

The RoutledgeFalmer Reader in
Teaching and Learning
Edited by E.C. Wragg

The RoutledgeFalmer Reader in Gender and Education

Edited by
Madeleine Arnot and
Mairtin Mac an Ghaill

Routledge
Taylor & Francis Group

LONDON AND NEW YORK

First published 2006
by Routledge
2 Park Square, Milton Park, Abingdon, Oxon OX14 4RN

Simultaneously published in the USA and Canada
by Routledge
270 Madison Ave, New York, NY 10016

Reprinted 2007

*Routledge is an imprint of the Taylor & Francis Group,
an informa business*

© 2006 Madeleine Arnot and Mairtin Mac an Ghaill

Typeset in Sabon by
Newgen Imaging Systems (P) Ltd, Chennai, India
Printed and bound in Great Britain by
TJ International, Padstow, Cornwall

British Library Cataloguing in Publication Data
A catalogue record for this book is available from the British Library

Library of Congress Cataloging in Publication Data
A catalog record for this book has been requested

ISBN10: 0–415–34575–8 (hbk)
ISBN10: 0–415–34576–6 (pbk)

ISBN13: 978–0–415–34575–0 (hbk)
ISBN13: 978–0–415–34576–7 (pbk)

CONTENTS

ACKNOWLEDGEMENTS

The following articles have been reproduced with kind permission of the respective journals

L. Allen 'Beyond the birds and the bees: constituting a discourse of erotics in sexuality education', *Gender and Education*, 16, 2, 151–167, 2004.

B. Davies 'Identity, abjection and otherness: creating the self, creating difference' *International Jounal for Equity and Innovation in Early Childhood*, 2, 1, 58–80, 2004 (on line journal).

C. Haywood and M. Mac an Ghaill 'Materialism and deconstructivism: education and the epistemology of identity' *Cambridge Journal of Education*, 27, 2, 261–272, 1997 [original title of chapter 4].

G. Ivinson and P. Murphy 'Boys don't write romance: the construction of knowledge and social gender identities in English classrooms, *Pedagogy, Culture and Society*, 11, 1, 89–112, 2003.

M.J. Kehily and A. Nayak ' "Lads and laughter": humour and the production of heterosexual hierarchies' *Gender and Education*, 9, 1, 69–88, 1997.

J. Kenway and L. Fitzclarence 'Masculinity, violence and schooling: challenging "poisonous pedagogies" ' *Gender and Education*, 9, 1, 117–133, 1997.

H. Lucey, J. Melody and V. Walkerdine 'Uneasy hybrid: psychosocial aspects of becoming educationally successful for working-class young women' *Gender and Education*, 15, 3, 285–299, 2003.

J. McLeod 'Working out intimacy – young people and friendship in an age of reflexivity' *Discourse: studies in the cultural politics of education*, 23, 2, 211–226, 2002.

C. Paechter 'Power, bodies and identity: how different forms of physical education construct varying masculinities and femininities in secondary schools', *Sex Education*, 3, 1, 47–59, 2003.

L. Raphael Reed 'Troubling boys and disturbing discourses on masculinity and schooling: a feminist exploration of current debates and interventions concerning boys in school' *Gender and Education*, 11, 1, 93–110, 1999.

D. Reay "Spice girls", "nice girls", "girlies", and "tomboys": gender discourses, girls' cultures and feminities in the primary classroom', *Gender and Education* 13, 2, 153–166, 2001.

M. Tamboukou and S. Ball 'Nomadic subjects; young black women in Britain, *Discourse: studies in the cultural politics of education* 23, 3, 267–284, 2002

C. Wright, D. Weeks and A. McGlaughlin, 'Gender-blind racism in the experience of schooling and identity formation', *International Journal of Inclusive Education*, 3, 4, 293–307, 1999.

The following chapters have been reproduced with kind permission of the respective publishers

P. Bourdieu 'Masculine domination: permanence and change' Extract Chapter 3: *Masculine Domination*, Polity Press, 81–108, 2001.

J. Butler 'Performative acts and gender constitution: an essay in phenomenology and feminist theory' in C.R. McCann and K. Seung-Kyung (eds) *Feminist Theory Reader*, Rouledge, 2003. Copyright held by Theater Journal, 1997, Columbia University Press.

R.W. Connell 'The big picture: masculinities in recent world history' in A. Halsey, H. Lauder, P. Brown and A. Stuart Wells (eds) *Education, Culture, Economy and Society*, Oxford University Press, 605–619, 1997. Originally published in *Theory and Society*, 22, 597–623, 1993.

J.A. Dillabough 'Gender theory and research in education: modernist traditions and emerging contemporary themes' in B. Francis and C. Skelton (eds) *Investigating Gender: contemporary perspectives in education*, Open University Press, 11–26, 2001.

A. Harris 'Citizenship and the self-made girl', Chapter 3, *Future Girl: young women in the twenty first century,* Routledge, 63–95, 2004.

CHAPTER 1

(RE)CONTEXTUALISING GENDER STUDIES IN EDUCATION
Schooling in late modernity

Madeleine Arnot and Mairtin Mac an Ghaill

Currently, across western societies, there is great anxiety that the existing gender settlement between men and women has broken down. In response, popular media images simplistically suggest a new social order in which old gender hierarchies of industrial society have been inverted with women emerging as late modernity winners. These accounts fail to engage with the increasing complexity of contemporary social relations. In contrast to such popular accounts, as this anthology illustrates, feminist and gender theorists have produced systematic investigations of the contemporary social organisation of gender and the cultural production of diverse images of femininities and masculinities. These critical inquiries demonstrate the complexity of gender relations and male and female positionings within contemporary educational contexts and the uneven and difficult effects on boys and girls of social and educational politics and power. Most significantly, in these analyses, gender has a central dynamic location in making sense of wider social and cultural transformation within conditions of late modernity (Connell, 1987; Haywood, 1996).

Behind recent research on gender in education lies the conundrums associated with the restructuring of educational institutions and the governance, the changing curriculum, the differential patterns of educational performance, the transformation of teacher's work and shifting community, family and work relations. The gender outcomes of schooling especially in the UK demonstrate both continuities and change (Arnot et al., 1999) although only one story tends to be written about the greater success of girls in the school performance. These national patterns are much debated not least since they have fed so forcefully a global debate about boys' underperformance and underachievement, thus swinging the tide of concern towards what has been called a 'crisis of masculinity' (Lingard, 2003).

Associated with these debates have been suggestions of the feminisation of public institutions, such as schooling and the accompanying de-masculinisation of male students. On the other hand, the educational reforms introduced, for example in the UK in the late 1980s, and the neo-liberal processes of marketisation and commodification of education in the US, Australia and the UK have suggested a re-masculinisation of schooling and the extension of male domination through tightened disciplining and surveillance of individuals and the reduction in child-centred progressive or democratic tendencies associated often with feminist egalitarian movements (Arnot and Miles, 2005). In this overview we discuss these tensions in greater depth, setting a context for the continuing development of gender studies in education and the studies we have selected for this volume. We have not taken the traditional strategy of describing each section in turn, but rather have presented an overview of the explicit or implicit themes of the chapters in our argument. At the end of this chapter we reflect back on our choices for this volume of readings. First, we focus on three key themes. They are: *gender in late modernity; feminisation and 'the crisis in masculinity'; and, the (re)masculinisation of schooling and girls' education.*

Gender in late modernity

German social theorists Ulrich Beck and Elizabeth Gernsheim Beck (2002)[1] identify what they call the two 'epochal forces of second modernity'. Taking a rather upbeat tone, they argue that:

> Two epochal processes above all others, individualisation and globalisation, are changing the foundations of living together in all spheres of social action....cultural individualisation and globalisation create precisely that historical orientation and those preconditions for an adaptation of institutions to a coming second modernity.

> (Beck and Beck-Gernsheim, 2002, p. 169)

They maintain that in this new 'second' stage of modernity, the 'quality of the social and the political' will be changed so that individuals no longer locate themselves in traditional communities, with traditional identities of class, gender and ethnicity. Ascribed statuses, such as class, gender, ethnicity and regionality (which traditionally have been associated with social inequality) arguably will pale in significance – *normative* biographies will be replaced by *choice* biographies and new alliances will be formed by individuals on the basis of shared common risks rather than any restrictive notion of social contract (Beck, 1992).

This new culture is described as *a self-culture* which combines the 'indeterminancy of self and of the ensuing conflicts, crises and developmental opportunities and a binding or bonding of self-oriented individuals to, with and against one another' (op.cit., p. 42). Central to this self-culture are the processes of reflexive individualisation in which individuals come to see themselves as centres of their own life world. People's lives become an art form – something to be created. In the first stage of modernity, the ethos was of *'being individual'* and reflective – in contrast, the new generation of youth are now *'becoming individual'* through reflexivity. The new credo is not 'I think therefore I am' but rather 'I am I' (Bauman, 1999, vii).

Evidence of the development of this self-culture is already visible in a variety of social changes such as the new forms of social movements that act as forms of 'resistance within civil society'; 'the many kinds of moral and aesthetic experimentation' by people on how they live their lives, and their emotions, their personal relationships, and 'parenthood, sex and love'; the 'great unfinished experiment' with healthy eating shifting people's relationship to nature and their bodies; 'the new forms of active empathy' with animal rights, asylum seekers, AIDs victims, drug addicts; and, the new forms of vigilantes protecting niches of prosperity' (Beck and Beck-Gernsheim, op.cit., p. 44).

Self-culture is also epitomised in the 'conflicts...between men and women in all spheres' (ibid., p. 44). Gender change has become iconic for change in late modernity. In a 'risk society', Beck argues that the economic order has been fundamentally transformed as have the mechanisms for maintaining the social order. Families now have to renegotiate their norms and, in many cases, links between family and occupation have been broken. In this context, Beck (1992) argues that young people will experience a 'social surge of individualisation' associated with a *de-normalisation* of roles. Traditional forms of segmentations and stratification will be replaced by an 'individualisation of social inequality'. Giddens (1992, p. 3) also argues that such detraditionalisation will unsettle patterns of relationships, calling into question fixed notions of the sex/gendered self and identity. A transformation of intimacy within the context of men and women compelled to forge their own identity, raises the possibility of a radical democratising of intimate relations, 'in a manner compatible with democracy in the public sphere'.

As young people are 'set free' from the social forms connected with industrial society, success and failure will become the responsibility of individuals alone. The relationship of gender to education is, from this perspective, transformed into individualised subjectivity and desire rather than predetermined socialisation patterns. The patterns of gender reproduction are understood to have been disrupted, but not necessarily replaced since the sustenance of traditional gender identities may become the means of survival within a continuously shifting social order. As Beck (1992) argues, in a risk society, young men may well find themselves attempting to cling onto traditional male roles, traditional family structures and local (territorial and community) identities:

> All the factors which dislodge women from their traditional role are missing on the male side. In the context of male life, fatherhood and career, economic independence and familial life are not contradictions that have to be fought for and held together against the conditions in the family and society: instead their compatibility with the traditional male role is prescribed and protected. But this meant that individualisation...strengthens masculine role behaviour.
> (Beck, 1992, p. 112)

As modernisation proceeds, it is also said to have specific implications for women, who are positioned as the reflexivity winners. As Walkerdine (2003) argues, the task of neo-liberals is to 'become somebody' – somebody who is commodified and made 'Other' through the experiences of an upward social mobile trajectory. On the one hand, female agency (e.g. that of the 'new' educated working class woman) is understood as freedom from the inherited ascriptions of institutional structures. On the other hand, feminisation is represented as a response to suggested shifts in Western societies. Late modernity theories use an expanding concept of feminisation within the context of the mutually constitutive interplay between new ways of work and alternative ways of 'doing gender'; or more specifically, the aligning of a new aesthetics of doing work and a cultural re-valuing of the feminine. Importantly, these notions of feminisation suggest a more complex analytical understanding that goes beyond the simpler framework of male and female employment participation rates.

Evidence of the tensions between detraditionalisation and individualisation in relation to gender can be found throughout this collection of articles. The extent to which individualisation can be found amongst boys and girls while at school are currently a recurrent theme in contemporary gender education research. So too is the theme of reflexivity, self-culture, and its relationship to gendered youth cultures and educational motivations. Much of the interest in performance and gender by boys and girls highlights the tensions between continuities and social changes of the sort described by such social theorists. However, reading through the body of literature in this field, we were struck by the extent to which girls' and boys' educational responses and their identifications and identities drew upon an understanding of the complexity of these processes, rather than evidence of the success of individualisation. Recent studies of social mobility highlight the interface of traditional identities of social class and gender, particularly amongst working class girls and women and their identifications or disidentifications with the processes of change (cf. Weis, 2004; Walkerdine *et al.*, 2001). They reveal in effect that the processes of late modernity are worked on rather than the driving force of young people's experiences.

Individualisation in this context, although found in the voices of young people today, can act as a mythologising discourse which hides the continuing impact of social stratifications, or ways of accepting fate. Much gender research is an attempt to get behind such discourse and investigate the gendered realities and the continuities of male domination and power which are retained within schooling but, today, in different form. The ways in which such domination continues to exert itself are also now understood in different ways from the gender analyses of twenty years ago. The research represented in this collection demonstrates a strong emphasis on the multiplicities and fluidities of gender identity formation and identifications of both male and female youth and of differences, discontinuities and tensions *within* each gender category. Relational worlds are no longer portrayed as merely proscribed by strong structural determinants derived from economic and state formations. Instead gender relations are portrayed as the product of substantial identity work, constructed, policed and challenged on and in and through various discursive positionings, such as those pertaining to sexuality, ethnicity, religion as well as through time, space and locality. The epistemological and political shifts associated with poststructuralism, and in particular the use of Foucauldian theories of power and knowledge and psychoanalytic concepts of identity and subjectivity, ruptures the original modernist political agendas. They create new theoretical spaces in which to study the social-psychological domains of regulation, disciplining and surveillance, the discursive positionings of subjects and the framing of fantasy, desire, engagement and reaction to gender orderings. Gender, as so much of contemporary research understands, is conceptualised now as an embodiment of social, cultural and historical constructions. Contemporary research explores the physical embodiment and socio-psychological anxieties around gender identities – the expression if you like of individualisation and reflexivity in society. At the same time, sociological studies of the interface between social class, gender and ethnicity challenge the extent to which individualisation has in reality shifted the material bases of gender power. Feminist research demonstrates the historical continuities of gender politics into late modernity especially through the imposition of dominant norms of heterosexuality, male violence and economic subordination of women.

What unites the examples of research selected for this collection is a concern fundamentally with the notion of gender lens with which to explore these social tensions in late modernity. Such a lens today is careful not to exclude the analysis of other social differences such as those of social class, ethnicity, race, religion and sexuality. Indeed most authors today work with notions of multiplicity and diversity, exploring through the eyes of multipositioned and multivocal subjects the complexity of social formations. Gender, however, remains their starting point and one which allows the reader to think through the procedures which sustain difference, over and above the fluidities and trajectories of late modernity. Gender as boundary maintenance, as examples of border work and classifications, gender as the means of regulation, experience and resistance is never the complete narrative, it is only the beginning of a sophisticated analysis of the operation of social power within a transforming social order.

Below, we explore two contemporary themes which shape contemporary gender analyses (which themselves are the expression of such 'modernisation'), first through a discussion of 'feminisation' of school and the boys' education debate and secondly through a discussion of the increasing (re)masculinisation of state schooling. Both these debates contextualise the explicit or implicit concerns of the contributors in the book.

Feminisation of schooling and the 'crisis of masculinity'

Although gender change is fundamental to the nature of a risk society, it is concern about masculinity, and in particular the problem of boys that has dominated public attention and academic research. Gender educational researchers are aware that the boys' education debate has become part of our common sense and in that sense their choice of research topic or focus is part of their response to this public debate. Any interrogation of contemporary gender dynamics in education cannot resist address-ing, explicitly or implicitly the pervasive reporting of a masculinity crisis. Many of the authors included in this volume would have had at the back of their minds, if not privileged in their research, the dilemmas associated with this political turn. Some authors actively engage with the boys' educational debate, whilst others take over the structures (such as single sex classes) which were designed to address boys' under-achievement. Boys, no longer just a sub-sample in gender (*sic* women's) studies, have become the ground on which contemporary gender research has been built and have occasioned the development of interest in masculinity as a gender form.

The transformation of social democracy in Europe, the need to respond to increasing globalisation and the desire to sustain neo-liberal agenda around choice and excellence were not conducive to modernist egalitarian understandings of this issue. Social democratic merged with neo-liberal agenda in the use of standard mod-els of gender difference as explanation of educational success and failure. By the mid-to late 1980s in the UK, the statistical narrative documented how girls had turned the tide of credentialism (even if only temporarily, in their favour) – however this pattern could not be celebrated. Instead it was read as exemplifying the increas-ing feminisation of the school system. Public concern articulated worries about the failure of boys as category to keep up with girls even though some boys from par-ticular social and ethnic groups excel. A more subtle approach would have asked *which girls and which* boys succeed and which fail (e.g. Teese *et al.*, 1995). The main focus has been the extent to which the gender balance has shifted with boys losing their historical advantage in the Sciences and in Mathematics at school level – girls appeared to be invading the 'space' in which men were able to sustain their historical advantage (Foster, 1996). Boys continue to perform relatively poorly in traditionally female subjects such as English and Modern Languages thus failing also to reduce female advantage in these language related subjects – a worry that reflected the growing value of communicative competence in late modernity.

Such is the success of girls in the school system that every summer in the UK, journalists go into a frenzy as they seek to establish the latest changes in examina-tion performances between girls and boys. Many feminist academics in the UK ponder over this extraordinary media debate with its incitement of government to act in the name of boys and retrieve boys' advantage. To some extent, it represents a moral panic that is associated with uneven economic and political cleavages of late modernity. Social divisions here are reread either as individualised problems (the failure of independent learning and motivation) or as the consequence of over-arching equality agenda such as feminisation (or anti-racism). The problems of literacy teaching are conceptualised, therefore, as boys' problems leading to the view schools have become too feminised, favouring girls by remodelling the curriculum in line with their learning needs. Similarly there is concern that boys' disaffection is linked, not to the collapse of traditional male economic and community power nor to disengagement with the performance cultures of schooling, but rather with the dominance of women teachers particularly working with the younger age groups. One answer therefore has been to try and recruit more male primary teachers – a paradoxical move given the huge number of female teaching assistants recruited into schools to sustain the performance culture (Arnot and Miles, 2005). The challenge to school pedagogies also reflected concern about the 'feminine' influences of child-centred progressive modes of teaching. The emphasis on boys' immaturity and their 'essential' characteristics (lack of concentration, motivation, independence, emotional development etc) encouraged teachers to adopt more traditional highly structured and teacher controlled pedagogies (Skelton, 1996; Arnot and Gubb, 2001).

The state gender agenda in the UK, according to Pat Mahony (2003), is 'morally bankrupt' not least because of this displacement of egalitarian agenda. Feminism was portrayed by Thatcherism as part of the problem not part of the solution (ibid., p. 75) – a view that might have been challenged by the allegedly more 'inclusive' policy making of New Labour. However, in reality, Labour's commitment to policy continuity meant that a similar aversion to feminist egalitarianism was hidden in the 'softer less aggressive and overtly threatening version of the politics of the Third Way'. Gender became part of the redistributionist discourse in which poverty is explained in cultural terms, in which inclusion means 'labour market attachment', in which inequality is redefined as social exclusion and gender means boys (Arnot and Miles, 2005).

It is reassuring to know, however, that such aggressive marginalising of gender concerns has not diminished the academic tradition of critical gender research. Feminists have sustained their critique of gender power, engaging issues of masculinity as integral to women's position in society and their civic, political and cultural well being (if not gender equality then some version of a renegotiated gender order is assumed). Feminist approaches to masculinity are distinctive and not unsympathetic to the dilemmas facing male youth, especially male working class youth, in relation to the neo-liberal project of individualisation, increased surveillance and hostile economic and social policing. Alternative approaches encourage 'enabling' pedagogies, 'anti-violence' pedagogies, 'critical literacy' and 'narrative therapy' which were more likely to challenge rather than embed essentialist models of masculinity, and socialisation theories of identity formation. Feminist researchers, however, have not overly focused on the issues of masculinity *per se*, preferring to consider the predicament of young women faced both with this shift in educational discourse but also with what is seen as a *re-masculinisation* of schooling. Their analysis of classrooms, corridors and pathways suggest that neo-liberal project of restructuration has strengthened male domination through education rather than weakened it. The 'feminisation' thesis is challenged by evidence of the continued dominance of heterosexual, white class cultures of schooling and its negative impacts not just on marginalised boys but female pupils and women teachers. In this sense they sustain, although not in the same form and often in a different conceptual language, the legacy of critique associated with the second wave of feminism in the post war period.

The (re)masculinisation of schooling and girls' education

Paradoxically, despite the boys' education debate, institutional restructuring has involved the remasculinisation of primary and secondary schooling, which manifests itself in the sidelining of gender equality discourses and concerns (Haywood and Mac an Ghaill, 2001). The language of equal opportunities had been converted into performance discourses and social justice elements marginalised (Arnot *et al.*, 1999). By 2000, the publication *Whatever Happened to Equal Opportunities in Schools?* (Myers, 2000) suggested that the activism of the l980s around gender equality and particularly girls' education had been lost. Today, the discourse of academic/management standards has become permeated by 'masculinist and bellicose language and imagery'. The new policy language offers to use ' tough love',' hit squads', 'a name and shame approach', 'zero toler-ance of failure', 'silencing the doubts of cynics and the corrosion of the perpetual sceptics'. (Raphael Reed, 1998, p. 65) – 'improving schools and boys' performance seems to be predicated on the restitution of hegemonic forms of masculinity and gender oppressive practices' (ibid., p. 73). Not only are 'empowering and powerful counter discourses' not available, nor are broader curriculum approaches which could address the 'fears, anxieties, displacements' (ibid., p. 73) – the effects of this new pedagogic and political context of education. This masculine language of 'technical rationality' which privileges teacher accountability over professionalism also has major consequences for teachers who are made to feel powerless, for teacher training which now neglects equity issues and for management structures in schools which appear to have little interest in developing gender equality programmes (Mahony, 2003).

Social exclusion is another concept that has been (re)masculinised. When, in 1997, Blair set up the Social Exclusion Unit arguing that it would ensure 'social cohesion and not social division', the expectation was that gender inequalities in education would be addressed (Arnot and Miles, 2005). However school exclusion was defined as a boys' problem – either it is a problem for boys in general or for a particular group of boys, even though as Osler and Vincent (2004) found girls constitute quite a significant minority of those excluded. Between 1995 and 1999, over 10,000 secondary aged school girls were permanently excluded from school in England – this amounts to the equivalent of the population of a small town (p. 11). Girls represent 'one in four of those subject to formal, permanent disciplinary exclusion from secondary school' (DfES, 2002). Many more girls are subject to fixed term disciplinary exclusion, are unofficially excluded (e.g. when parents were asked to find alternative schooling for their daughters) or are self-excluding by truanting. Girls' feelings of isolation, personal, family and emotional problems, bullying, with-drawal or truancy, and the disciplinary action taken against them are masked in the dominance of this male agenda. Only recently have new ideas been developed to work with girls in addressing their particular learning needs. The prioritising of boys' education and the assumptions about girls' success 'masks a reality where there are vast differences in educational experiences and opportunities among girls' (op.cit., p. 1). Meanwhile, new approaches to tackle youth crime and truancy focus especially on parental (especially female) responsibilities in relation to deviant male youth. The mother is often held responsible for the 'out of control' and 'uneducable boy' (Raphael Reed, 1998, pp. 64–65) whilst at the same time, teenage mothers are discursively pathologisied as 'unfit subjects' (Harris, 2004; Pillow, 2004).

The resmasculinisation of schooling is associated with a complex reconfiguration of working class girls' education. Plummer (2000) documented the statistics of 'failing' working class girls and there is considerable interest amongst gender researchers to retrieve their experiences within education. The production of girls, in this context, is now 'complex and problematic' – girls and women are being remade into the 'modern neo-liberal subject, the subject of self-invention and transformation who is capable of surviving within the new social, economic and political system (Walkerdine *et al.*, 2001, p. 3). However, this new concept of the autonomous, self-managing 'new psychological subject' (ibid., p. 2) is only applicable to middle class girls, particularly those from the professional middle classes:

> The terrible and central fact is this: it is social class that massively divides girls and young women in terms of their educational attainment and life trajectories…the gains of the 1960s and 1970s have been shown to be ephemeral and it is wishful thinking,…to pretend that class has disappeared either as a tool of analysis or as a concrete fact.
>
> (Walkerdine *et al.*, 2001, p. 4)

Behind the boys' education debate remain the substantial gender inequalities of the labour market (Haywood and Mac an Ghaill, 1996). The government has encouraged the economic sector to create a more diverse, less male-centric domain, improve the rights of access to all forms of employment, create more conducive 'micro-cultural' work conditions for men and women and ensure a better work-family balance. A stream of reports give employers incentives to modernise their gender profiles, to recruit women, and foster female enterprise. However, the problem of female low pay, part-time work and continuing correlations of motherhood with childcare has not been effectively tackled. Women still outnumber men in service industry employment, whilst men outnumber women in managerial and administrative positions. David (2004) points out that the 'mother gap' which disadvantages women with children is large by international standards, and badly affects teenage mothers and low skilled women. Further as David points out, the 'ideological push for individuality, the adult worker model combining family-work balance…may also distance women from the educational development of their children' (p. 48).

As Arnot and Miles (2005) comment, government ambitions of raising national skill levels continues to be thwarted by continuing patterns of gender differentiation in choices of vocational courses and careers. The gender skills gap is embedded in young people's sex stereotypical choices of pre-vocational programmes and further/higher education courses. Twenty five years after the Sex Discrimination Act 1975, sex stereotyping is extensive in vocational course choices with large groups of girls 'still choosing to train as hairdressers and boys as car mechanics and computer specialists'. (EOC, 2001) Care, childcare, hairdressing and beauty therapy are predominantly female whilst the overwhelming majority of students on construction, manufacturing, information technology, and motor industry courses are male. Yet despite such extensive gender differentials, plans are being developed to uncouple the National Curriculum, introducing a more flexible range of work related courses for 14–16 year olds. Increased flexibility in the school curriculum will run counter to the desire to degender the work force and working practices in the UK economy. At this point we can expect more gender theorists to return to the matter of curriculum differentiation and gender choices.

Gender theory in education

The relationship between unprecedented social and cultural transformations in the social relations of gender in Britain, much of Europe, the Antipodes and the United States and gender theory is hard to disentangle. For example, Phillips (1998, p. 1) in her edited collection *Feminism and Politics*, writes about: 'Transformations that can be measured in the global feminisation of the workforce, the rapid equalisation between the two sexes (at least in richer countries) in educational participation and qualifications, and a marked increase in women's self-confidence and self-esteem that is probably the most lasting legacy of the contemporary women's movement'. Yet, Segal (1999, p. 203), while acknowledging such changes, notes the continuities of sexual divisions, including women's average earnings being less than that of men persisting throughout the world; women having less leisure time than men with housework and childcare still the primary responsibility of women; and the increased reporting of men's violence against women and children since the mid 1980s, while conviction rates have decreased.

Men's studies projects a crisis masculinity across Western contemporary societies that is marked by bitter debates about the assumed changing social location of men and the accompanying threatened male subjectivities (see Kimmel and Messner, 1989). The anti-assimilation stance of queer activism suggests a reconceptualisation of what we understand by the political. This involves a shift away from challenging structural inequalities and power relations between relatively given or fixed sexual/gender categories to deconstructing the categories themselves: 'their fixity, separateness or boundedness' and a move 'towards seeing the play of power as less binary and less uni-directional' (Epstein and Johnson, 1998, p. 38). At the same time, such a move sensitises us to the tensions between the mobilisation of the collective political subject and the pluralisation of identities, involving processes of fragmentation and dislocation within the contexts of different geographies and histories of change at the local level of the nation or state (Hall, 1992; Mac an Ghaill, 1999).

Part of the difficulty in discussing these alternative explanations is that gender relations are one of the most contested areas of human behaviour. However, confronted by the lack of consensus about these much-debated issues, it is easy to overlook the fact that a fundamental transformation in social theory has occurred. Perhaps the most important advance in feminist theory is that gender relations have been problematised. In other words, gender can no longer be seen as a simple natural fact (Flax, 1990). Hence the gendered sensibility is no longer the preserve of political minority of activists, such as feminists and pro-feminist men. Rather, it has become naturalised at a collective subjective level, as an epistemological organisational theme of how men and women articulate their understanding of being subjects in and objects of a world in flux (Haywood, 1996).

The collection of articles we have selected for this book, as we have attempted to show, are part of these wider social and cultural transformations. By framing gender relations as part of the crisis of late modernity, we suggest a global focus as it explores the differential impact that social change has upon femininities and masculinities – across time and space – within different societies and cultures (Massey, 1994; Archetti, 1999). Simultaneously, by taking this perspective, we can generate more comprehensive accounts of gender relations, including making sense of the interconnectedness between multiple relations of power, such as gender, class, sexuality and ethnicity and the making of subjective identities. From the theoretical investigation emerges an evaluation of past understanding and analysis of implications for contemporary political and professional practices. Informed by empirical research, this provides a critical yet constructive diagnosis of the origins and development of current conditions and controversies within institutional sites, such as schools, family life and work.

Selecting material for this collection at this pivotal time has not been easy nor has it been satisfactory. The principles of exclusion were as difficult as the princip of inclusion. We were faced with a field that had developed substantially si late 1980s in the Anglophone world. More journals are published, more empirical research is conducted even if there appear to be fewer opportunities for researchers to address educational practice and to engage with professional audiences. In order to capture such a field, made up of marginalised voices at the same time, today as expert voices, we would have needed a series of major anthologies. Such is the richness of the field, that no one collection of material is capable of indicating its wealth.

Our task was to capture the field in flight, representing but not defining the field. Such a field is characterised by its diversity, its opposition and positions, its contradictions, its synchronic and diachronic nature. The field has evolved, gone through conjunctures and disjunctures, been positioned by government interest and lack of interest, from critique to possibilities for action. It is never static nor simple. Our selection therefore is also idiosyncratic, reflecting our own positioning with the field of gender and education, as sociologists, as sympathetic to feminist/ pro-feminist positions, as engaged in educational research over the last twenty years and as marked by our own publications around feminist theory, gender codes, and equality policies (Arnot, 2000) and around masculinities, social class and ethnicities (Mac an Ghaill 1994, 1996; Haywood and Mac an Ghaill, 2003). Our selection of material addresses the need:

- to capture the gender critiques of schooling and society;
- to engage readers in a dialogue with the strands of theorising, the types of research and the sense of direction; and
- to encourage gender studies as important aspects of critical social analysis of education.

We have worked up a selection of material which we believe has a contemporary story to tell. Its narrative is based on a focus on *gender* as a concept which is in use in commonsense locations now, but also in academia. From the moment that Anne Oakley (1974) separated in our minds, sex from gender, there has been an interplay of positions, some attempting to explore as deeply as possible the nature of gender as classification, categorisation, a social phenomenon which is constructed and reconstructed, contextualised and recontextualised, which has its own historical dynamic, but also its contemporary transformation. It is now represented as unstable, fluid, complex not unitary and understood as an identity, identification, and subjectivity, a positioning within society. The study of gender in education has grown like topsy, sometimes cumulatively and by accretion but mostly by new insights into how it works, when it works. The articles in this collection focus less on what it is and more about how it imposes on individuals who have to aspire to its standards of masculinity and femininity.

Gender relations arguably shape gender categorisations, but the question is how, when and where and with what consequences? What shapes gender relations and h~ re they established and reinforced across generations? Who is involved i~   lations – heterosexuals, homosexuality, lesbians, dominant and subor-
                ns, within gender across gender, with other social relations such as
            ? Gender is now understood to be of great significance in shaping
            terns and we have some idea of how it works in practice. At the
            ant to know when it is called into play, when it becomes signifi-
            'on or lack of action. Gender researchers in this volume offer
            ' as embodiment, gender as identity and identification, gender
            1, and projection, gender as resolution to conflicts.

In Part 1, we offer three different views of the development of gender theory in education. Dillabough draws out attention to the dynamics of feminist theory of identity, making the leap to poststructuralism with political consequences. Raphael Reed explores the discursive construction of the boys' education debate and feminist responses to this new agenda whilst Haywood and Mac an Ghaill explore the contradictions between materialist (neo-marxist) and poststructural accounts of identity and the possibility of a rapprochement. These articles indicate the depth of theoretical engagement with social scientific theory but also with the contemporary political context in which gender education researchers work. Discursive shifts in the field represent a recontextualisation of the politics of the women's movement, anti-racist and to some extent the development of post-colonial theory and queer theory. Contemporary research on gender draws heavily on particular understandings of 'difference'. In the second section therefore we have selected a range of theoretical pieces which explore difference and power. These authors offer ways of engaging with the symbolic, discursive, material and physical dimensions of gender. Butler, for example, explores phenomological and feminist theory and offers her own understanding of the performative nature of gender. Davies extends the analysis of gender dualism by exploring Freudian notion of abjection in relation to gender border work. Her illustrations suggests the moments of engagement, performance and rejection of gender identities, for children even at very young ages. Her examples illustrate the power of combining psychoanalytic concepts with poststructuralism, whilst Bourdieu challenges the primary use of performative identity by emphasising the material and symbolic homologies between social institutions, economic and political agencies and the continuities of the structures of male domination. His conceptual framework has been used to explore gender both as a system of power and as a classification struggle which shape young peoples dispositions to gender (habitus) (cf. Dillabough, 2004). In *Masculinities* (1995), Connell drawing on Gramsci's notion of hegemony to consider the definitional struggles over masculinity and its consequences for various social groups. He illustrates this powerful notion historically and in relation to contemporary economic transformations.

Part 3 focuses on gender identity work. Reay's study reveals primary aged girls working with various definitions of femininity. Her analysis demonstrates the power of ethnographic research in uncovering the contexts, engagements and limitations of young girls' struggle to define themselves within the gender dynamics of schooling. Similarly, Kehily and Nayak's study of the work of heterosexual masculinity in shaping boys' identities and their mechanisms of engagement including humour and self-demonstrate the power of researching identities in their complexity. In these studies, schools are rediscovered as complex sites for the production of identity but also spaces in which new identities can be worked on and performed. Wright, Weekes and McGlaughlin, building on the findings of Mirza (1992) remind us of the power of teachers and racialisation processes which frame gender relations and the moments in which African-Carribean girls express solidarity in relation to race and other moments in schooling when gender structures underly racial tensions.

Part 4 of the collection focuses on the issues of curriculum knowledge, pedagogy and power in a context where, in the neo-liberal framework, the curriculum is represented as 'gender neutral'. In our selection of articles, we hope to indicate the styles, foci and methodologies of gender researchers who have returned to focus on the underlying discursive shaping of curriculum and teaching. Current research in the field of gender and education focuses in particular on the gendered construction of learning whether visible or invisible. Ivinson and Murphy engage directly with the boys' education debate by evaluating the assumptive worlds of single sex classes and different teaching styles, revealing the gendered production of English. Louisa Allen's research suggests how sexuality education would need to be reframed by a discourse of erotics and desire if it is to engage with the worlds of young women and men. Paechter goes behind the range of physical education activities to uncover differential constructions of the male and female body. Kenway and Fitzclarence, in a seminal article, ask what it means to engage with male violence, how it could be understood as gendered and addressed through anti-violence pedagogies.

Parts 5 shares a view that the conditions of a risk society discussed earlier require extensive research. Julie McLeod's study of reflexity explores the shaping of boys' friendships, whilst June Melody, Helen Lucey and Valerie Walkerdine engage critically and reflexively with working class girls' ambivalent educational successes. This theme is explored further in Maria Tamboukou and Stephen Ball's analysis of the nomadic subjectivities and choices of black women in Britain. The moment of critique exposed by researchers in the 1980s is subsumed within the oppressive constraints they face. Anita Harris' chapter on citizenship and the self-made girl vividly demonstrates the political and cultural representational work involved in such incorporation. The tension between past and present, between gender as subordination and as transformation provides the motif.

This collection signals both the continuities and changes in the field of gender studies in education. The analysis of gender is shown to be a powerful lens through which to understand how power works at the societal level and how power works through men and women's lives at the deepest and most personal level. Educational institutions, contexts and processes are the prism in which power is refracted and as the field of gender studies has shown, it is lived with and through. The political and economic contradictions of late modernity encourages one of the most challenging and exciting stages of gender theory in education.

Note

1   This theme is discussed extensively in Arnot (2006).

References

Archetti, E.P. (1999) *Masculinities: Football, polo and the tango in Argentina*, Oxford: Berg.
Arnot, M. (2000) *Reproducing Gender? Essays on educational theory and feminist politics*, London: RoutledgeFalmer.
Arnot, M. (2006) Freedom's Children: a gender perspective on the education of the learner citizen, *Review of Education*, 52, 1–2, 1–21.
Arnot, M., David, M. and Weiner, G. (1999) *Closing the gender gap: postwar social and educational reforms*, Cambridge: Polity Press.
Arnot, M. and Gubb, J. (2001) *Adding value to boys' and girls' education: a gender and achievement project in West Sussex*, Chicester: West Sussex County Council.
Arnot, M. and Miles, P. (2005) 'A reconstruction of the gender agenda: the contradictory gender dimensions in New Labour's educational and economic policy', *Oxford Review of Education*, 31,1, 173–189.
Bauman, Z. (1999) 'Individually, together Foreword to U. Beck and E. Beck Gernsheim' *Individualisation*, London: Sage.
Beck, U. (1992) *Risk Society: towards a new modernity*, London: Sage.
Beck, U. and Gernsheim Beck, E. (2002) *Individualisation: institutionalised individualism and its social and political consequences*, London: Sage.
Connell, R.W. (1987) *Gender and power: society, the person and sexual politics*, Cambridge: Polity Press.

Connell, R.W. (1995) *Masculinities*, Cambridge: Polity Press.

David, M.E. (2004) *Personal and political: feminisms, sociology and family lives*, London: Trentham.

Dillabough, J. (2004) 'Class, culture and the "predicaments of masculine domination" encountering Pierre Bourdieu', *British Journal of Sociology of Education*, 25, 4, 489–506.

Department for Education and Science (DfES) (2002) *Permanent exclusions from school and exclusion appeals: England 2000/2001*, Provisional Estimates, 23 May, London, DfES.

Epstein, D. and Johnson, R. (1998) *Schooling and sexualities*, Buckingham: Open University Press.

Equal Opportunities Commission (2001) Women and Men in Britain. Sex stereotyping from school to work, Manchester: EOC.

Flax, J. (1990) 'Postmodernism and gender relations in feminist theory', in L.J. Nicholson (ed.) *Feminism/postmodernism*, London: Routledge.

Foster, V. (1996) 'Space invaders: desire and threat in the schooling of girls', *Discourse: Studies in the Cultural Politics of Education*, 17,1, 43–63.

Giddens, A. (1992) *The transformation of intimacy: sexuality, love and eroticism in modern societies*, Cambridge: Polity Press.

Hall, S. (1992) 'The question of cultural identity', in S. Hall, D. Held and T. McCrew (eds) *Modernity and its futures*, London: Polity/The Open University.

Harris, A. (2004) *Future girl: young women in the twenty-first century*, London: Routledge.

Haywood, C. (1996) ' "Out of the curriculum": Sex talking, talking sex', *Curriculum Studies*, 4, 2, 226–249.

Haywood, C. and Mac an Ghaill, M. (1996) 'What about the boys? Regendered local labour markets and the recomposition of working class masculinities', *British Journal of Education and Work*, 9, 19–30.

Haywood, C. and Mac an Ghaill, M. (2001) 'The significance of teaching English boys: exploring social change, modern schooling and the making of masculinities', in W. Martino and B. Meyenn (eds) *What about the Boys?* Buckingham: Open University Press.

Haywood, C. and Mac an Ghaill, M. (2003) *Men and masculinities: theory, research and social theory*, Buckingham: Open Univeristy Press.

Kimmel, M. and Messner, M. (1989) *Men's Lives*, New York: Macmillan.

Lingard, B. (2003) 'Where to in gender policy in education after recuperative masculinity politic', *International Journal of Inclusive Education*, 7, 33–56.

Mac an Ghaill, M. (1994) *The making of men: masculinities, sexualities and schooling*: Buckingham: Open University Press.

Mac an Ghaill, M. (1996) *Understanding masculinities*, Milton Keynes: Open University Press.

Mac an Ghaill, M. (1999) *Contemporary racisms and ethnicities: social and cultural transformations*, Buckingham: Open University Press.

Mahony, P. (2003) 'Recapturing imaginations and the gender agenda: reflections on a progressive challenge from an English perspective', *International Journal of Inclusive Education*, 7, 75–81.

Massey, D. (1994) *Space, place and gender*, London: Polity Press.

Mirza, H. (1992) *Young female and black*, London: Routledge.

Myers, K. (ed.) (2000) *Whatever happened to educational opportunities in schools? Gender equality initiatives in education*, Buckingham: Open University Press.

Oakley, A. (1974) *The sociology of housework*, Oxford: Martin Robertson.

Osler, A. and Vincent, K. (2004) *Girls and exclusion: rethinking the agenda*, London: RoutledgeFalmer.

Phillips, A. (ed.) (1998) *Feminism and politics*, Oxford: Oxford University Press.

Pillow, W.S. (2004) *Unfit subjects: educational policy and the teen mother*, New York: RoutledgeFalmer.

Plummer, G. (2000) *Failing working class girls*, London: Trentham Books.

Raphael Reed, L. (1998) Zero tolerance: gender performance and school failure, in: and D. Epstein, J. Elwood, V. Hey and J. Maw (eds) *Failing Boys: Issues in Gender and Achievement*, Buckingham: Open University Press.

Segal, L. (1999) *Why feminism? Gender, psychology and politics*, New York: Columbia University Press.

Skelton, C. (1996) Learning to be tough: the fostering of maleness in one primary school, *Gender and Education*, 8, 185–197.

Teese, R., Davies, M., Charlton, M. and Polesel, J. (1995) *Who Wins at School? Boys and girls in Australian secondary education*, Department of Education Policy and Management, Melbourne: University of Melbourne.

Weis, L. (2004) *Class Reunion: the remaking of the American white working class*, New York: Routledge.

Walkerdine, V. (2003) 'Reclassifying upward mobility: femininity and the neo-liberal subject', *Gender and Education*, 15, 3, 237–248.

Walkerdine, V., Lucey, H. and Melody, J. (2001) *Growing up girl: psychosocial explorations of gender and class*, London: Palgrave.

PART 1

GENDER AND EDUCATIONAL THEORY

CHAPTER 2

GENDER THEORY AND RESEARCH IN EDUCATION

Modernist traditions and emerging contemporary themes

Jo-Anne Dillabough, in B. Francis and C. Skelton (eds) *Investigating gender: contemporary perspective in education,* Open University Press, 2001

Introduction

This chapter explores theoretical developments in the study of gender in education. Its primary purpose is to examine such developments over the last two decades, with a particular concentration on the most recent trends in the field. As one element of this task, I also consider some of the changes and continuities which have marked feminist thought and its application to the study of gender in education. In so doing, I argue that gender research in education has moved away from its initial concern with gender socialization patterns, the reproduction of gender inequality in schools and gender equity reforms towards an engagement with social and cultural theory and its analysis of the contested nature of gender identities in schools.

In tracking gender research in education over time, I focus on contemporary gender theory not because it presents a complete picture of feminist educational research or all of its contending positions, but because it characteristically displays, like other fields of humanities research, theoretical conflicts which are apparent in the broader sphere of contemporary social theory. Without an understanding of the relationship between theoretical conflicts in social theory and education as a domain of study, the development of gender analyses in education will remain elusive. It is with the elucidation of this relationship that this chapter is concerned.

I begin with an informal historical sketch of gender research in education followed by a brief reflection on the impetus behind the theoretical shifts in the application of feminist theory to educational research over the last two decades.

The development of gender in education as a field of study

Some may argue that the field of gender in education has its origins in the theoretical work of Ann Oakley (1972) and education feminists investigating links between gender, school structures and broader social arrangements. Oakley's key argument, for example, was that the social category 'gender' in the study of inequality was preferable to a focus on sex differences, since it perceived gender as a social construction rather than as a fixed biological in entity. To put this another way, if gender, as opposed to sex, was ultimately a social construct, then its links to socialization could be understood primarily as an aspect of gender identity formation.

In keeping with this shift, education feminism in the late 1970s and early 1980s moved beyond the distinctive concerns of liberal and radical feminists to an analysis of education's role in gender socialization patterns and the reproductive functions of education in shaping gender relations (Dillabough and Arnot, 2002). It was in these respects that Oakley's (1972) work provided feminists with the conceptual tools for expanding the boundaries of gender research.

Second-wave feminist concerns influenced the direction in which this kind of gendered analysis of education might go. For example, research documenting the manifestation of sexual discrimination in schools began to emerge (see Wolpe, 1976; Byrne, 1978; Deem, 1978, 1980; Stanworth, 1981) alongside studies highlighting the links between the form of girls' education and capitalism (Barrett, 1980; MacDonald, 1980). In such studies, gender and class differentiation and patriarchal school structures were major concerns, as were the consequent equity issues for education. In following the work of radical feminists, early gender analyses examined the patriarchal language of school subjects and school structures (Mahony, 1983, 1985) and exposed what Spender (1980) dubbed the 'patriarchal paradigm of education'. Influenced by a strong Marxist inflection, many education feminists sought to expose the gender and class inequities emerging from sex-segregated schooling, while others identified important links between the aims of educational policy, male domination and a capitalist economy (David, 1980; Walker and Barton, 1983). By the early 1980s, the most significant motifs were a notion of gender as a theoretical construct, education as a site for the cultivation of gender inequalities (Delamont, 1980) and a concentration on the relationship between the state, national policy and the economy in shaping girls' education.

As we will see, the theoretical premises – whether Marxist, structuralist or functionalist – associated with this work emphasized schools as sites for the *potential* democratization of gender relations even though gender socialization was understood to be shaped, above all, by residual patriarchal relations rather than by a dynamic of social *change*. This meant that earlier liberal preoccupations with sex differences and roles began to give ground to deeper concerns about the relation between gender and social structure. Critical forms of gender equity research sought, in part, to challenge those early liberal positions focusing on the psychological characteristics seen as 'intrinsic' to girls and women. In their place came new emphases upon the gendered nature of social structures and the particularity of gender identity formation.

Such concerns contributed to the building of a new theoretical agenda for studying gender in education from a broad social and political perspective to which many education feminists from the late 1970s have remained committed. This was an agenda dedicated to the project of uncovering the gendered nature of school knowledge/curriculum (Bernstein, 1978), and revealing its role in shaping girls' and boys' identities and aspirations. It was also an attempt to address the pragmatic problems of gender inequity and feminist pedagogy in schools, drawing upon wider social concerns for, and about, women (Weiner and Arnot, 1987; Weiner, 1994). In each of these respects, much of the early equity research work represented a sustained attempt to expose sexist school practices, engage in school reform and to challenge what Dale Spender (1980), Bob Connell (1987) and others had identified as patriarchal school structures.

While this early phase of education feminism undoubtedly contributed substantially to the field, its initiatives were not without their difficulties. Indeed, many feminists began to disassociate from mainstream 'equity research' that focused too narrowly on girls' education and issues of discrimination, access and attainment. Such work, it was argued, was entrenched in middle-class values and narrowly defined visions of the category 'female'. As such, it was ill-equipped to address questions about issues of identity, culture and women's differences (Carby, 1982; Brah and Minhas, 1985). For this reason, the study of identity began to emerge as central to a reconfiguration of the field.

Gender, educational structures and social reproduction

In this early stage of change, education, as a mediating structure of the economy, was still seen as a major site for the reproduction of class culture rather than as a site for the construction of broader social identities associated with, for example, race and sexuality. Innovative gender research within this tradition was principally concerned with the part played by education in *reproducing* dominant class structures, codes and corresponding classed identities. A theoretical interest in the notion of schools as sites for the cultural reproduction and development of social identities (chiefly relating to class and gender), while distanced from earlier functionalist traditions, therefore continued to emphasize the importance of mapping economic structures onto school structures (Dillabough and Arnot, 2002).

Within this framework, significant attention was given to issues of gender politics/inequity in schools (Arnot and Weiner, 1987) and to women's education as training a 'hierarchically stratified workforce' for the 'reserve army of labour'. Such work highlighted the role of education in constructing women teachers and female pupils as servants to the state (Steedman, 1985). It also revealed the gender hierarchies of educational management and the masculine expectations by which they were framed. In sum, the achievement of such work was to expose the reproductive role of education in maintaining symbolic representations of male rationality and female subservience.

Emphasis on the reproduction of the social and economic order through education led towards a feminist version of *reproduction theory*:

> In 'hard' versions of social reproduction theory (Bowles and Gintis 1976), education was conceptualized as an instrument of capitalism through which the subordination of women and working class girls was reproduced. As might be expected, class culture appeared with great regularity as the social formation which not only pre-figured, but determined, girls' educational experiences, identities and forms of consciousness.
>
> (Dillabough and Arnot, 2002: 12)

Later versions of reproduction theory took on somewhat different theoretical inflections, and mark a shift in our understanding of social theory generally, and feminist thinking more specifically. Such accounts of reproduction theory drew widely upon theories of class hegemony (Gramsci, 1971), cultural capital (Bourdieu and Passeron, 1977) and educational codes (Bernstein, 1977, 1978). Of particular significance was the attention which these approaches gave to the role of masculinity and femininity in shaping class relations and gender inequality in schools, with disaffection expressed as a celebration of resistant masculinities (Willis, 1977) or a 'cult of femininity' (McRobbie, 1978). Here, the cultural reproduction of class and gender positioning in the state emerged as a kind of 'parallelism' (Willis, 1977) between young people's resistance to élitist school norms and an apparent class commitment to the construction of traditional gender positions.

As expressed in the now seminal works of Willis (1977) and McRobbie (1978), the emergence of gender inequality in school cultures was not as straightforward as social reproduction theorists such as Bowles and Gintis (1976) had suggested. Male and female youth were also involved in the active construction of their own complex identity positions. Such work revealed the critical importance of diverse school experiences and the cultural identities and social positioning which prefigured them. Cultural identity therefore began to emerge as a much more complex element in the study of male and female youth's lived experiences of schooling.

Cultural reproduction theorists were not without their critics. Their approach tended to devalue women's political agency and the part played by both education and women's movements in the recontextualization of gender and class relations. Nor did they address issues of difference – beyond class – broadly or seriously enough. In particular, the category 'gender' was under reconstruction in some feminist research in this period. Yet cultural reproduction theorists had started gender research on a course which began to resist narrow and overly deterministic understandings of educational processes and school cultures and their role in shaping diverse and resistant identities. Such shifts in educational research were indicative of a larger interest within cultural and social theory of moving beyond 'the charge of essentialism' and challenging what was seen as a conceptually impoverished and reductive way of thinking about identity formation. In the place of cultural reproduction came a broader understanding of gender as a more permeable social construct held together through elements of discourse.

Transformations in gender theory and educational research

In the light of these broad theoretical shifts, new questions could now be raised about modern feminist theory and its application to the study of gender in education. In looking to these shifts – in effect, the movement from modernist to postmodernist/poststructuralist analyses, or what Francis (1999) has described as a move from a realist to a relativist feminist framework – a number of important theoretical questions have emerged. While still concerned to a degree with gender equity, curriculum and gender reform policies, these newer questions settle their key problematic upon a philosophical concern about the nature of gender identity and the ways in which educational discourses shape the modern individual.

Some of the most salient questions which have arisen about gender in education concern the 'meaning and significance of identity', and 'relationships between identity and difference' (Weir, 1996, p. 1). As a key representative of one side of the debate regarding the formative place of identity in social theory, Judith Butler (1990, p. 39) writes that the 'heterosexual imperative enables certain sexual identifications and forecloses and/or disavows other identifications'. Butler's words reveal a concern with social difference and notions of female identity 'in which sexuality is the main axis of operation and normative heterosexuality as the main obsession' (Anderson, 1998, p. 8). If we do not wish to repress difference, how, as education feminists, might we theorize it in relation to gender and other social formations 'without making false claims to authority and authorship' (Weir, 1996). These questions have played a substantial role in recasting the debates about gender equity in 'education feminism', though more traditional sociological and pedagogical questions have also maintained much of their force. Gender research has, moreover, continued to shed light on the shifting and constructed nature of curricular knowledge in relation to educational practices over time (Measor and Sikes, 1992; Murphy and Gipps, 1996; Paechter and Head, 1996), as well as on sociological, cultural and historical analyses of women teachers' and teacher educators' working lives (Acker and Feurverger, 1997).

Despite the range of topics spanning the field, the argument I now wish to pursue suggests that an emphasis on gender identity rather than equity *per se* has emerged, in part as a response to larger transformations in social theory and the evolution of education within the humanities and social sciences. Some of the key issues which have emerged as a result of these transformations include the viability of the modem democratic education project, the 'death of the female subject' (i.e. a uniform notion of female identity), and the question of whether social and cultural theory can serve as grounds for struggle over values inherent in education feminism, such as the goal of gender equity.

At the same time, it is important to remember that there remain education feminists who argue that there is a continuing need to examine the relationship between gender identity both as a *category of analysis* and as a coherent narrative which is shaped, in part, through educational forces. By contrast, those who are more formally entrenched in assessing the shifting nature of gender identity in schools (e.g. poststructuralists) argue that we need to get beyond viewing gender as a core element of selfhood and instead examine the equity implications for education policy of *understanding multiple positions on identity*. Still others argue that equity itself is framed within a liberal humanist or liberal democratic project that honours some female groupings (i.e. the middle class) and marginalizes others. There are, then, many diverse positions from which to engage the significance of gender identity for education.

Emerging themes/theoretical orientations in gender and education

Four major themes mark contemporary theory in *gender in education*. ... It is to a consideration of each of these themes, their related research and theory, and their impact on education that I now turn.

Gender, poststructuralism and the 'sexed identity' in education

The mid- to late 1980s represented a transformative period in the study of gender and education, when it could be suggested, for example, that the category 'woman' or 'girl' was either illusory or could no longer speak for all women in the name of a straightforward or simplistic notion of social and cultural reproduction. Modernist feminist perspectives in education could therefore be 'seen as rationalistic explanations and master narratives' – which not only identified the causes of gender inequality but had uniformly described the core premises of gender identity formation in modernity' (Dillabough and Arnot, 2002). Such explanations, as the work of Willis (1977) and McRobbie (1978) had suggested, bore little relation to the complexity of gender identities and experiences in schools.

In the struggle against essentialism in 'education feminism', a more explicit research interest in the *multiple forms of gender identity* and their manifestations in education began to emerge. Such analyses took a variety of forms, including studies of the part played by the 'sexed identity' (Butler, 1990) in school performance (Epstein *et al.*, 1998), the role of identity formation in influencing the effectiveness of gender equity policies (Kenway, 1997) or definitions of teacher professionalism and accounts of the lives and experiences of female teachers and teacher educators (Acker, 1994).

Within this emergent tradition, one strand of identity research has proliferated in recent years and has addressed the ways in which educational discourses lead to multiple forms of masculinity and femininity in schools. In this section, I highlight how the study of femininity and masculinity – perhaps more than other domains of educational research – is an example of how 'education feminism' has attempted to grapple with changes in social/cultural theory stimulated by poststructural thinking, particularly in relation to shifting gender identities. This shift could be charted as a move away from the 'sociology of women's education' and political and pedagogical concerns with gender equity (as pragmatic issues) towards a broader theoretical concern with the formation of gender identities and novel *gender theories* of education.

One of the most prominent theories drawn upon in recent years to problematize uniform understandings of 'gender' has been feminist poststructuralism.... In short, that which distinguishes poststructuralism from *rational* forms of structuralism or other modernist feminisms is its link to deconstruction as a conceptual tool for critiquing language, and its insistence that gender identity is not a coherent or stable narrative to be known in any ultimate sense.

Several terms favoured by poststructuralists, such as 'discourse', 'deconstruction', 'subjectivity' and 'regimes of truth' have been much drawn upon by education feminists to examine the gendered nature of educational language. The aim here has been to reveal the cultural elements of educational life (e.g. peer culture, teachers' talk, school text) as discourses (i.e. as embedded in language) rather than rigid social forces, shaping masculinity and femininity. One of the earliest illustrations of this theoretical shift in education was the work of Bronwyn Davies. Davies (1989 pp. 1–2, 13) writes: 'In learning the discursive practices of their society, children learn that they must be socially identifiable as [either male of female]. Positioning oneself as male or female is done through discursive practices and through the subject positionings which are available within those (linguistic) practices'.

While Davies' work was principally concerned educational life in Australia, it drew upon earlier projects on the construction of femininity in the UK. For example, Valerie Walkerdine (1981) and Walkerdine and Lucey (1989), drawing upon both psychoanalytic and poststructural approaches, championed the idea that historical images of women which mirror the private sphere are mobilized within education *discourses* to propogate the subordination of women and girls. Following Foucault, they argued that a 'regime of truth' about gender identity which people understand to be historically continuous and unitary is thus always present in classrooms. In this sense, femininity and masculinity are merely performed in honour of the discourses that construct them. For Walkerdine, dominant understandings of gender identity represent fictional accounts of an old and rather unimaginative reincarnated story about men and women across time and space.

As a further development of this earlier work, the study of masculinity has emerged as central to identity research in education. Often drawing upon aspects of poststructural theory, this research suggests that there is no one form of masculinity in schools; rather, there are many competing and contradictory forms, each of which is contingent on the conditions of gender *regulation* in schools. Examples of this work include studies of the gendered language which is drawn upon by male youth to legitimize various positions on masculinity, a practice which ultimately privileges some dominant 'identity' forms over others – for example, the difference between being a 'swot' or 'wimp' (Mac an Ghaill, 1994; Haywood and Mac an Ghaill, 1996; Davies, 1997; Kehily and Nayak, 1997; Skelton, 1997). Other studies address how, for example, homophobia is constructed through the heterosexist language of boys' everyday practices in school cultures (Epstein, 1997). Recent work drawing on poststructuralism has also examined the language forms of educational policy and the media, such as the 'underachieving boy', and the implications such language has for reproducing gender inequity in reactive policy measures such as 'saving' the 'underachieving boy' through educational support offered up by famous footballers (Raphael Reed, 1999).

Why has such a sustained focus on masculinity in education taken place in recent years? Even though feminists have explored the lives of girls and women, and described a 'cult of femininity' (McRobbie, 1978), they have not until recently fully explored what it meant to study gender (as opposed to sex) in the broadest social sense; to study girls alone cannot address the issue of gender relations. While Willis (1977) entered this territory over 20 years ago, he remained committed to masculinist theories of reproduction to explain masculinity (grounded in notions of class conflict). The contemporary trends in tackling issues of masculinity have attempted to challenge such positions by drawing upon theoretical work which offers new understandings of competing gender discourses and their role in shaping diverse gender identities.

Masculinity research in education also relates directly to the broader preoccupation with identity debates in social and cultural theory. It has exposed novel equity issues associated with a range of masculinities emerging in schools and paved the way for viewing gender as more permeable and changing than in previous periods of educational research. A special concern with the gendered elements of educational discourse has also meant that key issues such as 'failing boys' and 'boys', underachievement' have been examined from a poststructural perspective. Ironically, most poststructuralists were hoping to do away with identity as a category of analysis, but it seems to loom large in most of this work. [...] Yet it is clear that this work has been extremely effective in charting the everyday language regulating the lives of male and female pupils and teachers. And in conducting micro-feminist analyses of gender in education and moving beyond liberal, maternal and Marxist accounts, it has achieved much that had seemed beyond the reach of mainstream education feminists.

Gender, ethnicity and social exclusion: the transformative power of black, post-colonial and standpoint feminisms

Another example of alternative feminist theorizing which has gained greater prominence over the last decade is 'black feminism' and variants on 'stand-point feminism' (Hill-Collins, 1990), some of which are aligned to a greater, or lesser extent with 'feminist critical realism' or 'post-colonial feminism' (Brah and Minhas, 1985; hooks, 1989; Mirza, 1993). Key educational ideas which have been central to such analysis can be summarized as follows: (1) women and girls' education is formulated within a colonial narrative where the 'other' emerges as the marginal identity to be gazed upon; (2) colonial models of education reproduce the cross-cultural domination of women and girls through conformity to values and ideals embedded in white narratives of educational success; and (3) educational research fails to recognize the key question of difference – that black and minority ethnic girls' experiences and family life are distinct from the white cultural narrative and therefore cannot be measured in relation to it (Mirza, 1992). Much of this research analyses the relationship of black families (Phoenix, 1987), communities (Mirza and Reay, 2000) and black women and girls to capitalism and imperialism (Hill-Collins, 1990). In so doing, the Eurocentric and racist elements of a good deal of earlier feminist theorizing have been exposed (Wright *et al.*, 1998).

From its inception, black feminist analysis has revealed the ways in which the liberal democratic education project has constructed stereotypes of the 'black girl and boy' (Phoenix, 1987; Blair, 1995; Blair and Holland, 1995). It also went beyond the school context to explore black family life and its impact on the formation of black students' identities. It therefore challenged traditional and stereotypical notions that black girls suffered from problems of self-esteem against an image of the confident, white, middle-class girl. Instead, it highlighted the positive and subversive power of families in shaping young girls' identities (Mirza, 1992). It also castigated liberal and Marxist feminist research for focusing too narrowly on a stereotypical view of black youth that often projected 'black failure'.

Mirza's (1992) work was perhaps the most influential in moving mainstream education accounts of 'black female youth and achievement' studies beyond the schooling context. Her purpose was to critique the liberal emphasis on black female achievement and instead highlight the significance of other contextual, cultural and political issues more broadly linked to identity. Her work therefore exposed the importance of school culture and family as important mediators of girls' racialized identities. Black femininity and masculinity could no longer be solely understood on the basis of what many education feminists had referred to as the 'gender binary' – colonial and class distinctions between male and female or the public and private spheres. Alongside the work of others (e.g. Blair, 1995; Wright *et al.*, 1998), Mirza also exposed the racialized and gendered elements of upward social mobility and illustrated how rationalized strategies of school success served only to reinstate the various educational and labour market constraints that black men and women encountered in the workforce.

In recent years, black feminists have been instrumental in defining a new category of educational research on the 'social exclusion' of black and minority ethnic youth. For example, recent gender/race research conducted by Callander and Wright (2000) has moved beyond a concern with 'girls' and 'women' to an engagement with the ways in which working-class black boys and girls are constructed by exclusionary school processes within 'cycles of confrontation and underachievement' (Wright *et al.*, 1998, p. 85). Such processes include the cultural politics of school sanctions and teacher discipline, and the interactive place of race and gender in the formation of exclusionary school hierarchies.

Perhaps the greatest significance of this important body of work lies neither in the image of black girls resisting power structures nor their compliance in conforming to the achievement standards of an educational system. It rests instead on black feminist emphases on the potentially coercive role of external constructions (the colonial narrative, racism) and exclusions in shaping the gendered and racialized pupil. Gender identity within black feminist perspectives thus emerges as a product of social and cultural experience. It is invoked to highlight the communicative and interactive elements of collective, cultural self-understandings. It is understood as culturally contingent yet indispensable for moving beyond the masculine gaze of an education system premised on colonial practices. In highlighting difference, the question of who benefits from gender equity policies moves to the forefront. As Mirza (1992) suggests, this work should not therefore be viewed as an attempt to accommodate the mainstream. It is an attempt to define what Mirza and Reay (2000) have called the 'third space' – not one which is necessarily embedded in the colonialist tension between the public and private spheres, but one which identifies 'other' worlds. These 'other worlds' represent the value of knowledge claims which emerge from a different cultural standpoint. In charting 'other worlds', both the potential and the limits of purportedly liberating gender school reform policies come sharply into focus.

Gender, markets and educational processes

Another recent contemporary theme in gender theory and educational research is feminist analyses of 'marketization', or what is sometimes referred to as post-Fordist analysis. A renewed emphasis on the study of educational markets has been ignited by a return to 'class' issues in ways which move beyond locating class within the individual (e.g. 'working-class girls') or viewing class solely as divisive (such as class conflict, social stratification). This return to class is instead concerned with the role of market forces in *regulating* education. While some of this research is grounded in poststructuralist theory (regulation, governance), it also serves as a critique of market theory and its influence over the field of education (Ball *et al.*, 1992).

In this model of research, there is a shift away from the study of exclusion as an issue of identity towards a concern with *social inequality* in relation to instituted market policies such as examination performance, school choice, achievement and standards in 'an ostensibly open market' (Brown, 1997, p. 394). Much of this work appears to be concerned with a very particular notion of social inequality that unfolds as an interaction between class positioning and market forces, largely at the expense of a study of race and gender (Carter, 1997). The impact of marketization on the formation and regulation of identities positioned differently by race, class and gender is therefore an element of this research that deserves greater attention.

The principal actors in analyses of school markets are consumers (students) and workers (teachers, administrators, policy discourse). It is argued that the interactions between these groups reflect the social and global relations (or language) of production. Key questions therefore arise around notions of identity in market school cultures. Recent work by Ball and Gewirtz (1997), for example, has highlighted the importance of seeing school markets as elements of entrepreneurship which view girls not as students with needs but as commodified 'objects and consumers of the market' (Ball and Gewirtz, 1997, p. 208). In the past, women were constructed as symbolic of the private sphere or objectified as sexualized service providers. In this new school context, governed by market policies, girls and women teachers are presented as consumers and rationalized as a commodity.

Post-Fordist theories have also stimulated feminist research which charts the relationship between family life, education and the market. For example,

David *et al.*'s (1994) recent work on mothers and school choice and Reay's (1998) research on mothers' involvement in school markets have exposed the gendered nature of 'school choice' as an element of marketization. They have also high-lighted the reproduction of traditional ideals and expectations attached to labels such as 'femininity' and 'motherhood' in schools. Other studies examining the marketization of education focus more directly on educational policy as a form of *regulating* women and girls (see Kenway and Epstein, 1996). This work has raised important questions about the regulative role of market discourse (rationality, expediency) and the 'new managerialism' in reconfiguring gender hierarchies in diverse educational contexts (Kenway and Epstein, 1996; Blackmore, 1997; Mahony and Hextall, 1997). Education feminism is also beginning to examine the forces of globalization, and their impact on the way gender is viewed in educa-tional policy under the influence of market cultures (Unterhalter, 2000).

In summary, this assembly of work has exposed the gendered nature of market forces in the radical restructuring of schools and their impact on girls and women. It examines how 'education markets' and new right politics undermine gender reforms and create novel forms of gender inequality (Ball and Gewirtz, 1997; David, 2001). At the same time, such research has exposed the novel forms of male rationality found at the basis of new reform policies, school choice and the like (see Dillabough, 1999). As a result, the asymmetry between markets, school cultures and gender equity has come more clearly into view. Feminist post-Fordist critiques of education have effectively demonstrated how neo-liberal educational policies mediate both the economy and gender relations in the interests of the global state.

In analyses of this sort, it can be difficult to discern whether the category of identity sustains any conceptual and theoretical relevance. It is worth noting that researchers such as Ball and Gewirtz (1997) might argue that gender inequality – as one element of social inequality – emerges as more significant in post-Fordist approaches, particularly because market policies, rather than identity, loom large. By contrast, it might also be argued that this work precisely exposes the interaction between school policy and identity (Dillabough, 1999). It is, in other words, torn between fixed and more permeable understandings of gender identity in the critique of market ideology.

New gender identifications and theories of social change

Feminist youth studies and the study of social change – what Madeleine Arnot and I have called '*critical modernization* studies' (Dillabough and Arnot, 2001) – are two related and ongoing areas of study in gender education research. This work is firmly rooted in more traditional sociological emphases, since its main concerns are with tracking social change and its impact on male and female youth identities. Broadly speaking, this work is concerned with representing, through the study of youth themselves, both the continuities and transformations in gender identity over time.

Beck's (1992) examination of the 'the risk society' and the 'hidden pressures it places on individuals to engage in a process of "reflexive individualization"' (Dillabough and Arnot, 2001, p. 44) appears to be the point of departure for many gender researchers. In such analyses, feminism is seen as only one of many ele-ments of modernity which have transformed male and female identities. Proponents of this view argue that modernity (as a historical period of social change) has provided a more flexible social context for the construction of gender identity, particularly for girls. However, in a fractured moral society where the benefits of modernity (e.g. equal opportunity policies) are only accorded to the privileged few, social theorists such as Beck argue that only particular groups of women and men will benefit from such changes. In the 'risk society', the social world becomes increasingly fractured and gaps between the middle and working classes widen.

Much of the research which falls under the category 'youth, gender and social change' suggests that young girls stand at the intersection of a range of highly contradictory messages deriving, in part, from broad economic and social changes and modem transformations in gender relations (Chisholm and Du Bois Reymond, 1993). Such messages highlight, on the one hand, the significance of new patterns of educational attainment, a more flexible and open workforce (Arnot *et al.*, 1999), transformations in gender relations and state commitments to the education of women. On the other hand, such messages coexist alongside reductions in social and educational support for particular groups of female youth, the rise in new right social policies and the escalation in national levels of female poverty. Such tensions are seen as key factors contributing to the increasing levels of school/social exclusion experienced by impoverished female youth and the reconfiguration of youth identities in schools (Hey, 1997; Dillabough, 2001). Research of this kind therefore tracks the contradictory social changes in education and their *differential* impact on female youth identities (Wilkinson, 1996).

At the same time, such research also alludes to changes in class structures and their positive impact on the achievement of girls. For example, Chris Mann's (1996, 1998) work on class and educational attainment highlights the key role of shifting family structures in enhancing working-class girls' chances of educational success. These studies point to the movement of working families into higher level income categories through the educational mobility of parents – what could be identified as the social transformation of, or 'intra-class' changes in, the culture of poverty itself. In these studies, families (largely mothers) who ultimately transcend their own class boundaries are seen to place greater pressure upon schools and teachers to encourage working-class girls to persist with education despite the barriers of class positioning.

Another aspect of this work is the study of gender and performance in schools (Arnot *et al.*, 1998, 1999; Francis, 2000). This work is also concerned with broader debates about gender identity theorizing in social theory, although not explicitly so. Largely through social analyses of changing patterns of male and female achievement, it has brought to centre stage the novel ways in which young people identify with and respond to changes in social, political and educational cultures across time. For example, Arnot *et al.*'s (1999) explanatory account of performance patterns tracks the movement from a Victorian model of women's education to the contemporary moment, revealing key forces of social change in the achievement patterns of girls. It highlights the symbolic power of the feminist movement in shaping female identities, exposes intra-class changes in working-class families, reveals subsequent influences on girls' achievement patterns and highlights the restructuring of equal opportunity policies.

Education feminists have also recently concentrated on clarifying the changing nature of gender hierarchies in schools and higher education, and the changing patterns of women teachers' careers and their experiences of exploitation in the workplace (Acker and Feurverger, 1997). Such work has therefore revealed both continuities and changes in the social order, and exposed the enduring stability of the gender order in girls' and women's working lives, despite transformations in contemporary gender relations. Education feminists concerned with social change have thus embraced both the old and the new traditions in gender research in education, viewing them in dialectical relation. No exploration of identity, no analysis of social change can be done without an awareness of the other.

In short, what emerges from this work is new gender knowledge about young people's transitions and the gendered processes of identification at work in social change. Simultaneously, however, it has identified the ways in which 'girls' identities are still mediated by the continuing effects of social reproduction (particularly social class inequalities) (Dillabough and Arnot, 2001, p. 45). At the level of social analysis, the historicity of women and girls' oppression comes clearly into view as an ongoing force in the processes of social change. As Calhoun (1995, p. 155) suggests, it also addresses precisely those problems identified in social critiques of postmodernist perspectives on identity:

> They [postmodernists] address various changes in media...the shift from production oriented consumerism to...seduction oriented consumerism but they do not address the empirical question of whether in fact social relations, most basically relations of power, are undergoing fundamental transformations – and whether those transformations affect more the systematic character of indirect [social] relations.

Conclusion

Despite the diversity of thinking in the early stages of education feminism, most feminists remained concerned with women's education, the reproduction of gender inequality in schools, women teachers' work and gender equity policies. Since the mid-1980s, however, education feminism has become more explicitly concerned with issues of gender identity, even though 'gender' has been viewed as a social category since the development of the concept by Ann Oakley (1972). My own argument has focused, in part, on the use by education feminists of 'identity' as a conceptual device for transforming the practice of educational research. I have argued that shifts over time in social theory have influenced the ways in which identity has been taken up as both a critique of education in modernity and as a category of analysis. As a result, identity has been deployed in diverse and contesting ways across the different domains of emerging research traditions over the last two decades. It has also been called upon both to sustain traditional theoretical positions and establish new ones.

At the same time, research traditions in the study of gender and education continue to reflect modernist goals such as class and race analyses. The dual properties of much of this research highlight the importance of understanding that while the development of alternative research approaches represented by poststructuralism may involve a paradigmatic shift, they do not necessarily jettison all aspects of the preceding paradigm. Hence, modernist ideals in education feminism (such as gender equity) will persist to the extent that they drive a relevant research agenda, and are likely to be contested when they undermine shifts in other domains of social theory. The process of change in the progress of education feminism is, like change in other domains, a dialectical one producing a synthesis which is not an abrupt break with the past but moves categorically beyond it.

What then can we make of the diversity of trends in the study of gender in education over the last two decades? How, as feminists and scholars who remain concerned with the positioning of women, should we respond to such trends at the level of theory and practice? These are difficult questions to answer in the short term. However, research which embraces the best of both theoretical worlds – modernist and postmodernist/poststructural theories – will be, in my judgement, the most useful in moving forward. But in so doing, we should avoid consumer-oriented and trendy 'pick and choose' approaches that ultimately possess limited theoretical integrity and analytical cohesion. Educational research needs to wrestle with the tensions in feminist theory and attempt to resolve them. [...] In my view, we ought to come to terms with the impasses that are presented to us in social theory in the name of the political issues still at stake in education feminism. It is time now to get beyond gender 'identity' – both the fluid and the stable – not to repress particularity, but in the true spirit of social analysis in education feminism. We need new terms of reference through which to explore the broad range of exciting research topics which have arisen in recent years. Clearly, identity, as a conceptual tool (if we wish to call it that) cannot be used to situate the range of issues which need exploring, particularly if we wish to sustain an emphasis on gender equity in education.

In light of the collapse of recent gender equity school reforms in Australia and the UK (Arnot *et al.*, 1999), a sustained focus on the social and political elements of schooling is important. We need to broaden our theoretical vocabulary in the study of gender and education. In so doing, we may explore unknown territory while remaining committed to the role that feminist educational theory ought to play in our work. Without it, we will be ill-equipped to deal with the challenges which lie ahead and deprived of a clear vision of precisely where we hope to go.

References

Acker, S. (1994) *Gendered Education*. Buckingham: Open University Press.

Acker, S. and Feurverger, G. (1997) Doing good and feeling bad: the work of women university teachers, *Cambridge Journal of Education*, 26(3): 401–422.

Anderson, A. (1998) Debatable performances: restaging contentious feminisms, *Social Text*, 54, 16(1): 1–24.

Arnot, M. and Weiner, G. (eds) (1987) *Gender and the Politics of Schooling*. London: Hutchinson.

Arnot, M., Gray, J., James, M. and Rudduck, J. (1998) *A Review of Recent Research on Gender and Educational Performance*, Ofsted Research Series. London: HMSO.

Arnot, M., David, M. and Weiner, G. (1999) *Closing the Gender Gap*. Cambridge: Polity Press.

Ball, S. and Gewirtz, S. (1997) Girls in the education market: choice, competition and complexity, *Gender and Education*, 9(2): 207–223.

Ball, S., Bowe, R. and Gold, A. (1992) *Reforming Education and Changing Schools: Case Studies in Policy Sociology*. London: Routledge.

Barrett, M. (1980) *Women's Oppression Today: Problems in Marxist Feminist Analysis*. London: Verso.

Beck, U. (1992) *Risk Society: Towards a New Modernity*. London: Sage.

Bernstein, B. (1977) *Class Codes and Control*, 3rd edn. London: Routledge & Kegan Paul.

Bernstein, B. (1978) Class and pedagogies: visible and invisible, in J. Karabel and A. Halsey (eds) *Power and Ideology in Education*. Oxford: Oxford University Press.

Blackmore, J. (1997) The gendering of skill and vocationalism in twentieth-century Australian education, in A. Halsey, H. Lauder, P. Brown and A. Wells (eds) *Education: Culture, Economy, Society*. New York: Oxford University Press.

Blair, M. (1995) Race, class and gender in school research, in J. Holland, M. Blair and S. Sheldon (eds) *Debates and Issues in Feminist Research and Pedagogy*. Clevedon: Multilingual Matters.

Blair, M. and Holland, J. (eds) (1995) *Identity and Diversity*. Clevedon: Multilingual Matters.

Bourdieu, P. and Passeron, J.C. (1977) *Reproduction in Education, Society and Culture*. London: Sage.

Bowles, S. and Gintis, H. (1976) *Schooling and Capitalist America*. London: Routledge & Kegan Paul.

Brah, A. and Minhas, R. (1985) Structural racism or cultural difference: schooling for Asian girls, in G. Weiner (ed.) *Just a Bunch of Girls: Feminist Approaches to Schooling*. Buckingham: Open University Press.

Brown, P. (1997) The 'third wave': education and the ideology of parentocracy, in A. Halsey, H. Lauder, P. Brown, and A. Wells (eds) *Education: Culture, Economy, Society*. New York: Oxford University Press.

Butler, J. (1990) *Gender Trouble*. New York: Routledge.

Byrne, E. (1978) *Women and Education*. London: Tavistock.

Calhoun, C. (1995) *Critical Social Theory*. Oxford: Blackwell.

Callander, C. and Wright, C. (2000) Discipline and democracy: Race, gender, school sanctions and control, in M. Arnot and J. Dillabough (eds) *Challenging Democracy: International Perspectives on Gender, Education and Citizenship*. London: Routledge.

Carby, H. (1982) Schooling in Babylon, in Centre for Contemporary Cultural Studies (eds) *The Empire Strikes Back*. London: Hutchinson.

Carter, J. (1997) Post-Fordism and the theorisation of educational change: what's in a name? *British Journal of Sociology of Education*, 18(1): 45–62.

Chisholm, L. and Du Bois Reymond, M. (1993) Youth transitions, gender and social change, *Sociology*, 27(2): 259–279.

Connell, R.W. (1987) *Gender and Power*. London: Routledge.

David, M. (1980) *Women, Family and Education*. London: Routeldge.

David, M. (2001) Gender equity issues in educational effectiveness in the context of global, social and family life changes. Plenary paper presented to the 14th International Congress for School Effectiveness and Improvement, Toronto, Canada, 5–9 January.

David, M., West, A. and Ribbens, J. (1994) *Mother's Intuition? Choosing Secondary Schools*. London: Falmer.

Davies, B. (1989) *Frogs and Snails and Feminist Tales*. London: Allen & Unwin.

Davies, B. (1997) Constructing and deconstructing masculinities through critical literacy, *Gender and Education*, 9(1): 9–30.

Deem, R. (1978) Women and schooling, in R. Deem (ed.) *Schooling for Women's Work*. London: Routledge & Kegan Paul.

Deem, R. (ed.) (1980) *Schooling for Women's Work*. London: Routledge & Kegan Paul.

Delamont, S. (1980) *Sex Roles and the School*. London: Methuen.

Dillabough, J. (1999) Gender politics and conceptions of the modern teacher: women, identity and professionalism, *British Journal of Sociology of Education*, 20(3): 373–394.

Dillabough, J. (2001) Gender, social change and the study of impoverished youth in Ontario schools. Social Sciences and Humanities Research Council Grant Proposal, under review. Ottawa: Canada.

Dillabough, J. and Arnot, M. (2001) Feminist sociology of education: dynamics, debates, directions, in J. Demaine (ed.) *Sociology of Education Today*. London: Macmillan.

Dillabough, J. and Arnot, M. (2002) Feminist perspectives continuity and contestation in the field, in D. Levinson, A. Sadovnik and P. Cookson (eds) *Encyclopaedia: Sociology of Education*. New York: Garland.

Epstein, D. (1997) Boyz' own story: masculinities and sexualities in schools, *Gender and Education*, 9(1): 105–116.

Epstein, D., Elwood, J., Hey, V. and Maw, J. (eds) (1998) *Failing Boys? Issues in Gender and Achievement*. Buckingham: Open University Press.

Francis, B. (1999) Modernist reductionism or poststructuralist relativism: can we move on? An evaluation of the arguments in relation to feminist educational research, *Gender and Education*, 11(4): 381–394.

Francis, B. (2000) *Boys, Girls and Achievement: Addressing the Classroom Issues*. London: Routledge/Falmer.

Gramsci, A. (1971) *Selections from the Prison Notebooks of Antonia Gramsci*. London: Lawrence & Wishart.

Haywood, C. and Mac an Ghaill, M. (1996) Schooling masculinities, in M. Mac an Ghaill (ed.) *Understanding Masculinities*. Buckingham: Open University Press.

Hey, V. (1997) *The Company She Keeps: An Ethnography of Girls' Friendship*. Buckingham: Open University Press.

Hill-Collins, P. (1990) *Black Feminist Thought: Knowledge, Consciousness, and the Politics of Empowerment*. Boston, MA: Unwin Hyman.

hooks, b. (1989) *Talking Back: Thinking Feminist, Thinking Black*. Boston, MA: South End Press.

Kehily, M.J. and Nayak, A. (1997) Lads and laughter: humour and the production of heterosexual hierarchies, *Gender and Education*, 9(1): 69–87.

Kenway, J. (1997) Taking stock of gender reform policies for Australian schools: past, present, future, *British Educational Research Journal*, 23(3): 329–344.

Kenway, J. and Epstein, D. (eds) (1996) Introduction: the marketisation of school education: feminist studies and perspectives, *Discourse*, 17(3): 301–314.

Mac an Ghaill, M. (1994) *The Making of Men*. Buckingham: Open University Press.

MacDonald, M. (1980) Schooling and the reproduction of class and gender relation, in L. Barton, R. Meighan and S. Walker (eds) *Schooling, Ideology and the Curriculum*. Lewes: Falmer.

McRobbie, A. (1978) Working class girls and the culture of femininity, in Women's Studies Group Centre for Contemporary Cultural Studies, University of Birmingham (eds) *Women Take Issue: Aspects of Women's Subordination*. London: Hutchinson.

Mahony, P. (1983) How Alice's chin really came to be pressed against her foot: sexist processes of interaction in mixed sexed classrooms, *Women's Studies International Forum*, 16(1): 107–115.

Mahony, P. (1985) *Schools for the Boys: Coeducation Reassessed*. London: Hutchinson.

Mahony, P. and Hextall, I. (1997). Sounds of silence: the social justice agenda of the teacher training agency, *International Studies in Sociology of Education*, 7(2): 137–157.

Mann, C. (1996) '*Finding a Favourable Front: The Contribution of the Family to Working-class Girls' Achievement*', unpublished PhD dissertation. University of Cambridge.

Mann, C. (1998) The impact of working class mothers on the educational success of their adolescent daughters at a time of social change, *British Journal of Sociology of Education*, 19(2): 211–126.

Measor, L. and Sikes, P. (1992) *Gender and Schooling*. London: Cassell.

Mirza, H. (1992) *Young, Female, and Black*. Buckingham: Open University Press.

Mirza, H. (1993) The social construction of black womenhood in British educational research: towards a new understanding, in M. Arnot and K. Weiler (eds) *Feminism and Social Justice in Education: International Perspectives*. London: Falmer.

Mirza, H. and Reay, D. (2000) Redefining citizenship: Black women educators and the 'third space', in M. Arnot and J. Dillabough (eds) *Challenging Democracy: International Perspectives on Gender, Education and Citizenship*. London: Routledge.

Murphy, P. and Gipps, C. (eds) (1996) *Equity in the Classroom: Towards an Effective Pedagogy for Girls and Boys*. London: Falmer.

Oakley, A. (1972) *Sex, Gender and Society*. London: Temple Smith.

Paechter, C. and Head, J. (1996) Power in the staffroom, *British Educational Research Journal*, 22(1): 57–69.

Phoenix, A. (1987) Theories of gender and black families, in G. Weiner and M. Arnot (eds) *Gender Under Scrutiny: New Inquiries in Education*. London: Hutchinson.

Raphael Reed, L. (1999) Troubling boys and disturbing discourses on masculinity and schooling: a feminist exploration of current debates and interventions concerning boys in school, *Gender and Education*, 11(1): 93–110.

Reay, D. (1998) *Class Work: Mothers' Involvement in their Children's Schooling*. London: UCL Press.

Skelton, C. (1997) Primary boys and hegemonic masculinities, *British Journal of Sociology of Education*, 18(3): 349–370.

Spender, D. (1980) *Man Made Language*. London: Routledge & Kegan Paul.

Stanworth, M. (1981) *Gender and Schooling: A Study of Sexual Divisions in the Classroom*. London: Women's Research and Resources Centre Publications Collective.

Steedman, C. (1985) 'The mother made conscious': the historical development of primary school pedagogy, *History Workshop Journal*, 20: 149–163.

Unterhalter, E. (2000) Transnational visions of the 1990s: contrasting views of women, education and citizenship, in M. Arnot and J. Dillabough (eds) *Challenging Democracy: International Perspectives on Gender, Education and Citizenship*. London: Routledge Falmer.

Walker, S. and Barton, L. (eds) (1983) *Gender, Class and Education*. Lewes: Falmer.

Walkerdine, V. (1981) Sex, power and pedagogy, *Screen Education*, 38: 14–24.

Walkerdine, V. and Lucey, H. (1989) *Democracy in the Kitchen: Regulating Mothers and Socialising Daughters*. London: Virago.

Weiner, G. (1994) *Feminisms in Education: An Introduction*. Buckingham: Open University Press.

Weiner, G. and Arnot, M. (eds) (1987) *Gender Under Scrutiny*. London: Hutchinson.

Weir, A. (1996) *Sacrificial Logics: Feminist Theory and the Critique of Identity*. New York: Routledge.

Willis, P. (1977) *Learning to Labour*. Aldershot: Saxon House.

Wolpe, A. (1976) The official ideology of education for girls, in M. Flude and J. Ahier (eds) *Educability, Schools and Ideology*. London: Croom Helm.

Wright, C., Weekes, D., McGlaughlin, A. and Webb, D. (1998) Masculinised discourses within education and the construction of black male identities amongst African Caribbean youth, *British Journal of Sociology of Education*, 19(1): 75–87.

CHAPTER 3

TROUBLING BOYS AND DISTURBING DISCOURSES ON MASCULINITY AND SCHOOLING

A feminist exploration of current debates and interventions concerning boys in school

Lynn Raphael Reed, *Gender and Education*, 11, 1, 1999

Introduction

Everywhere we look we find the apparition of the lost boys. My starting point is that as feminist educators, walking towards the twenty-first century, we need to discuss how we might read this formulation; as ever, to find our own ground upon which to enquire into the phenomenon of the underachieving and alienated male and resist the inscriptions that draw us towards some unproblematised acceptance of the 'truth'. At the same time, we need to explore forms of practice that engage with masculinities in education from a feminist perspective.

This is not a theoretical debate alone; it is a challenge to each and every teacher who daily inhabits and contests the patriarchal spaces of our educational institutions. It is a matter of ideas and actions. It is an issue of *discourse* and *praxis*.

I am using the idea of *discourse* here to mean a regulated and regulative body of ideas and sets of knowledges which delimit the kinds of questions we can ask, the ways in which we might make sense of the world, the potential pathways for further development and insight, with powerful discourses becoming 'regimes of truth' (Foucault, 1972) and competing discourses delineating domains of conflict, disjuncture and change. Discourse is more than a matter of ideas. It arises out of and affects practices; it mediates and adumbrates actions; it speaks of history and context. Every discourse is: 'the result of a practice of production which is at once material, discursive and complex, always inscribed in relation to other practices of production of discourse'. (Henriques *et al.*, 1984, p. 106) By reference to discourse I am also invoking a particular interpretation of power. From this perspective power is located within and reproduced by knowledge, embodied in a complex of relationships and practices, productive as well as obstructive. It operates through normalisation, surveillance and discipline as well as desire, pleasure and complicity:

> Power produces knowledge. Power and knowledge directly imply one another. There is no power relation without the correlative constitution of a field of knowledge, nor any knowledge that does not presuppose and constitute at the same time, power relations.
> (Foucault, 1977, p. 93 quoted in Kenway, 1995a, p. 133)

Power operates through people's actions, which moves us towards the importance of *praxis*; critically informed and reflexive action, making and remaking meanings and experience (Lather, 1986). From a feminist standpoint, such a praxis-oriented approach to concerns of masculinity and schooling necessitates that we interrogate from a gender-critical perspective the discursive complex currently defining the terrain, reflect upon the problematics we experience in practice, and explore new ways forward around our engagements with boys in school.

Composing the subject: orchestrating the crisis

The subject of our enquiry, the 'underachieving boy', is composed in a particular way in current popular debate and practitioner-oriented circles, with specific forms of evidence and explanatory paradigms being drawn upon, related to influential discourses in psychology and sociology. This is not an argument over whether male educational underachievement exists or not: its 'reality' is a measure of its productivity in reshaping the landscape of educational policies and practices and there is considerable evidence of its current effects (Equal Opportunities Commission (EOC) and Office for Standards in Education (OFSTED), 1996; Morris, 1996; Qualifications and Curriculum Authority (QCA), 1998). Rather, it is an attempt to deconstruct the elements of signification at a particular historical juncture and as part of a specific genealogy, accepting that: 'the reality represented does not determine the representation or the means of representation. Instead, the process of signification itself gives shape to the reality it implicates' (Henriques *et al.*, 1984, p. 99).

Whilst the main focus of this article is on the British context, similar debates and perspectives are also current in other settings (Yates, 1997).

Descriptive parameters to the 'underachieving boy'

Current pedagogic practices are increasingly affected by the determination of measurable outcomes where the imperative to 'reach the grade' disciplines the actions of teachers and elevates productivity by unproblematised output in the register of pupil experience. This imperative crosses the primary–secondary divide, and although there is evidence that primary teachers are still attempting to mediate between the Plowdenesque principles of child-centred pedagogy and centralised control of curriculum experience (Pollard *et al.*, 1994), increasing pressure to shift ground towards a more 'authoritative' and subject-centred practice is apparent (Alexander *et al.*, 1992; Boaler, 1997; Raphael Reed, 1998).

It is of significance, then, that the principal source of descriptive evidence cited for a crisis in relation to boys and schooling, is their measurable performance in assessment tasks during the period of compulsory education (particularly it the point of transition at 16 around the General Certificate of Secondary Education (GCSE)), with their achievement always posed in relation to the achievement of girls. This was the representation put forward in the Annual Report for 1995 of the Chief Inspector for Schools, a report which marks the beginning of this period of intense interest in the performance of boys:

> The gap between the GCSE achievements of girls and boys remains wide. In 1985 some 27.4% of girls and 26.3% of boys were awarded 5 or more grades equivalent to GCSE grades A* to C. More recently the equivalent figures have

been, respectively, 38.4% and 30.8% in 1990, and 47.8% and 39.1% in 1994, and the provisional figures for 1995 are 48.1% and 39%.

(OFSTED, 1996)

The relatively stronger performance of girls is claimed across all areas of the curriculum, including subjects traditionally considered boys' subjects, although the differential is usually less marked in these areas and boys still appear to outperform girls in some aspects of science (EOC and OFSTED, 1996) and mathematics (Elwood, 1995).

In particular, concern is widely expressed about the performance of boys in English (QCA, 1998), especially in relation to reading and writing (OFSTED, 1993), with figures from the National Consortium for Examination Results being quoted to claim a 19.3 point gap by gender in English Language GCSE in 1996, with 41.6 per cent of boys passing compared with 60.6 per cent of girls (Morris, 1996). This concern about the relative achievement of boys and girls is not in itself new (Walden and Walkerdine, 1981). However, its composition at this moment in time has specificity which we need to unravel and critique.

First, we should question the reliability and validity of reported achievement data on a national scale. Segments of statistical data are selected in secondary writings, to make a specific case, for example about the relative achievement in GCSE by individual subjects, with different figures appearing on different occasions for different audiences and from differnt sources. A parallel debate about the degree of comparability of standards or otherwise across different examination boards, undermines the claim to have standard national tests at GCSE. This is mirrored by reported concerns over the implementation of Standard Assessment Tasks (SATs) at Key Stages 1–3 (at ages 7, 11, 14) where only recently questions have been asked about the quality of assessments made by diverse markers in a relatively unmoderated system at Key Stage 3. With an ever-changing framework for assessment processes combined with the context variability of application of those assessments, it is hard to have confidence in the demonstration of trends – or longitudinal demonstration of underachievement of cohorts over time. Low scores of socially defined groups certainly indicate an area for investigation; they do not necessarily indicate underachievement *per se*.

Second, the lack of sound national achievement data looking at the intersection of gender with social class and ethnicity conceals further markers of social differentiation. Whilst Gillborn and Gipps (1996) provide useful evidence that the pattern of girls outperforming boys may only hold uniformly for white pupils across all social class backgrounds and they highlight specific concerns about the levels of achievement of African-Caribbean boys, they admit to the frailty of the data sources available. This latter point allows the declaration of a different agenda by the Chief Inspector for Schools: 'the failure of boys and *in particular white working class boys* is one of the most disturbing problems we face, within the whole education system' (Woodhead, quoted in the *Times Educational Supplement*, 15 March 1996). The erosion of attention to the positioning of black working-class boys is interesting, when set within the competing ideologies around 'New Labour' perspectives on education, largely informed by the school effectiveness and school improvement movement. Here, ethnicity and equality issues have been subsumed into a depoliticised agenda which denies the significance of cultural difference and conflicts of power and where: 'ethnic differences in achievement are assimilated into a universal discourse of raising standards, in which the curriculum is seen as unproblematic and pupil cultures as irrelevant'

(Hatcher, 1997, p. 123). Equally, despite the identification of social class as a descriptive issue here, the significance of social class and inequality is open to similar erosion through reduction of this issue into an issue of 'effective schooling' and value-added parameters. This is illustrated by the most recent shift of attention towards the measurable 'gender gap' across local education authorities (LEAs), where the gap of nearly 15 percentage points between proportions of girls and boys achieving 5 + A* − C at GCSE in the wealthy borough of Richmond is equated with the similar gender gap in impoverished Hackney, despite the fact that the overall levels of achievement are significantly different. This allows the Schools Standards Minister, Stephen Byers, to declare that the phenomenon is not necessarily caused by poverty (Bright, 1998). Indeed, Yates (1997), reviewing parallel concerns about boys' underachievement in the Australian context, argues one critical factor influencing recent reform agendas is the growing concern of middle-class parents and their families that their sons should not be outclassed.

Third, overly simplistic use of GCSE and other assessment data conceals important questions about the socially situated nature of assessment practices. Gipps and Murphy (1994) remind us that issues of equity in assessment are highly complex, and that differential outcomes indicate potentially important differences in underlying social and curricular experiences of different groups, including different orientations to learning and pedagogic experiences. Any underlying assumption that we should be looking for or anticipating equity of outcomes for different groups as part of a social justice agenda, needs to be problematised (Gipps, 1995).

At the same time, Elwood (1995) challenges the commonly held belief that the forms of assessment at GCSE themselves have been prejudicially favourable to girls, specifically the use of coursework, claiming that in fact coursework marks contribute more to the grade distributions of boys than girls. Parallel to this she examines the gender-related effects of strategic decisions that teachers make on the setting of pupils and entry by tier in examination. Traditional gender expectations and outcomes arise post-16 where, for example, the tendency to play safe with examination entries of girls in mathematics at GCSE means more girls than boys achieve grade C from the Intermediate tier, but mathematics departments in schools only encourage continuation with maths at A level with a B or C grade gained from the Higher tier.

This takes us on to a fourth area of concern, that the concentration on measurable achievement across Key Stages 1–4 removes attenton from the reversed gender differential apparent in post-16, where certain subjects along gender stereotype lines still recruit a significantly higher number of boys and the ach: evement levels for boys may still outstrip girls, even in 'girl-friendly' subjects (Elwood, 1995). In particular it is interesting to note that the differential achievement in favour of boys seems most pronounced amongst pupils achieving high GCSE scores. In 1994, 32 per cent of boys and 22 per cent of girls achieved A/AS scores of 30 or more, where both had achieved GCSE point scores of 60 or more in 1992 (EOC and OFSTED, 1996). This may well foreshadow issues of social class. Despite middle-class anxieties, it is hard to conclude that middle-class boys from professional backgrounds are failing in school. [...]

Fifth, the current emphasis on boys' performance in schools might suggest that boys are disadvantaged when it comes to progress through employment hierarchies. In fact, it is still the case that a glass ceiling operates for women and, on average across the employment sector, men's pay is significantly higher than women's, with large numbers of women trapped in low paid and part-time work (Hewitt, 1993; Wylie and Papworth, 1996).

Finally, it must also be remembered that a narrow focus on measurable outcomes inadequately captures the complexity of gender issues in education, and that a broader concern with the 'hidden curriculum' and social processes of schooling should remain a key priority. To quote Riddell (1992, p. 46): 'Unless this wider social context is taken into account, the conclusion from girls' examination performance could suggest there is really no problem'. Despite these criticisms and critiques to be made of the composition of the underachieving boy by comparative achievement outcomes, it has potent material effects. There is an increasing industry generating in-service materials and events to look at 'improving boys' performance'; school development plans proliferate which target resources at 'raising the achievement of boys'. These initiatives are informed in part by the school improvement movement, although a residual problem for that movement remains the evidence that suggests improving school profiles are predominantly made up by higher levels of achievement from the girls. Education policies across the political spectrum in Britain identify the targeting of educational resources to increasing the motivation and inclusion of boys in school.

This points to another element in the current descriptive positioning of 'problematic boys'; the coalescence of concern about boys' academic performance with concerns about their social behaviours and social alienation. Whilst some boys in the system may be going on to degrees of success, more boys than girls leave school with no qualifications at all, and a lower proportion stay on in full-time education or training at 16 (Morris, 1996). This reported statistic is combined with preoccupations with school exclusion, truancy and crime. Data on pupil exclusion are considered highly sensitive by schools and LEAs and a clear picture is therefore not easy to acquire. However, it appears that the majority of excluded pupils are boys, and that the majority of them are excluded for 'emotional and behavioural difficulties' (Cohen *et al.*, 1994; Gardiner, 1996). In certain LEAs the vast majority of pupils excluded from school are black, working-class boys, particularly boys of African-Caribbean heritage (Blair, 1995; Department for Education and Employment (DFEE), 1995), although it is interesting that the most widely publicised individual cases in the last few years have involved white working-class boys.

At the same time we have an increasing identification of certain psychological and physiological syndromes affecting boys and their behaviours in far greater numbers than girls (e.g. Attention Deficit Hyperactivity Disorder, and Asperger's Syndrome). Whilst this tendency to 'syndromatise' challenging and difficult behaviours of boys in school urgently requires a sociological analysis, taken together with reading difficulties, such diagnoses partially account for the predominance of boys in special educational needs (SEN) units, groups and classes in school, where boys can outnumber girls by as much as six to one, creating a highly gendered dynamic to special needs policies and practices, with material and social effects (Daniels *et al.*, 1996; Riddell, 1996). Boys absorb far more special educational needs support and resources than girls, with evidence that girls in need are not being identified so readily. For example, there is some evidence that girls absent from school are more frequently labelled as 'non-attenders' because of domestic commitments and become invisible, whereas boys are labelled as 'truants' and are pursued and disciplined as such. The high profile attention to difficult boy behaviours in school and problems of school exclusions is only likely to reinforce this trend.

This articulation of the 'problem' with boys in school resonates with some widely publicised concerns over boys and young men in society at large. The vast majority of pupils identified as truants are boys and a recent Home Office survey on youth crime found that 78 per cent of males who admitted truanting once a week or more had committed an offence (Morris, 1996). The ratio of males to females offending widens dramatically with age; with juveniles it is 1:1; with older teenagers it is 4:1; with those in their early twenties it is 11:1 One in three men in the UK will have a conviction for a serious offence by the age of 31 (Stanko, 1995). Again, feminist criminologists have problematised the 'male norm' in defining offending, and the gender inequalities around sentencing and remediation. However, the popular imagination is captured by high profile cases which claim to demonstrate a critical breakdown in law and order, engendering a 'moral panic' (Hall, 1978) over the actions of boys and young men in society. The Exerted study on weapon-carrying in school (Schools Health Education Unit, 1996) reinforces this perception of masculinity as dangerous and out of control.

An important further element of the discursive positioning of boys and young men introduces the notion that they are not just 'bad' but 'sad'. Suicide rates for young men appear to be on the increase, with recent statistics quoted to claim that boys in their mid- to late teens and early twenties are almost twice as likely to commit suicide as they were 20 years ago, while the suicide rate for girls of the same age has declined by 23 per cent over the same period (Duval Smith, 1994; Gardiner, 1995b). Rates of depression amongst boys are on the increase, whilst unwillingness to consult doctors over mental and physical health problems sustain shorter life expectancy for men (Aggleton, 1995). Testicular cancer, for example, is the commonest cancer in men between 20 and 34, with an 85 per cent chance of full cure if caught early enough – yet resistance to self-examination persists (Dillner, 1995).

These, then, form the elements of description of the 'underachieving boy' in education; in school, but not reaching high enough levels of achievement and whose performance is eclipsed by girls even in subjects boys once could take as their own; or alienated, unhappy and excluded, marginalised into the half-light of society as part of a youth culture disarticulated from society: what the DEMOS report, *Freedom's Children*, called the 'underwolves' (Wroe, 1995).

Popular explanatory paradigms for the 'underachieving boy'

To understand the discursive complex at work here, we need to look further at the most common and influential explanations proffered for why these problems with boys 'exist'. Particular explanatory paradigms imply certain forms of intervention; how you understand the 'nature of the problem' determining your prescription for 'remedy'. It is here too that we can see the articulation of perspectives on boys with wider perspectives on gender relations in society. As feminists, we need to unpack this suitcase of effects.

(a) The dominant psychological explanation and related interventions. Popularised explanations for boys' perceived failure often include the notion that by nature, boys and girls are different and bring with them different individual aptitudes and orientations to the learning environment. Crude cognitive psychology is invoked by Geoff Hannan, an educational consultant increasingly quoted as a practitioner 'expert' on improving boys' performance (BBC, 1994; CSGS Programme of

Events, 1996/97), who claims that from birth boys' development is slower than girls, and that their mental processes develop along different pathways. By adulthood, their brains are structured and operate differently. In particular the 'male brain' finds it hard to deal with reflective emotional-centred tasks; their preference is for speculative thinking and action (Gardiner, 1995a; Hannan, 1996). In his in-service presentation Hannan bolsters his argument with reference to dubious and unreferenced research 'evidence', but successfully mines the audience preconceptions about gender difference. The fact that 'women want to talk about problems, but men just want to run away' (*group laughter*) (presentation: Redbridge Teachers' Centre, 24 May 1996) is explained by 'the fact that in women strong feelings activate pathways to the higher cerebral cortext; in men they trigger the primitive "fight or flight" response'. His claim, then, is that predominant classroom practices favour the reflective and language-rich approach to learning of girls and seriously disadvantage boys, with boys naturally poorer on things which require reflection and carefully throught-through organisation and sequential planning. This perspective was further picked up by the School Curriculum and Assessment Authority, with Nicholas Tate, Chief Executive, urging schools to use more structured teaching methods to stop boys falling further behind in school subjects (Macleod, 1995).

There are important elements of this paradigm to unravel. To some extent, this represents part of a shift in the dominant individualist pedagogic perspective, building on Piagetian preoccupations with the emergence and activation of innare developmental stages, and heavily influenced by the work of Howard Gardner on multiple intelligences (Gardner, 1993). The related interest in 'accelerated learning strategies', reflected again in popular in-service courses of the moment (Smith, 1995; O'Connor, 1996), provides a rearticulation of child-centred pedagogy, where the teacher is responsible for identifying and matching individual pupil learning needs by preferred learning style, or by failing to do so being responsible for pupil failure (Walkerdine, 1984).

This way of looking at classroom experience is fundamentally apolitical and asocial; gender as a social practice is replaced by idiographic descriptions of learner orientations, with gendered preference embedded in the brain. It also reinforces the relational argument of male disadvantage; that girls and women are somehow causing boys' failure (the title of one *Times Educational Supplement* article on boys' underachievement, '*Male brain rallied by curriculum oestrogen*' (15 March 1996) even invokes the reported concern that reductions in male fertility are a consequence of increased oestrogen in the water cycle, caused by female oral contraceptives in women's urine!).

Combined with a call to make the curriculum more relevant in content to boys' interests, this discursive element may well lead to a further masculinisation of teaching styles and classroom environments, particularly in secondary schools. In primary classrooms too there may be a return to teaching in more didactic and structured ways (phonics-based approaches to literacy; whole-class inculcation of mathematical rules etc.) with the reinvention of a narrow 'elementary' curriculum of basic skills in English, mathematics, science and information technology through the implementation of the National Literacy Hour, the National Numeracy Hour and a reduced curriculum framework (DfEE, 1997). One could see this as a reinforcement of hegemonic masculinity through the form of pedagogy; privileging rationality and the 'mastery of reason' as individual power, over emotional and intuitive connectedness through social and linguistic practices (Walkerdine, 1988).

Of course, the extent to which the domination of hegemonic masculinity in education has *ever* been seriously destabilised in practice is debatable. It is quite hard to find a secondary school classroom which provides a 'reflective and language rich environment'; the allocation of time to subjects under the National Curriculum since 1988 has privileged logocentrie subjects, and forms of discipline in most schools (primary and secondary) are profoundly male-oriented (Skelton, 1996). However, what I believe we are witnessing is a discursive reformulation of masculinist ascendancy through historically specific forms of epistemological and pedagogic control.

(b) The dominant sociological explanation and related interventions. Developments in academic perspectives on how to understand the complexities of gender and masculinities invite us to recognise diverse masculinities as discursive practices and social relations in specific contexts, with 'relations of alliance, dominance and subordination' (Connell, 1995, p. 37) between hegemonic and non-hegemonic forms of masculinity. However, this perspective has little purchase on the popular perception of what is happening with boys where the dominant sociological paradigm informing current school programmes remains primarily a simplistic and normative theory of social role. Commonly accounts tend to emphasise the significance of material and ideological changes to men's position and role in society. Increasing male unemployment and particularly high rates of unemployment amongst black and working-class young men are used to explain boys' disaffection with schooling and young men's oppositional stances (Wilkinson, 1995; Morris, 1996) as well as the growing incidence of psychosocial disorders, although Rutter and Smith (1995) argue that some of the most popular theories of causation between sociological factors and increasing incidence of psychosocial disorders amongst young people are not supported by reliable evidence and that further research is urgently needed.

Linked to this perspective, and arising from a sex-role socialisation thesis about the creation and sustenance of gender identity, is media anxiety about the lack of positive male, role models for boys. This is articulated most clearly in relation to African-Caribbean boys, where deficit models still predominate, through a crude sociological proposition that absent black fathers in the home must be substituted for by positive black role models in the classroom (Jeffreys and Bradley, 1995; Holland/Channel 4, 1995; Parry, 1995) and that African-Caribbean boys suffer from overdomination by the black matriarch in the family. Overall most reports assume that boys consider it 'uncool' to be successful at school (Williams, 1995), with schoolboy cultures unmediated by work-oriented male models or unsupported by family aspirations and standards.

Such a perspective on the 'problem' leads to a particular educational solutions, themselves potentially problematic. The intervention of black male mentors proposed by Stephen Holland has been criticised for diverting attention away from institutionalised racism, and for undermining the integrity of female teachers (Hutchinson and John, 1995), and the whole construction of 'black underachievement' and gender relations in African-Caribbean families has been critiqued by Mirza (1993), as has a tendency to oversimplify and over-essentialise black male student identities and experiences in school (Sewell, 1997).

Furthermore, unproblematised notions of masculinity are embedded in certain 'positive' role models. One school in Rochdale has established a mentoring scheme for boys to shadow business people in industry, so that 'boys will see what being busy and organised at work really means' (Haigh, 1995). This includes being picked up by a male manager at 6.45 am in the morning to attend a business meeting over breakfast; a questionable and highly gendered practice to emulate and one which reasserts traditional hegemonic notions of masculinity. The idea of returning to a 'self-discipline through authoritative male practices' is equally evidenced in recent suggestions that what badly behaved ad and unmotivated boys need is a compulsory period in the cadet corps (Harding and Fairhall, 1997).

This articulation of regulation and surveillance has wider significance when put together with suggestions of curfews for young troublemakers, home–school contracts on behaviours and fining parents for their children's (sons') misdemeanours (Home Office, 1997). This points to the repositioning of family and state responsibilities; at a time when family poverty remains a critical issue for more than one in five children in school, and family child welfare and support services are being cut back by cash-strapped local authorities, the penalisation of working-class families remains a vindictive and inadequate response. Equally, welfare reform policies of the current era project blame onto women, who are now both blamed for causing family poverty through not working if they are single parents on benefits, or by working, undermining the role of the traditional male breadwinner or destablising their sons' education (Raphael Reed, 1998). In the much debated North London University study by Margaret O'Brien on the relationship between parental working patterns and pupil achievement, it was reported that boys in particular in the sample appeared to be affected by both parents working full-time (Harding, 1997).

Finally, some calls for increasing the employment of male primary school teachers to counteract the feminising effects of primary education and provide positive role models for young children, have failed to ask questions about the type of masculinity being reproduced by male teachers, the constraints around destablising hegemonic masculinity as a male primary school teacher (Charlesworth, 1996) or the consequences of their swift elevation to headship once engaged in the primary domain (Foster, 1995).

Perspectives on literacy and boys reveal the intersection of beliefs about role, culture and cognition in many of the current school-based strategies (QCA, 1998). Schools are encouraged to provide positive role models of men reading, represented by a series of posters from the National Literacy Trust showing popular footballers reading books (fortunately not Gazza: when asking a group of boys recently what they thought about Paul Gascoigne being chosen for the England football squad having recently physically assaulted his wife, one boy said, 'Well, it shows he can kick, doesn't it?'). The reference to football as a medium for motivating boys is echoed in the Labour Government's recent deal with four Premier League clubs to open after-school study centres for pupils where 'leading footballers would be able to work with switched-off boys in a bid to get them back to their books' (Macleod, 1997a).

This is matched by advice from English teachers and advisers in a plethora of publications to redefine what counts as 'reading', to recognise that the social and cultural specificity around literate practices for many boys mean that they emerge as 'differently literate', disadvantaged by educational practices which fail to acknowledge this (Millard, 1997). Such concern combines with previous observations that English teachers often seem to value girls' tendency to produce written work that looks neat and conforms to expected content, rather than boys' tendency to be more rushed but take more intellectual risks. This, of course, could equally be seen as an attempt to reassert the perspective that girls only succeed by hard work not flair, but boys succeed through impetuous and challenging ability, 'where evidence of failure itself is produced as evidence in support of understanding' (Walkerdine, 1988, p. 209). The promotion of information technology in the classroom is also proposed as a strategy to 'turn boys on' to working (EOC and OFSTED, 1996) despite evidence that information technology educational and employment contexts continue to disadvantage women and girls (Bell, 1995). [...]

Though the histories and theoretical referents of these dominant explanatory paradigms are diverse, the overall effect is to force our gaze on the 'underachieving boy' as a subject constructed in need of our help. His 'existence' overly determines the interpretation of gender concern amongst teachers and schools, including the allocation of resources. His production is a consequence of teachers' failure (especially female teachers, predominant in the primary school, the English faculty or special educational needs provision) to meet his individual learning needs. His 'masculinity' is problematised by the changing world order post feminism; it is not itself the problem. His crisis is always understood in relation to female independence and success. How the subject is constructed thereby affects the questions being asked and actions being taken.

In conclusion, the dominant discursive complex currently evident in the public debate on boys and schooling has the following effects.

- It reinforces capture of the 'social justice' agenda as part of the market-oriented 'achievement' perspective of the new centre (neo-liberal Conservative and neo-social democratic Labour), blind to real issues of social differentiation and inequality, consolidating a new and frightening political consensus on education where the 'ideologies' of 'feminism' and 'socialism' are deemed outmoded and obstructive.
- At the same time it provides a rearticulation of child-centred individualist perspectives on pedagogy, divorced from social context, and used to discipline teachers – particularly female teachers – for their failure to meet boy's needs.
- It provides a medium for the reassertion of particular forms of hegemonic masculinity built around social and pedagogic practices of 'discipline' and structure (through social roles and identities, orientations to learning, curricular focus, forms of knowledge etc.) and legitimates the continuing appropriation of resources to support that agenda.
- In promoting social deficit theories about African-Caribbean and white working-class families, and shifting responsibility and blame towards those sectors of society for behaviours and performance of their boys and young men, it provides important validation for increased surveillance and regulation of these social groups. Situated within this, mothers are blamed for either dominating or neglecting their sons, or for undermining the male role by becoming the principal wage-earner.

A feminist's perspective on masculinities and schooling

In the final part of this chapter I want to identify some possible elements of a feminist perspective on masculinity and schooling, to inform our practices as feminist pedagogues in varied educational contexts. This is not easy, since this arena seems relatively undertheorised in feminist literature (Kenway, 1995b). I am not presuming here to offer a feminist theory of masculinity, but to offer some reflections as part of the debate. [...]

Luke and Gore (1992) quoting Irigaray (1985) remind us of the liberatory effect of deconstructing the power of logocentric and phallocentric discourse, of naming our place outside these refractions:

> the years of looking straight into a straight mirror have reflected back clearly only the spectacle and rule of the father. We know it well. But we also know our otherness by virtue of being in the dark and on the outside of those refractions: knowing ourselves in the hidden and oblique spaces accessible through the curved specular mirror.
>
> (Luke and Gore, 1992, p. 3)

Indeed, we need to recognise the effects of our differential positioning through discourse as female and male in the world of education, to better understand the 'wants and needs', the 'drives and desires' which inform our actions.

I am not suggesting an essentialist experience we could name 'masculinity' and 'femininity'. Feminist writings over the last three decades and recent writings on masculinities, have richly described the multiplicity of forms and qualities of experiences encompassed by context specific gender relations. We are all shaped by a myriad of influences, and continually reform our subjectivities through our actions and engagements with others. However, shared contexts for experiences exist and we are never entirely individual in our appropriation of the world of meaning. What I touch on here has resonance with accounts of being positioned as a boy and as a girl at the same time and its effects upon the unconscious:

> within our present system of schooling, the success of working-class children and girls depends upon the effectivity of disavowal and therefore upon intense and persecutory pain...we might predict a terrifying experience consequent upon effects of simultaneous desire for identification and fear of total loss and annihilation.
>
> (Walkerdine, 1985, pp. 225–226)

Peter Redman presents one insightful exploration of the unconscious process at work in his adolescent gender identification with 'muscular intellectualness' in a particular school context, drawing on the analytical perspective of Lacan and centralising the importance of sexuality (Redman and Mac an Ghaill, 1996). What we need now, I would suggest, are more feminist accounts of the production of sexualised identities in and through education for teachers and pupils, in particular looking at the relationship between adult and child processes across the masculine/feminine divide and including the complexities of the unconscious.

This, I believe, would bring specific insight to our understanding of the circulation of sexualised power in classroom spaces and would allow a different reading of the significance female and male teachers bring to their interactions with and interpretations of both boys and girls. One female teacher I currently work with (mainstream secondary science) described the different feelings experienced in working with each:

> With Gary, well, I'll ask him to do something I think he will settle down to do. There's no point in doing anything else. I haven't got the time or energy to cope with the confrontation. If I ask him to move I always say 'Thank you, Gary', but it is irony really. His tutor told me he beats up his mum. No. I'm not frightened of him, but I'm frightened of the situation escalating and sparking him off.

> The girls are gorgeous. They are so motivated. They work well, they come and check their work and then get back on with it. And their books are so neat. Even Michelle. She is a truant but she has gorgeous doe eyes.

> Kevin. I don't like him. Sly eyes – I don't trust him. He makes the hairs stand up on the back of my neck. [...]

I think this account has a number of important referents: female complicity with obstructive male behaviour; the threat of imaginary violence; the lack of trust in masculinity; the positive desirous identification with girls and negative projection onto boys; the feeling of being played with and taken for a ride; the feeling of powerlessness; the corporeality of pedagogic encounter (McWilliam, 1996). ...

In stressing the significance of teachers I am also suggesting further enquiry into the interactions between teachers and pupils to explore in greater depth the ways in which classroom process are active in the construction of and sustenance of particular forms of gender identity, with masculine identities as an important part of this. [...] The significance of the teacher becomes particularly crucial to the exploration of feminist pedagogic perspectives on working with boys. Such a perspective needs to centralise the deconstruction of the 'father' in dominant pedagogic discourse, without romanticising the creation of alternative critical pedagogic practices. In an earlier research project which I have undertaken, gathering life histories of teachers committed to social justice and working in socially deprived contexts, a recurrent theme in their accounts was the difficulties and tensions experienced around working with boys, particularly in working-class and multiethnic contexts (Raphael Reed, 1995). Models of how to work in an emancipatory way with girls do not easily transfer across the gender divide, and dilemmas created by working from a radical or feminist perspective with pupils whose masculine identities in school often manifest as domineering and disruptive illuminate some significant limitations to existing perspectives on gender work in schools and unproblematised notions of critical pedagogy. At the same time, it highlights the need to move beyond the prescriptions of a rigid binary categorisation of experience and build links across that divide, reading against the grain of how things are 'supposed to be'.

Elements of a way forward are now apparent. First, we need to listen to and acknowledge the real and multiple interests and subject positions of different boys rather than importing a political identity (politically correct or otherwise) and placing it upon them (Askew and Ross, 1988). The 'underachieving boy' forced beneath our gaze by the dominant discourses on masculinity and schooling, is not immediately recognisable in the range of boys we encounter in the classroom, including the painfully quiet boy who rarely speaks to a teacher at all, and who does not jump out at us as part of a recognisable male typology. As Salisbury and Jackson acknowledge, boys themselves are seriously damaged by the expectations and labels of hegemonic forms of masculinity, and given the chance, have gendered issues of serious import to share with teachers and each other in sorting out their senses of themselves (Salisbury and Jackson, 1996). In part, this is about supporting contexts where the 'private self' can be integrated with the 'public self' (Walker, 1997).

Second, we need to look at pedagogic practices that encourage the building of critical learning dialogues and the internalisation of self-control, as a challenge to masculinised forms of knowledge, learning and social interaction. This includes the need to assert authority and appropriately powerful actions as teachers in establishing the parameters of safe spaces for others (liberatory pedagogy does not have to mean anti-authoritarian pedagogy), but for women in particular we need to share examples of how this can also be a process of returning responsibility to boys (and girls) for the consequences of particular actions, rather than shouldering responsibility for them. At times this may engender argument and passion, as part of the struggle to make 'the power of discourse visible to them' (Davies, 1997, p. 13). [...]

We need to share examples of feminist teachers working the space of deconstruction so that in magical moments we can see ourselves in each other and envision other ways to be. In one teacher's written account of her drama work with a group of boys, the possibility of this comes to life:

> The best example I can describe to you is working with a group of boys in drama on pregnancy and termination. It is important in this work to go deep. Towards the end of the afternoon they are deep in role. One 'mother' will not accept that her unborn child may be born with cerebral palsy. She is supported sympathetically by her 'husband', though he confides he is in despair. She, in addressing the 'doctors' who have recommended a termination, makes a powerful speech for her right to have a child. We are all moved. [...]
>
> The lesson could have gone deeper and deeper – but time is always a factor. As we sum up and evaluate together at the end of the lesson, they comment both in and out of role. What emerges is the isolation many of the 'women' felt coping with the lack of tolerance and understanding from male doctors and pressure from social workers. Many of the 'men' did not like their feelings of powerlessness, or felt inadequate in knowing how to support, or resentful that attention had been taken away from them. All agreed it was hard to make a decision. Listening to them go out I understood that they had been moved, but I also watched as their bodies shifted into their roles as being boys in an East End school...shoulders reaching into the space to fill the corridors.
>
> (Raphael Reed, 1995, p. 86)

This, I would suggest, is an excellent example of what Bronwyn Davies calls 'critical literacy' through social actions:

> critical literacy...is the capacity to make language live, to bring oneself to life through language and, *at the same time*, bring to bear on language a critique

which makes visible the powerful force of rationality and of linear patterns of thought, of usual speech patterns and usual metaphors, and a recognition of their constraints and limitations. Critical literacy enables one to understand how culture(s) and discourse(s) shape the body, desire and deeply felt personal knowledges.

(Davies, 1997, p. 28)

At the same time this is critical thinking combined with a 'pedagogy of the emotions' (Kenway and Fitzclarence, 1997) where an extraordinary relationship built between one group of pupils and their teacher facilitated emotional growth across the divide of gender, all the more remarkable for the predominance of 'poisonous pedagogy' elsewhere in the school.

Such stories give us inspiration. Let us be roused. In such a way we might truly come to trouble boys and disturb discourses on masculinity and schooling; dreaming new dreams of how the world might be and animating our visions through our creative and social actions.

References

Aggleton, P. (1995) *Young Men Speaking Out* (London, Health Education Authority and London Institute of Education).

Alexander, R., Rose, J. and Woodhead, C. (1992) *Curriculum Organisation and Classroom Practice in Primary Schools: A Discussion Paper* (London, Department of Education and Science).

Askew, S. and Ross, C. (1988) *Boys Don't Cry: Boys and Sexism in Education* (Milton Keynes, Open University Press).

BBC (1994) The future is female, *Panorama*, 24 October BBCI.

Bell, M. (1995) National Council for Educational Technology presentation to *National Conference at INSTED Targeting Underachievement: Boys or Girls?* London, November.

Blair, M. (1995) Race, class and gender in school research, in: J. Holland, M. Blair with S. Sheldon (Eds) *Debates and Issues in Feminist Research and Pedagogy* (Clevedon, Multilingual Matters and Open University Press).

Boaler, J. (1997) *Experiencing School Mathematics: Teaching Styles, Sex and Setting* (Buckingham, Open University Press).

Bright, M. (1998) Caught in the gender gap, *The Observer*, 4 January.

Centre for the Study of Comprehensive Schools (1996) Programme of Events.

Charlesworth, P. (1996) *The Other Side of Silence: The Experiences of Four Gay Primary School Teachers*, MEd dissertation, University of the West of England.

Cohen, R. and Hughes, M. with Ashworth, L. and Blair, M. (1994) *School's Out: The Family Perspective on School Exclusion* (London, Family Service Unit and Barnardos).

Connell, R.W. (1995) *Masculinities* (Cambridge, Polity Press).

Daniels, H., Hey, V., Leonard, D. and Smith, M. (1996) Underachievement and 'special educational needs': the gendering of special needs practices, paper presented at *Economic and Social Research Council Seminar Series on: Gender and Schooling: Are Boys Now Underachieving?* INSTED, 17 May.

Davies, B. (1997) Constructing and deconstructing masculinities through critical literacy, *Gender and Education*, 9, pp. 9–30.

Department for Education and Employment (1995) *National Survey of Local Education Authorities' Policies and Procedures for the Identification of, and Provision for, Children who are Out of School by Reason of Exclusion or Otherwise* (London, HMSO).

Department for Education and Employment (1997) *Excellence in Schools* (London, HMSO).

Dillner, L. (1995) The life in your man, *The Guardian*, 10 October.

Duval, Smith, A. (1994) Giving up on life, *The Guardian*, 3 December.

Elwood, J. (1995) Undermining gender stereotypes: examination and coursework performance in the UK at 16, *Assessment in Education*, 2, pp. 283–303.

Equal Opportunities Commission and Office for Standards in Education (1996) *The Gender Divide: Performance Differences between Boys and Girls at School* (London, HMSO).

Foster, T. (1995) You don't have to be female on this course but it helps, *The Redland Papers*, 3, pp. 35–43.

Foucault, M. (1972) *The Archaeology of Knowledge* (London, Tavistock).

Gardiner, J. (1995a) Females do better on reflection, *Times Educational Supplement*, 20 October.

Gardiner, J. (1995b) Not asking for the moon, just a bedsit, *Times Educational Supplement*, 20 October.

Gardiner, J. (1996) Exclusions rise relentlessly, *Times Educational Supplement*, November.

Gardner, H. (1993) *Frames of Mind; The Theory of Multiple Intelligences*, 2nd edn (London, Fontana Press).

Gillborn, D. and Gipps, C. (1996) *Recent Research on the Achievements of Ethnic Minority Pupils*, OFSTED Reviews of Research (London, HMSO).

Gipps, C. (1995) What do we mean by equity in relation to assessment? *Assessment in Education*, 2, pp. 271–281.

Gipps, C. and Murphy, P. (1994) *A Fair Test? Assessment, Achievement and Equity* (Buckingham, Open University Press).

Haigh, G. (1995) Not for wimps, *Times Educational Supplement*, 6 October.

Hall, S. (1978) Racism and reaction, in: *Five Views on Multiracial Britain* (London, Commission for Racial Equality).

Hannan, G. (1996) *Improving Boys' Performance*, INSET materials.

Harding, L. (1997) Working mums blamed, *The Guardian*, 3 February.

Harding, L. and Fairhall, D. (1997) Labour repels lads' army, *The Guardian*, 24 January.

Hatcher, R. (1997) Social justice in education after the Conservatives: the relevance of Barry Troyna's work, in: P. Sikes and F. Rizvi (Eds) *Researching Race and Social Justice in Education* (Stoke-on-Trent, Trentham Books).

Henriques, J., Holloway, W., Urwin, C., Venn, C. and Walkerdine, V. (1984) *Changing the Subject: Psychology, Social Regulation and Subjectivity* (London, and New York, Methuen).

Hewitt, P. (1993) *About Time: The Revolution in Work and Family Life* (London, IPPR/ Rivers Oram Press).

Holland, S. (1995) *Frontline*, Channel 4, 13 September.

Home Office (1997) *No More Excuses: A New Approach to Tackling Youth Crime in England and Wales* (London, HMSO).

Hutchinson, M. and John, G. (1995) Enter the role model, *Guardian Education*, 26 September.

Jeffreys, D. and Bradley, L. (1995) They're poisoning our kids: the new rap backlash, *The Independent*, 31 July.

Kenway, J. (1995a) Feminist theories of the state: to be or not to be? in: M. Blair and J. Holland with S. Sheldon (Eds) *Identity and Diversity: Gender and the Experience of Education* (Clevedon, Multilingual Matters).

Kenway, J. (1995b) Masculinities in schools: under siege, on the defensive and under reconstruction, *Discourse*, 16, pp. 59–79.

Kenway, J. and Fitzclarence, L. (1997) Masculinity, violence and schooling: challenging 'poisonous pedagogies', *Gender and Education*, 9, pp. 117–133.

Lather, P. (1986) Research as praxis, *Harvard Educational Review*, 56, pp. 257–277.

Luke, C. and Gore, J. (Eds) (1992) *Feminisms and Critical Pedagogy* (New York and London, Routledge).

Macleod, D. (1995) Schools told to stop boys' slide, *The Guardian*, 20 October.

Macleod, D. (1997a) Schoolboys get soccer boost, *The Guardian*, 24 March.

Macleod, D. (1997b) Sums before soccer, *The Guardian*, 20 February.

McWilliam, E. (1996) Admitting impediments: or things to do with bodies in the classroom, *Cambridge Journal of Education*, 26, pp. 367–378.

Millard, E. (1997) *Differently Literate: Boys, Girls and the Schooling of Literacy* (London, Falmer Press).

Mirza, H. (1993) The social construction of black womanhood in British educational research: towards a new understanding, in: M. Arnot and K. Weiler (Eds) *Feminism and Social Justice in Education* (London, Falmer Press).

Morris, E. (1996) *Boys will be Boys? Closing the Gender Gap* (Labour Party Consultation Document).

O'Connor, M. (1996) Green light for faster progress, *Times Educational Supplement*, 4 October.

Office for Standards in Education (1993) *Boys and English* (London, HMSO).

Office for Standards in Education (1996) *The Annual Report of Her Majesty's Chief Inspector of Schools: Standards and Quality in Education* (London, HMSO).

Parry, O. (1995) What's sex got to do with it? *Guardian Education*, 5 September.

Pollard, A., Broadfoot, P., Croll, P., Osborn, M. and Abbott, D. (1994) *Changing English Primary Schools?* (London, Cassell).

Qualifications and Curriculum Authority (1998) *Can Do Better; Raising Boys' Achievements in English* (London, QCA).

Raphael Reed, L. (1995) Reconceptualising equal opportunities in the 1990s: a study of radical teacher culture in transition, in: M. Griffiths and B. Troyna (Eds) *Antifascism, Culture and Social Justice in Education* (Stoke-on-Trent, Trentham Books).

Raphael Reed, L. (1996) Re-searching: re-finding; re-making: exploring the unconscious as a pedagogic and research practice, paper presented to the *British Educational Research Conference*, Lancaster, September.

Raphael Reed, L. (1998) 'Zero tolerance', gender performance and school failure, in: D. Epstein, J. Elwood, V. Hey and J. Maw (Eds) *Failing Boys? Issues in Gender and Achievement* (Buckingham, Open University Press).

Redman, P. and Mac an Ghaill, M. (1996) Schooling sexualities: heterosexual masculinities, schooling and the unconscious, *Discourse*, 17, pp. 243–256.

Riddell, S. (1992) Gender and education: progressive and conservative forces in the balance, in: S. Brown and S. Riddell (Eds) *Class, Race and Gender in Schools* (Edinburgh, Scottish Council for Research in Education).

Riddell, S. (1996) Gender and special educational needs, in: G. Lloyd (Ed.) *Knitting Progress Unsatisfactory: Gender and Special Issues in Education* (Edinburgh, Moray House Institute of Education).

Rutter, M. and Smith, D. (1995) *Psychosocial Disorders in Young People: Time Trends and Their Causes* (London, Wiley & Sons).

Salisbury, J. and Jackson, D. (1996) *Challenging Macho Values: Practical Ways of Working with Adolescent Boys* (London, Falmer Press).

Schools Health Education Unit (1996) *Cash and Carry* (Exeter, Exeter University).

Sewell, T. (1997) *Black Masculinities and Schooling: How Black Boys Survive Modem Schooling* (Stoke-on-Trent, Trenthan Books).

Skelton, C. (1996) Learning to be 'tough': the fostering of maleness in one primary school, *Gender and Education*, 8, pp. 185–197.

Smith, A. (1995) *Accelerated Learning in the Classroom* (Basingstoke, Network Educational Press).

Stanko, B. (1995) Gender and crime, *Criminal Justice Matters*, 19, pp. 3–4.

Walden, R. and Walkerdine, V. (1981) *Girls and Mathematics: She Early Years*, Bedford Way Papers 8 (London, Institute of Education).

Walker, B. (1997) Young men behaving sadly, *Times Educational Supplement*, 7 March.

Walkerdine, V. (1984) Developmental Psychology and the child-centred pedagogy: the insertion of Piaget into early education, in: J. Henriques, W. Holloway, C. Urwin, C. Venn and V. Walkerdine *Changing the Subject: Psychology, Social Regulation and Subjectivity* (London and New York Methuen).

Walkerdine, V. (1985) On the regulation of speaking and silence: subjectivity, class and gender in contemporary schooling, in: C. Steedman, C. Urwin and V. Walkerdine (Eds) *Language, Gender and Childhood* (London, Routledge & Kegan Paul).

Walkerdine, V. (1988) *The Mastery of Reason: Cognitive Development and the Production of Rationality* (London, Routledge).

Williams, E. (1995) Lapped by girls, *Times Educational Supplement*, 14 July.

Wilkinson, C. (1995) *The Drop-out Society: Young People on the Margin* (London, National Youth Agencey).

Wroe, M. (1995) Bitter howl of the underwolf, *The Observer*, 1 October.

Wylie, I. and Papworth, J. (1996) Are women still being squeezed? *The Guardian*, 26 October.

Yates, L. (1997) Gender equity and the boys debate: what sort of challenge is it? *British Journal of Sociology of Education*, 18, pp. 337–347.

CHAPTER 4

EDUCATION AND GENDER IDENTITY
Seeking frameworks of understanding

Chris Haywood and Mairtin Mac an Ghaill, *Cambridge Journal of Education*, 27, 2, 1997

We are living at a time of rapid global socio-economic and cultural changes in a period of late capitalism (Harvey, 1989; Giddens, 1990; Jamieson, 1991). These changes, such as de-industrialisation, feminisation of local labour markets and the diversification of family forms, are contesting and fragmenting traditional lifestyles. Alongside this, education as a post-war representation of the modernist project, involving comprehensive re-organisation, child centred pedagogy, anti-racism and anti-sexism underpinned by a belief in universalism, collectivism, humanism, rational progression and social justice, is being destabilised by this emerging socio-economic uncertainty. For example, fundamental changes in the relationship between the reward structures of the school and the labour market seem to be leading to great confusion among large sectors of male and female students concerning the purpose of school in preparing them for occupational and social destinies (Stanley, 1989). However, education continues to be a social and cultural refuge for the projection and temporary resolution of English social anxieties, as media representations of school standards are portrayed as national exemplars of the social, moral and economic standards. At the same time, schools are actively involved in the production of these anxieties. Current controversies around boys' under-achievement and middle class students' disaffection are shifting concern away from social minorities to a re-examination of social majorities, with the implication that we are no longer sure about the purpose of education. This may be read as part of a broader social and cultural interregnum that we are presently experiencing. As Rutherford (1990, p. 23) proposes:

> We are caught between the decline of the old political identifications and the new identities that are in the process of becoming or yet to be born. Like Laurie Anderson's 'urbanscape' in her song 'Big Science' the imagery traces of the future are present, but as yet have no representation or substance.

It is within this process of political and media displacement that educational researchers are using different epistemological frameworks to explain the formation of young people's identities.

While dominant conceptions of schooling continue to erase the contribution of critical social scientific accounts, alternative conceptualisations of identity formations within educational sites are increasingly engaging with philosophical questions. An important contribution to this engagement is the growing influence of feminist poststructuralism, which places underlying assumptions of identity formation at the centre of their work (Butler, 1993; Sedgewick, 1994; Fuss, 1996). Alongside this influence, we have argued in previous work for the need to re-connect the theorising of identities and education to the wider changing socio-economic and cultural landscape (Haywood and Mac an Ghaill, 1996a,b). This work has focused on examining the interplay between changing social and economic conditions and young people's gender/sexual identities. Importantly, this interplay of material conditions and student subjectivities has highlighted the limitations of earlier theoretical positions. In earlier work we have found it productive to hold together what we identify as materialist and deconstructionist identity epistemologies, in order to access the structures and the categories of identities within educational arenas. While this chapter is informed by this work, we will emphasise, through theorising gender/sexual identities in education sites, some of the broader tensions that ate emerging between these different philosophical accounts.

Materialist and deconstructionist identity epistemologies

Zaretsky (1994) suggests that the central philosophical dilemmas involved in conceptualising identity are based upon, first, what gives a thing or a person its essential nature and, second, what makes a thing or a person the same. These dilemmas are significant, in that they capture the continuities that run through contemporary theorising of gender/sexual identities in education. What remains constant between materialist and deconstructionist accounts of identity formation is the idea that education institutions impact (including through their absence) upon the formation of identities. [...]

Materialist in our chapter refers to social movements that perceive the organisation and normalisation of gender and sexual identities as deriving from fixed bases of social power. Such bases of social power are seen to work logically and predictably, often being illustrated through the subject's occupation of fixed categorical and hierarchical positions, such as dominant and subordinate or oppressed and empowered couplets. We locate materialist conceptualisations of identities within both the political interventionism of the New Social Movements and conceptual discussions of the inter-relationship between structure and agency. In contrast, our discussion of deconstructivism explores aspects such as multiple relations of power, the inversion of power relations and the binaric formation of identity categories. As Davies and Hunt (1994, p. 389) assert: 'Deconstruction is a strategy for displacing the hierarchy, for revealing the dependence of the privileged or ascendant term on its other for its own meaning: deconstruction moves to disrupt binary logic and its hierarchical oppositional constituitive force'. As indicated above, we argue that in order to generate more comprehensive accounts of educational identities, critical analysis needs to engage with both philosophical approaches.

Materialist accounts of identity: politics, structure and agency

An important development in the social sciences over the last 20 years has been the impact of the New Social Movements on re-theorising institutional arenas, such as education. The impact of these New Social Movements has been to re-conceptualise the structural and phenomenological aspects of schooling. In general, these social movements have retained the theoretical and conceptual foundations of earlier social scientific theories, such as Marxism, and thus inherited certain epistemological foundations. Of central importance is how New Social Movements examine the mutually informing relationship between prescribed/proscribed social and cultural status of specific collectivities and the corresponding social relationships and practices that they generate within different institutions and broader social groups. For instance, innovative feminist work stressed the importance of examining how particular areas of school life, such as the occupation of geographical space, the form and content of the curriculum materials and relationships between teachers and students, contributed to the reproduction of gender inequalities within and beyond schooling arenas (Stanworth, 1981; Barrett, 1980). More recently, academics have identified similar processes as operating in an oppressive way towards different sexual minorities, such as gays or lesbians (Jones and Mahony, 1989; Epstein and Johnson, 1994). In this way, New Social Movements tend to concentrate on the processes that reproduce inequalities and the corresponding effects of identity on social equality. It is through the processes of reproduction of inequalities that identity formations take place. As a result, particular social injustices impart the essential nature or identity of different social groups.

Of central concern to the understanding of the formation of gender identities has been to highlight the particular social structures that are used to reproduce social inequality. For example, the use of patriarchy as a conceptual framework to explain gender relations continues to be influential, albeit often unacknowledged, in understanding identity formations in education. Patriarchy, as a complex and multi-levelled distribution of automatic power for men located in interpersonal relations and institutional structures, is seen as a key dynamic in structuring unequal relations between males and females within education (Herbert, 1992). Social positions between men and women are hierarchically ordered, with men's unequal access to disproportionate amounts of power resulting in the oppression of men over women. Similarly, in terms of sexuality, compulsory heterosexuality is used to characterise the ways that education arenas structurally discriminate against people with different sexual identities. More specifically, there is a focus on how the organisation and management of the curriculum benefits heterosexuals (Jones and Mahony, 1989; Appleby, 1996). Of primary importance in this work are the ways that different collectivities, males and females, heterosexuals and gays/lesbians, exist in unequally structured oppositions. In these oppositions, the defining features of identity tend to be intrinsically located within the position occupied.

Methodologically, one important form of researching identities from a materialist position has been to employ standpoint epistemologies. This allows an alternative conceptualisation of educational experience that serves to displace the explanatory power of dominant accounts. For instance, Halson (1989), carrying out research with 14-year-old white lower middle class girls in a co-educational school, locates their experience of sexual harassment within broader structural sources of social power. The girls' position as powerless is seen to derive from an organised/normalised structured relation between men and women. Critically analysing this theoretical position, Jones and Moore (1992, p. 247) assert:

> This theory associated the acquisition of school knowledge with identity formation on the basis of the internalisation of stereotypically 'appropriate' raced and gendered 'images', principally transmitted through the curriculum and reinforced by teacher expectations and the influences of various 'significant others' in the family, peer group and media.

From this it follows that, philosophically, the task is to challenge the dominant masculine ideologies that circumscribe school life. At the same time, from a strategic point of view, this alternative conceptualisation of gender relations suggests the need to remove pupils' and teachers' 'false consciousness' (Askew and Ross, 1988; Jones and Mahony, 1989; Davidson, 1990). In this way, gender/sexual identity becomes strategically connected to the ideologies that different social groups adopt. Hence, a change in the norms and values contained within particular ideologies will serve to change identities.

Materialist accounts of masculinity have identified how at a general level, capitalist economic structures *reproduce* masculinity (Hearn, 1987). Other theorists working within this philosophical tradition, such as Connell (1987, 1995), have emphasised the strategic importance of local institutional sites in the *production* of masculinities. Connell argues that patriarchy, that is the structured subordination of women by men, is the key source of identity formation. However, he develops a conception of identity that differs from biological *or* cultural essentialism, considering how '...personal life and collective social arrangements – are linked in a fundamental and constitutive ways' (1987, p. 17). Connell provides an important contribution to the materialist conceptualisation of gender relations by emphasising the compatibility and complementarity between structures and lived experiences. From this perspective, the institutional structures of schooling, such as qualification hierarchies and streaming mechanisms, are seen as creating a correspondence between the accompanying ideologies and the lived out experience of those who are subject to those ideologies. As a more sophisticated materialist account, institutions are seen to be structured by particular gender regimes; regimes that are historically based and open to change. This begins to contest the universalising fixed binary positioning of males and females. The theoretical shift to *the local level*, as a definitive feature of social relations, allows Connell to illustrate the multiple and varied ways in which the 'fact' of male domination over females can be articulated. Most significantly, this results in opening up categories that were conceptualised as closed. For example, in relation to the formation of gender identities, local institutions are portrayed as active in making available a range of masculinities that may be occupied. In this way, identity reflects the institutional dynamics; it is a mirror image or an effect of certain social mechanisms. Although Connell points to a relative autonomy in the formation of gender identities, a main organising principle of materialist analysis remains, namely that the nature of social being can be logically read off from the institutional infrastructure.

The conceptual limitations of these materialist approaches can be located at the level of their socio-political history. The success of identity politics is based upon its explanatory power in uncovering the logic behind the organisation of social inequalities. The force of materialist explanations are often located through the centrality of particular aspects of social power, such as gender, sexuality or race. However, ultimately, materialist positions are limited in being able to accomodate different forms of social power. For instance, Lees' (1986) discussion of sexual harassment through the use of abusive language/focuses on males' use of the label 'slag' to police female sexuality. Importantly, this sexual policing primarily exists as a gendered process; sexual policing serves the gender hierarchy. Within this framework sexuality cannot exist as a fundamental dynamic of identity formation. Furthermore, the framework is unable to realise the significant challenges of the New Social Movements, which are to create theoretical frameworks that can accommodate a range of social inequalities, such as race/ethnicity, gender, sexuality and class. In short, holding on to a materialist epistemological point of entry into the enquiry of identity formation produces conceptual difficulties in articulating an inclusive account of multiple forms of social power.

The development of deconstructionist accounts of the formation of gender identities, which informs the shift from identity politics to the cultural politics of difference, has gone some way in reconciling this tension. This is now examined with reference to theoretical work on sexuality.

Deconstructionist accounts of identity formation: multiplicity, inversion and binaries

Post-structuralist theorising has had a major influence on sexuality as an area of research. Studies such as Walkerdine (1990), Skeggs (1991), Mac an Ghaill (1994a,b) and Kehily and Nayak (1996) have suggested that the site of schooling involves a more fluid, fragmented and uncertain formation of gender/sexual identities than materialist accounts allow. With an emphasis on de-centred relations of power, concepts such as class, age and race/ethnicity have greater visibility in the theorising of gender/sexual identities. Being informed by French philosophical thinkers such as Derrida, Lacan and Foucault and contemporary North American feminist cultural theorists, including the work of Judith Butler, Eve Kosofky Sedgwick, Diana Fuss and Elspeth Probyn, deconstructionist accounts represent a shift from a highly visible political impetus to one that can be seen as more abstracted or academically orientated. Deconstructivists' argument against the notion of a singular identity manifested through the possession of a unitary self contributes to the absence of a collective political critique. For instance, Flax (1993) points out that Western conceptions of the self have been grounded in a notion of coherence. She argues that psychic structures are constituted by the inter-weaving of many heterogeneous experiences and capacities. These include: complex clusters of capabilities, modes of processing, altering and retaining experience and foci of affect, somatic effects and the transformation of process into various kinds of language, fantasy, delusion, defence, thought and modes of relating to self and others (ibid., pp. 93–94). As a result, an identity 'expresses the simultaneously determined multiple and agentic qualities of subjectivity' (ibid., p. 93).

One of the shifts from a materialist to a deconstructivist position in examining the formation of educational identities has been to focus on the constitutive dynamics of subjectivity. Foucault (1988) has suggested exploring identity as a technology of tae self, where subjectivity is a socio-historical formation of dispersed institutional arenas of power. At a social level, this perspective suggests that having a singular 'identity' is inadequate, because social situations produce varied subjective positions that may be occupied. In its philosophical sense, identity as a form of identification of essential being is inappropriate. What constitutes identity is a range of subject positions that cannot be contained within a singular category. For instance, such subjective positions, Davies (1993) suggests, are constituted by a range of narratives that speak identities. These narratives regulate normative subjective positions. As an individual can be located in a range of social relations at one time, the formation of identities through a range of discursive positions is a highly complex, ambivalent and unfinished process. In this way, subjectivity is conceptualised as a process of *becoming*, characterised by fluidity, oppositions and alliances between particular narrative positions. Exploring the simultaneous relationship between analytic concepts such as age, race/ethnicity, gender, sexuality and class is a significant facet of deconstructivist strategies. This suggests that in order to understand identities in educational sites, researchers need to examine the simultaneous articulations of a dispersed and localised shifting nexus of social power. In short, we need to understand how sexual identities are simultaneously racialised and gendered. For example, Mac an Ghaill (1994b) and Haywood (1996) have explored the ways that gay identities are often juxtaposed with authentic 'Englishness' (see Fuss, 1996). Furthermore, the simultaneous speaking of race/ethnicity and sexuality can also be mapped out as class based, as certain styles of gay identities resonate with forms of middle class Englishness.

Another philosophical position held by deconstructivists has been to invert predictable logocentric assumptions that surround the formation of gender/ sexual identities that appear in materialist analysis. Skeggs (1991) provides a clear illustration of the explanatory power of this theoretical position. As pointed out earlier, materialist approaches to the formation of identity in educational arenas have positioned females as both subordinated females and students. Skeggs' work on young women within a further education college suggests that being female students did not necessitate a double oppression. Rather, the female students in her study were able to contest the dominant institutional gender/sexual hierarchies. For example, the female students would openly challenge the teachers' sexuality. In doing so, they re-positioned themselves with an active positive female sexuality and simultaneously challenged the implicit student position as being the object of teaching. Importantly, Skeggs argues that such displays of power by the young women constituted resistance. As resistance, she suggests that the discursive space won by the female students, in contesting the dominant gender/sexual categories, were not momentary disruptions to an all encompassing dominant gender/sexual discourse (see Aggleton, 1987). Rather, the repositioning by the female students was an effective means of maintaining and defending their own identities. Similar work by Mac an Ghaill (1994a,b) with black and Asian young gays and lesbians has highlighted their contradictory position within educational arenas that actively proscribe sexuality. As a consequence, the gay students articulated the isolation, confusion, marginalisation and alienation they experienced in a secondary school that privileged a naturalised heterosexuality. However, this account became more complex because their dissonant institutional location also contained a positive and creative experience. In particular, the gay and lesbian students had an insight into the contradictory constitution of a naturalised heterosexuality that was structured through ambivalent misogyny and homophobia: In this way, gay and lesbian students were able to occupy positions of power that allowed the contestation and inversion of heterosexual power. As Mathew, a young gay man, illustrates:

> Mathew: The RE teacher said one day in class that teenage boys go through a homosexual phase just like earlier on they go through an anti-girls' phase.... I told him, I didn't think that boys go through phases. I said that if boys go through an anti-girls' phase, it was a long phase because men were abusing women all of their lives.... The teacher went mad. It was gays that were supposed to be the problem and I turned it round to show the way that it really is....
>
> (Ibid., p. 168)

The final aspect of a deconstructivist philosophical position we wish to discuss is the function of binaries within the formation of gender/sexual identities. Bronwyn Davies (1995), using deconstructivism to explore boys' literacy, emphasises the need to challenge the male/female binaries that constitute educational practices. In particular, Davies concentrates on the stories employed by English teachers and the ways that male and female binaries are maintained throughout teaching practices. In a creative way, Davies uses alternative narratives in stories to contest traditional assumptions of maleness, namely that maleness equals aggressiveness, competence with females, misogyny, hedonism and toughness with stories that problematise such positioning. As a deconstructive strategy, it is not intended as a process of re-education, but rather as a simultaneous disruption of the traditional cultural resources employed to make masculinities. It attempts to highlight the discovery of the political and personal problems entailed in performing maleness. Through pedagogical practices Davies attempts to transcend, the binaric oppositions that she argues constitute dominant conceptions of gender/sexual identities. For example, she outlines a feminist pirate story, where the female pirate is in competition with a male pirate. The story ends with the male pirate giving up his claims to being mean and dangerous. Davies then illustrates how the boys rejected the pirate's initial claim to an authentic aggressive masculinity. This process involves deconstructing how males gain ascendant positions in relation to other males and females, through these binaries. In doing this, Davies suggests that gender/sexual identity formation is performative. Performative from this position suggests that gender/sexual identities are a continual establishment and articulation of binaries. In response, materialists have criticised deconstructivists for assuming that identities are available to everyone, with the opportunity to take up, reposition themselves and become powerful. Butler (1993) has challenged this interpretation. She argues that the very conditions of identity formation are the interrelated cultural matrices of institutional and psychic gender/sexual practices. As lived-out and state-regulated cultural representations, these practices in themselves become ontological evidence of an essential identity; even though, according to Bulter, such evidence is illusory.

Adopting a different emphasis, Dollimore (1991) examines the particular dynamics of binaries in the structures and categories of identities. In direct conflict with the notion of identity formed through its inherent or intrinsic nature, Dollimore suggests that identities can only exist in a symbiotic relationship to what they are not. What Dollimore calls the 'perverse dynamic' is a conceptualisation of identities depending on and giving ontological priority to other identities. This perspective provides a more complex understanding of gender/sexual identities within the context or educational sites. For instance, it suggests that heterosexual identities can only articulate themselves in relation to gay and lesbian identities. Furthermore, it can be argued that the discriminatory practices against gays and lesbians are articulations of heterosexual claims to an authentic identity. From this philosophical position, identities are not formed through an 'essential being' or 'separateness', but through the containment and promotion of oppositions. It is through the promotion of oppositions and their displacement that various identities are established. At a more general level, this epistemological stance fundamentally employs an anti-ontological position. As Woodwiss (1990, p. 31) asserts in relation to post-structuralism: '... the position rests upon a claim to know an epistemological truth; that is, epistemology offers no satisfactory route to the truth'. It is part of the contradictions within this approach that materialism may be used to counter such limitations. It is within such a theoretical framework that we have found it productive to hold on to the tensions between materialism and deconstructivism. One way this may be achieved is by recognising the philosophical limitations of contemporary social scientific conceptualisations of gender/sexual identity formations. We also suggest materialist and deconstructionist accounts need to be complemented by psychoanalytic perspectives (see Benjamin, 1988; Fuss, 1991; Redman and Mac an Ghaill, 1996).

Conclusion

Placing ourselves within the conditions of late modernity, marked by notions of fragmentation, dislocation and hybridity, we have illustrated a hybrid form of philosophising that brings together a traditional concern of philosophy, namely the question of identity, with recent theoretical and conceptual frameworks developed within sociology and cultural studies. Importantly, in order to develop philosophically informed sociological and cultural studies' perspectives that engage comprehensively with the range of theoretical and epistemological perspectives of identity formation there is a need for a continual referral to social relations themselves. In so doing, this will not only test out theorising, but also provide alternative avenues of enquiry. If social science is to continue to make sense of social phenomena at a time of rapid global and local social change, there is a need to explore both socio-historical continuities and discontinuities within different epistemologies of identity. In this way, the challenge centres not so much upon underlying different representations of identity formations, but a need to address more fundamental issues of the processes involved in identity formation.

References

Aggleton, P. (1987) *Rebels Without a Cause?: Middle Class Youth and the Transition from School to Work* (Lewes, Falmer).

Appleby, Y. (1996) 'Decidedly different': Lesbian women and education, *International Studies in the Sociology of Education*, 6, pp. 67–87.

Askew, S. and Ross, C. (1988) *Boys Don't Cry: Boys and Sexism in Education* (Milton Keynes, Open University).

Barrett, M. (1980) *Women's Oppression Today* (London, Verso).

Benjamin, J. (1988) *The Bonds of Love: Psychoanalysis, Feminism and the Problem of Domination* (London, Virago).

Butler, J. (1993) *Bodies that Matter, On the Discursive Limits of 'Sex'* (London, Routledge).

Connell, R.W. (1987) *Gender and Power* (Cambridge, Polity).

Connell, R.W. (1995) *Masculinities* (Cambridge, Polity).

Davidson, N. (1990) *Boys Will Be...? Sex Education and Young Men* (London, Bedford Square: Press).

Davies, B. (1993) *Shards of Glass: Children, Reading and Writing Beyond Gendered Identities* (Sydney, Unwin and Allen).

Davies, B. (1995) What about the boys? The parable of the bear and the rabbit, *Interpretations*, 28, 2, pp. 1–7.

Davies, B. and Hunt, R. (1994) Classroom competencies and marginal positioning, *British Journal of Sociology of Education*, 15, pp. 389–408.

Dollimore, J. (1991) *Sexual Dissidence: Augustine to Wilde, Freud to Foucault* (Oxford, Clarendon Press).

Epstein, D. and Johnson, R. (1994) On the straight and narrow: the heterosexual presumption, homophobias and schools, in: D. Epstein (Ed.) *Challenging Lesbian and Gay Inequalities it Education* (Buckingham, Open University).

Flax, J. (1993) *Disputed Subjects: Essays on Psychoanalysis, Politics and Philosophy* (New York, Routledge).

Foucault, M. (1988) Technologies of the self, in: L. H. Martin, H. Gutman and P. H. Hutton (Eds) *Technologies of the Self: A Seminar with Michael Foucault* (London, Tavistock).

Fuss, D. (1991) Decking out: performing identities, in: D. Fuss (Ed.) *Inside/Out: Lesbian Theories, Gay Theories* (New York, Routledge).

Fuss, D. (1996) *The Identification Papers* (New York, Routledge).

Giddens, A. (1990) *The Consequences of Modernity* (Cambridge, Polity).

Halson, J. (1989) Young women, sexual harassment and heterosexuality: violence, power relations and mixed sex schooling, in: P. Abbot and C. Wallace (Eds) *Gender, Power and Sexuality* (London, Macmillan),

Harvey, D. (1989) *The Conditions of Post-Modernity* (Oxford, Basil Blackwell).

Haywood, C. (1996) Out of the curriculum: sex talk, talking sex, *Curriculum Studies*, 4, pp. 229–249.

Haywood, C. and Mac an Ghaill, M. (1996a) The sexual politics of the curriculum: contested values, *International Studies in the Sociology of Education*, 5, pp. 231–236.

Haywood, C. and Mac an Ghaill, M. (1996b) What about the boys?, *British Journal of Education and Work*, 9, pp. 19–30.

Hearn, J. (1987) *The Gender of Oppression: Men, Masculinity and the Critique of Marxism* (Brighton, Wheatsheaf).

Herbert, C.M.H. (1992) *Sexual Harassment in Schools: A Guide for Teachers* (London, David Fulton).

Jamieson, F. (1991) *Postmodernism or the Cultural Logic of Late Capitalism* (London, Sage).

Jones, C. and Mahony, P. (Eds) (1989) *Learning Our Lines: Sexuality and Social Control in Education* (London, The Women's Press).

Jones, L. and Moore, R. (1992) Equal opportunities: the curriculum and the subject, *Cambridge Journal of Education*, 22, pp. 243–253.

Kehily, M. and Nayak, A. (1996) 'Playing it straight': masculinities and homophobias and schooling, *Journal of Gender Studies*, 5, pp. 211–230.

Lees, S. (1986) *Losing Out: Sexuality and Adolescent Girls* (London, Hutchinson).

Mac an Ghaill, M. (1994a) *The Making of Men: Masculinities, Sexualities and Schooling* (Buckingham, Open University).

Mac an Ghaill, M. (1994b) (In)visibility: sexuality, masculinity and 'race' in the school context, in: D. Epstein (Ed.) *Challenging Lesbian and Gay Inequalities in Education* (Buckingham, Open University).

Redman, P. and Mac an Ghaill, M. (1996) Schooling sexualities: heterosexual masculinities, schooling and the unconscious, *Discourse*, 17, pp. 243–256.

Rutherford, J. (1990) A place called home: identity and the cultural politics of difference, in: J. Rutherford (Ed.) *Identity: Community, Culture and Difference* (London, Lawrence and Wishart).

Sedgwick, E.K. (1994) *Tendencies* (London, Routledge).

Skeggs, B. (1991) Challenging masculinity and using sexuality, *British Journal of Sociology of Education*, 12, pp. 127–140.

Stanley, J. (1989) *Marks on the Memory* (Buckingham, Open University Press).

Stanworth, M. (1981) *Gender and Schooling* (London, Women's Research and Resource Centre).

Walkerdine, V. (1990) *Schoolgirl Fictions* (London, Verso).

Woodwiss, A. (1990) *Social Theory after Postmodernism: Rethinking Production, Law and Class* (London, Pluto).

Zaretsky, E. (1994) Identity theory, identity politics: psychoanalysis, Marxism, post-structuralism, in: C. Calhoun (Ed.) *Social Theory and the Politics of Identity* (Blackman, Oxford).

PART 2

DIFFERENCE AND POWER

CHAPTER 5

PERFORMATIVE ACTS AND GENDER CONSTITUTION
An essay in phenomenology and feminist theory

Judith Butler, in C.R. McCann and K. Seung-Kyung (eds)
Feminist Theory Reader, Routledge, 2003

Philosophers rarely think about acting in the theatrical sense, but they do have a discourse of 'acts' that maintains associative semantic meanings with theories of performance and acting. For example…the phenomenological theory of 'acts', espoused by Edmund Husserl, Maurice Merleau-Ponty, and George Herbert Mead, among others, seeks to explain the mundane way in which social agents *constitute* social reality through language, gesture, and all manner of symbolic social sign. Though phenomenology sometimes appears to assume the existence of a choosing and constituting agent prior to language (who poses as the sole source of its constituting acts), there is also a more radical use of the doctrine of constitution that takes the social agent as an *object* rather than the subject of constitutive acts.

When Simone de Beauvoir claims, 'one is not born, but, rather, *becomes* a woman', she is appropriating and reinterpreting this doctrine of constituting acts from the phenomenological tradition.[1] In this sense, gender is in no way a stable identity of locus of agency from which various acts proceed; rather, it is an identity tenuously constituted in time – an identity instituted through a stylized repetition of acts. Further, gender is instituted through the stylization of the body and, hence, must be understood as the mundane way in which bodily gestures, movements, and enactments of various kinds constitute the illusion of an abiding gendered self. This formulation moves the conception of gender off the ground of a substantial model of identity to one that requires a conception of a constituted *social temporality*. Significantly, if gender is instituted through acts which are internally discontinuous, then the *appearance of substance* is precisely that, a constructed identity, a performative accomplishment which the mundane social audience, including the actors themselves, come to believe and to perform in the mode of belief. If the ground of gender identity is the stylized repetition of acts through time, and not a seemingly seamless identity, then the possibilities of gender transformation are to be found in the arbitrary relation, between such acts, in the possibility of a different sort of repeating, in the breaking or subversive repetition of that style.

Through the conception of gender acts sketched above, I will try to show some ways in which reified and naturalized conceptions of gender might be understood as constituted and, hence, capable of being constituted differently. In opposition to theatrical or phenomenological models which take the gendered self to be prior to its acts, I will understand constituting acts not only as constituting the identity of the actor, but constituting that identity as a compelling illusion, an object of *belief*. In the course of making my argument, I will draw from theatrical, anthropological, and philosophical discourses, but mainly phenomenology, to show that what is called gender identity is a performative accomplishment compelled by social sanction and taboo. In its very character as performative resides the possibility of contesting its reified status.

Sex/gender: feminist and phenomenological views

Feminist theory has often been critical of naturalistic explanations of sex and sexuality that assume that the meaning of women's social existence can be derived from some fact of their physiology. In distinguishing sex from gender, feminist theorists have disputed causal explanations that assume that sex dictates or necessitates certain social meanings for women's experience. Phenomenological theories of human embodiment have also been concerned to distinguish between the various physiological and biological causalities that structure bodily existence and the *meanings* that embodied existence assumes in the context of lived experience. In Merleau-Ponty's reflections in *The Phenomenology of Perception* on 'the body in its sexual being', he takes issue with such accounts of bodily experience and claims that the body is 'an historical idea' rather than 'a natural species'.[2] Significantly, it is this claim that Simone de Beauvoir cites in *The Second Sex* when she sets the stage for her claim that 'woman', and by extension, any gender, is an historical situation rather than a natural fact.[3]

In both contexts, the existence and facticity of the material or natural dimensions of the body are not denied, but reconceived as distinct from the process by which the body comes to bear cultural meanings. For both Beauvoir and Merleau-Ponty, the body is understood to be an active process of embodying certain cultural and historical possibilities, a complicated process of appropriation which any phenomenological theory of constitution needs to describe. In order to describe the gendered body, a phenomenological theory of constitution requires an expansion of the conventional view of acts to mean both that which constitutes meaning and that through which meaning is performed or enacted. In other words, the acts by which gender is constituted bear similarities to performative acts within theatrical contexts. My task, then, is to examine in what ways gender is constructed through specific corporeal acts, and what possibilities exist for the cultural transformation of gender through such acts.

Merleau-Ponty maintains not only that the body is an historical idea but a set of possibilities to be continually realized. In claiming that the body is an historical idea, Merleau-Ponty means that it gains its meaning through a concrete and historically mediated expression in the world. That the body is a set of possibilities signifies (a) that its appearance in the world, for perception, is not predetermined by some manner of interior essence, and (b) that its concrete expression in the world must be understood as the taking up and rendering specific of a set of historical possibilities. Hence, there is an agency which is understood as the process of rendering such possibilities determinate. These possibilities are necessarily constrained by available historical conventions. The body is not a self-identical or merely factic materiality; it is a materiality that bears meaning, if nothing else, and the manner of this bearing is fundamentally dramatic. By dramatic I mean only that the body is not merely matter but a continual and incessant *materialization* of possibilities. One is not simply a body, but, in some very key sense, one does one's body and, indeed, one does one's body differently from one's contemporaries and from one's embodied predecessors and successors as well.

It is, however, clearly unfortunate grammar to claim that there is a 'we' or an 'I' that does its body, as if a disembodied agency preceded and directed an embodied exterior. More appropriate, I suggest, would be a vocabulary that resists the substance metaphysics of subject-verb formations and relies instead on an ontology of present participles. The 'I' that is its body is, of necessity, a mode of embodying, and the 'what' that it embodies is possibilities. But here again the grammar of the formulation misleads, for the possibilities that are embodied are not fundamentally exterior or antecedent to the process of embodying itself. As an intentionally organized materiality, the body is always an embodying *of* possibilities both conditioned and circumscribed by historical convention. In other words, the body *is* a historical situation, as Beauvoir has claimed, and is a manner of doing, dramatizing, and *reproducing* a historical situation.

To do, to dramatize, to reproduce, these seem to be some of the elementary structures of embodiment. This doing of gender is not merely a way in which embodied agents are exterior, surfaced, open to the perception of others. Embodiment clearly manifests a set of strategies or what Sartre would perhaps have called a style of being or Foucault, 'a stylistics of existence'. This style is never fully self-styled, for living styles have a history, and that history conditions and limits possibilities. Consider gender, for instance, as *a corporeal style*, an 'act', as it were, which is both intentional and performative, where 'performative' itself carries the double-meaning of 'dramatic' and 'non-referential'.

When Beauvoir claims that 'woman' is a historical idea and not a natural fact, she clearly underscores the distinction between sex, as biological facticity, and gender, as the cultural interpretation or signification of that facticity. To be female is, according to that distinction, a facticity which has no meaning, but to be a woman is to have *become* a woman, to compel the body to conform to an historical idea of 'woman', to induce the body to become a cultural sign, to materialize oneself in obedience to an historically delimited possibility, and to do this as a sustained and repeated corporeal project. The notion of a 'project', however, suggests the originating force of a radical will, and because gender is a project which has cultural survival as its end, the term '*strategy*' better suggests the situation of duress under which gender performance always and variously occurs. Hence, as a strategy of survival, gender is a performance with clearly punitive consequences. Discrete genders are part of what 'humanizes' individuals within contemporary culture; indeed, those who fail to do their gender right are regularly punished. Because there is neither an 'essence' that gender expresses or externalizes nor an objective ideal to which gender aspires; because gender is not a fact, the various acts of gender, and without those acts would be no gender at all. Gender is, thus, a construction that regularly conceals its genesis. The tacit collective agreement to perform, produce, and sustain discrete and polar genders as cultural fictions is obscured by the credibility of its own production. The authors of gender become entranced by their own fictions whereby the construction compels one's belief in its necessity and naturalness. The historical possibilities materialized through various corporeal styles are nothing other than those punitively regulated cultural fictions that are alternately embodied and disguised under duress.

How useful is a phenomenological point of departure for a feminist description of gender? On the surface it appears that phenomenology shares with feminist analysis a commitment to grounding theory in lived experience, and in revealing the way in which the world is produced through the constituting acts of subjective experience. Clearly, not all feminist theory would privilege the point of view of the subject (Kristeva once objected to feminist theory as 'too existentialist'),[4] and yet, the feminist claim that the personal is political suggests, in part, that subjective experience is not only structured by existing political arrangements, but effects and structures those arrangements in turn. Feminist theory has sought to understand the way in which systemic or pervasive political and cultural structures are enacted and reproduced through individual acts and practices, and how the analysis of ostensibly personal situations is clarified through situating the issues in a broader and shared cultural context. Indeed, the feminist impulse, and I am sure there is more than one, has often emerged in the recognition that my pain or my silence or my anger or my perception is finally not mine alone, and that it delimits me in a shared cultural situation which in turn enables and empowers me in certain unanticipated ways. The personal is thus implicitly political inasmuch as it is conditioned by shared social structures, but the personal has also been immunized against political challenge to the extent that public/private distinctions endure. For feminist theory, then, the personal becomes an expansive category, one which accommodates, if only implicitly, political structures usually viewed as public. Indeed, the very meaning of the political expands as well. At its best, feminist theory involves a dialectical expansion of both of these categories. My situation does not cease to be mine just because it is the situation of someone else, and my acts, individual as they are, nevertheless reproduce the situation of my gender, and do that in various ways. In other words, there is, latent in the personal is political formulation of feminist theory, a supposition that the life-world of gender relations is constituted, at least partially, through the concrete and historically mediated *acts* of individuals. Considering that 'the' body is invariably transformed into his body or her body, the body is only known through its gendered appearance. It would seem imperative to consider the way in which this gendering of the body occurs. My suggestion is that the body becomes its gender through a series of acts which are renewed, revised, and consolidated through time. From a feminist point of view, one might try to reconceive the gendered body as the legacy of sedimented acts rather than a predetermined or foreclosed structure, essence or fact, whether natural, cultural, or linguistic.

The feminist appropriation of the phenomenological theory of constitution might employ the notion of an *act* in a richly ambiguous sense. If the personal is a category which expands to include the wider political and social structures, then the *acts* of the gendered subject would be similarly expansive. Clearly, there are political acts which are deliberate and instrumental actions of political organizing, resistance, and collective intervention with the broad aim of instating a more just set of social and political relations. There are thus acts which are done in the name of women, and then there are acts in and of themselves, apart from any instrumental consequence, that challenge the category of women itself. Indeed, one ought to consider the futility of a political program which seeks radically to transform the social situation of women without first determining whether the category of woman is socially constructed in such a way that to be a woman is, by definition, to be in an oppressed situation. In an understandable desire to forge bonds of solidarity, feminist discourse has often relied upon the category of woman as a universal presupposition of cultural experience which, in its universal status, provides a false ontological promise of eventual political solidarity. In a culture in which the false universal of 'man' has for the most part been presupposed as coextensive with humanness itself, feminist theory has sought with success to bring female specificity into visibility and to rewrite the history of culture in terms which acknowledge the presence, the influence, and the oppression of women. Yet, in this effort to combat the invisibility of women as a category, feminists run the risk of rendering visible a category which may or may not be representative of the concrete lives of women. As feminists, we have been less eager, I think, to consider the status of the category itself and, indeed, to discern the conditions of oppression which issue from an unexamined reproduction of gender identities which sustain discrete and binary categories of man and woman.

When Beauvoir claims that woman is an 'historical situation', she emphasizes that the body suffers a certain cultural construction, not only through conventions that sanction and proscribe how one acts one's body, the 'act' or performance that one's body is, but also in the tacit conventions that structure the way the body is culturally perceived. Indeed, if gender is the cultural significance that the sexed body assumes, and if that significance is codetermined through various acts and their cultural perception, then it would appear that from within the terms of culture it is not possible to know sex as distinct from gender. The reproduction of the category of gender is enacted on a large political scale, as when women first enter a profession or gain certain rights, or are reconceived in legal or political discourse in significantly new ways. But the more mundane reproduction of gendered identity takes place through the various ways in which bodies are acted in relationship to the deeply entrenched or sedimented expectations of gendered existence. Consider that there is a sedimentation of gender norms that produces the peculiar phenomenon of a natural sex, or a real woman, or any number of prevalent and compelling social fictions, and that this is a sedimentation that over time has produced a set of corporeal styles which, in reified form, appear as the natural configuration of bodies into sexes which exist in a binary relation to one another.

Binary genders and the heterosexual contract

To guarantee the reproduction of a given culture, various requirements, well-established in the anthropological literature of kinship, have instated sexual reproduction within the confines of a heterosexually based system of marriage which requires the reproduction of human beings in certain gendered modes which, in effect, guarantee the eventual reproduction of that kinship system. As Foucault and others have pointed out, the association of a natural sex with a discrete gender and with an ostensibly natural 'attraction' to the opposing sex/gender is an unnatural conjunction of cultural constructs in the service of reproductive interests.[5] Feminist cultural anthropology and kinship studies have shown how cultures are governed by conventions that not only regulate and guarantee the production, exchange, and consumption of material goods, but also reproduce the bonds of kinship itself, which require taboos and a punitive regulation or reproduction to effect that end. Levi-Strauss has shown how the incest taboo works to guarantee the channeling of sexuality into various modes of heterosexual marriage.[6] Gayle Rubin has argued convincingly that the incest taboo produces certain kinds of discrete gendered identities and sexualities.[7] My point is simply that one way in which this system of compulsory heterosexuality is reproduced and concealed is through the cultivation of bodies into discrete sexes with 'natural' appearances and 'natural' heterosexual dispositions. Although the enthnocentric conceit suggests a progression beyond the mandatory structures of kinship relations as described by Levi-Strauss, I would suggest, along with Rubin, that contemporary gender identities are so many marks or 'traces' of residual kinship. The contention that sex, gender, and heterosexuality are historical products which have become conjoined and reified as natural over time has received a good deal of critical attention not only from Michel Foucault, but Monique Wittig, gay historians, and various cultural anthropologists and social psychologists in recent years.[8] These theories, however, still lack the critical resources for thinking radically about the historical sedimentation of sexuality and sex-related constructs if they do not delimit and describe the mundane manner in which these constructs are produced, reproduced, and maintained within the field of bodies.

Can phenomenology assist a feminist reconstruction of the sedimented character of sex, gender, and sexuality at the level of the body? In the first place, the phenomenological focus on the various acts by which cultural identity is constituted and assumed provides a felicitous starting point for the feminist effort to understand the mundane manner in which bodies get crafted into genders. The formulation of the body as a mode of dramatizing or enacting possibilities offers a way to understand how a cultural convention is embodied and enacted. But it seems difficult, if not impossible, to imagine a way to conceptualize the scale and systemic character of women's oppression from a theoretical position which takes constituting acts to be its point of departure. Although individual acts do work to maintain and reproduce systems of oppression, and, indeed, any theory of personal political responsibility presupposes such a view, it doesn't follow that oppression is a sole consequence of such acts. One might argue that without human beings whose various acts, largely construed, produce and maintain oppressive conditions, those conditions would fall away, but note that the relation between acts and conditions is neither unilateral nor unmediated. There are social contexts and conventions within which certain acts not only become possible but become conceivable as acts at all. The transformation of social relations becomes a matter, then, of transforming hegemonic social conditions rather than the individual acts that are spawned by those conditions. Indeed, one runs the risk of addressing the merely indirect, if not epiphenomenal, reflection of those conditions if one remains restricted to a politics of acts.

But the theatrical sense of an 'act' forces a revision of the individualist assumptions underlying the more restricted view of constituting acts within phenomenological discourse. As a given temporal duration within the entire performance, 'acts' are a shared experience and 'collective action'. Just as within feminist theory the very category of the personal is expanded to include political structures, so is there a theatrically based and, indeed, less individually oriented view of acts that goes some of the way in defusing the criticism of act theory as 'too existentialist.' The act that gender is, the act that embodied agents *are* inasmuch as they dramatically and actively embody and, indeed, *wear* certain cultural significations, is clearly not one's act alone. Surely, there are nuanced and individual ways of *doing* one's gender, but *that* one does it, and that one does it in *accord with* certain sanctions and proscriptions, is clearly not a fully individual matter. Here again, I don't mean to minimize the effect of certain gender norms which originate within the family and are enforced through certain familial modes of punishment and reward and which, as a consequence, might be construed as highly individual, for even there family relations recapitulate, individualize, and specify preexisting cultural relations; they are rarely, if ever, radically original. The act that one does, the act that one performs, is, in a sense, an act that has been going on before one arrived on the scene. Hence, gender is an act which has been rehearsed, much as a script survives the particular actors who make use of it, but which requires individual actors in order to be actualized and reproduced as reality once again. The complex components that go into an act must be distinguished in order to understand the kind of acting in concert and acting in accord which acting one's gender invariably is.

In what senses, then, is gender an act? As anthropologist Victor Turner suggests in his studies of ritual social drama, social action requires a performance which is *repeated*. This repetition is at once a reenactment and reexperiencing of a set of meanings already socially established; it is the mundane and ritualized form of their legitimation.[9] When this conception of social performance is applied to gender, it is clear that although there are individual bodies that enact these significations by becoming stylized into gendered modes, this 'action' is immediately public as well. There are temporal and collective dimensions to these actions, and their public nature is not inconsequential; indeed, the performance is effected with the strategic aim of maintaining gender within its binary frame. Understood in pedagogical terms, the performance renders social laws explicit.

As a public action and performative act, gender is not a radical choice or project that reflects a merely individual choice, but neither is it imposed or inscribed upon the individual, as some post-structuralist displacements of the subject would contend. The body is not passively scripted with cultural codes, as if it were a lifeless recipient of wholly pregiven cultural relations. But neither do embodied selves preexist the cultural conventions which essentially signify bodies. Actors are always already on the stage, within the terms of the performance. Just as a script may be enacted in various ways, and just as the play requires both text and interpretation, so the gendered body acts its part in a culturally restricted corporeal space and enacts interpretations within the confines of already existing directives.

Although the links between a theatrical and a social role are complex and the distinctions not easily drawn (Bruce Wilshire points out the limits of the comparison in *Role-Playing and Identity: The Limits of Theatre as Metaphor*),[10] it seems clear that, although theatrical performances can meet with political censorship and scathing criticism, gender performances in nontheatrical contexts are governed by more clearly punitive and regulatory social conventions. Indeed, the sight of a transvestite onstage can compel pleasure and applause while the sight of the same transvestite on the seat next to us on the bus can compel fear, rage, even violence. The conventions which mediate proximity and identification in these two instances are clearly quite different. I want to make two different kinds of claims regarding this tentative distinction. In the theatre, one can say, 'this is just an act', and derealize the act, make acting into something quite distinct from what is real. Because of this distinction, one can maintain one's sense of reality in the face of this temporary challenge to our existing ontological assumptions about gender arrangements; the various conventions which announce that 'this is only a play' allows strict lines to be drawn between the performance and life. On the street or in the bus, the act becomes dangerous, if it does, precisely because there are no theatrical conventions to delimit the purely imaginary character of the act, indeed, on the street or in the bus, there is no presumption that the act is distinct from a reality, the disquieting effect of the act is that there are no conventions that facilitate making this separation. Clearly, there is theatre which attempts to contest or, indeed, break down those conventions that demarcate the imaginary from the real (Richard Schechner brings this out quite clearly in *Between Theatre and Anthropology*).[11] Yet in those cases one confronts the same phenomenon, namely, that the act is not contrasted with the real, but *constitutes* a reality that is in some sense new, a modality of gender that cannot readily be assimilated into the preexisting categories that regulate gender reality. From the point of view of those established categories, one may want to claim, but oh, this is *really* a girl or a woman, or this is *really* a boy or a man, and further that the *appearance* contradicts the *reality* of the gender, that the discrete and familiar reality must be there, nascent, temporarily unrealized, perhaps realized at other times or other places. The transvestite, however, can do more than simply express the distinction between sex and gender, but challenges, at least implicitly, the distinction between appearance and reality that structures a good deal of popular thinking about gender identity. If the 'reality' of gender is constituted by the performance itself, then there is no recourse to an essential and unrealized 'sex' or 'gender' which gender performances ostensibly express. Indeed, the transvestite's gender is as fully real as anyone whose performance complies with social expectations.

Gender reality is performative which means, quite simply, that it is real only to the extent that it is performed. It seems fair to say that certain kinds of acts are usually interpreted as expressive of a gender core or identity, and that these acts either conform to an expected gender identity or contest that expectation in some way. That expectation, in turn, is based upon the perception of sex, where sex is understood to be the discrete and *factic datum* of primary sexual characteristics. This implicit and popular theory of acts and gestures as *expressive* of gender suggests that gender itself is something prior to the various acts, postures, and gestures by which it is dramatized and known; indeed, gender appears to the popular imagination as a substantial core which might well be understood as the spiritual or psychological correlate of biological sex.[12] If gender attributes, however, are not expressive but performative, then these attributes effectively constitute the identity they are said to express or reveal. The distinction between expression and performativeness is quite crucial, for if gender attributes and acts, the various ways in which a body shows or produces its cultural signification, are performative, then there is no preexisting identity by which an act or attribute might be measured; there would be no true or false, real or distorted acts of gender, and the postulation of a true gender identity would be revealed as a regulatory fiction. That gender reality is created through sustained social performances means that the very notions of an essential sex, a true or abiding masculinity or femininity, are also constituted as part of the strategy by which the performative aspect of gender is concealed.

As a consequence, gender cannot be understood as a *role* which either expresses or disguises an interior 'self', whether that 'self' is conceived as sexed or not. As performance which is performative, gender is an 'act', broadly construed, which constructs the social fiction of its own psychological interiority. As opposed to a view such as Erving Goffman's which posits a self which assumes and exchanges various 'roles' within the complex social expectations of the 'game' of modern life,[13] I am suggesting that this self is not only irretrievably 'outside', constituted in social discourse, but that the ascription of interiority is itself a publicly regulated and sanctioned form of essence fabrication. Genders, then, can be neither true nor false, neither real nor apparent. And yet, one is compelled to live in a world in which genders constitute univocal signifiers, in which gender is stabilized, polarized, rendered discrete and intractable. In effect, gender is made to comply with a model of truth and falsity which not only contradicts its own performative fluidity, but serves a social policy of gender regulation and control. Performing one's gender wrong initiates a set of punishments both obvious and indirect, and performing it well provides the reassurance that there is an essentialism of gender identity after all. That this reassurance is so easily displaced by anxiety, that culture so readily punishes or marginalizes those who fail to perform the illusion of gender essentialism should be sign enough that on some level there is social knowledge that the truth or falsity of gender is only socially compelled and in no sense ontologically necessitated.

Feminist theory: beyond an expressive model of gender

This view of gender does not pose as a comprehensive theory about what gender is or the manner of its construction, and neither does it prescribe an explicit feminist political program. Indeed, I can imagine this view of gender being used for a number of discrepant political strategies. Some of my friends may fault me for this and insist that any theory of gender constitution has political presuppositions and implications, and that it is impossible to separate a theory of gender from a political philosophy of feminism. In fact, I would agree, and argue that it is primarily political interests which create the social phenomena of gender itself, and that without a radical critique of gender constitution, feminist theory fails to take stock of the way in which oppression structures the ontological categories through which gender is conceived. Gayatri Spivak has argued that feminists need to rely on an operational essentialism, a false ontology of women as a universal in order to advance a feminist political program.[14] She knows that the category of 'women' is not fully expressive, that the multiplicity and discontinuity of the referent mocks and rebels against the univocity of the sign, but suggests it could be used for strategic purposes. Kristeva suggests something similar, I think, when she prescribes that feminists use the category of women as a political tool without attributing ontological integrity to the term, and adds that, strictly speaking, women cannot be said to exist.[15] Feminists might well worry about the political implications of claiming that women do not exist, especially in light of the persuasive arguments advanced by Mary Anne Warren in her book, *Gendercide*.[16] She argues that social policies regarding population control and reproductive technology are designed to limit and, at times, eradicate the existence of women altogether. In light of such a claim, what good does it do to quarrel about the metaphysical status of the term, and perhaps, for clearly political reasons, feminists ought to silence the quarrel altogether.

But it is one thing to use the term and know its ontological insufficiency and quite another to articulate a normative vision for feminist theory which celebrates or emancipates an essence, a nature, or a shared reality which cannot be found. The option I am defending is not to redescribe the world from the point of view of women. I don't know what that point of view is, but whatever it is, it is not singular, and not mine to espouse. It would only be half-right to claim that I am interested in how the phenomenon of a men's or women's point of view gets constituted, for while I do think that those points of views are, indeed, socially constituted, and that a reflexive genealogy of those points of view is important to do, it is not primarily the gender episteme that I am interested in exposing, deconstructing, or reconstructing. Indeed, it is the presupposition of the category of 'woman' itself that requires a critical genealogy of the complex institutional and discursive means by which it is constituted. Although some feminist literary critics suggest that the presupposition of sexual difference is necessary for all discourse, that position reifies sexual difference as the founding moment of culture and precludes an analysis not only of how sexual difference is constituted to begin with but how it is continuously constituted, both by the masculine tradition that preempts the universal point of view, and by those feminist positions that construct the univocal category of 'women' in the name of expressing or, indeed, liberating a subjected class. As Foucault claimed about those humanist efforts to liberate the criminalized subject, the subject that is freed is even more deeply shackled than originally thought.[17]

Clearly, though, I envision the critical genealogy of gender to rely on a phenomenological set of presuppositions, most important among them the expanded conception of an 'act' which is both socially shared and historically constituted, and which is performative in the sense I previously described. But a critical genealogy needs to be supplemented by a politics of performative gender acts, one which both redescribes existing gender identities and offers a prescriptive view about the kind of gender reality there ought to be. The redescription needs to expose the reifications that tacitly serve as substantial gender cores or identities, and to elucidate both the act and the strategy of disavowal which at once constitute and conceal gender as we live it. The prescription is invariably more difficult, if only because we need to think a world in which acts, gestures, the visual body, the clothed body, the various physical attributes usually associated with gender, *express nothing*. In a sense, the prescription is not utopian, but consists in an imperative to acknowledge the existing complexity of gender which our vocabulary invariably disguises and to bring that complexity into a dramatic cultural interplay without punitive consequences.

Certainly, it remains politically important to represent women, but to do that in a way that does not distort and reify the very collectivity the theory is supposed to emancipate. Feminist theory which presupposes sexual difference as the necessary and invariant theoretical point of departure clearly improves upon those humanist discourses which conflate the universal with the masculine and appropriate all of culture as masculine property. Clearly, it is necessary to reread the texts of western philosophy from the various points of view that have been excluded, not only to reveal the particular perspective and set of interests informing those ostensibly transparent descriptions of the real, but to offer alternative descriptions and prescriptions; indeed, to establish philosophy as a cultural practice, and to criticize its tenets from marginalized cultural locations. I have no quarrel with this procedure, and have clearly benefited from those analyses. My only concern is that sexual difference does not become a reification which unwittingly preserves a binary restriction on gender identity and an implicitly heterosexual framework for the description of gender, gender identity, and sexuality. There is, in my view, nothing about femaleness that is waiting to be expressed; there is, on the other hand, a good deal about the diverse experiences of women that is being expressed and still needs to be expressed, but caution is needed with respect to that theoretical language, for it does not simply report a prelinguistic experience, but constructs that experience as well as the limits of its analysis. Regardless of the pervasive character of patriarchy and the prevalence of sexual difference as an operative cultural distinct, there is nothing about a binary gender system that is given. As a corporeal field of cultural play, gender is a basically innovative affair, although it is quite clear that there are strict punishments for contesting the script by performing out of turn or through unwarranted improvisation. Gender is not passively scripted on the body, and neither is it determined by nature, language, the symbolic, or the overwhelming history of patriarchy. Gender is what is put on, invariably, under constraint, daily and incessantly, with anxiety and pleasure, but if this continuous act is mistaken for a natural or linguistic given, power is relinquished to expand the cultural field bodily through subversive performances of various kinds.

Notes

1 For a further discussion of Beauvoir's feminist contribution to phenomenological theory, see my 'Variations on Sex and Gender: *Beauvoir's The Second Sex*', *Yale French Studies* 172 (1986).
2 Maurice Merleau-Ponty, 'The Body in its Sexual Being', in *The Phenomenology of Perception*, trans. Colin Smith (Boston: Routledge and Kegan Paul, 1962).

3 Simone de Beauvoir, *The Second Sex*, trans. H.M. Parshley (New York: Vintage, 1974), p. 38.

4 Julia Kristeva, *Histoire d'amour* (Paris: Editions Denoel, 1983), p. 242.

5 See Michel Foucault, *The History of Sexuality: An Introduction*, trans. Robert Hurley (New York: Random House, 1980), p. 154: 'the notion of 'sex' made it possible to group together, in an artificial unity, anatomical elements, biological functions, conducts, sensations, and pleasures, and it enabled one to make use of this fictitious unity as a causal principle'.

6 See Claude Levi-Strauss, *The Elementary Structures of Kinship* (Boston: Beacon, 1965).

7 Gayle Rubin, 'The Traffic in Women: Notes on the "Political Economy" of Sex', in *Toward an Anthropology of Women*, ed. Rayna R. Reiter (New York: Monthly Review Press, 1975), pp. 178–185.

8 See my 'Variations on Sex and Gender: Beauvoir, Wittig, and Foucault', in *Feminism as Critique*, ed. Seyla Benhabib and Drucila Cornell (London: Basil Blackwell, 1987 (distributed by the University of Minnesota Press)).

9 See Victor Turner, *Dramas, Fields, and Metaphors* (Ithaca: Cornell University Press, 1974). [...]

10 Bruce Wilshire, *Role-Playing and Identity: The Limits of Theatre as Metaphor* (Boston: Routledge and Kegan Paul, 1981).

11 Richard Schechner, *Between Theatre and Anthropology* (Philadelphia: University of Pennsylvania Press, 1985). See especially, 'News, Sex, and Performance', pp. 295–324.

12 In *Mother Camp: Female Impersonators in America* (Englewood Cliffs: Prentice-Hall, 1972), Anthropologist Esther Newton gives an urban ethnography of drag queens in which she suggests that all gender might be understood on the model of drag. In *Gender: An Ethnomethodological Approach* (Chicago: University of Chicago Press, 1978), Suzanne J. Kessler and Wendy McKenna argue that gender is an 'accomplishment' which requires the skills of constructing the body into a socially legitimate artifice.

13 See Erving Goffmann, *The Presentation of Self in Everyday Life* (Garden City: Doubleday, 1959).

14 Remarks at the Center for Humanities, Wesleyan University, Spring, 1985.

15 Julia Kristeva, 'Woman Can Never Be Defined', trans. Marilyn A. August, in *New French Feminisms*, ed. Elaine Marks and Isabelle de Courtivron (New York: Schocken, 1981).

16 Mary Anne Warren, *Gendercide: The Implications of Sex Selection* (New Jersey: Rowman and Allanheld, 1985).

17 Ibid.; Michel Foucault, *Discipline and Punish: The Birth of the Prison*, trans. Alan Sheridan (New York: Vintage, 1978).

CHAPTER 6

IDENTITY, ABJECTION AND OTHERNESS
Creating the self, creating difference

Bronwyn Davies, *International Journal of Equity and Innovation in Early Childhood*, 2, 1, 2004

In *Frogs and Snails and Feminist Tales: preschool children and gender* (Davies, 1989/2003) and also in my book with Hiroyuki Kasama, *Japanese Preschool Children and Gender. Frogs and Snails in Japan* (Davies and Kasama, 2004) I explored how children take up their gendered identities, and in doing so constitute and maintain the binary and hierarchical gender order. I wanted to know how identity comes to be tied to biological difference, and genital difference in particular, in the construction and maintenance of 'male' and 'female' identities. I was curious about how gender is taken up as one of a pair of binary opposites with male as dominant and female as subordinate, despite discourses of gender equity being readily available. I was fascinated in these studies by the moments of transgression, when individual children successfully disrupted the apparent inevitability of this binary division of identities. I was interested in the work they did on themselves and each other to prevent these transgressions, and to recreate the binary and hierarchical gender order once it had been breached. I analysed those responses to transgression as children engaging in 'category-maintenance work'. I argued that they engaged in this work in order to be able to take up their own identities in meaningful and predictable ways within a known order:

> ...individuals *can* deviate, but their deviation will give rise to *category-maintenance work* around the gender boundaries. This category-maintenance work is aimed partly at letting the deviants know they've got it wrong – teasing is often enough to pull someone back into line – but primarily it is aimed at maintaining the category as a meaningful category in the face of the individual deviation that is threatening it.

> (Davies, 1989, p. 29)

The desire for order – for familiarity and predictability – is a common feature of the children in these studies. The children actively engage in category-maintenance work even in response to fictional stories that challenge the gender order. In the Japanese study, for example, where children were read *Oliver Button is a Sissy*, a group of three boys object to Oliver Button being saved by girls. In mounting their objection to this break with usual storylines the boys also assert their dominant position over the female interviewer, Chika, by telling her she is 'uncool'.

Chika:	So Oliver was helped by girls wasn't he?
Takero:	Yes! Uncool!
Chika:	Uncool? Why?
Wataru:	(points to Chika) This person is uncool.
Chika:	(points to self) This person is uncool?
Wataru:	Because you are a woman
Kentaro:	It's the end to be helped by a woman.
Chika:	Oh really? Be helped by a woman is the end?
Wataru:	Yes, it's the end.
Chika:	It's the end?
Wataru:	No, it's bad.
Kentaro:	It's the end.

Not only is Oliver positioned as in the wrong for being saved by girls but the boys read the situation of listening to this story as one in which they should perform themselves as strong and cool, demonstrating that Oliver and the interviewer are *other* to them. In this way, they *abject* the character of Oliver and the femaleness of Chika.

Border-work and abjection: constituting the other

In this section, I want to expand the concept of category-maintenance work by adding the border-work children do in constructing their own identities. This border-work involves the process of *abjection*. The practice of abjection in psycho-analytic theory begins with the violent vomiting out of the mother's milk as a way of abjecting her, making her other to the self of the child. The milk has the double status of having become part of oneself and of representing the mother. Abjecting the other is a way of establishing the 'I', and it is also part of the 'I' that is being cast out. Referring to vomiting as an early form of abjection of the mother, of the milk, Kristeva writes:

> I expel myself, I spit myself out, I abject myself within the same motion through which 'I' claim to establish myself. During that course in which 'I' become, I give birth to myself amid the violence of sobs, of vomit.
>
> (Kristeva, 1982, p. 3)

The boys' abjection of Oliver and of Chika seemed to me extraordinarily violent and sexist when I first heard it. I felt a gut level horror at being placed, along with Chika and Oliver, in the category of that which is to be spat out. At the same time I could reason that the violence of the spitting is to do with both the necessity of establishing an 'I' – with abjecting the weak, the dependent, and the feminine – and with establishing the coherence and legitimacy of the dominant male 'I'. The femi-nine and the dependent must be continually expelled from that 'I' if one is to accomplish, and go on accomplishing, dominant masculinity. It is an othering that can never be finally accomplished, the 'not-I' being part of oneself at one's abject borders.

My suggestion here is that category-maintenance work is actively going on as part of the hard work that individual subjects engage in to separate themselves out into the binary category to which they have been assigned. Since the categories are multiple and fluid, and since we are always in some sense both and neither of the binary categories, the accomplishment of unequivocal membership of one and not the other, and the simultaneous accomplishment of the 'I' as *this* person and not any other, involves the expulsion of the other.

In order to grasp this expulsion as an expulsion of some aspect of the self, it is interesting to re-visit some of the moments of category-maintenance work that I observed in the earlier study. Each moment was accompanied by a fluid movement outside the child's assigned gender category. Sometimes the category-maintenance work was done on oneself and sometimes it was done by another. Sometimes it led to a recovery by the transgressing subject of their membership in their assigned category, and sometimes it did not. Sometimes it was painful and emotional and at other times it had a tinge of fear and excitement: [...]

- Joanne, who has previously told me she would like to be a member of the dominant boys' group, though not as the feminine victim of their play, has entered into a game where she and her friend Tony, from the dominant boys' group, defend their takeover of a new tree-house. They defend their space (from which the dominant boys have been evicted by the teachers who say the space is for everyone) by dropping sawdust in the potential invaders' eyes. When Joanne sees me watching she tells me they are just cleaning up the tree-house.

  Joanne clearly takes pleasure in this dominant territorial activity, but on seeing it through adult eyes she 'knows' it is wrong, and relocates herself in a virtuous domestic storyline in which the gender order is kept intact. She thus maintains the binary difference as meaningful, by expelling the possible interpretation of herself as dominant male, and in doing so, she re-inhabits her body as female, with male as other to whom she might imaginably be.

- George comes into the home corner where Catherine is playing with a smaller boy, John. George steals Catherine's dolly and runs off with it. Catherine pursues him and tearfully asks for her dolly back. When George refuses to give it to her, she returns to the home corner, puts on a male waistcoat from the dressing-up cupboard, tucks it into the dress up skirts she has on, then marches off to find George and get her dolly back. On returning to the home corner she sheds the waistcoat, drops it on the floor, puts on a feminine cape, and happily plays at "cooking" with John.

  George disrupts the gender order by carrying off Catherine's dolly. Catherine uses male signifiers on her body to enable a different kind of performance, to give her a dominant kind of power over George and outside of the domestic sphere of the home corner. Once she has accomplished her task she re-signifies herself as female as if to make up for the momentary breach, abjecting the waistcoat, which is left lying on the floor.

[...] The practices of category-maintenance work might be interpreted as a rational, cerebral, linguistic strategy. Yet if one looks at the examples, there is a lot of emotion and movement of bodies going on that involves more than the rational maintenance of the gender order. The structure of the gender order, the formation of the 'I' with its particular boundaries, the maintenance of the binary form of discourse, are all going on simultaneously and through the same practices. The practices involve a negation and use of others who are constituted as different, in the establishment and maintenance of the borders of the 'I' as a knowable, recognizable subject (Davies, 2000).

Through category-maintenance work, we might say that the self *deciphers* itself through available discourses (to decipher is to determine the meaning of something obscure and illegible). As Rose says: 'Through such practices [as self-evaluation, self-scrutiny, self-regulation], individuals [are] subjected not by an alien gaze but through a reflexive hermeneutics' (Rose, 1998, p. 77). These technologies of the self, as Foucault has called them,

> permit individuals to effect by their own means or with the help of others a number of operations on their own bodies and souls, thoughts, conduct and ways of being, so as to transform themselves in order to attain a certain state of happiness, purity, wisdom, perfection or immortality.
>
> (Foucault, 1988, p. 18)

Those technologies of the self are used to work on the hopes and dreams of one who successfully becomes – and goes on becoming – a subject.

The pursuit of that certain state, it would seem, requires that we abject from ourselves those possibilities that do not fit with our understanding of the individual 'I' that is to be accomplished – the 'I' that makes sense within the particular social structures and discourses in which it takes up its existence. That which we abject is that which becomes unimaginable for ourselves, that which is removed to the outside borders of the subject's identity. In Judith Butler's (1993) terms, we guard the borders of our own identity (we engage in border-work), for on the other side of the border lies that which it is not possible to be:

> The normative force of performativity – its power to establish what qualifies as 'being' – works not only through reiteration, but through exclusion as well. And in the case of bodies, those exclusions haunt signification as its abject borders or as that which is strictly foreclosed: the unlovable, the nonnarrativizable, the traumatic.
>
> (Butler, 1993, p. 188)

Or in the words of Elizabeth Grosz (1994):

> The abject is not that which is dirty or impure about the body: nothing in itself.... is dirty. Dirt, for her, is that which is not in its proper place, that which upsets or befuddles order... Dirt signals a site of possible danger to social and individual systems, a site of vulnerability insofar as the status of dirt as marginal and unincorporable always locates sites of potential threat to the system *and to the order it both makes possible and problematises.*
>
> (Grosz, 1994, p. 192, my italics)

Let us take another example of category-maintenance work combined with border-work.

Two boys start aggressive wrestling and punching. Geoffrey, the bigger of the two, seems to be getting the worst of it. He is dressed in a black velvet skirt.

He starts to cry and shouts at the smaller boy, 'you're yukky! You made me ( )' He stands up and takes the skirt off angrily and throws it on the ground. He kicks the smaller boy, saying, 'now I've got more pants on!' The smaller boy starts to cry, no longer willing to fight back, he cowers away from Geoffrey's kicking. Once he has kicked him several times Geoffrey walks away, seemingly satisfied and no longer tearful. The black velvet skirt is left lying on the ground.

(Davies, 1989/2003, p. 16)

In this story of the black velvet skirt, Geoffrey opens the possibility of imagining himself in an-other space, as able to try on (try out?) the feminine. More often seen as a dominant figure, for example as the fire-fighter threatening to burn babies, on *this* morning Geoffrey entertains an 'I' who can wear the gorgeous black velvet skirt. In entertaining this possible 'I' he can be seen as disrupting the gender order and the idea that identities are stable and fixed. Though he is willing to explore the feminine, a smaller boy sees this as an invitation to attack him, and discovers in doing so that he can beat him. (How does Geoffrey's adoption of the feminine give the smaller boy such power? It is an interesting question.) Geoffrey is outraged. He yells. He abjects the feminine, throwing the skirt on the floor. He magnifies his masculinity, standing up in a tough posture, drawing attention to his pants, kicking the smaller boy. The black velvet skirt, signifying the feminine is flung from him, lying on the floor, signifying what he is not and cannot, for now, imaginably be. Geoffrey's taking on of the feminine could be read by the small boy as *befuddling the order*, signalling a 'site of possible danger to himself and to social systems' (Grosz, 1994, p. 192). Abjecting Geoffrey in the black velvet skirt, and then Geoffrey's abjection of the feminine both *makes the binary gender order possible and problematises it.*

Subject/embodiment

What implications does this have for the processes of social change? Do category-maintenance work and border-work together maintain hierarchies of difference as inevitable, as necessary to the formation of selves? When we encourage children to accept differences in each other, what exactly are we asking them to do in relation to their own identity work? Is it possible to better understand these processes of identity formation in order to work more effectively in the development of acceptance of multiplicity – of genders and of other differences – in our schools? In order to address these questions, I will try to set up an analytic framework for researching transgressive practices.

An analytic framework for researching transgressive practice

Poststructuralist theory is interested in social structure, discourse and the subject. It is interested in the processes whereby the individual becomes a subject. It does not limit its analytic gaze to any one of these three areas carved out as independent arenas and spheres of action by sociology, linguistics and psychology. Rather, poststructuralist theory incorporates all three arenas as inseparable aspects of human practice. But more than this, these arenas do not exist as separate objects in the world, but are constituted simultaneously through and in relation to each other in ongoing *practice*:

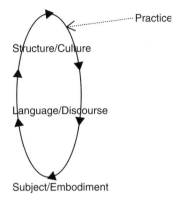

This focus on practice is contrary to the idea of the over-determined subject of structuralism, since practice is necessarily, to some extent, open-ended. This point is similar to the point made by Connell, Radican and Martin (1987) who point out that individual subjects' practice is constrained by structure and yet 'practice can be turned against what constrains it':

> ...practice, while presupposing structure...is always responding to a *situation*. Practice is the transformation of that situation in a particular direction. To describe structure is to specify what is in a particular situation that constrains the play of practice. Since the consequence of practice is a transformed situation which is the object of new practice, 'structure' specifies the way practice (over time) constrains practice.

Since human action involves free invention...and human knowledge is reflexive, practice can be turned against what constrains it; so structure can deliberately be the object of practice. But practice cannot escape structure, cannot float free from its circumstances... It is always obliged to reckon with the constraints that are the precipitate of history (Connell, Radican, and Martin, 1987).

Poststructural theorists both problematise and dwell on such concepts as 'free invention'. As human subjects we are always circumscribed by particular situations, by the discourses at play, by the subject positions we may or may not take up, by the inscriptions on our bodies of emotions, of attitudes, of commitments, of understandings. To turn practice against those inscriptions is complex work. We are always vulnerable to the constitutive normalising work that it counterposes – that normalising work coming from ourselves as well as from others. As Hillevi Lenz-Taguchi (2000) wrote about the hard work of transgression:

> Feelings of transgression give me a temporary feeling of freedom, which fades away. In the very process of persistent weaving, I am always in a state of resistance, where knots untied will stick up their grinning faces again and again, and where I as a weaving subject will always struggle with being meshed within the fabric – wanting it badly and hating it! But simultaneously – with joy, fear and pain – I spin those delicate threads that necessarily 'go against

the grain,' making the fabric uneven or leaving it with mysterious holes of uncertainties, doubts, desires and excitements.

(Davies, 2000, p. 169)

The cloth is both woven and unpicked and it unfuriatingly re-weaves itself at the site of our unpicking. The way power works in poststructural theory is not one of total domination, but is theorised as movement, as force and counter-force. Since we are thinking beings we can see and analyse those forces and we can generate counter-forces – in discourse, in structure, in ways of being embodied – or more precisely, simultaneously in discursive practices, in ways of making structures, in practices of embodiment.

Discourses (which include politics, medicine, economics, history, education, psychology and so on) generate universalities, binaries, forums of truth and specific ways of being human. 'Discourses regulate and discipline by constituting fields of knowledge, instituting truths, constituting subjectivities in particular ways, positioning people within discourses and subjecting them to normalizing judgements' (Malson, 1998, p. 29). *The power of those normalising judgements, of the gaze of the small girl, on ourselves, on others, in the media, are interesting, here, precisely because their force indicates a counter-force, an energy, a possibility, and even an intention to deviate, to transgress, to do and be otherwise.*

In poststructuralist theory, discourse is not the transparent medium of reporting that we find in many of the social sciences, which have borrowed the realist and empiricist practices of the physical sciences. Words carefully and rationally chosen to do not *reveal* real worlds; rather, the practices of speaking open up ways of being and create intelligibility in those ways of being:

> Discourse is not merely spoken words, but a notion of signification which concerns not merely how it is that certain signifiers come to mean what they mean, but how certain discursive forms articulate objects and subjects in their intelligibility. In this sense 'discourse' is not used in the ordinary sense... Discourse does not merely represent or report on pregiven practices and relations, but it enters into their articulation and is, in that sense, productive.
>
> (Butler, 1995, p. 24)

The productive force of discourse does not mean that it is all-powerful, or fixed, or that it works independently of counter-force. Just how we might enter into and use counterforce against the desire for particular forms of order and intelligibility is a central question for those interested in social change. Let us dwell for a moment on that desire for order and intelligibility. I was sitting in my local café working on this chapter when the following scene unfolded:

> A toddler, perhaps 18 months old, is squealing and squawking. It is ear splitting. Her parents get the message – she wants to leave. On the way out she is toddling ahead of her parents who are wheeling her stroller. She stops, transfixed, staring. Her gaze has alighted on a man, sitting near the exit of the café, who wears an eye patch. She stands stock still and stares. Her parents encourage her to move on. The exit from the café is blocked. They gently push her. She cannot be moved. It is as if she cannot hear them. It is a moment of syncope – time out. She appears to no longer hear or see anything except the man with the eye patch. He looks back at her smiling. Everyone's attention is drawn to

the transfixed child. Her parents keep nudging. Suddenly she starts, as if she is waking, becoming aware of the others around her. She starts to cry loudly, as if she is afraid of the man at whom she has been staring. The man with the patch and his companion laugh, and the child and her parents leave.

The small girl's attention is drawn to something that is out of the familiar order of things. She understands people have two eyes. The man with one eye exists outside of the order she knows. In that moment of gazing, transfixed, she becomes absorbed in the difference. She absorbs the difference. In that space she has momentarily entered outside of her everyday world. She is transfixed by a man with one eye. But then she 'comes to', and she cries. Her crying is perhaps a form of abjection: she expels the stranger with his difference from her. It is both: a double movement – incorporation and expulsion.

In all probability, the two-eyed nature of the human form has not been spoken into existence in the life of this child. While the orderly nature of the world is accomplished by giving each object 'the status of an object... making it manifest, nameable, describable' (Foucault, 1972, p. 41), objects are not only spoken *about* in particular ways, described as specific kinds of object. They are also evoked indirectly, by discourses which operate *as if* objects had particular universal qualities. Such constitutive work can be invisible, not something one can directly oppose, or even easily detect. The small girl's transfixed gaze reveals a moment in which she discovers that not everyone has two eyes and discovers, perhaps, that she thought that they did. The work of catching discourse at work in particular ways, of seeing what it accomplishes is a large part of the discourse analytic work that poststructuralists engage in. The constitutive work through which subjects become subjects, through which social structures become particular kinds of structure, and the way these are woven together, is what is of particular interest.

I am interested not only in the power of constitutive forces but also the transgressive possibilities to be found in oneself as embodied subject, in text, in the practices of others. In the diagram below I focused on practice and the way it weaves and unpicks the fabric of human existence, on its forces and counter-forces, with the knots that seem to bind the woven fabric in place. In the following diagram, I break this line up into three different kinds of practice through which the subject is discursively constituted. These are conceptually separated here, but cannot really be separated in practice. The first of these loops I characterise as the process of *subjectification*; the second as the process of *deconstruction*; and the third, as *syncope* where we enter into another space, open to another possibility of knowing the self and the other.

The subject who is constituted through the processes of subjectification, deconstruction and syncope is the specific desiring subject – with particular attitudes and emotions. It is the rational, thinking subject, and it is also the embodied subject.

Subjectification

In this first loop of practice, these are the processes through which the appropriate(d) self is shaped up. The subject is both dominated and shaped and, at the same time and through the same practices, actively takes up the possibilities of the self that are available in recognised/recognisable discourses and practices. To emphasize the *doubleness* of this process (one is subjected *and* becomes an agentic subject), I want to emphasise the fluidity and room for movement in this loop. As part of that active taking up the subject is not limited to the gendered signs of skirts and

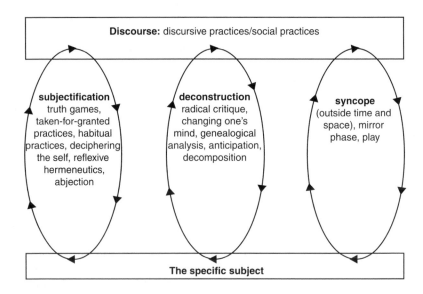

pants already discussed. Identity can be taken up within a wide and fluid range of possibilities. As Grosz (1994) points out:

> ...the body image is capable of accommodating and incorporating an extremely wide range of objects...External objects, implements, and instruments with which the subject continually interacts become, while they are being used, intimate, vital, even libidinally cathected parts of the body image.
> (Grosz, 1994, p. 80)

Let me illustrate this fluidity with an example from the Japanese study on a morning when a new box of dressing up clothes appeared in the kindergarten:

> When the dressing up box is brought out Yuya puts on a gladiator helmet and flourishes a whip. He finds a mobile phone in the box, which he holds in one hand, whip in the other...He appears happy as he runs around flourishing his whip. Fumiko has also dressed as a gladiator and she has an axe. They begin mock battle, but the axe actually hits Yuya's face. He stands still, holding his face, looking very upset, appearing to try not to cry, but unable to get past the moment of shock or hurt. Fumiko runs off, perhaps to get a teacher, as shortly afterwards a teacher comes and takes him kindly by the hand. Yuya then re-enters the play, appearing happy, running around, now with the mobile phone fitted neatly in his pocket. Then another boy comes up from behind him and steals the mobile phone from his pocket. Yuya flings himself upon the thief and grabs the phone back. Just as he is putting it back in his pocket, the music comes on that announces the end of play-time. Yuya stumbles into the hallway, out of people's view, and crumples in a heap on the floor sobbing. One of the bigger boys comes over to comfort him but the flood of sobbing does not stop. Then a teacher comes by and bends down to talk to him. He keeps on crying. The other boy runs off. The teacher asks him what is wrong and eventually he tells her 'I had the telephone and the other boy took it. I got it back but then it was the end of play-time and I couldn't play with the

telephone any more. So I cried'. The teacher takes him by the hand and he stands up and walks with her. He brushes the tears off his face with the palm of his hand, then pulls off his gladiator helmet and lets it drop to the floor.

(Davies and Kasama, 2004, pp. 106–107)

Deconstruction/geneaology

The second loop is one that reflexively stands back from and gazes at the first loop to see how it works and what it does. According to poststructuralist theory, the self is an ongoing project: we are engaged in selving, or continually becoming selves (Davies, 2000). To the extent that this is so, there are multiple possibilities for reflection on the discourses through which the self is constituted, that reflection opening up new possibilities of resistance to those discourses, and thus to change (Davies, 1993). Such change is not understood to be the same project as the project of the constantly reforming humanist self repeatedly taking itself up in yet another heteronomous code. Rather it is a self in process who finds the gaps and tensions in existing dominant discourses, who subjects them to critique, who thus transforms the codes themselves by making them more visible and open to scrutiny. A poststructuralist critique is in itself transformative:

> ....I don't think that criticism can be set against transformation, "ideal" criticism against "real" transformation.... . A critique does not consist in saying that things aren't good the way they are. It consists in seeing on what type of assumptions, of familiar notions, of established, unexamined ways of thinking, the accepted practices are based.
> ...There is always a little thought occurring even in the most stupid institutions; there is always thought even in silent habits.... Criticism consists in uncovering that thought and trying to change it; showing that things are not as obvious as people believe, making it so that what is taken for granted is no longer taken for granted. To do criticism is to make harder those acts which are now too easy.... Understood in these terms, criticism (and radical criticism) is utterly indispensable for any transformation.
> ...as soon as people begin to have trouble thinking things the way they have been thought, transformation becomes at the same time very urgent, very difficult, and entirely possible.
>
> (Foucault, 2000, pp. 456–457)

This work of radical poststructural critique involves a refusal of the inevitability of the constituted world. What deconstruction and genealogical analyses do is make visible the arbitrariness of institutions and their practices. We create spaces of freedom by thinking beyond accepted knowledges, and as Nikolas Rose says, even: '...if we cannot disinvent ourselves, we might at least enhance the contestability of the forms of being that have been invented for us, and begin to invent ourselves differently' (Rose 1998, p. 197). Foucault sees such work as central to the work of intellectuals:

> My role – and that is too emphatic a word – is to show people that they are much freer than they feel, that people accept as truth, as evidence, some themes that have been built up at a certain moment during history, and that this so-called evidence can be criticized and destroyed. To change something in the minds of people – that's the role of an intellectual.
>
> (Foucault, cited in Martin, 1988, p. 10)

Foucault also emphasises in his own life his openness to new forms of being and the task of throwing off the need to *have* a recognisable identity:

> I don't feel it is necessary to know exactly what I am. The main interest in life and work is to become someone else that you were not in the beginning.... The game is worthwhile insofar as we don't know what will be the end.
>
> (Foucault, cited in Martin, 1988, p. 7)

[...] *Poststructural writing practices also open up strategies for resisting, subverting, decomposing the discourses themselves through which one is being constituted* (Barthes, 1977). *In that writing, the rational conscious subject is decentred and the play of desire and the unconscious are given space. Old ways of knowing, such as through master or grand narratives, are subjected to play and resisted as sole arbiters of meaning. It is not that the grand narratives with their humanist heroes become irrelevant, but their storylines may be taken in directions that go against the grain of dominant ways of seeing. New subjectivities are not opened up through simple acts of opposition and resistance but through a series of escapes, of small slides, of plays, of crossings, of flights – that open (other, slippery) understandings* (Cixous and Derrida, 2001). *Agency in poststructuralist writing is not understood solely in terms of individuals or collectives standing outside or against social structures and processes. It involves as well a recognition of the power of discourse, a recognition of one's love of, immersion in and indebtedness to that discourse, and also a fascination with the play of meanings through which new life-forms may be generated: life-forms capable of disrupting the hold of old gendered meanings and desires.*

Syncope

The third loop is where time stops for a moment. The everyday world and the processes of subjectification are on hold. Something else becomes possible as Catherine Clément (1994) describes in her wonderful book *Syncope. The Philosophy of Rapture*:

> 'Syncope' is a strange word. It pivots from the clinic to the art of dance, tilts towards poetry, finally ends up in music. In each of these fields, syncope takes on a definition. At first there is a shock, a suppression: something gets lost, but no one says what is won. Suddenly, time falters... There is no dance without syncope – without syncopation...
>
> Physical time never stops. That may be, but syncope seems to accomplish a miraculous suspension. Dance, music, and poetry traffic in time, manipulate it, and even the body manages to do that by an extraordinary short circuit... But inside, what is going on? Where is the lost syllable, the beat eaten away by the rhythm? Where does the subject go who later comes to, 'comes back'? Where am I in syncope?
>
> (Clement, 1994, pp. 1–4)

The small girl in the coffee shop appeared to move into just such a syncopated state where another reality was apprehended. Clement takes as a first experience of syncope what Lacing calls the mirror phase, where the child comes to know itself as both separate from the adult in the mirror and as part of humanity. Clément renders the mirror phase in a non-reductive specificity. Her focus is on the laughter, and the rapture of the moment:

> This is the moment the *infans* catches sight of his reflection in the mirror, turns to the adult who stands close to him, and manifests signs of intense exultation. He already knows how to laugh, and that is what he does. He laughs, in a delighted preoccupation that contributes to the successful exploit. Nothing else happens except for this image in the mirror, this pause, and this sudden rapture. It is a fleeting and precise moment.... He grasps that the reversed image is his own. And yet he can neither walk nor talk.... the mirror phase allows the baby to make a major leap. He recognizes himself simultaneously as a unique individual and as part of this 'all' into which he has been born, the world of people.
>
> (1994, pp. 118–119)

Clément compares this moment to the pause, the syncope, the moment the heart stops, in music and in dance:

> Here the imago has the effect of a syncope. Remember the definition of syncope in music: a note lags behind and anticipates the rest of the movement. That is the dynamic of the imago: caught in the mirror, 'captured' in the organic gaze, it is prolonged and anticipates the human figure of the animal who thinks. Everything matches: the original clash 'between the ego and the being,' the twisting that is created by leaning on the delay, and the leaping ahead, the projection toward a future that is as yet unthinkable.
>
> (Clement, 1994, pp. 119–120)

What interests me here is the possibility that the moment of syncope holds. It has in its first expression, joy; the self as separate and the self as the same – same-different – an openness to the new, to the 'future that is as yet unthinkable'. No need in this moment to lock the self into the binary war of difference and limitation. In each of the children's transgressive moments in their play, they step outside of the everyday. They open themselves up to the possibility of a joyous moment: of rupture and of rapture. They move towards the not yet known. In this third loop, there is a kind of freedom that is reigned back in by the work that is being done in the first loop. It is to the work in the middle, deconstructive loop that we must turn in order to catch these moments of syncope and to begin the work of undoing the weaving back up of binary structures and hierarchies.

The tickle in the brain: bringing the analytic framework to bear on practice

In the final part of this chapter, I am going to examine in detail an interview that I carried out for the earlier study with Anika, a five-year-old girl. We were reading *Oliver Button is a Sissy* and were discussing whether she could say and do the things that are usually regarded as what boys say and do. Anika told me about a tickle in her brain that would prevent her from doing what boys do. In the original analyses of Anika's tickle in the brain, I read her description of the tickle and the subsequent laughter in negative terms, as category maintenance work that closed down the freedom for her to transgress the gender order. Now, using the concept of syncope, and drawing on this imaging of the subject as itself, I want to add another layer to the analysis.

In relation to looking at subjects' accounts of their life and the discourses through which they constitute themselves as subjects in relation to the other subjects and objects with which they interact, there is a temptation always to see those accounts as the products of the rational subject: the subject who consciously knows not only that it speaks, but that also knows how to mobilise the systems of thought through which that speaking is done. It knows how to analyse the way systems of thought work as well as the precise nature of the subjects/objects that are being discursively constituted. In conducting and then analysing interviews, it is not only this rational knowing subject that is important, but also the emotional, desiring, embodied subject. Subjects – and the objects they speak into existence – are not to be understood in a Foucauldian analysis as having an empirical status that can be examined independent of their discursive construction. Yet, in the act of interviewing and transcribing and engaging in 'discourse analysis', we are always at risk of constituting them as such, and in the process, constituting ourselves as the rational knowing researcher. What we already know through rational analysis is not enough. It is a beginning. It engages the discourses through which we constitute the world and are constituted. To find the moment of insight that goes beyond, that is another matter. Cixous (1998) likens this search for the moment beyond the rational analysis to drawing and to her own writing:

> What are we trying to grasp between the lines, in between the strokes, in the net that we're weaving, that we throw, and the dagger blows? Not the person, but the precious in that person, not the Virgin, not the child, but what is between them in this very moment, linking them – a secret. That which mysteriously renders those two unforgettable. I sense: it's not divinity, it's whim. That little grain of meanness which *makes* the little boy. Do you see?

Leonardo da Vinci's drawing *Vierge a l'enfant*

It's not a question of drawing the contours, but of what escapes the contour, the secret movement, the breaking, the torment, the unexpected.

The drawing wants to draw what is invisible to the naked eye. It's very difficult. The effort to write is always beyond my strength. What you see here, these lines, these strokes, are rungs on the ladder of writing, the steps which I have cut with my fingernails in my own wall, in order to hoist myself up above and beyond myself.

(Cixous, 1998, p. 23)

[...] What the individual subject knows may lie in the gaps and silences as much as in what is said:

Silence itself – the things one declines to say, or is forbidden to name, the discretion that is required between different speakers – is less the absolute limit of discourse, the other side from which it is separated by a strict boundary, than an element that functions alongside the things said, with them and in relation to them within over-all strategies. There is no binary division to be made between what one says and what one does not say; we must try to determine the different ways of not saying such things, how those who can and those who cannot speak of them are distributed, which type of discourse is authorized, or which form of discretion is required in either case.

(Foucault, 1978, p. 27)

Foucault's writing here errs in favour of the conscious rational subject. That which is unsayable here is characterised as 'the things one declines to say' – as if this were a conscious refusal (which it may sometimes be) – or as the thing that one is 'forbidden to name' as if a rule and a ruler were consciously in mind. The discursive acts are called 'strategies' and subjects act with 'discretion' ('the quality of behaving or speaking in such a way as to avoid social embarrassment or distress', Collins English Dictionary). Of course, we do act discreetly and we may even sometimes be able to articulate the precise discursive act that was carried out, or not carried out, in order to avoid a particular kind of embarrassment or distress. At other times, we may just feel a dumb panic around certain words, or a gut level disgust that prohibits speaking. Or more subtly, a certain meanness, or a certain resistance to a cliché, an imposition. That detail may lie behind or embedded in the romantic surface – difficult to read, but there nonetheless.

To turn then to Anika and the story of the 'tickle in the brain' and the story of Oliver Button is a Sissy. Oliver wants to do the things that girls usually do. He wants to dance and sing and play with paper dolls. In response to my questioning, Anika says she would laugh at David, her brother, if he did what only girls normally do. I express surprise. Anika had elsewhere produced a liberal feminist discourse about girls being free to do anything and I presume this belief must extend to boys. (I thus provide a discursive space, inside rationality, for her to make sense of her take-up of contradictory discursive positions.) She provides some reasoned analysis of her inclination to laughter in relation to my why questions. He would be, she explains, a 'tomboy' if he did girl things, and he has no friends that are tomboys. Here she competently uses and extends a third gender category and explains that occupying such a category requires others who are doing the same, who occupy that same category. She actively constitutes herself in this analysis as the rational knowing subject. I then pursue the desire to laugh as a topic of conversation, still using why questions, but then moving to a discussion of feelings:

BD: So why would you laugh at him?
Anika: Because it's sort of a girls' thing.
BD: Right, and you would feel funny about him doing a girls' thing?
Anika: Mmm, I feel, you know, funny.
BD: Feel...
Anika: Feel funny.
BD: Yeah...
Anika: And when people, when people, when the wrong kind of human being does that, I get a (pause) tickle in my brain.
BD: Do you? When?
Anika: Mmm
BD: And what about if a girl does a boy thing?
Anika: I get (pause) the same thing.
BD: It makes you feel really funny?
Anika: Mmm, and it makes me laugh
BD: Does it?
Anika: Mmm, and it's like a little man is in my brain, tickling my brain.
BD: Does it feel horrible or funny?
Anika: Funny
BD: Funny
Anika: Like it's a piece of string like this tickling from side to side (motions as if drawing a piece of string back and forth through her brain).
BD: And that tickling makes you laugh?
Anika: Mmm
BD: Does it make you feel unhappy at all?
Anika: No.

My words weave off her words, as if we are jointly putting together the reading of her embodied response. In doing so, I constitute her as one who can read her own emotions and find appropriate language to make them describable. Working off the word 'funny' that I offer, I stop for the moment asking for reasons, and ask for an embodied reading, and she gives it – or rather we produce it together. In the ensuing elaboration, the complexity of the laughter, of who laughs when, of control of the laughter in front of others, the hard work of constituting oneself appropriately as a gendered subject becomes visible. The laughter is a rupture (a rapture), which may need to be brought under control, or which may serve to bring others back into the known order. It comes from a physical sensation in the brain, a tickling associated with dissonance, disruption to what is known. David imaginably disrupts the gender order. This disruption erupts in her in laughter. The same laughter might erupt if she herself moves over into "boys'" activity. She imagines pleasurably moving toward a disruption of the gender order. She desires that movement. In the moment of its pleasurable accomplishment she is at risk of her body erupting in laughter. That laughter may bring too much attention to the act, to its transgressive potential, to her own potential wrong location in the world. The laughter must be controlled to avoid this possible shame, yet the laughter may at the same time be an expression of the pleasurable disjunction between the known order and another possibility:

BD: So if you were to do a boy thing and it made you laugh, but you really wanted to do it and it started making you tickle and laugh, would you keep on doing it?
Anika: Oh no.
BD: Is the tickling enough to make you stop?
Anika: Yeah, because I'd only do it when I was practising and no girl or boy is around, no-one because they might laugh at me.
BD: And if you were practising it alone, and um, say, like what, what would be a boy thing you would really like to do?
Anika: Um, fly a racing, fly an aeroplane.
BD: And if you were flying that aeroplane and you were practicing it all by yourself where nobody could watch you, would you get a tickling in your brain then?
Anika: Yeah
BD: You would, but you wouldn't care?
Anika: No
BD: If your mum or dad was watching you would that matter?
Anika: Oooh, if I got a ticklish thing I wouldn't laugh
BD: You wouldn't?
Anika: Because they might hear me.

This is a complex construction/observation. She is free to and desires to fly an aeroplane. There is a risk, however, that others will laugh in seeing her do it. To do it alone would generate *in her* the tickling feeling and the laughter. But to laugh in that way in front of others would be to get it wrong. As an appropriate subject she can do something that boys do if she desires it, but she has to do it *as if* it is normal, and to accomplish that she must practice it (get it right in her body) and also not laugh – not signal openly the disjuncture that she is experiencing. The possible shame of getting it wrong, of not being practised enough, of not bringing the laughter under control, is enough to shift desire, to not want to do it under conditions where others would get the tickling feeling and laugh at her, or where she was not able to control her own laughter. This is a detailed observation of her body as text, her body as a text that erupts uncontrollably in the dissonant moment of moving across gender boundaries. Clément defines such moments of syncope as depriving 'the body of its obedience to the mind' (1994, p. 7). 'Those [philosophers] who have come near to laughter', Clement says,

have declared that it springs from the ruptures, the 'differences in level' (*dénivellations*), as Bataille says, or from the short circuits, according to Roger Bastide: risky or deliberate collisions... Laughter intrigues by its course: a short and beneficent ecstasy; it moves towards anguish... when one is tickled. It moves between the poles of agony and ecstasy.

(Clément, 1994, p. 8)

Unfortunately, I move the interview away from this reading of the embodied moment of rupture. I invoke a rational subject who can analyse and hypothesise the moments of its occurrence:

> BD: So you would just go on playing the plane, flying the plane, if they were there, but you wouldn't if there were other boys or girls there?
> Anika: Mmm. I mean if there were boys or girls there I still wouldn't laugh because you know I, you know…(pause) let's just get on with the story.
> BD: Right OK. It's hard to explain isn't it?
> Anika: Mmm. Very.

In this case, the silence that she requires of herself in order not to be seen laughing is not something she can produce an account of in terms of what it is that prohibits, or that is prohibited. It is not, in this case, a choice to be discreet, or a sense of being forbidden. She sees in herself the will to laugh. She sees it in others.

She reads the will to laugh as related to movement across gender borders. One might say in this sense that the entry by a girl into boy activity is forbidden and at the same time, intensely pleasurable. Further, her own take-up of feminist discourse and her parents' take-up of feminist discourse give rise to another desire and gives permission to move across this boundary. She is both encouraged and forbidden. There is both permission and taboo. The taboo acts like string pulling through her brain. The permission can be spoken about. The silence thus operates at the level of conscious awareness and rationality and at the same time and in a different way as a taboo working on the body and through the embodied reactions of others. Her parents don't reason with her 'you can't do that', instead they may erupt in laughter as might she. And even if they don't, she fears that she or they will do so, so disrupting her performance of herself as a competent subject. That potential disruption works at the level of her desire to be a particular kind of subject.

Notes for an enabling pedagogy

There is much to be learned from this conversation with Anika. She tells us by implication, for example, what would make it OK for David to be different from other boys. He can enter a third category, breaking up gender's binary form if he has friends that do similar things, and if he has a chance to practise the new skills in a non-threatening environment and so not be self conscious when he does them. Such conditions can be created not just around gender difference but other differences as well. I once saw a wonderful documentary, which moved me deeply, about a small country school where one of the new students was deaf. He was at risk of being othered, abjected, because he belonged in a new category, with no-one else to share it and where others could not imaginably be like him. 'Not speaking' is unimaginable if no work has been done to shift its definition and to make it imaginable. Without that work, his not speaking (in the way others generally do) creates potential disorder and disruption with the deaf boy needing to be abjected in order to restore order. Instead, the school initiated a programme in which every child in the school became bilingual, with sign language as their second (and in some cases, third) language. Once this was set in place the deaf boy had high status and became a desirable friend. He was no longer incomprehensible, no longer someone to be abjected. He spoke the language they were learning better than they did. They could learn from him – and there was a hidden bonus. The new language could be used as a secret language in settings outside the school, as others did not speak it. The children regarded sign language as a very special form of communication and used it voluntarily in the playground alongside usual speech whenever the deaf boy was present, and even when he wasn't.

The pedagogy the school adopted not only familiarised difference, but it actively made available and legitimate the practices of the other. It made the strange, that which may have been perceived as frightening and in need of abjection, familiar. It was not enough that the children learned sign language superficially. The programme could only work if sign language was valued, time made available to practice it and a new fluency developed.

We have seen throughout this paper the openness of children to the new, the pleasure, even rapture of entering into possibilities outside of usual time and space. We have seen how they love to play with different modes of signification and enter into their possibilities. We have also looked at the conditions under which such fluidity and openness is closed down. Without denying the tension between openness to the new and a desire for order, it is possible to contemplate a pedagogy that opens up learning of the new, not just as a romanticised or politically correct imposition, but as a genuine opening up of new skills and practices. And with it, new attitudes, emotions, forms of embodiment and understandings. Teachers need to develop a capacity for deconstruction, but at the same time, they cannot ignore each of the overlapping loops of practice that go to make and remake the social order and the individuals within it.

References

Barthes, R. (1977). *Roland Barthes*. Berkeley: University of California Press.

Butler, J. (1993). *Bodies that matter: on the discursive limits of sex*. New York, Routledge.

Butler, J. (1995). For a careful reading. In S. Benhabib, J. Butler, D. Cornell, and Fraser, N. (Eds), *Feminist contentions: a philosophical exchange* (pp. 127–143). New York: Routledge.

Cixous, H. (1998). *Stigmata: escaping texts*. Routledge, London.

Cixous, H., and J. Derrida (2001). *Veils: cultural memory in the present*. Stanford: Stanford University Press.

Clément, C. (1994). *Syncope. The philosophy of rapture*. Minneapolis: University of Minnesota Press.

Connell, B., Radican, N., and Martin, P. (1987). *The changing faces of masculinity*. Sydney: Macquarie University. Unpublished paper.

Davies, B. (1989/2003). *Frogs and snails and feminist tales: preschool children and gender*. Sydney/Cresskill NJ: Allen and Unwin/Hampton Press.

Davies, B. (1993). *Poststructuralist theory and classroom practice*. Geelong: Deakin University Press.

Davies, B. (2000). *A body of writing, 1990–1999*. Walnut Creek: Alta Mira Press.

Davies, B., and Kasama, H. (2004). *Japanese preschool children and gender. Frogs and snails and feminist tales in Japan*. Creskill, NJ: Hampton Press.

Foucault, M. (1972). *The archaeology of knowledge*. London: Routledge.

Foucault, M. (1978). *The will to knowledge: the history of sexuality*. London: Penguin.

Foucault, M. (1988). Technologies of the self. In L.H. Martin, H. Gutman, and P.H. Hutton (Eds), *Technologies of the self: a seminar with Michel Foucault* (pp. 16–49). Massachusetts: University of Massachusetts Press.

Foucault, M. (2000). So is it important to think? In J.D. Faubion (Ed.), *Michel Foucault* (pp. 454–458). New York: The New York Press.

Grosz, E. (1994). *Volatile bodies: toward a corporeal feminism*. Sydney: Allen and Unwin.

Kristeva, J. (1982). *Powers of horror: an essay on abjection.* (Trans. Leon S. Roudiez). Columbia: Columbia University Press.

Malson, H. (1998). *The thin woman: feminism, post-structuralism, and the social psychology of anorexia nervosa.* London: Routledge.

Martin, R. (1988). Truth, power, self: an interview with Michel Foucault. In L.H. Martin, H. Gutman, and P.H. Hutton (Eds), *Technologies of the self: a seminar with Michel Foucault*, pp. 9–15. Massachusetts: University of Massachusetts Press.

Rose, N. (1998). *Inventing our selves. psychology, power and personhood.* Cambridge: Cambridge University Press.

CHAPTER 7

MASCULINE DOMINATION
Permanence and change

Pierre Bourdieu, *Masculine Domination*, Polity Press, 2001

It is indeed astonishing to observe the extraordinary autonomy of sexual structures relative to economic structures, of modes of reproduction relative to modes of production. The same system of classificatory schemes is found, in its essential features, through the centuries and across economic and social differences.... Researchers, almost always schooled in psychoanalysis, discover, in the psychic experience of the men and women of today, processes, for the most part very deeply buried, which, like the work needed to separate the boy from his mother or the symbolic effects of the sexual division of tasks and times in production and reproduction, are seen in the full light of day in ritual practices, which are publicly and collectively performed and are integrated into the symbolic system of a society organized through and through according to the principle of the primacy of masculinity. How can we explain why the uncompromisingly androcentric vision of a world in which ultra-masculine dispositions often find the conditions most favourable to their actualization in the structures of agrarian activity – organized according to the opposition between male working time and female production time – and also in the logic of a fully developed economy of symbolic goods, has been able to survive the profound changes which have occurred in productive activities and in the division of labour, relegating the economy of symbolic goods to a small number of islands, surrounded by the 'icy waters of self-interest and calculation'? How do we take account of this apparent perennity, which moreover plays a considerable part in giving the appearances of a natural essence to a historical construction, without running the risk of ratifying it by inscribing it in the eternity of a nature?

The historical labour of dehistoricization

In fact, it is clear that the eternal, in history, cannot be anything other than the product of a historical labour of eternalization. It follows that, in order to escape completely from essentialism, one should not try to deny the permanences and the invariants, which are indisputably part of historical reality; but, rather, one must *reconstruct the history of the historical labour of dehistoricization*, or, to put it another way, the history of the continuous (re)creation of the objective and subjective structures of masculine domination, which has gone on permanently so long as there have been men and women, and through which the masculine order has been continuously reproduced from age to age. In other words, a 'history of women' which brings to light, albeit despite itself, a large degree of constancy, permanence, must, if it wants to be consistent with itself, give a place, and no doubt the central place, to the *history of the agents and institutions which permanently contribute to the maintenance of these permanences*, the church, the state, the educational system, etc., and which may vary, at different times, in their relative weights and their functions. It cannot be content, for example, to record the exclusion of women from this or that occupation, this or that branch or discipline; it must also take note of and explain the reproduction both of the hierarchies (occupational, disciplinary, etc.) and of the hierarchical dispositions which they favour and which lead women to contribute to their own exclusion from the places from which they are in any case excluded.

Historical research cannot limit itself to describing the transformations over time of the condition of women, or even the relationship between the sexes in the different epochs. It must aim to establish, for each period, the state of the system of agents and institutions – family, church, state, educational system, etc., which, with different weights and different means at different times, have helped to remove the relations of masculine domination *more or less completely from history*. [. . .]

In short, in bringing to light the transhistorical invariants of the relationship between the 'genders', historical study is obliged to take for its object the historical labour of dehistoricization which has continuously produced and reproduced them, in other words, the constant work of *differentiation* to which men and women have never ceased to be subject and which leads them to distinguish themselves by masculinizing or feminizing themselves. In particular it should aim to describe and analyse the endlessly renewed social (re)construction of the principles of vision and division that generate 'genders' and, more broadly, the various categories of sexual practices (heterosexual and homosexual, in particular), heterosexuality itself being socially constructed and socially constituted as the universal standard of any 'normal' sexual practice, that is one that has been rescued from the ignominy of the 'unnatural'. A genuine understanding of the changes that have occurred both in the condition of women and in relations between the sexes can, paradoxically, be expected only from an analysis of the transformations of the mechanisms and institutions charged with ensuring the perpetuation of the order of genders.

The work of reproduction was performed, until a recent period, by three main agencies, the family, the church and the educational system, which were objectively orchestrated and had in common the fact that they acted on unconscious structures. The family undoubtedly played the most important part in the reproduction of masculine domination and the masculine vision; it is here that early experience of the sexual division of labour and the legitimate representation of that division, guaranteed by law and inscribed in language, imposes itself. As for the church, pervaded by the deep-seated anti-feminism of a clergy that was quick to condemn all female offences against decency, especially in matters of attire, and was the authorized reproducer of a pessimistic vision of women and womanhood, it explicitly inculcates (or used to inculcate) a familialist morality, entirely dominated by patriarchal values, with, in particular, the dogma of the radical inferiority of women. In addition it acts, more indirectly, on the historical structures of the unconscious, notably through the symbolism of the sacred texts, the liturgy and even religious space and time (the latter marked by the correspondence between the structure of the liturgical year and that of the farming year). In some periods, it has been able to draw on a series of ethical oppositions corresponding to a cosmological model in order to justify the hierarchy within the family, a monarchy by divine right based on the authority of the father, and to impose a vision of the social world of woman's place within it through what has been called 'iconographic propaganda'.

Finally, the educational system, even when it had freed itself from the grip of the church, continued to transmit the presuppositions of the patriarchal representation (based on the homology between the man/woman relationship and the adult/child relationship) and, perhaps most importantly, those that are inscribed in its own hierarchical structures, all sexually characterized, between the various schools or faculties, between the disciplines ('soft' or 'hard' – or, closer to the original mythical intuition – 'desiccating'), between specialisms, that is, between ways of being and ways of seeing, or seeing *oneself*, one's aptitudes and inclinations, in short, everything that combines to form not only social destinies but also self-images. In fact the whole of learned culture, transmitted by the educational system, whether in its literary, philosophical, medical or legal variants, has never ceased, until a recent period, to convey archaic modes of thought and models (with, for example, the weight of the Aristotelian tradition, which makes man the active principle and woman the passive principle) and an official discourse on the second sex to which theologians, jurists, doctors and moralists have all contributed and which aims to restrict the autonomy of the wife, especially as regards work, on the grounds of her 'childish' and feeble nature. [. . .]

To complete the catalogue of the institutional factors of the reproduction of the gender division one should also take into account the role of the *state*, which has ratified and underscored the prescriptions and proscriptions of private patriarchy with those of a *public patriarchy*, inscribed in all the institutions charged with managing and regulating the everyday existence of the domestic unit. Without reaching the extremes of paternalist, authoritarian states . . ., full-scale realizations of the ultra-conservative vision which makes the patriarchal family the principle and model of the social order interpreted as a *moral order*, based on the absolute pre-eminence of men over women, adults over children, and on identification of morality with the strength, courage and self-control of the body, the seat of temptations and desires, modern states have inscribed all the fundamental principles of the androcentric vision in the rules defining the official status of the citizens. The essential ambiguity of the state derives in part from the fact that in its very structure, with the opposition between financial ministries and spending ministries, between its paternalist, familialist, protective right hand, and its socially oriented left hand, it reproduces the archetypal division between male and female, with women being linked to the left hand as its administrators and as the main recipients of its benefits and services. [. . .]

The factors of change

The major change has doubtless been that masculine domination no longer imposes itself with the transparency of something taken for granted. Thanks, in particular, to the immense critical effort of the feminist movement, which, at least in some regions of the social space, has managed to break the circle of generalized mutual reinforcement, it now appears, in many contexts, as something to be avoided, excused or justified. The calling into question of the self-evident comes hand in hand with the substantive transformations seen in the condition of women, especially in the most advantaged social categories. There are, for example, increased access to secondary and higher education and waged work, and, through this, to the public sphere; and a degree of distancing from domestic tasks and reproductive functions (linked to the development and generalized use of contraception and the reduction of family size), with, in particular, the postponement of marriage and procreation, reduction of the interruption of professional activity due to childbirth, and also increased divorce and a lower rate of marriage.

Of all the factors of change, the most important are those that are linked to the decisive transformation of the function of the educational system in reproducing the differences between the genders, such as women's increased access to education and, consequently, to economic independence, and the transformation of family structures (resulting, in particular, from increased rates of divorce). It is true that even when the real family has changed, the inertia of habitus, and *of law*, tends to perpetuate the dominant model of family structure and, by the same token, of legitimate sexuality – heterosexual and oriented towards reproduction – in relation to which socialization and with it the transmission of the traditional principles of division were tacitly organized; but the appearance of new types of family, such as 'composite' families, and the public visibility of new (particularly homosexual) models of sexuality help to break the *doxa* and expand the space of what is possible in terms of sexuality. In addition, and in a more banal way, the increased number of working women could not fail to affect the division of household tasks and therefore the traditional male and female models, which has no doubt had consequences for the acquisition of the sexually differentiated dispositions within the family. It has been observed, for example, that the daughters of working mothers have higher career aspirations and are less attached to the traditional model of a woman's role.

But one of the most important changes in the status of women and one of the most decisive factors of change is undoubtedly the increased access of girls to secondary and higher education, which, together with the transformations of the structures of production (particularly the development of large public and private bureaucracies and the social technologies of management), has led to a very important modification of the position of women in the division of labour. Women are now much more strongly represented in the intellectual professions, in administration and in the various forms of sale of symbolic services – journalism, television, cinema, radio, public relations, advertising, design and decoration; and they have intensified their presence in the occupations closer to the traditional definition of female activities (teaching, social work and paramedical activities). This having been said, while female graduates have found their main career openings in intermediate middle-range occupations (middle management, technical staff, medical and social personnel), they remain practically excluded from positions of authority and responsibility, particularly in industry, finance and politics. [. . .]

The same logic governs access to the various professions and to the various positions within each of them: in work as in education, the progress made by women must not conceal the corresponding progress made by men, so that, as in a handicap race, the structure of the *gaps* is maintained. The most striking example of this *permanence in and through change* is the fact that positions which become feminized are either already devalued (the majority of semi-skilled workers are women or immigrants) or declining, their devaluation being intensified, in a snowball effect, by the desertion of the men which it helped to induce. Moreover, while it is true that women are found at all levels of the social space, their chances of access (and rate of representation) decline as one moves towards the rarest and most sought-after positions (so that the rate of actual and potential feminization is no doubt the best index of the relative position and value of the various occupations).

Thus, at each level, despite the effects of hyper-selection, the formal equality between men and women tends to disguise the fact that, other things being equal, women always occupy less favoured positions. For example, while it is true that women are more and more strongly represented among the employees of central and local government, it is always the lowest and most insecure positions that are reserved for them (there is a particularly high proportion of women among non-established and part-time staff, and in local government service, for example, they occupy junior and ancillary positions as assistants and 'carers' – cleaners, canteen staff, nursery assistants, etc.) The clearest indication of the uncertainties of the status granted to women in the labour market is no doubt the fact that they are always paid less than men, other things being equal, that they are appointed to lower positions with the same qualifications, and above all that they are proportionately more affected by redundancies and insecurity of employment and more often relegated to part-time posts – which has the effect, among other things, of almost invariably excluding them from access to decision-making and career prospects. Given that their interests are bound up with the 'left hand' of the state and with 'social' positions within the bureaucratic field as well as with those sectors of private companies which are most vulnerable to 'flexible labour' policies, there is every reason to expect that they will be the main victims of the neoliberal policy aimed at reducing the welfare role of the state and favouring the 'deregulation' of the labour market. [. . .]

For a full understanding of the statistical distribution of powers and privileges between men and women and the way it has changed over time, one has to bear in mind, simultaneously, two properties which may at first sight appear contradictory. On the one hand, whatever their position in the social space, women have in common the fact that they are *separated from men by a negative symbolic coefficient* which, like skin colour for blacks, or any other sign of membership of a stigmatized group, negatively affects everything that they are and do, and which is the source of a systematic set of homologous differences: despite the vast distance between them, there is something in common between a woman managing director who needs a massage every morning to give her the strength to cope with the stress of exercising power over men – or among men – and the woman production-line worker in the metal industry who has to look to the solidarity of her female workmates for support against the ordeals of work in a male environment, such as sexual harassment, or, quite simply, the damage done to her self-image and self-esteem by the ugliness and dirt imposed by her working conditions. On the other hand, despite the specific experiences which bring them together (such as the small change of domination received in the countless, often subliminal, wounds inflicted by the masculine order), women remain *separated from each other* by economic and cultural differences which affect, among other things, their objective and subjective ways of undergoing and suffering masculine domination – without, however, cancelling out all that is linked to the diminution of symbolic capital entailed by being a woman.

For the rest, even the changes in the condition of women always obey the logic of the traditional model of the division between male and female. Men continue to dominate the public space and the field of power (especially economic power – over production) whereas women remain (predominantly) assigned to the private space (domestic space, the site of reproduction), where the logic of the economy of symbolic goods is perpetuated, or to those quasi-extensions of the domestic space, the welfare services (especially medical services) and education, or to the domains of symbolic production (the literary, artistic or journalistic fields, etc.).

If the old structures of the sexual division seem still to determine the very direction and form of these changes, this is because, as well as being objectified in disciplines, careers and jobs that are more or less strongly characterized sexually, they act through *three practical principles* which women, and also their social circles, apply in their choices. The first is that the functions appropriate to women are an extension of their domestic functions – education, care and service. The second is that a woman cannot have authority over men, and, other things being equal, therefore has every likelihood of being passed over in favour of a man for a position of authority and of being confined to subordinate and ancillary functions. The third principle gives men the monopoly of the handling of technical objects and machines.

Through the experience of a 'sexually' ordered social order and the explicit reminders addressed to them by their parents, teachers and peers, themselves endowed with principles of vision acquired in similar experiences of the world, girls internalize, in the form of schemes of perception and appreciation not readily accessible to consciousness, the principles of the dominant vision which lead them to find the social order, such as it is, normal or even natural and in a sense to anticipate their destiny, refusing the courses or careers from which they are anyway excluded and rushing towards those for which they are in any case destined. The constancy of habitus that results from this is thus one of the most important factors in the relative constancy of the structure of the sexual division of labour: because these principles are, in their essentials, transmitted from body to body, below the level of consciousness and discourse, to a large extent they are beyond the grip of conscious control and therefore not amenable to transformations or corrections (as is shown by the frequently observed discrepancies between declarations and practices – for example, those men most favourable to equality between the sexes make no greater contribution to housework than others); moreover, being objectively orchestrated, they confirm and reinforce one another. [. . .]

The economy of symbolic goods and reproduction strategies

But another decisive factor in the perpetuation of differences is the permanence that the economy of symbolic goods (of which marriage is a central component) owes to its relative autonomy, which enables masculine domination to perpetuate itself within it unaffected by the transformations of the economic modes of production – and to do so aided by the constant, explicit support that the family, the guardian of symbolic capital, receives from the churches and from law. The legitimate exercise of sexuality, although it may appear increasingly freed from the matrimonial obligation, remains ordered by and subordinated to the transmission of the patrimony, through marriage, which remains one of the legitimate routes for the transfer of wealth. As Robert A. Nye endeavours to show, bourgeois families have not ceased to invest in reproduction strategies, especially matrimonial ones, aimed at conserving or increasing their symbolic capital. They do so much more than the aristocratic families of the ancien régime, because the maintenance of their position depends strongly on the reproduction of their symbolic capital through the production of inheritors capable of perpetuating the heritage of the group and through the acquisition of prestigious allies.[1] [. . .]

Being excluded from the universe of serious things, of public and especially economic affairs, women long remained confined to the domestic universe and the activities associated with the biological and social reproduction of the lineage. Even if these activities (especially the maternal ones) are apparently recognized and sometimes ritually celebrated, they are so only in so far as they remain subordinated to the activities of production, which alone receive a true economic and social sanction, and ordered in relation to the material and symbolic interests of the lineage, that is, of the men. Thus, a very large part of the *domestic work* which falls to women is, in many milieux, aimed at conserving the solidarity and integration of the family by maintaining kin relationships and all the social capital through the organization of a whole series of social activities – ordinary ones, such as meals which bring together the whole family, or extra-ordinary, such as the ceremonies and celebrations (birthdays, etc.) designed to ritually celebrate the bonds of kinship and to ensure the maintenance of social relations and the prestige of the family, the exchanges of gifts, visits, letters or postcards and telephone calls.

This domestic work remains largely unnoticed or deprecated (with, for example, the ritual denunciation of women's taste for chatter, especially on the telephone . . .) and, when it is noticed, it is derealized by the transfer on to the terrain of spirituality, morality or feeling, which its non-profit-making and 'disinterested' character facilitates. The fact that women's domestic labour has no monetary equivalent does indeed help to devalue it, even in their own eyes, as if this time without a market value were also without importance and could be given without recompense, and without limits, first to the members of the family, and especially the children (thus it has been observed that a mother's time is more easily interrupted), but also outside it, for voluntary tasks, in the church or in charitable organizations, or, increasingly, in associations or political parties. . . .

Just as, in the least differentiated societies, women were treated as means of exchange enabling men to accumulate social and symbolic capital through marriages, which functioned as investments leading to the creation of more or less extensive and prestigious alliances, so too today they make a decisive *contribution* to the production and reproduction of the symbolic capital of the family, first by manifesting the symbolic capital of the domestic group through everything that contributes to their appearance (cosmetics, clothing, bearing, etc.); by virtue of this, they are situated on the side of appearances and charm. The social world functions (to a greater or lesser extent, depending on the field) as a market in symbolic goods, dominated by the masculine vision: for women, as has been noted, to be is to be perceived, and perceived by the male eye or by an eye informed by masculine categories – those that one implements, without being able to state them explicitly, when one praises a woman's work as 'feminine' or, on the contrary, 'not at all feminine'. To be 'feminine' means essentially to avoid all the properties and practices that can function as signs of manliness, and to say of a woman in a position of power that she is 'very feminine' is just a particularly subtle way of denying her the right to the specifically masculine attribute of power.

The particular position of women in the symbolic goods market explains the greater part of female dispositions: if every social relationship is, in one respect, the site of an exchange in which each participant invites the other to evaluate his or her perceptible appearance, then in this being-perceived, the proportion which pertains to the body reduced to what is sometimes called (potentially sexualized) 'physique', relative to less directly perceptible properties, such as speech, is greater for women than for men. Whereas, for men, cosmesis and clothing tend to efface the body in favour of social signs of social position (dress, decorations, uniform, etc.), in women they tend to highlight it and make it a language of seduction. This explains why the investment (in time, money, effort, etc.) in cosmetic work is much greater for women. [. . .]

Being assigned to the management of the symbolic capital of the family, women are quite logically called upon to transport this role into the company, which almost always asks them to provide the functions of presentation and representation, reception and hospitality ('air hostess', 'exhibition hostess', 'conference hostess', 'receptionist', 'courier', etc.), and also the management of the major bureaucratic rituals which, like domestic rituals, help to maintain and enhance the social capital of relationships and the symbolic capital of the company. [. . .]

The strength of the structure

A truly *relational* approach to the relation of domination between men and women as it establishes itself *in the whole set of social spaces and subspaces*, that is, not only in the family but also in the educational world and the world of work, in the bureaucratic universe and in the field of the media, leads one to explode the fantastical image of the 'eternal feminine', in order to bring to light more clearly the constancy of the structure of the relation of domination between men and women which is maintained beyond the *substantive* differences in condition linked to moments in history and positions in social space. And this noting of the *transhistorical continuity of the relation of masculine domination*, far from producing an effect of dehistoricization, and therefore of naturalization, as some people sometimes pretend to believe, in fact requires one to reverse the traditional problematic, based on the observation of the most visible changes in the *condition* of women. It forces us to pose the – always ignored – question of the endlessly recommended historical labour which is necessary in order to wrench masculine domination from history and from the historical mechanisms and actions which are responsible for its apparent dehistoricization and which any politics of historical transformation needs to be aware of if it is not to be condemned to powerlessness.

Finally, and above all, it forces one to see the futility of the strident calls of 'postmodern' philosophers for the 'supersession of dualisms'. These dualisms, deeply rooted in things (structures) and in bodies, do not spring from a simple effect of verbal naming and cannot be abolished by an act of performative magic, since the genders, far from being simple 'roles' that can be played at will (in the manner of 'drag queens'), are inscribed in bodies and in a universe from which they derive their strength.[2] It is the order of genders that underlies the performative efficacy of words – and especially of insults – and it is also the order of genders that *resists* the spuriously revolutionary redefinitions of subversive voluntarism.

Like Michel Foucault, who sought to rehistoricize sexuality against psychoanalytic naturalization, by describing, in a *History of Sexuality* conceived as 'an archaeology of psychoanalysis', a genealogy of Western man as a 'subject of desire', I have tried here to link the unconscious which governs sexual relations, and, more generally, the relations between the sexes, not only to its individual ontogeny but to its collective phylogeny, in other words to the long and partly immobile history of the androcentric unconscious. [. . .]

Sexuality as we understand it is indeed a historical invention, but one which has developed progressively as the various fields and their specific logics became differentiated. It was first necessary for the sexed (and not sexual) principle of division which constituted the fundamental opposition of mythic reason to cease to be applied to the whole order of the world, both physical and political, defining for example the foundations of cosmology [. . .]

The schemes of the sexually characterized habitus are not 'fundamental structuring alternatives', as Goffman would have it, but historical and highly differentiated structures, arising from a social space that is itself highly differentiated, which reproduce themselves through learning processes linked to the experience that agents have of the structures of these spaces. Thus insertion into different fields organized according to oppositions (strong/weak, big/small, heavy/light, fat/thin, tense/relaxed, hard/soft, etc.) which always stand in a relation of homology with the fundamental distinction between male and female and the secondary alternatives in which it is expressed (dominant/dominated, above/below, active-penetrating/passive-penetrated) is accompanied by the inscription in the body of a series of sexually characterized oppositions which are homologous among themselves and also with the fundamental opposition. [. . .]

It follows that the genetic sociology of the sexual unconscious is logically extended into the analysis of the structures of the social universes in which this unconscious is rooted and reproduces itself, whether it be the divisions embodied in the form of principles of division or the objective divisions that are established between social positions (and their occupants, who are preferentially male or female: doctors/nurses, employers/intellectuals, etc.), the most important of which, from the point of view of the perpetuation of these divisions, is undoubtedly the one which distinguishes the fields devoted to symbolic production. The fundamental opposition. . ., is 'geared down' or diffracted in a series of homologous oppositions, which reproduce it, but in dispersed and often almost unrecognizable forms (such as sciences/humanities or surgery/dermatology). These specific oppositions channel the mind, in a more or less insidious way, without ever allowing themselves to be seen in their unity and for what they are, namely, so many facets of one and the same structure of relations of sexual domination.

It is however on condition that one holds together the totality of the sites and forms in which this kind of domination is exercised – a domination which has the particularity of being able to be exercised on very different scales, in all social spaces, from the most restricted, such as families, to the broadest – that it becomes possible to grasp its structural constants and the mechanisms of its reproduction. The visible changes that have affected the condition of women mask the permanence of the invisible structures, which can only be brought to light by relational thinking capable of *making the connection between the domestic economy, and therefore the division of labour and powers which characterizes it, and the various sectors of the labour market* (the fields) in which men and women are involved. This is in contrast to the common tendency to consider *separately* the distribution of tasks, and especially ranks, in domestic work and in non-domestic work. [. . .]

Only when one takes account of the constraints that the structure of the (actual or potential) domestic space brings to bear on the structure of the occupational space (for example, through the representation of a necessary, unavoidable, or acceptable gap between the husband's position and the wife's) does it become possible to understand the homology between the structures of the male positions and the female positions in the various social spaces, a homology which tends to be maintained even when the terms constantly change their substantive content, in a chase in which women never overcome their handicap.

The making of this connection enables one to understand how the same relation of domination may be observed, in different forms, in the most contrasting social conditions, from the voluntary devotion of the women of the grande bourgeoisie of money and business to their homes or their charitable activities, to the ancillary and 'mercenary' devotion of domestic servants, or, in between, at the level of the petite bourgeoisie, a waged job complementary to that of the husband, and compatible with it, and almost always performed in a minor mode. The structure of masculine domination is the ultimate principle of these countless singular relationships of domination/submission, which, while they differ in their form according to the position in space of the agents concerned – sometimes immense and visible, sometimes infinitesimal and almost invisible, but homologous and therefore united by a family resemblance – separate and unite men and women in each of the social universes, thus maintaining between them the 'mystic boundary' to which Virginia Woolf referred [in *A Room of One's Own*].

Notes

1   R.A. Nye, *Masculinity and Male Codes of Honor in Modern France* (New York: Oxford University Press, 1993), p. 9.
2   Judith Butler herself seems to reject the 'voluntaristic' view of gender that she seemed to put forward in *Gender Trouble*, when she writes: 'The misapprehension about gender performativity is this: that gender is a choice, or that gender is a role, or that gender is a construction that one puts on, as one puts clothes on in the morning' (J. Butler, *Bodies that Matter: On the Discursive Limits of 'Sex'* (New York: Routledge, 1993), p. 94).

CHAPTER 8

THE BIG PICTURE
Masculinities in recent world history

R.W. Connell, in A. Halsey, H. Lauder, P. Brown and
A. Stuart Wells (eds) *Education, Culture, Economy and
Society,* Oxford University Press, 1997

This chapter addresses the question of how we should study men in gender relations, and what view of modern world history an understanding of masculinity might give us. I start with the reasons why 'masculinity' has recently become a cultural and intellectual problem, and suggest a framework in which the intellectual work can be better done. The historicity of 'masculinity' is best shown by cross-cultural evidence on the differing gender practices of men in different social orders. The core of the chapter is a sketch of the historical evolution of the forms of masculinity now globally dominant. This shows their imbrication with the military, social, and economic history of North Atlantic capitalist states, and especially with imperialism. This history provides the necessary basis for an understanding of the major institutionalized forms of masculinity in contemporary 'first world' countries, and the struggles for hegemony among them. I conclude with a brief look at the dynamics of marginalized and subordinated masculinities.

Studying 'Masculinity'
Masculinity as a cultural problem

The fact that conferences about 'masculinities' are being held is significant in its own right. Twenty-five years ago no one would have thought of doing so. Both the men-and-masculinity literature that has bubbled up in the interval (Carrigan *et al.,* 1985; Ford and Hearn, 1988; Hearn and Morgan, 1990) and the debates at conferences and seminars, testify that in some part of the Western intelligentsia, masculinity has become problematic in a way it never was before.

There is no doubt what cued the discovery of this problem. It was, first, the advent of Women's Liberation at the end of the 1960s and the growth of feminist research on gender and 'sex roles' since. Second – as important intellectually though of less reach practically – it was the advent of Gay Liberation and the developing critique of heterosexuality of lesbians and gay men.

While much of the key thinking about masculinity continues to be done by radical feminists and gay activists, concern with the issue has spread much more widely. The nature and politics of masculinity have been addressed by the new right, by heterosexual socialists, and by psychotherapists of wondrous variety. (Johnson, 1974; Gilder, 1975; Ellis, 1976; Connell, 1982)....

Something is going on; but what? Writers of the masculinity literature of the 1970s pictured change as a break with the old restrictive 'male sex role,' and the rapid creation of more equal relations with women. They were far too optimistic – and missed most of the politics of the process. Segal has aptly called the pace of change among heterosexual men 'slow motion,' and she has shown the political complexities of reconstructing masculinity in the case of Britain. The leading style of gay masculinity in English-speaking countries went from camp to 'clone' in a decade, and gay politics then ran into the wall of the new right and the HIV epidemic. Commercial popular culture, in the era of Rambo movies and Masters of the Universe toys, has reasserted musclebound and destructive masculinity and has made a killing (Farrell, 1975; Nichols, 1975; Segal, 1990; Humphries, 1985).

So, to say masculinity has become 'problematic' is not necessarily to say gender relations are changing for the better. It is, rather, to say that cultural turbulence around themes of masculinity has grown. An arena has opened up. What direction gender relations move will in part be determined by the politics that happens in this arena. And this very much involves the intelligentsia. Intellectuals are bearers of the social relations of gender and makers of sexual ideology. The way we do our intellectual work of inquiry, analysis, and reportage has consequences; epistemology and sexual politics are intertwined (Connell, 1987).

Masculinity as an intellectual problem

Such awareness is not common in the English-language literature on men-and-masculinity. Indeed the implicit definitions of masculinity in this literature have limited its intellectual and political horizons quite severely.

Closest to common-sense ideas is the notion of masculinity as a *psychological essence*, an inner core to the individual. This may be inherited, or it may be acquired early in life. In either case it is carried forward into later life as the essence of a man's being. Pseudo-biological versions of this concept abound. A more sophisticated version draws on psycho-analytic ideas to present masculinity as an identity laid down in early childhood by family constellations. Stoller's conception of 'core gender identity' is probably the most influential. It has had a good run in blaming mothers for transsexuality, and psychologizing the anthropology of masculinity (Stoller, 1968, 1976; Tiger, 1969; Stoller and Herdt, 1983).

The conception of masculinity as a psychological essence obliterates questions about social structure and the historical dynamic of gender relations. At best, the formation of masculinity within the family is treated as a moment of reproduction of the gender order. At worst, an ahistorical masculine essence, as unchanging as crystal, is set up as a criterion against which social arrangements are judged, and generally found wanting....

The conception of a male *sex role*, the staple of American masculinity literature in the 1970s and early 1980s, promises better than this. It places definitions of masculinity firmly in the realm of the social, in 'expectations,' 'stereotypes,' or 'role models.' This allows for change. There may be role strain, conflict within or about the role, shifting role definitions. It also allows for a certain diversity. Role theorists can acknowledge that the 'black male role' may be different from the 'white male role' (David and Brannon, 1976; Pleck, 1976; Harrison, 1979; Franklin, 1987).

But these gains are slight. Sex-role theory is drastically inadequate as a framework for understanding gender. The role concept analytically collapses into an assertion of individual agency; it squeezes out the dimension of social structure. It gives no grip on the distribution of power, on the institutional organization of gender, on the gender structuring of production. Role theory rests on a superficial analysis of human personality and motives. It gives no grip on the emotional contradictions of sexuality, or the emotional complexities of gender in everyday life, which are revealed by fine-textured field research.[1]

A third body of work locates masculinity in *discourse* or treats it via cultural *representations*. Early writing on media stereotypes has now been transcended by a much more supple and penetrating account of the symbolic structures operating within particular genres. One of the best pieces of recent North American writing about masculinity, Jeffords's *The Remasculinization of America* (1989), traces the reshaping of the collective memory of the Vietnam War by novelists and filmmakers. This is a striking reversal of the slow desanitizing of the Second World War traced by Fussell in *Wartime* (1989). Theweleit's much quoted *Male Fantasies* (1987) similarly locates sources of German fascism in discourses linking war and sexuality. These studies are politically sophisticated, even politically vibrant, in a way the discourse of 'sex roles' never has been. They attend to issues of power, to nuances and complexities in the representation of masculinity, to contradiction and change. But because they operate wholly within the world of discourse they ignore their own conditions of existence in the practices of gender and in the social structuring of those practices. Their politics is inevitably reactive. One can get from such criticism no pro-active idea of how to *change* oppressive gender relations – except perhaps to fly back in time and write a better war novel.

The limitations of our current approaches to masculinity are summed up by the startling ethnocentrism of most of the English-language literature. By this I don't only mean white, middle-class writers' habit of taking white, middle-class experience as constituting reality and marginalizing or ignoring men who work with their hands or who come from other ethnic groups. That habit exists, of course. Class and race blindness is particularly blatant in the therapeutic literature on masculinity. It has been under challenge for some time, with little effect.[2] Rather, I mean the more startling ethnocentrism by which a discourse of 'masculinity' is constructed out of the lives of (at most) 5 per cent of the world's population of men, in one culture-area, at one moment in history. [. . .]

A cure is at hand, in a body of research that has developed quite separately from the men-and-masculinity literature. Ethnographers in a number of culture areas, doubtless sensitized to gender by feminism though rarely pursuing feminist themes, have come up with accounts of local constructions of masculinity very different from the mid-Atlantic norm. [. . .] Putting such accounts together might lead to a comparative sociology of masculinity capable of challenging many of our culture's received notions. ... But the familiar comparative method rests on an assumption of intact, separate cultures; and that assumption is not defensible any more. European imperialism, global capitalism under US hegemony, and modern communications have brought all cultures into contact, obliterated many, and marginalized most. Anthropology as a discipline is in crisis because of this. The dimension of *global history* must now be a part of every ethnography. And that is true for ethnographies of masculinity as well.

Towards a new framework: a political sociology of men in gender relations

To grasp the intellectual and political opportunity that is now open requires a shift in the strategic conception of research and in our understanding of the object of knowledge. The object of knowledge is not a reified 'masculinity' (as encapsulated, with its reified partner 'femininity,' in the psychological scales measuring M/F and androgyny). The object of knowledge is, rather, *men's places and practices in gender relations*. It is true that these places may be symbolically constructed (the subject of representation research); and that these practices are organized transactionally and in the life course (the subject of sex role and personality research). Thus the main topics of existing men-and-masculinity studies are included in this conception of the field. But these topics can only be understood in relation to a wider spectrum of issues that must now be systematically included in the field of argument.

First, masculinity as personal practice cannot be isolated from its institutional context. Most human activity is institutionally bound. Three institutions – the state, the workplace/labor market, and the family – are of particular importance in the contemporary organization of gender.

Thus we cannot begin to talk intelligibly about 'masculinity and power' without addressing the institutionalized masculinization of state élites, the gender differentiation of parts of the state apparatus (consider the military in the Gulf deployment), the history of state strategies for the control of populations via women's fertility. The sexual division of labor in production, the masculinized character of the very concept of 'the economic,' the levels of income and asset inequality between men and women, make it impossible to speak about 'masculinity and work' as if they were somehow separate entities being brought into relation. Hansot and Tyack have correctly emphasized the importance of 'thinking institutionally' in the case of gender and schooling, and their point has much wider relevance. It is not too strong to say that *masculinity is an aspect of institutions*, and is produced in institutional life, *as much as it is an aspect of personality* or produced in interpersonal transactions (Connell, 1986; Hansot and Tyack, 1987; Burton, 1991: ch. 1).

Second, masculinities as cultural forms cannot be abstracted from sexuality, which is an essential dimension of the social creation of gender. Sexuality has been leeched out of much of the literature on masculinity. This perhaps reflects an assumption that sexuality is pre-social, a natural force belonging to the realm of biology. But while sexuality addresses the body, it is itself social practice and constitutive of the social world. There is no logical gap between sexuality and organizational life. [. . .]

These arguments are consistent with a position in social theory that insists on the historicity of social life. Practice is situational (it responds to a particular configuration of events and relationships) and transformative (it operates on a given situation and converts it into a differently configured one). One cannot be masculine in a particular way (which is to say, engage in particular practices constructing a given form of masculinity) without affecting the conditions in which that form of masculinity arose: whether to reproduce them, intensify them, or subvert them.

Since gender relations produce large-scale inequalities – in most contemporary cultures, collective advantages for men and disadvantages for women – masculinity understood in this way must be understood as political. I mean 'political' in the simple, conventional sense of the struggle for scarce resources, the mobilization of power and the pursuit of tactics on behalf of a particular interest. Interests are constituted within gender relations by the facts of inequality. They are not homogeneous, indeed are generally extremely complex, but they are powerful determinants of social action.

Different masculinities arise in relation to this structure of interests and embody different commitments and different tactics or strategies. I have suggested elsewhere that hegemonic masculinity in patriarchy can be understood as embodying a successful strategy for the subordination of women (Connell, 1990). I would now add to that formula that when the historical conditions for a strategy's success have altered, the hegemonic form of masculinity is vulnerable to displacement by other forms.

To construct such an analysis requires a standpoint, and I take the most defensible one to be the commitment to human equality. The standpoint of equality is not an end-point but a starting-point for social analysis. In relation to masculinity it defines the enterprise as one of 'studying up,' a matter of studying the holders of power in gender relations with a view to informing strategies for dismantling patriarchy. Given the interweaving of structures of inequality, it should also yield significant information on strategic questions about capitalism, race relations, imperialism, and global poverty. This is no new observation, but it bears repeating. [. . .]

Masculinities in history

An important negative conclusion can be drawn immediately. The models of masculinity familiar in Euro/American discourse simply do not work for the realities of gender in other cultures, so far as these cultures can be reconstructed before colonial or commercial domination by the Euro/American world. [. . .] To speak of 'masculinity' as one and the same entity across these differences in place and time is to descend into absurdity. Even a modest study of this evidence wipes out sociobiology, any scheme of genetic determination, or any ontological or poetic account of male essences, as credible accounts of masculinity.

Indeed I am forced to wonder whether 'masculinity' is in itself a culture-bound concept that makes little sense outside Euro/American culture. Our conventional meaning for the word 'masculinity' is a quality of an individual, a personal attribute that exists in a greater or lesser degree; in the mental realm an analogue of physical traits like hairiness of chest or bulk of biceps. The connection of such a concept with the growth of individualism and the emerging concept of the self in early-modern European culture is easy to see. A culture not constructed in such a way might have little use for the concept of masculinity.

Nevertheless, it is Euro/American culture that is dominant in the world now, and which must be addressed first in any reckoning with our current predicament. Imperialism was a massively important event in gender history. Some cultures' gender regimes have been virtually obliterated by imperialism. . . . All have been abraded by it. Surviving cultures have attempted to reconstruct themselves in relation to Euro/American world dominance, an explosive process that is perhaps the most important dynamic of gender in the contemporary world. . . .

To make this point is not to accept that gender effects simply follow from class causes. Stacey convincingly argues that Confucian China was a patriarchal class order in which the crisis of the politico-economic system was inherently also a crisis of the family and gender relations. Similarly, I argue that European imperialism and contemporary world capitalism are gendered social orders with gender dynamics as powerful as their class dynamics. The history of how European/American culture, economy, and states became so dominant and so dangerous is *inherently* a history of gender relations (as well as, interwoven with class relations and race relations). Since the agents of global domination were, and are predominantly men, the historical analysis of masculinity must be a leading theme in our understanding of the contemporary world order.

Having made that large claim, I should back it up with a dozen volumes of evidence, and they have not yet been written. Serious historical work on themes of masculinity is extremely rare. All I can offer here is yet another sketch, a historical hypothesis about the course of events that produced contemporary Euro/American masculinities. This sketch is informed by the decent research I have been able to locate, but is necessarily very tentative.

Transformations of hegemonic forms

The history of hegemonic forms of Euro/American masculinity in the last two hundred years is the history of the displacement, splitting, and remaking of gentry masculinity. Because I have limited space I am very summary at this point. Political revolution, industrialization, and the growth of bureaucratic state apparatuses saw the displacement of gentry masculinity by more calculative, rational, and regulated masculinities. The bureaucrat and the businessman were produced as social types. The economic base of the landed gentry declined, and with it the orientation of kinship and honor. Violence was split off from political power, in the core countries; Mr Gladstone did not fight duels, nor lead armies. Rather, violence became a specialty. As mass armies were institutionalized so was the officer corps. This became the repository of much of the gentry code. The Dreyfus affair in France was shaped by this code; the Prussian officer corps was perhaps its most famous exemplar. But violence was now combined with an emphasis on rationality: we see the emergence of military science. If Las Casas's *History of the Indies* was a key document of early-modern masculinity, perhaps the nineteenth century equivalent was Clausewitz's *On War* (1827; 1976 edn.) – Clausewitz being one of the reformers of the Prussian army. It was bureaucratically rationalized violence as a social technique, just as much as superiority of weapons, that made European states and European settlers almost invincible in the colonial frontier expansion of the nineteenth century.

But this technique risked destroying the society that sustained it. Global war led to revolutionary upheaval in 1917–1923. In much of Europe the capitalist order was only stabilized, after half a generation of further struggle, by fascist movements that glorified irrationality and the unrestrained violence of the front-line soldier. And the dynamics of fascism soon enough led to a new and even more devastating global war. The defeat of fascism in the Second World War cut off the institutionalization of a hegemonic masculinity marked by irrationality and personal violence. But it certainly did not end the bureaucratic institutionalization of violence. [. . .] The growth of destructive capability through the application of science to weapons development has, however, given a new significance to technical expertise.

This paralleled developments in other parts of the economy. The enormous growth of school and university systems during the twentieth century, the multiplying number of 'professional' occupations with claims to specialized expertise, the increasing political significance of technology, and the growth of information industries, are aspects of a largescale change in culture and production systems that has seen a further splitting of nineteenth-century hegemonic masculinity.

Masculinity organized around *dominance* was increasingly incompatible with masculinity organized around *expertise* or technical knowledge. 'Management' split from 'professions,' and some analysts saw power increasingly in the hands of the professionals. Factional divisions opened in both capitalist ruling classes and communist élites between those pursuing coercive strategies towards workers (conservatives/hard-liners) and those depending on technological success and economic growth that allow integrative strategies (liberals/reformers). The emotional pattern of Reaganite politics in the United States centered on a revival of the first of these inflections of masculinity and a rejection of the second. In the 1992 US presidential campaign, both Bush and Clinton image-makers seemed to be trying to blend the two (Galbraith, 1971; Gouldner, 1979).

Subordinated forms

So far I have been sketching the hegemonic masculinities of the dominant class and race in the dominant countries of the world-system. But this, obviously, is far from being the whole picture. The hegemonic form of masculinity is generally not the only form, and often is not the most common form. Hegemony is a question of relations of cultural domination, not of head-counts.

On a world scale this is even more obviously true. The patterns of masculinity just outlined are formed in relation to the whole complex structure of gender relations. In terms of other masculinities, they exist in tension with the hegemonic masculinities of subordinated classes and races, with subordinated masculinities in their own class and race milieu, and with the patterns of masculinity current in other parts of the world order. To offer even a sketch of this structure, let alone analyze its dynamics, is a tall order; again I shall have to settle for indications.

The historical displacement of the gentry by businessmen and bureaucrats in core countries was plainly linked to the transformation of peasants into working classes and the creation of working-class hegemonic masculinities as cultural forms. The separation household from workplace in the factory system, the dominance of the wage form, and the development of industrial struggle, were conditions for the emergence of forms of masculinity organized around wage-earning capacity, skill and endurance in labor, domestic patriarchy, and combative solidarity among wage earners.

The expulsion of women from industries such as coalmining, printing, and steelmaking was a key moment in the formation of such masculinity. The craft union movement can be seen as its institutionalization. The growing power of organized labor in the last decades of the nineteenth and first decades of the twentieth century was one of the main pressures on the masculinity of the dominant class that led to the splits between political alternatives (fascist, liberal, conservative) already mentioned (Seccombe, 1977; Cockburn, 1983).

At much the same time the masculinity of the dominant class was purged in terms of identity and object choice. As gay historians have shown, the late nineteenth century was the time when 'the homosexual' as a social type was constructed, to a considerable extent through the deployment of medical and penal power. At earlier periods of history sodomy had been officially seen as an act, the potential for which existed in any man who gave way to libertinage. From the point of view of hegemonic masculinity, this change meant that the potential for homoerotic pleasure was expelled from the masculine and located in a deviant group (symbolically assimilated to women or to beasts). There was no mirror-type of 'the heterosexual'; rather, heterosexuality became a required connotation of manliness. The contradiction between this rapidly-solidifying definition and the actual conditions of emotional life among men in military and paramilitary groups reached crisis level in fascism. [. . .]

On the frontier of settlement, regulation was ineffective, violence endemic, physical conditions harsh. Industries such as mining offered spectacular profits on a chancy basis. A very imbalanced sex ratio allowed a homosocial masculinization of the frontier. Phillips, in an important study of the New Zealand case, draws the contrast between two groups of men and two images of masculinity: the brawling single frontiersman and the settled married pioneer farmer. The distinction is familiar in the American and Canadian west too. The state, Phillips argues, was hostile to the social disorder generated by the masculine work and pub culture of the former group. Accordingly, it encouraged family settlement and might promote women's interests. It is notable that such frontier areas were the earliest where women won the vote. Nevertheless cults of frontier masculinity (Daniel Boone, the cowboys, Paul Bunyan, the diggers, the shearers, the Voortrekkers) continued as a characteristic part of sexual ideology in former colonies of settlement such as the United States, South Africa, and Australia (Phillips, 1980, 217–243).

In colonies where local populations were not displaced but turned into a subordinated labor force (much of Latin America, India, East Indies) the situation was more complex again. It is a familiar suggestion that Latin American 'machismo' was a product of the interplay of cultures under colonialism. The conquistadors provided both provocation and model; Spanish Catholicism provided the ideology of female abnegation; and oppression blocked other claims of men to power. Pearlman shows that this pattern is also a question of women's agency. Machismo is *not* the ideology governing men's relations with women in the subsistence-farming Mazatec people, where gender relations are much more egalitarian. Outmigration and commodification are changing this, but even so, the young Mazatec men who are picking up a hyper-masculine style from the wider Mexican culture are forced into codeswitching at home because older women and men will not play along (Pearlman, 1983; Adolph, 1985).

Nevertheless, it is the Mazatec gender order that is under pressure in the interaction, not the national Mexican. Internationally it is Euro/American culture and institutions that supply the content of global mass media, design the commodities and the labor process of producing them, and regulate the accumulation of resources. This power is the strongest force redefining men's place in gender relations outside the North Atlantic world.

Contemporary politics

The present moment

If this historical outline has some validity, it should give us purchase on what is happening in the lives of men and women in the 'first world' at the present time.

It suggests, most obviously, that we should see contemporary changes in masculinity not as the softening (or hardening) of a unitary 'sex role,' but as a field of institutional and interpersonal changes through which a multilateral struggle for hegemony in gender relations, and advantage in other structures, is pursued.

The distinctive feature of the present moment in gender relations in first-world countries is the fact of open challenges to men's power, in the form of feminism, and to institutionalized heterosexuality, in the form of lesbian and gay men's movements. We must distinguish between the *presence* of these movements from the operating *power* they have won, which is often disappointingly small. Whatever the limits to their gains, and the success of the conservative backlash, the historic fact that these movements are here on the scene structures the whole politics of gender and sexuality in new ways.

These challenges are being worked out in a context of technological change and economic restructuring (e.g. the decline of heavy industry in old industrial centers), globalization of market relationships and commercial mass communication (e.g. the crumbling of Eastern-European command economies), widening wealth inequalities and chronic tensions in first-world/third-world relations (e.g. the Vietnam war, the debt crisis, the Gulf War). Each of these processes has its gender dimension.

Contestation in hegemonic masculinity

Earlier in the twentieth century a split began to open in the hegemonic masculinity of the dominant classes, between a masculinity organized around interpersonal dominance and one organized around knowledge and expertise. Under the pressure of labor movements and first-wave feminism, and in the context of the growing scale of mass production, dominance and expertise ceased to be nuances within the one masculinity and became visibly different strategies for operating and defending the patriarchal capitalist order. In some settings distinct institutional bases for these two variants hardened: line management versus professions, field command versus general staff, promotion based on practical experience versus university training. Political ideologies and styles – conservatism versus liberalism, confrontation versus consensus politics – also clustered around this division.

Feminism in the 1970s and 1980s often found itself allied with the liberal/ professional side in this contestation, for a variety of reasons. Notions of equal opportunity and advancement by merit appealed in a technocratic style of management. Much feminist activity was located in universities and professions. Liberal feminism (the strongest current in feminism) as an enlightenment project found itself on the same terrain, and using much the same political language, as progressive liberalism and reformist labor.

The patriarchal counter-attack on feminism, conversely, rapidly became associated with the masculinity of dominance. Early attempts to find a scientific basis for the counter-attack, such as Goldberg's *The Inevitability of Patriarchy* (1973), were faintly ludicrous and had little influence. Much more powerful was the cultural backing given by authoritarian patriarchal churches. Perhaps the most successful of all antifeminist operations in the last 20 years has been the Catholic church's attacks on contraception, abortion, and sexual freedom for women.

The reassertion of a dominance-based masculinity has been much discussed in popular culture. To my mind its most interesting form is not Rambo movies but the 1980s cult of the 'entrepreneur' in business. Here gender imagery, institutional change, and political strategy intersect. The deregulation policies of new-right governments in the 1980s dismantled Keynesian strategies for social integration via expert macro-economic regulation. The credibility of the new policies rested on the image of a generation of entrepreneurs whose wealth-creating energies were waiting to be unleashed. That this stratum was masculine is culturally unquestionable. Among other things, their management jargon is full of lurid gender terminology thrusting entrepreneurs, opening up virgin territory, aggressive lending, etc.

New-right ideology naturalizes these social practices, that is, treats them as part of the order of nature. But in fact the shift of economic power into the hands of this group was very conjunctural. The operations of the entrepreneurs were essentially in finance, not production. Key practices such as the leveraged management buy-out (in the United States and the construction of highly geared conglomerates (in Australia) depended on the institutional availability of massive credit at high rates of interest (junk bonds and bank consortium loans). The political interest in sustaining a huge diversion of funds from productive investment was limited, but the 'entrepreneurs' could not stop. The growing contradiction between this particular inflection of the masculinity of dominance and the need of the rest of the dominant class for economic stability led to denunciations of greed and in the later 1980s to a virtual withdrawal of political support.

The political damage-control has generally taken the form of attempts to show these episodes were an aberration, not that they resulted from a mistaken strategy. Deregulation and the roll-back of the welfare state remains a powerful agenda in the politics of the rich countries, and neoconservative regimes continue to be electorally successful. It is in the internal politics of the state that we see most clearly the new direction in the contest between dominance and expertise. What Yeatman calls the 'managerialist agenda' in the reconstruction of the state occupies the terrain of expertise. Its ideology is provided by neoclassical economics, and its operating language is provided by a management science legitimated by university business schools and rapidly spreading through the universities themselves. But it detached the notion of expertise from the liberal/reformist politics of the Keynesian era and the humanist commitments that had allowed at least a partial alliance with feminism (Yeatman, 1990; Pusey 1991).

Managerialists and technocrats do not directly confront feminist programs but under-fund or shrink them in the name of efficiency and volunteerism. Equal-opportunity principles are accepted as efficient personnel management ideas, but no funds are committed for affirmative action to make equal opportunity a vehicle of social change. Research and training funds are poured into areas of men's employment (for instance the Australian government is currently pushing science and technology) because of the perceived need to make the country 'competitive in international markets.'

Speculating a little, I think we are seeing the construction of a new variant of hegemonic masculinity. It has a technocratic rather than confrontationist style, but it is misogynist as before. It characteristically operates through the indirect mechanisms of financial administration. It is legitimated by an ideology centering on an economic theory whose most distinctive feature is its blanket exclusion from the discourse of women's unpaid work – which, as Waring (1988) bitterly but accurately puts it, 'counts for nothing' in economic science.

Challenges: 'alternative' masculinities

Contestation for the hegemonic position is familiar. What is novel, in Euro/American history, is open challenge to hegemonic masculinity as such. Such challenges were sparked by the challenge to men's power as a whole made by contemporary feminism. Feminism may not have been adopted by many men, but an *awareness* of feminism is very widespread indeed. In the course of a recent life-history study among Australian men, this point emerged clearly. Almost all the men we interviewed had some idea of what feminism was and felt the need to take some position on it. Their positions ranged from essentialist rejection... via endorsement, usually making an exception of bra-burning extremiste,... to full-blown acceptance of feminism. The last kind of response is rare, though it is important in defining political possibilities. The life stories of men who reached this point via environmental politics show the importance of a direct encounter with feminist activism among women. Given the massive bias of media against feminism, more indirect acquaintance is extremely unlikely to lead to a positive response from men (Connell 1989).

The challenge to hegemonic masculinity among this group of men mainly takes the form of an attempt to re-make the self. Most of them started off with a fairly conventional gender trajectory, and they came to see a personal reconstruction as required. This turns out to be emotionally very difficult. The growth-movement techniques available to them do not deliver the political analysis, support, or follow-through that the project actually requires. Only a few, and those only marginally, have moved beyond this individualist framework to the search for a collective politics of gender among men.

A collective politics is precisely the basis of the challenge to hegemonic heterosexuality mounted by gay liberation. At one level this challenge was delivered simply by the presence of an open gay milieu based on sex and friendship. 'Coming out' is experienced as entering a social network, not just as entering a sexual practice. As a gay man in the same study put it: 'Rage, rage, rage – let's do everything you've denied yourself for 25 years – let's get into it and have a good time sexually, and go out partying and dancing and drinking' (Transport worker, gay, 25).

The collective work required was to construct the network and negotiate a social presence for it. This meant dealings with the state authorities, for example the police; economic mobilization, the so-called 'pink capitalism'; and organizing political representation, the most famous representative being Harvey Milk in the United States (Altman, 1982; Adam, 1987).

Most of this went no further than a politics of pluralist accommodation, analogous, as Altman has pointed out, to claims for political space by ethnic minorities in the United States. It was this assimilationist program that was disrupted in the early 1980s by the HIV epidemic and the need for a renewed struggle against the medicalization and criminalization of homosexuality.

But in gay liberation, from very early on, was a much more radical, indeed revolutionary, challenge to hegemonic masculinity. The slogan 'Every straight man is a target for gay liberation!' jokingly catches both an openended libertarianism and the point that gays cannot be free from oppression while heterosexual masculinity remains as it is. Drawing on Freudian ideas, some gay theorists argued that the repression of homosexual affect among straight men was a key source of their authoritarianism and violence. These ideas have never been turned into an effective practical politics; but they remain an important moment of critique (Mieli, 1980).

Deconstructions of working-class masculinity

'Rage, rage, rage' is exactly what the settled married farmer, or the respectable married working man, cannot do. Donaldson argues that the link between the family household and the workplace, rather than the workplace itself, is the axis on which working-class masculinity is formed. It finds political expression in a community-based, formally organized labor movement and is sustained by a sharp gender division of labor between wage-earning husband and child-raising wife. These points have been well documented in recent Australian research on sexual politics in working-class communities (Williams, 1981; Donaldson, 1987; Metcalfe, 1988).

But with the collapse of the postwar boom, the abandonment of full employment as a policy goal by modern states, and the shift to market discipline by business strategists (an aspect of the contestation discussed earlier), the conditions of this gender regime in working-class communities have changed. Significant proportions of the working class face long-term structural unemployment. Traditional working-class masculinity is being deconstructed by impersonal forces, whether the men concerned like it or not.

Young men respond to this situation in different ways. They may attempt to promote themselves out of the working class, via education and training. They may accept their poor chances of promotion and develop a slack, complicit masculinity. Or they may fight against the powers that be, rejecting school, skirmishing with the police, getting into crime (Connell, 1989, 1991).

The tattoo-and-motorcycle style of aggressive white working-class masculinity is familiar enough; Metcalfe even comments on the 'larrikin mode of class struggle.' It has generally been understood as linked with stark homophobia, misogyny, and domestic patriarchy. Our interviews with young unemployed men suggest that this pattern too is being deconstructed in a significant way. The public display of protest masculinity continues. But it can coexist with a breakdown in the *domestic* gender division of labor, with an acceptance of women's economic equality, and an interest in children, which would not be expected from traditional accounts (Willis, 1978; Metcalfe, 1988; Hopper and Moore, 1989).

Since structural unemployment in first-world countries is most likely to affect members of oppressed ethnic groups, such a deconstruction must interweave with race politics. American discussions of masculinity in urban black ghettos show this interplay in one dramatic form. In other parts of the world it does not necessarily follow the same course. For instance, some Australian work on the making of masculinity in multi-ethnic innercity environments suggest a more negotiated, though still racially structured, outcome (Staples, 1978; Contrast Walker, 1988; Majors, 1989).

What the evidence does show unequivocally is that working-class masculinities are no more set in concrete than are ruling-class masculinities – though in a bourgeois culture they are much more liable to stereotyped representation. The conscious attempts at building a counter-sexist heterosexual masculinity have mainly occurred in middle-class milieux. Some socialist explorations did occur but are now mostly forgotten. I would argue that a progressive sexual politics cannot afford to be class-blind. It must look to the settings of working-class life, and existing forms of working-class collective action, as vital arenas of sexual politics (Tolson, 1977).

Notes

1   For the conceptual critique see Connell (1987). Fine examples of field research are Hochschild (1989) and Stacey (1990).
2   Attempts are now being made to take class and race issues aboard: see the recent collections Kimmel, M.S., and Messner, M.A. (eds) (1989); Messner, M.A., and Sabo, D. (eds) (1990).

References

Adam, B.D. (1987), *The Rise of a Gay and Lesbian Movement* (Boston: Hall).

Altman, D. (1982), *The Homosexualization of America, the Americanization of the Homosexual* (New York: St Martin's Press).

Burton, C. (1991), *The Promise and the Price: The Struggle for Equal Opportunity in Women's Employment* (Sydney: Allen and Unwin), ch. 1: 'Masculinity and Femininity in the Organisation'.

Carrigan, T., Connell, R.W., and Lee, J. (1985), 'Toward a New Sociology of Masculinity', *Theory and Society*, 14/5: 551–604.

Clausewitz, K. (1827; 1975 edn.) *On War* (Princeton, NJ: Princeton University Press.)

Cockburn, C. (1983), *Brothers: Male Dominance and Technological Change* (London: Pluto Press).

Connell, R.W. (1982), 'Men and Socialism', in G. Evans and J. Reeves (eds), *Labor Essays* (Melbourne: Drummond), 53–64.

—— (1987), *Gender and Power: Society, the Person and Sexual Politics* (Stanford, Calif.: Stanford Univ. Press), 253–258.

—— (1986), 'The State, Gender, and Sexual Politics: Theory and Appraisal', *Theory and Society*, 15/5: 507–544.

—— (1989), 'Cool Guys, Swots and Wimps: The Interplay of Masculinity and Education', *Oxford Review of Education*, 15/3: 291–303.

—— (1990), 'A Whole New World: Remaking Masculinity in the Context of the Environmental Movement', *Gender and Society*, 4/4: 452–478.

—— (1991), 'Live Fast and Die Young: The Construction of Masculinity Among Young Working-Class Men on the Margin of the Labour Market', *Australian and New Zealand Journal of Sociology*, 27/2: 141–171.

David, D.S., and Brannon, R. (1976), *The Forty-Nine-Percent Majority: The Male Sex Role* (Reading, MA: Addison-Wesley).

Donaldson, M. (1987), 'Labouring Men: Love, Sex and Strife', *Australian and New Zealand Journal of Sociology*, 23/2: 165–184.

Ellis, A. (1976), *Sex and the Liberated Man* (Secaucus, NJ: Lyle Stuart).

Farrell, W. (1975), *The Liberated Man: Beyond Masculinity: Freeing Men and their Relationships with Women* (New York: Bantam).

Ford, D., and Hearn, J. (1988), *Studying Men and Masculinity: A Sourcebook of Literature and Materials* (Bradford: Univ. of Bradford Dept. of Applied Social Studies).

Franklin, C.W., II (1987), 'Surviving the Institutional Decimation of Black Males: Causes, Consequences, and Intervention', in H. Brod (ed.), *The Making of Masculinities* (Boston: Allen and Unwin), 155–169.

Fussell, P. (1989), Wartime: *Understanding and Behavior in the Second World War* (New York, Oxford University Press).

Galbraith, J.K. (1971), *The New Industrial State* (Boston, MA: Houghton Mifflin).

Gilder, G. (1975), *Sexual Suicide* (New York: Bantam).

Goldberg, S. (1973), *The Inevitability of Patriarchy* (New York: Morrow).

Gouldner, A.W. (1979), *The Future of Intellectuals and the Rise of the New Class* (New York: Seabury Press).

Hansot, E., and Tyack, D. (1987), 'Gender in Public Schools: Thinking Institutionally', *Signs*, 13/4: 741–760.

Harrison, J.B. (1979), 'Men's Roles and Men's Lives', *Signs*, 4/2: 324–336.

Hearn, J., and Morgan, D.H.J. (eds) (1990), *Men Masculinities and Social Theory* (London: Unwin Hyman).

Hochschild, A. (1989), *The Second Shift: Working Parents and the Revolution at Home* (New York: Viking).

Hopper, C.B., and Moore, J. (1989), 'Women in Outlaw Motorcycle Gangs', *Journal of Contemporary Ethnography*, 18/4: 363–387.

Humphries, M. (1985), 'Gay Machismo', in A. Metcalf and M. Humphries (eds), *The Sexuality of Men* (London: Pluto), 70–85.

Jeffords, S. (1989), *The Remasculinization of America: Gender and the Vietnam War* (Bloomington, IN: Indiana Univ. Press).

Johnson, R. (1974), *He: Understanding Male Psychology* (New York: Harper and Row).

Kimmel, M.S., and Messner, M.A. (eds) (1989), *Men's Lives* (New York: Macmillan).

Majors, R. (1989), 'Cool Pose', in M.S. Kimmel and M.A. Messner (eds), *Men's Lives* (New York: Macmillan).

Metcalfe, A.F. (1988), *For Freedom and Dignity: Historical Agency and Class Structure in the Coalfields of NSW* (Sydney: Allen and Unwin).

Mieli, M. (1980), *Homosexuality and Liberation Elements of a Gay Critique* (London: Gay Men's Press).

Nichols, J. (1975), *Men's Liberation: A New Definition of Masculinity* (New York: Penguin).

Pearlman, C.L. (1983), 'Machismo, Marianismo and Change in Indigenous Mexico: A Case Study from Oaxaca', *Quarterly Journal of Ideology*, 8/4: 53–59.

Phillips, J. (1980), 'Mummy's Boys: Pakeha Men and Male Culture in New Zealand', in P. Bukle and B. Hughes (eds), *Women in New Zealand Society* (Auckland: Allen and Unwin), 217–243.

Pleck, J.H. (1976), 'The Male Sex Role: Definitions, Problems, and Sources of Change', *Journal of Social Issues*, 32/3: 155–164.

Pusey, M. (1991), *Economic Rationalism in Canberra: A Nation-Building State Changes Its Mind* (London: Cambridge Univ. Press).

Seccombe, W. (1977), 'Patriarchy Stabilized: The Construction of the Male Breadwinner Wage Norm in Nineteenth-Century Britain', *Social History*, 2/1: 53–75.

Segal, L. (1990), *Slow Motion: Changing Masculinities, Changing Men* (London: Virago).

Stacey, J. (1990), *Brave New Families* (New York: Basic Books).

Staples, R. (1978), 'Masculinity and Race: The Dual Dilemma of Black Men', *Journal of Social Issues*, 34/1: 169–183.

Stoller, R.J. (1968), *Sex and Gender*, i. *On the Development of Masculinity and Femininity* (London: Hogarth Press and the Institute of Psychoanalysis).

—— (1976), *Sex and Gender*, ii. *The Transsexual Experiment* (New York: Jason Aronson).

Stoller, R.J. and Herdt, G.H. (1983), 'The Development of Masculinity: A Cross-Cultural Contribution', *American Psycho-Analytical Association Journal*, 30/1: 29–59.

Theweleit, K. (1987), *Male Fantasies* (Cambridge: Polity Press).

Tiger, L. (1969), *Men in Groups* (London: Nelson).

Tolson, A. (1977), *The Limits of Masculinity* (London: Tavistock).

Walker, J. (1988), *Louts and Legends: Male Youth Culture in an Inner-City School* (Sydney: Allen and Unwin).

Waring, M. (1988), *Counting for Nothing: What Men Value and What Women are Worth* (Wellington: Allen and Unwin and Port Nicholson Press).

Williams, C. (1981), *Open Cut: The Working Class in an Australian Mining Town* (Sydney: Allen and Unwin).

Willis, P.E. (1978), *Profane Culture* (London: Routledge and Kegan Paul).

Yeatman, A. (1990), *Bureaucrats, Technocrats, Femocrats: Essays on the Contemporary Australian State* (Sydney: Allen and Unwin).

PART 3

IDENTITY WORK

CHAPTER 9

'SPICE GIRLS', 'NICE GIRLS', 'GIRLIES', AND 'TOMBOYS'

Gender discourses, girls' cultures and femininities in the primary classroom

Diane Reay, *Gender and Education*, 13, 2, 2001

Introduction

This chapter attempts to demonstrate that contemporary gendered power relations are more complicated and contradictory than any simplistic binary discourse of 'the girls versus the boys' suggests (Heath, 1999). Although prevailing dominant discourses identify girls as 'the success story of the 1990s' (Wilkinson, 1994), this small-scale study of a group of 7 year-old girls attending an inner London primary school suggests that, particularly when the focus is on the construction of hetero-sexual femininities, it is perhaps premature always to assume that 'girls are doing better than boys'. While girls may be doing better than boys in examinations, this chapter indicates that their learning in the classroom is much broader than the National Curriculum and includes aspects that are less favourable in relation to gender equity. Although masculinities are touched on in this article, this is only in as far as they relate to girls. This deliberate bias is an attempt to refocus on femininities at a time when masculinities appear to be an ever-growing preoccupation within education.

However, although the subjects of this research are 14 girls, the position the chapter takes is that femininities can only be understood relationally. There is a co-dependence between femininities and masculinities which means that neither can be fully understood in isolation from the other. The chapter therefore explores how a particular group of primary-aged girls is positioned, primarily in relation to dominant discourses of femininity but also in relation to those of masculinity. There is also an attempt to map out their relationships to transgressive but less prevalent discourses of femininity, which in a variety of ways construct girls as powerful. The findings from such a small-scale study are necessarily tentative and no generalised assertions are made about girls as a group. Rather, the aim is to use the girls' narratives and their experiences in school and, to a lesser extent, those of the boys, to indicate some ways in which the new orthodoxy, namely that girls are doing better than boys, does not tell us the whole story about gender relations in primary classrooms. [. . .]

The research study

The chapter is based on data from a 1-year study, conducted over the academic year 1997/98, of children in a Year 3 class in an inner-city primary school. 3R comprised

26 children, 14 girls and 12 boys. There were five middle-class children, three girls and two boys, all white apart from Amrit who was Indian. The 21 working-class children were more ethnically mixed. As well as one Somalian and two boys of mixed parentage, there were four Bengali children, three boys and one girl. The social class attribution of the children was based on parental occupations but was also confirmed by information provided by the class teacher. Fifteen of the children were entitled to free school meals. The school is surrounded by 1960s and 1970s public housing estates from which most of its intake is drawn, and indeed, 14 of the children in 3R lived on one of these five estates.

I spent one day a week over the course of the year engaged in participant observation in both the classroom and the playground, amassing over 200 pages of field notes. Additionally, I interviewed all the children, both individually and in focus groups. I also carried out group work activities in which children both wrote and drew on a range of topics from playground games to best friends. As James *et al.* point out:

> Talking with children about the meanings they themselves attribute to their paintings or asking them to write a story allows children to engage more productively with our research questions using the talents which they possess.
> (James *et al.*, 1998, p. 189)

The unequal relationship between researcher and researched is compounded when the researcher is an adult and the researched a child. In order to mitigate at least some of the power differentials I organised workshops for the children in which I taught simple questionnaire design and interviewing techniques. The children then compiled their own questionnaires so that they could interview each other. These interviews, as well as those I conducted, 84 overall, were tape-recorded and transcribed. The class teacher and I also collected sociogram data, which enabled us to map out the children's friendship networks and work relationships.

Gender discourses

Many writers on education have attempted to provide a variety of conceptual tools in order to understand educational contexts and processes (Ball, 1994; Maclure, 1994). A key debate amongst educational researchers has been between structuralist and post-structuralist approaches. Although often these two conceptual approaches are seen as opposing perspectives, in this chapter, I use and combine what I perceive to be the strengths of both positions to illuminate the ways in which girls both construct themselves, and are constructed, as feminine (see also, Walkerdine, 1991, 1997; Williams, 1997; Walkerdine *et al.*, 2000 for similar approaches). As Davies *et al.* (1997) assert, power is both located in the structural advantage of individuals and also exercised partly through the construction of discourses.

Multiple discourses contribute not only to how researchers appreciate the conditions of childhood but also to how children come to view themselves (James *et al.*, 1998). Post-structuralist feminists have explored extensively the ways in which different discourses can position girls (Davies, 1993; Hey, 1997; Walkerdine, 1997). It is important to recognise that there are many competing gender discourses, some of which have more power and potency than others for particular groups of girls (Francis, 1998). Such processes of discursive recognition, of feeling a better fit within one discourse than another (Francis, 1999), are influenced by social class. Similarly, gender discourses are taken up differentially by different ethnic groupings. It is also important to stress that girls can position themselves differently in relation to gender discourses according to the peer group context they find themselves in. For example, it soon became evident in my research that girls assume different positions depending on whether they are in single- or mixed-sex contexts. As Gee and his colleagues assert:

> There are innumerable discourses in modern societies: different sorts of street gangs, elementary schools and classrooms, academic disciplines and their sub-specialities, police, birdwatchers, ethnic groups, genders, executives, feminists, social classes and sub-classes, and so on and so-forth. Each is composed of-some set of related social practices and social identities (or positions). Each discourse contracts complex relations of complicity, tension and opposition with other discourses.
>
> (Gee *et al.*, 1996, p. 10)

I found similar 'complex relations of complicity, tension and opposition' in relation to the nexus of gender discourses that these girls draw on. Yet, any local discursive nexus is framed by a wider social context within which, as Valerie Hey (1997) points out, there is a lack of powerful public discourses for girls, leaving them caught between schooling which denies difference and compulsory hetero-sexuality which is fundamentally invested in producing it. If this gives the impression of a fluid situation in relation to how contemporary girls position themselves as female, there is also substantial evidence of continuities in which, at least for the girls in this research, conformist discourses continue to exert more power than transgressive or transformative ones.

Masculinities in the classroom: setting the context

Although the main focus of this chapter is how gender discourses position girls at school, in order to understand femininities in this primary classroom, the ways in which masculinities are being played out cannot be ignored. I want to start with two short excerpts from boys. Josh and David, two white, middle-class, 7 year-old boys, interviewed each other about what they like most and least about being a boy:

J: David, what do you like most about being a boy?

D: Well, it must be that it's much easier to do things than being a girl, that's what I think. You get to do much better things.

J: So you think you find being a boy more interesting than being a girl? Is that what you're saying?

D: Yes because it's boring being a girl.

J: OK, and what do you like least about being a boy?

D: Well, I don't know, I can't think of anything.

J: Well, can't you think really – there must be something.

D: I'll think [long pause]. Well, it's easier to hurt yourself.

D: OK What do you like most about being a boy?

J: I'd probably say that it's better being a boy because they have more interesting things to do and it's more exciting for them in life I find.

D: Yes, I see. What do you like least about being a boy?

J: Ohh I'd probably say not being so attractive as girls probably I'd say they're much more attractive than boys.

Josh and David were the only middle-class boys in a Year 3 class of predominantly working-class children. Existing research has found that the culturally exalted form of masculinity varies from school to school and is informed by the local community (Skelton, 1997; Connolly, 1998). These two boys were adjusting to a predominantly working-class, inner-city peer group in which dominant local forms of masculinity were sometimes difficult for both to negotiate, but in particular, for David (for one thing, he did not like football). They both also found the low priority given to academic work among the other boys problematic. Even so, they were clear that it was still better being a boy.

Both boys, despite their social class positioning, were popular among the peer group. In particular, Josh commanded a position of power and status in the peer group which was virtually unchallenged (see also Reay, 1990). Sociogram data collected from all the children in the class positioned him as the most, popular child, not only with the working-class boys in the class but also with the girls. David's positioning is more difficult to understand. His particular variant of middle-class masculinity was far less acceptable to his working-class peers than Josh's. He was studious and hated games. In the exercise where children drew and described their favourite playground activity, David sketched a single figure with a bubble coming out of his head with 'thoughts' inside. He annotated it with 'I usually like walking about by myself and I'm thinking'. However; within the confines of the classroom, for much of the time, he retained both status and power, paradoxically through a combination of being male and clever. When the girls were asked to nominate two boys and two girls they would most like to work with, David was the second most popular male choice after Josh. However, he was the most popular choice with the other boys. The complex issues as to why these two boys were popular when their masculinities did not fit the dominant one within the male peer group are beyond the brief of this chapter. Rather, what is salient is the relevance of their positioning within the peer group for the group of girls who are the chapter's main protagonists.

Although the focus has been on 'the others' within masculinity, black and white working-class boys (Willis, 1977; Sewell, 1997), it is the association of normativity with white, middle-class masculinity that seems most difficult for girls to challenge effectively. Disruptive, failing boys' behaviour has given girls an unexpected window of opportunity through which some variants of femininities can be valorised over specific pathologies masculinities, particularly within the arena of educational attainment. Both girls and boys were aware of discourses which position girls as more mature and educationally focused than boys and regularly drew on them to make sense of gender differences in the classroom (see also Pattman and Phoenix, 1999). What seems not to have changed is the almost unspoken acceptance of white, middle-class masculinity as the ideal that all those 'others' – girls as well as black and white working-class boys – are expected to measure themselves against. Popular discourses position both masculinity and the middle classes as under siege, suggesting an erosion of both male and class power bases (Bennett, 1996; Coward, 1999). While there have been significant improvements in the direction of increasing equity, particularly in the area of gender, the popularity

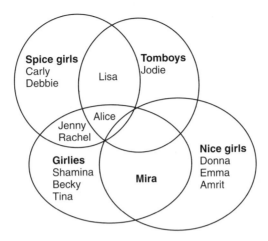

Figure 8.1 Girl groups in 3R.

of Josh and David, combined with the uniform recognition among the rest of the peer group that they were the cleverest children in the class, suggests that popular discourses may mask the extent to which white, middle-class male advantages in both the sphere of education and beyond continue to be sustained.

However, 10 of the 12 boys in 3R were working class. The 'failing boys' compensatory culture of aggressive 'laddism' (Jackson, 1998) had already started to be played out at the micro-level of this primary classroom. The working-class, white and mixed race boys were more preoccupied with football than the academic curriculum (see also Skelton, 1999). When they were not playing football in the playground, they would often be surreptitiously exchanging football cards in the classroom. Alongside regular jockeying for position within the male peer group, which occasionally escalated into full-blown fights, there was routine, casual labelling of specific girls as stupid and dumb. The three Bengali boys at the bottom of this particular male peer group hierarchy compensated by demonising, in particular, the three middle-class girls. Their strategy echoes that of the subordinated youth in Wight's (1996) study, where in order to gain the approval and acceptance of their dominant male peers, they endeavoured to become active subjects in a sexist discourse which objectified girls.

Sugar and spice and all things nice?

3R had four identifiable groups of girls – the 'nice girls', the 'girlies', the 'spice girls' and the 'tomboys' (see Figure 8.1).

The latter two groups had decided on both their own naming as well as those of the 'girlies' and the 'nice girls', descriptions which were generally seen as derogatory by both girls and boys. 'Girlies' and 'nice girls' encapsulate 'the limited and limiting discourse of conventional femininity (Brown, 1998), and in this Year 3 class, although there was no simple class divide, the 'nice girls' were composed of Donna, Emma and Amrit, the only three middle-class girls in 3R, plus a fluctuating group of one to two working-class girls. The 'nice girls', seen by everyone, including themselves, as hard-working and well behaved, exemplify the constraints of a gendered and classed discourse which afforded them the benefits of culture, taste and cleverness but little freedom. Prevalent discourses which work with binaries of mature girls and immature boys and achieving girls and underachieving boys appear on the surface to be liberating for girls. However, the constraints were evident in the 'nice girls'' self-surveillant, hypercritical attitudes to both their behaviour and their schoolwork; attitudes which were less apparent amongst other girls in the class. It would appear that this group of 7 year-old, predominantly middle-class girls had already begun to develop the intense preoccupation with academic success that other researchers describe in relation to middle-class, female, secondary school pupils (Walkerdine *et al.*, 2000).

Contemporary work on how masculinities and femininities are enacted in educational contexts stresses the interactions of gender with class, race and sexuality (Mac an Ghaill, 1988; Hey, 1997; Connolly, 1998). Sexual harassment in 3R (a whole gamut of behaviour which included uninvited touching of girls and sexualised name-calling) was primarily directed at the 'girlies' and was invariably perpetuated by boys who were subordinated within the prevailing masculine hegemony either because of their race or social class. However, while sexual harassment was an infrequent occurrence, identifying the 'nice girls' as a contaminating presence was not. In the playground, the three working-class Bengali boys were positioned as subordinate to the white and Afro-Caribbean boys; for example, they were often excluded from the football games on the basis that they were not skilful enough. These three boys constructed the 'nice girls' as a polluting, contagious 'other'. They would regularly hold up crossed fingers whenever one of these girls came near them. As a direct result, the 'nice girls' began to use the classroom space differently, taking circuitous routes in order to keep as far away from these boys as possible. Barrie Thorne (1993) found similar gender practices in which girls were seen as 'the ultimate source of contamination'. Like the girls in Thorne's research, the 'nice girls' did not challenge the boys but rather developed avoidance strategies which further circumscribed their practices.

Being one of the 'nice girls' had derogatory connotations for working-class girls as well as working-class boys. Alice, in particular, was adamant that she could not contemplate them as friends because they were 'too boring', while in one of the focus group discussions, Jodie, Debbie and Carly all agreed that 'no one wants to be a nice girl'. Their views reflect the findings of feminist research which position 'being nice' as specific to the formulation of white, middle-class femininity (Jones, 1993; Griffin, 1995; Kenway *et al.*, 1999). For a majority of the working-class girls in the class, being a 'nice girl' signified an absence of the toughness and attitude that they were aspiring to.

This is not to construct the 'nice girls' as passive in relation to other groups in the class. They often collaborated with Josh and David on classwork and were vocal about the merits of their approach to schoolwork over those of other girls in the class:

Emma: The other girls often mess around and be silly, that's why Alice and Lisa never get their work finished.
Donna: Yes we're more sensible than they are.
Emma: And cleverer.

However, the dominant peer group culture in the classroom was working class and, while this had little impact on the popularity of Josh and David, it did have repercussions for the status and social standing of the 'nice girls' within the peer group.

'The limited and limiting discourse of conventional femininity' also had a powerful impact on the 'girlies', a group of three working-class girls (two white and one Bengali). Kenway *et al.* (1999) write about 'the sorts of femininities which unwittingly underwrite hegemonic masculinity' (p. 120). Certainly, the 'girlies', with their 'emphasised femininity' (Connell, 1987, p. 187), were heavily involved in gender work which even at the age of 7 inscribed traditional heterosexual relations. Paul Connolly (1998) describes the ways in which sexual orientation and relations defined through boyfriends and girlfriends seems to provide an important source of identity for young children. This was certainly the case for the 'girlies'. These girls were intensely active in the work of maintaining conventional heterosexual relationships through the writing of love letters, flirting and engaging in regular discussions of who was going out with who. They were far more active in such maintenance work than the boys.

Both the 'girlies' and the 'nice girls' were subject to 'discourses of denigration' circulating among the wider peer group (Blackmore, 1999, p. 136). In individual interviews, many of the boys and a number of the other girls accounted for the 'nice girls'' unpopularity by describing them as 'boring' and 'not fun to be with', while the 'girlies' were variously described by boys as 'stupid' and 'dumb'. While the boys were drawing on a male peer group discourse which positioned the 'girlies' as less intelligent than they were, the 'girlies' were far from 'stupid' or 'dumb'. Although not as scholarly as the 'nice girls', they were educationally productive and generally achieved more highly that their working-class male counterparts. Rather, the working class discourse of conventional femininity within which they were enmeshed operated to elide their academic achievement within the peer group.

Discourses of conventional femininity also seemed to have consequences for the two Asian girls in the class. Amrit, who was Indian, was from a middle-class background while Shamina was Bengali and working class. Yet, both girls, despite their class differences, shared a high degree of circumscription in relation to the range of femininities available to them in the school context. As Shamina explained, 'the spice girls and the tomboys are naughty. I am a good girl'. In contrast to the other girls in the girls' focus group discussion, who all claimed to enjoy playing football, both Shamina and Amrit asserted that 'football was a boys' game', and Amrit said, 'It's not worth bothering with football. It's too boring. Me and my friends just sit on the benches and talk'.

Heidi Mirza (1992) argues that the cultural construction of femininity among African-Caribbean girls fundamentally differs from the forms of femininity found among their white peers. In the case of Amrit and Shamina, there were substantial areas of overlap rather than fundamental differences. However, neither managed to carve out spaces in which to escape gender subordination from the boys in the ways that the 'spice girls' and the 'tomboys', both all-white groups, did. Racism and its impact on subjectivities may well be an issue here. Although it is impossible to make generalisations on the basis of two children, ethnicity, as well as class, appears to be an important consideration in the possibilities and performance of different femininities.

Membership of the 'spice girls' revolved around two white, working-class girls, Carly and Debbie. Jenny, Rachel, Alice and Lisa were less consistently members of the group. Lisa and Alice would sometimes claim to be 'tomboys' while Jenny and Rachel, when playing and spending time with the 'girlies', and especially when Carly and Debbie were in trouble with adults in the school, would realign themselves as 'girlies'. Very occasionally, when she had quarrelled both with Carly and

Debbie, and with Jodie, the one consistent tomboy among the girls, Alice too would reinvent herself as a 'girlie'.

Although there were many overlaps between both the practices and the membership of the 'girlies' and the 'spice girls', aspects of the 'spice girls'' interaction with the boys appeared to transgress prevailing gender regimes, while the 'girlies'' behaviour followed a far more conformist pattern. Yet, the 'spice girls' were, for much of the time, also active in constructing and maintaining traditional variants of heterosexuality. Their espousal of 'girl power' did not exclude enthusiastic partaking of the boyfriend/girlfriend games. There was much flirting, letter writing, falling in and out of love and talk of broken hearts. However, they also operated beyond the boundaries of the 'girlies'' more conformist behaviour when it came to interaction with the boys. Debbie and Carly, the most stalwart members of the 'spice girls', both described the same activity – rating the boys – as their favourite playground game. As Carly explained, 'you follow the boys around and give them a mark out of ten for how attractive they are'.

The 'spice girls'' adherence to so-called girl power also allowed them to make bids for social power never contemplated by the 'girlies' or the 'nice girls'. During a science lesson which involved experiments with different foodstuffs, including a bowl of treacle, Carly and Debbie jointly forced David's hand into the bowl because, as Carly asserted, 'he is always showing off, making out he knows all the answers'. This incident, which reduced David to tears and shocked the other children, served to confirm the class teacher in her view that the two girls 'were a bad lot'. The 'girls with attitude' stance that Carly and Debbie so valued and their philosophy of 'giving as good as they got' were reinterpreted by adults in the school as both inappropriate and counterproductive to learning. Paul Connolly (1998) points out that girls' assertive or disruptive behaviour tends to be interpreted more negatively than similar behaviour in boys, while Robin Lakoff (1975) has described how, when little girls 'talk rough' like the boys do, they will normally be ostracised, scolded or made fun of. For the 'spice girls', 'doing it for themselves' in ways which ran counter to traditional forms of femininity resulted in them being labelled at various times by teachers in the staffroom as 'real bitches', 'a bad influence' and 'little cows'. The tendency Clarricoates found in 1978 for girls' misbehaviour to be 'looked upon as a character defect, whilst boys' misbehaviour is viewed as a desire to assert themselves' was just as evident in teachers' discourses more than 20 years later.

Debbie and Carly were doubly invidiously positioned in relation to the 'girls as mature discourse'. They were perceived to be 'too mature', as 'far too knowing sexually' within adult discourses circulating in the school but they were also seen, unlike the boys and the majority of the girls in 3R, as 'spiteful' and 'scheming little madams' for indulging in behaviour typical of many of the boys. There were several incidents in the playground of sexual harassment of girls by a small group of boys. Most of the adults dismissed these as 'boys mucking about'. However, Carly and Debbie's attempts to invert regular processes of gender objectification, in which girls are routinely the objects of a male gaze, were interpreted by teachers as signs of 'an unhealthy preoccupation with sex'. Their predicament exemplifies the dilemma for girls of 'seeking out empowering places within regimes alternatively committed to denying subordination or celebrating it' (Hey, 1997, p. 132). In this classroom, girls like Carly and Debbie seemed to tread a fine line between acceptable and unacceptable 'girl power' behaviour. Overt heterosexuality was just about on the acceptable side of the line but retaliatory behaviour towards the boys was not.

Valerie Walkerdine (1997) describes how playful and assertive girls come to be understood as overmature and too precocious. Girls like Debbie and Carly, no less than the girls in Walkerdine's advertisements, occupy a space where girls have moved beyond being 'nice' or 'girlie'. Rather, as sexual little women, they occupy a space where they can be bad. As Walkerdine points out, while it is certainly a space in which they can be exploited, it provides a space of power for little girls, although one which is also subject to discourses of denigration. The forms that denigration take are very different to those experienced by the 'nice girls' or the 'girlies' but become apparent in teachers' judgements of the two girls' behaviour.

'It's Better Being a Boy' – the Tomboys

The most intriguing case in my research was that of the 'tomboys'. The 'tomboys' in Becky Francis's research study were depicted by another girl in the class as traitors to girlhood:

> Rather than rejecting the aspiration to maleness because it is 'wrong' or 'unnatural', Zoe argues that 'girls are good enough', implying that her girl-friends want to be boys because they see males as superior, and that she is defending girlhood against this sexist suggestion.
>
> (Francis, 1998, p. 36)

As I have touched on earlier in the chapter, in 3R, there was a general assumption among the boys that maleness, if not a superior subject positioning, was a more desirable one. While, in particular the 'spice girls', but also at various times both the 'girlies' and 'nice girls' defended girlhood against such claims, their stance was routinely undermined by the position adopted by the tomboys.

Jodie was the only girl in the class who was unwavering in her certainty that she was not a girl but a 'tomboy', although a couple of the other girls in the class for periods of time decided that they were also 'tomboys':

Jodie: Girls are crap, all the girls in this class act all stupid and girlie.
Diane: So does that include you?
Jodie: No, cos I'm not a girl, I'm a tomboy.

On the one hand, Jodie could be viewed as a budding 'masculinised new woman at ease with male attributes' (Wilkinson, 1999, p. 37). Yet, her rejection of all things feminine could also be seen to suggest a degree of shame and fear of femininity. Jodie even managed to persuade Wayne and Darren, two of the boys in the class, to confirm her male status. Both, at different times, sought me out to tell me Jodie was 'really a boy'. It is difficult to know how to theorise such disruptions of normative gender positionings. Jodie's stance combines elements of resistance with recognition. She clearly recognised and responded to prevailing gender hierarchies which situate being male with having more power and status. Jodie appears to operate at the boundaries where femininity meets masculinity. She is what Barrie Thorne calls 'active at the edges'.

However, while Thorne reports that it was rarely used among her fourth and fifth graders, the term 'tomboy' is frequently used in 3M as a marker of respect by both boys and girls. Being a 'tomboy' seems to guarantee male friendship and male respect. Several of the working-class girls in the class, like Alice, appeared to move easily from taking up a position as a 'tomboy' through to assuming a 'girls with attitude' stance alongside Debbie and Carly to becoming a 'girlie' and back again. One week Alice would come to school in army fatigues with her hair scraped back, the next, in lycra with elaborately painted nails and carefully coiffured hair. However, Alice was unusual among the girls in ranging across a number of subject positions. For most of the girls, although they had choices, those choices seemed heavily circumscribed and provided little space for manoeuvre.

The regulatory aspects of the 'girlies' and the 'nice girls'' self-production as feminine were very apparent, yet the conformity of the 'tomboys' to prevailing gender regimes was far more hidden. While it is important to recognise the transgressive qualities of identifying and rejecting traditional notions of femininity in Jodie's behaviour, the empowering aspects of being a 'tomboy' also masked deeply reactionary features embedded in assuming such a gender position. Implicit in the concept of 'tomboy' is a devaluing of traditional notions of femininity, a railing against the perceived limitations of being female. This is particularly apparent in Jodie's comments:

> Jodie: I don't really have any friends who are girls cos they don't like doing the things I like doing. I like football and stuff like that.
> Diane: Don't girls like football?
> Jodie: Yeah, some of them, but they're no good at it.

Perhaps, in part, it is Jodie's obsession with football that contributes to her contradictory gender positionings. As Christine Skelton (1999) points out, there is a close association between football and hegemonic masculinities and, therefore, if Jodie is to be seen as 'a football star', she needs to assume a male rather than a female subject positioning.

But there is another possible reading in which Jodie's preoccupation with football facilitates, rather than is the cause of, her flight from femininity. Michelle Fine and Pat Macpherson define girls' identification with football as 'both a flight from femininity...and an association of masculinity with fairness, honesty, integrity and strength (Fine and Macpherson, 1992, p. 197). The girls in their study would call each other boys as a compliment: 'Girls can be good, bad or – best of all – they can be boys' (p. 200) and this was definitely a viewpoint Jodie adhered to. Jodie's individualised resistance can be set alongside Carly and Debbie's joint efforts to disrupt prevailing gender orders among the peer group. Yet, paradoxically, Jodie, no less than the 'girlies', seemed engaged in a process of accommodating the boys. The means of accommodation may differ but the compliance with existing gender regimes remains. Madeline Arnot (1982) writes of the ways in which boys maintain the hierarchy of social superiority of masculinity by devaluing the female world. In 3R, Jodie was also involved in this maintenance work. Although her practices are not rooted in subordination to the boys, she is still acquiescent in prevailing gender hierarchies. Her practices, no less than those of the 'girlies' and the 'nice girls', are confirmatory of male superiority.

Connell writes that 'it is perfectly logical to talk about masculine women or masculinity in women's lives, as well as men's' (Connell, 1995, p. 163). However, so-called 'masculine' girls do not seem to disrupt but rather appear to endorse existing gender hierarchies. All the girls at various times were acting in ways which bolstered the boys' power at the expense of their own. Even Jodie's performance of a surrogate masculinity works to cement rather than transform the gender divide. As a consequence, the radical aspects of transgressive femininities like those of Jodie's are undermined by their implicit compliance with gender hierarchies. Being one of the boys seems to result in greater social power but it conscripts Jodie into processes Sharon Thompson (1994) identifies as 'raging misogyny'. In my field notes, there are 16 examples of Jodie asserting that 'boys are better than girls'. Jodie's case is an extreme example of the ways in which girls' ventriloquising of the dominant culture's denigration of femininity and female relations can serve to disconnect them from other girls (Brown, 1998).

Conclusion

Performing gender is not straightforward; rather, it is confusing. The seduction of binaries such as male : female, boy : girl often prevents us from seeing the full range of diversity and differentiation existing within one gender as well as between categories of male and female. Both the girls and boys in 3R were actively involved in the production of gendered identities, constructing gender through a variety and range of social processes (Kerfoot and Knight, 1994). Yet, within this 'gender work', social and cultural differences generate the particular toolkit of cultural resources individual children have available to them. There is a multiplicity of femininities and masculinities available in this primary classroom. But this is not to suggest that these children have myriad choices of which variant of femininity and masculinity to assume. They do not. Class, ethnicity and emergent sexualities all play their part, and constrain as well as create options.

Pyke argues that:

> Hierarchies of social class, race and sexuality provide additional layers of complication. They form the structural and cultural contexts in which gender is enacted in everyday life, thereby fragmenting gender into multiple masculinities and femininities.
>
> (Pyke, 1996, p. 531)

Yet, despite the multiple masculinities and femininities manifested in 3R, there is evidence of hegemonic masculinity in this classroom no less than outside in the wider social world. Within such a context, it makes sense for girls to seek to resist traditional discourses of subordinate femininity. Yet, attempting to take up powerful positions through articulation with, and investment in, dominant masculinities serves to reinforce rather than transform the gender divide. As a consequence, the prevailing gender order is only occasionally disrupted, in particular by the 'spice girls' through their sex play and objectification of a number of the boys and also, paradoxically, through their working-class status. Unlike the 'nice girls' whose activities are circumscribed through being positioned by the boys as a contagious, polluting other, the 'spice girls'' positioning as 'rough' in relation to sensitive middle-class boys allows them to take up a 'polluting' assignment (Douglas, 1966) and use it as a weapon to intimidate the boys.

The girls' struggle to make meaning of themselves as female constitutes a struggle in which gendered peer group hierarchies such as those in 3R position boys as 'better' despite a mass of evidence to show they are neither as academically successful nor as well behaved as girls in the classroom. Peer group discourses constructed girls as harder working, more mature and more socially skilled. Yet, all the boys and a significant number of the girls, if not subscribing to the view that boys are better, adhered to the view that it is better being a boy. There are clearly confusions within the gender work in this classroom. To talk of dominant femininity is to generate a contradiction in terms because it is dominant versions of femininity which subordinate the girls to the boys. Rather, transgressive discourses and the deviant femininities they generate like Jodie's 'tomboy' and Debbie and Carly's espousal of 'girl power' accrue power in both the male and female peer group, and provide spaces for girls to escape gender subordination by the boys.

On the surface, gender relations in this classroom are continually churned up and realigned in a constant process of recomposition. But beneath, at a more subterranean level of knowing and making sense, both boys and girls seem to operate with entrenched dispositions in which being a boy is still perceived to be the more preferable subject positioning. Despite the contemporary focus, both within and without the classroom, on 'girl power' (Arlidge, 1999), as Jean Anyon (1983) found almost 20 years ago, it appears that girls' subversions and transgressions are nearly always contained within, and rarely challenge, the existing structures. For much of the time, girls are 'trapped in the very contradictions they would transcend'. Girls' contestation may muddy the surface water of gender relations, but the evidence of this classroom indicates that the ripples only occasionally reach the murky depths of the prevailing gender order. Within both the localised and dominant discourses that these children draw on, being a boy is still seen as best by all the boys and a significant number of the girls.

Children may both create and challenge gender structures and meanings. However, for much of the time for a majority of the girls and boys in 3R, gender either operates as opposition or hierarchy or most commonly both at the same time. As Janet Holland and her colleagues found in relation to the adolescents in their study, the girls just as much as the boys in this class were 'drawn into making masculinity powerful' (Holland *et al.*, 1998, p. 30).The contemporary orthodoxy that girls are doing better than boys masks the complex messiness of gender relations in which, despite girls' better educational attainment, within this peer group, the prevalent view is still that it's better being a boy.

Despite the all-pervading focus on narrow, easily measured, learning outcomes in British state schooling, learning in classrooms is much wider than test results suggest. While test results indicate that girls are more successful educationally than boys, it appears that in this primary classroom girls and boys still learn many of the old lessons of gender relations which work against gender equity. Sue Heath (1999, p. 293) argues that there is a need for school-based work that sensitively addresses issues of gender identity and masculinities within a pro-feminist frame-work. There is also an urgent need for work that addresses the construction and performance of femininities.

References

Anyon, J. (1983) Intersections of gender and class: accommodation and resistance by working-class and affluent females to contradictory sex-role ideologies, in: S. Walker and L. Barton (Eds) *Gender, Class and Education* (Lewes, Falmer Press).
Arlidge, J. (1999) Girl power gives boys a crisis of confidence, *Sunday Times*, 14 March.
Arnot, M. (1982) Male hegemony, social class and women's education, *Journal of Education*, 16, pp. 64–89.
Ball, S.J. (1994) *Educational Reform* (Buckingham, Open University Press).
Bennett, C. (1996) The boys with the wrong stuff, *Guardian*, 6 November.
Blackmore, J. (1999) *Troubling Women: Feminism, Leadership and Educational Change* (Buckingham, Open University Press).
Brown, L.M. (1998) *Raising Their Voices: The Politics of Girls' Anger* (Cambridge, MA, Harvard University Press).

Clarricoates, K. (1978) Dinosaurs in the classroom – a re-examination of some aspects of the 'hidden' curriculum in primary schools, *Women's Studies International Forum*, 1, pp. 353–364.

Connell, R.W. (1987) *Gender and Power* (Sydney, Allen and Unwin).

Connell, R.W. (1995) *Masculinities* (Cambridge, Polity Press).

Connolly, P. (1998) *Racism, Gender Identities and Young Children* (London, Routledge).

Coward, R. (1999) The feminist who fights for the boys, *Sunday Times*, 20 June.

Davies, B. (1993) *Shards of Glass* (Sydney, Allen and Unwin).

Davies, P., Williams, J. and Webb, S. (1997) Access to higher education in the late twentieth century: policy, power and discourse, in: J. Williams (Ed.) *Negotiating Access to Higher Education* (Buckingham, Open University Press).

Douglas, M. (1966) *Purity and Danger: An Analysis of Concepts of Pollution and Taboo* (London, Routledge and Kegan Paul).

Fine, M. and Macpherson, P. (1992) Over dinner: feminism and adolescent female bodies, in: M. Fine (Ed.) *Disruptive Voices: The Possibilities of Feminist Research* (Ann Arbor, MI, University of Michigan Press).

Francis, B. (1998) *Power Plays: Primary School Children's Construction of Gender, Power and Adult Work* (Stoke-on-Trent, Trentham Books).

Francis, B. (1999) Modernist reductionism or post-structuralist relativism: can we move on? An evaluation of the arguments in relation to feminist educational research, *Gender and Education*, 11, pp. 381–394.

Heath, S. (1999) Watching the backlash: the problematisation of young women's academic success in 1990's Britain, *Discourse*, 20, pp. 249–266.

Hey, V. (1997) *The Company She Keeps: An Ethnography of Girls' Friendship* (Buckingham, Open University Press).

Holland, J., Ramazanoglu, C., Sharpe, S. and Thomson, R. (1998) *The Male in the Head: Young People, Heterosexuality and Power* (London, Tufnell Press).

Gee, J.P., Hull, G. and Lankshear, C. (1996) *The New Work Order* (London, Allen and Unwin).

Griffin, C. (1995) Absences that matter: constructions of sexuality in studies of young women friendship groups, paper presented at the *Celebrating Women's Friendship Conference*, Alcuin College, University of York, 8 April.

Jackson, D. (1998) Breaking out of the binary trap: boys' underachievement, schooling and gender relations, in: D. Epstein, J. Elwood, V. Hey and J. Maw (Eds) *Failing Boys? Issues in Gender and Achievement* (Buckingham, Open University Press).

James, A., Jenks, C. and Prout, A. (1998) *Theorising Childhood* (Cambridge, Polity Press).

Jones, A. (1993) Becoming a 'girl': post-structuralist suggestions for educational research, *Gender and Education*, 5, pp. 157–166.

Kenway, J. and Willis, S. with Blackmore, J. and Rennie, L. (1999) *Answering Back: Girls, Boys and Feminism in Schools* (London, Routledge).

Kerfoot, D. and Knight, D. (1994) Into the realm of the fearful: identity and the gender problematic, in: H.L. Radtke and H.J. Stam (Eds) *Power/Gender: Social Relations in Theory and Practice* (London, Sage).

Lakoff, R.T. (1975) *Language and Woman's Place* (New York, Harper and Row).

Mac an Ghaill, M. (1988) *Young, Gifted and Black: Student–Teacher Relations in the Schooling of Black Youth* (Buckingham, Open University Press).

Maclure, M. (1994) Language and discourse: the embrace of uncertainty, *British Journal of Sociology of Education*, 15, pp. 283–300.

Mirza, S.H. (1992) *Young, Female and Black* (London, Routledge).

Pattman, R. and Phoenix, A. (1999) Constructing self by constructing the 'other': 11–14 year old boys' narratives of girls and women, paper presented at the *Gender and Education conference*, University of Warwick, 29–31 March.

Pyke, K.D. (1996) Class-based masculinities: the interdependence of gender, class and interpersonal power, *Gender & Society*, 10, pp. 527–549.

Reay, D. (1990) Working with boys, *Gender and Education*, 2, pp. 269–282.

Sewell, T. (1997) *Black Masculinities and Schooling: how Black Boys Survive Modern Schooling* (Stoke-on-Trent, Trentham Books).

Skelton, C. (1997) Primary boys and hegemonic masculinities, *British Journal of Sociology of Education*, 18, pp. 349–369.

Skelton, C. (1999) 'A passion for football': dominant masculinities and primary schooling, paper presented to the *British Educational Research Association Conference*, University of Sussex, 2–5 September.

Thompson, S. (1994) What friends are for: on girls' misogyny and romantic fusion, in: J. Irvine (Ed.) *Sexual Cultures and the Construction of Adolescent Identities* (Philadelphia, PA, Temple University Press).

Thorne, B. (1993) *Gender Play: Girls and Boys in School* (Buckingham, Open University Press).

Walkerdine, V. (1991) *Schoolgirl Fictions* (London, Verso).

Walkerdine, V. (1997) *Daddy's Girl: Young Girls and Popular Culture* (London, Macmillan).

Walkerdine, V., Lucey, H. and Melody, J. (2000) Class, attainment and sexuality in late twentieth-century Britain, in: C. Zmroczek and P. Mahony (Eds) *Women and Social Class: International Feminist Perspectives* (London: UCL Press).

Wight, D. (1996) Beyond the predatory male: the diversity of young Glaswegian men's discourses to describe heterosexual relationships, in: L. Adkins and V. Merchant (Eds) *Sexualising the Social: Power and the Organisation of Sexuality* (London, Macmillan).

Wilkinson, H. (1994) *No Turning Back: Generations and the Genderquake* (London, Demos).

Wilkinson, H. (1999) The Thatcher legacy: power feminism and the birth of girl power, in: N. Walters (Ed.) *On the Move – Feminism for a New Generation* (London, Virago).

Williams, J. (Ed.) (1997) *Negotiating Access to Higher Education* (Buckingham, Open University Press).

Willis, P. (1977) *Learning to Labour: How Working Class Kids Get Working Class Jobs* (Farnborough, Saxon House).

CHAPTER 10

'LADS AND LAUGHTER'

Humour and the production of heterosexual hierarchies

Mary Jane Kehily and Anoop Nayak, *Gender and Education*, 9, 1, 1997

Introduction

This chapter focuses on the use of humour among male pupils within two secondary schools in the UK where we conducted research. During the research period we were aware of humour as a common interaction of the young men we observed, interviewed and discussed school life with. However, with a few notable exceptions (Woods, 1976, 1990; Stebbins, 1980; Dubberley, 1993), relatively little attention has been paid to the social significance of these exchanges to the lives of pupils. Our study suggests that humour plays a significant part in consolidating male peer group cultures in secondary schools, offering a sphere for conveying masculine identities. By exploring a range of interactions involving young men, our work suggests that heterosexual masculinities are organised and regulated through humour. Using qualitative methods we look at the ways in which humour is used and expressed in the negotiation and contestation of heterosexual masculinities. Here, humour is frequently invoked to expose, police and create gender-sexual hierarchies within pupil cultures. We conclude by arguing that humour is a technique for the enactment of masculine identities and can be seen to produce differentiated heterosexualities. [...]

We are indebted to the insights of Woods (1976) and Willis (1976, 1977), where pupil humour can be understood, respectively, as both a coping strategy and a product of class cultural tensions. However, our study further suggests that humour is less an 'outcome' or 'effect' of working-class masculinity but, rather, is *constitutive of* these very identities. We argue that humour is a style utilised by young men to substantiate their heterosexual masculinities. It appeared that humour was used for *consolidating* heterosexual masculinities through game-play, storytelling and the practice of insults. Our study suggests that although pupil humour contains moments of subversion (to teachers, bourgeois values, compulsory education, etc.), it is also a compelling mode for sex/gender *conformity*. Although a resistance to the authorities of schooling, young men's humorous performances could have oppressive effects on other pupils. Significantly, young women were targets for male humorous insults (Jones, 1985; Lees, 1986, 1993) while young men who did not conform to dominant heterosexual codes of masculinity were also subject to its adverse consequences (Askew and Ross, 1988; Haywood, 1996; Nayak and Kehily, 1996). Although some styles of joking may enhance feelings of equality, we focus on the regulatory effects of humour on pupils' sex/gender identities. This may call for alternative ways of theorising working-class masculine resistance in the context of school.

Methodology

Our study is based in two secondary schools in predominantly working-class areas of the West Midlands, UK, where approximately 100 interviews were conducted with teachers and pupils between 1992 and 1994. The data are derived from a broader project exploring young people's sexuality in school.[1] We used many different qualitative approaches for data gathering including group discussions, participant observation and semi-structured interviews with groups and individuals. A tape-recorder was used for all sessions and combined with note-taking before and after the 2-year research period. This paper draws on ethnographic material from pupils aged between 15 and 16 years of age. In one school, pupils were selected for us by a teacher, while in the other we had scope to choose from a cross-section of the school population. The chapter does not attempt to address the contextual differences of humorous forms within each of the educational sites; rather we explore the commonalities of masculine power exchanges within English schools. Our focus in this paper is upon the role of humour in the lived cultures of young men in school. Although the groups were predominantly white, they included young women and men, some of whom were South Asian, African-Caribbean and of 'mixed heritage'. While there is not scope to consider methodological issues in this chapter, we acknowledge the influence of feminist praxis in this field, which stresses the role of subjects' experiences, self-reflexivity and grounded theory (Finch, 1984; Harding, 1987; Hollway, 1989; Stanley and Wise, 1993).

In our study, the research dynamic was specifically nuanced by our own differently located gendered and ethnic identities, as a white female and Asian male. Originally we had planned to conduct 'same sex' interviews where the researcher and the researched would occupy a shared gender identity. However, once in school we found this to be an impractical and inappropriate approach to fieldwork concerned with the interactions *between* gendered identities and the social relationships this produces. Recent work has problematised the extent to which a shared 'race' or gender identity can transform the unequal power relations between the researcher and respondents (Phoenix, 1994; Rhodes, 1994). Moreover, gender identities are classed, 'raced' and sexed in all kinds of complex and contradictory ways. Undoubtedly, our growing resistance to recourse to gender or racial 'matching' between interviewer and interviewee had an impact on the structure of responses we were given. As time went on, the placing of pupils within such crudely defined research categories appeared presumptuous and inappropriate for our study, though this may be a productive strategy for other fieldwork encounters.

Regimes of humour: masculinities, game-play and insults

A common style of interaction that male pupils engaged in was the elaborate use of game-play incorporating ritualised verbal and physical assaults. This involved young men using language and physicality in competitive ways where the 'game' became the arena for competing masculinities. Among the pupils we interviewed, such games involved forms of verbal sparring and physical 'play-fighting', which assimilated a range of linguistic and bodily practices. These included 'cussing' or 'blowing' matches, formulaic insults and punch-'n'-run. During the fieldwork period we encountered routine forms of physical game-play that young men undertook to demonstrate their dominance over young women and one another. These regular activities included hitting, pushing, kicking and tripping as frequent styles of physical gaming. Humphries and Smith (1984) refer to such activities as 'rough-and-tumble', identifying the lack of attention researchers have paid to these daily pupil exchanges. Meanwhile, Willis (1977) found *actual* violence outside the boundaries of play to be rare; fights were the final point of conflict used ultimately to define masculine status. Symbolic exchanges fusing violence with play occurred in the playground, school corridors and classrooms when teachers were not looking. In these examples the notion of humour could be invoked to avoid the charge of outright violence, aggression or abuse. Back explains:

> In operating this kind of play the sensitive line of significance is policed. On one side of this line is the meaning which the word/exchange stands for in wider usage, on the other is a meaningless denotation guaranteed in play. The tension in this kind of early and late adolescent play is centred around the issue of whether these practices mean what they stand for or not.
>
> (1990, p. 10)

The examples in this section show how the rituals of gaming and humour allow male competitive styles to continue relatively unabated in school. It is through these displays of verbal and physical performance that young men are able to exhibit their heterosexual masculinities.

'Cussing' matches

Hewitt identified a link between verbal sparring and masculinity. He commented that the 'ability to hold your own in a slanging match can be especially important once a boy moves into adolescence, and to do so the language has to be right' (1986, p. 158). The ritualisation of abuse was a central feature of 'cussing' or 'blowing competitions' in the masculine exchanges we studied, described here by one of the teachers, Mr Carlton.

> We get things like, we used to have, 'Your mom's a dog'. What does that mean, y'know? [*laughs*]
>
> 'Your mom's a sweaty armpit'.
>
> It is purely an insult and kids had competitions here called blowing competitions to see who could give the worst insult, right. Now we've managed to stamp it out, but my God, you should have heard some of the things that were said. And it was always about their mother right, because that is the one thing that everybody has in common. They all know their mother and that's very personal. They know where they come from, very personal and it hurts. And you get all these brash kids who've been reduced to tears by some of the comments that have been thrown at them.

'Blowing competitions' were hotly contested verbal duals that tended to occur between two invariably male opponents, usually in lunch periods away from the intervention of teachers. During our time in schools we did not encounter any examples of this activity between young women,[2] though as Back (1990) found, they commonly engaged in less structured 'cussing', slurs and name-calling. According to Mr Carlton, the object of 'blowing competitions' was 'to see who could give the worst insult'. The competition involved the giving and taking of ritualised insults where language became the stage for the performance of masculinity. Here, the ability to absorb 'very personal' comments with seeming indifference, and to respond sharply, are the weaponry required for successful verbal jousting. That 'brash kids' could be 'reduced to tears' indicates that a publicly recognised version of masculinity can be momentarily punctured and secured through these contests. These rituals show the techniques young men may utilise to make each other vulnerable, while emphasising the power of dominant versions of masculinity to produce anxieties within the structure of a competitive 'game'. 'Blowing competitions' have the effect of creating clear-cut masculine identities, crystallising who is 'hard' or 'soft' through the public exposition of power and vulnerability. The term 'blowing competition' is a metaphor that provides insight into the ways masculine egos are either inflated or ruptured during these contests. Layman's research into a US male fraternity suggests that 'dozens' – the ritual exchange of insults – perform a range of functions. His study indicates the way in which sexist jokes consolidate the bonds of an 'in-group' through mutual hostility against an 'out-group' (1987, pp. 159–160). In these exchanges the ability to keep control of your emotions in the face of a barrage of abuse is seen as essential for group membership and the demonstration of a competent, socially validated masculinity. As one of his respondents explains:

> If there's one theme that goes on, it's the emphasis on being able to take a lot of ridicule, of shit, and not getting upset about it. Most of the interaction we have is verbally abusing each other, making disgusting references to your mother's sexuality, or the women you were seen with, or your sex organ. And you aren't cool unless you can take it without trying to get back.
>
> (in Lyman, 1987, p. 155)

The description of 'blowing competitions' provided by Mr Carlton is similar to the volatile, verbal exchanges Lyman found, and those identified by Labov (1972) in his study of uses of black vernacular among adolescents in urban USA. Labov describes 'sounding' as a form of verbal duelling that involves the trading of ritual insults for prestige within the peer group. Those most skilled at employing sophisticated insults had higher status in the group[3] where the structured performances were constituted around abusing an opponent's mother. Mr Carlton noted how 'blowing competitions' were 'always about their mother' because it's 'the one thing that everybody has in common, they all know their mother and that's very personal'. In a *discursive manoeuvre*, young men are able to mobilise a sexist discourse of power against other males through a verbal attack on their mothers. The discursive shift is a way of accessing a privileged version of male sexual power to humiliate an opponent. The invocation of a boy's mother into the discourse of the male peer group taps into the contradictory 'private' emotions of maternal affection and the public disavowal of the 'feminine'. At the root of this contradiction may lie the impossibility of locating one's mother through the virgin/whore dichotomy used to define *all* women (Griffin, 1982). These contradictory feelings may contribute to the potency of mother insults, exacerbated when males are located as moral guardians of the sexual reputations of mothers, girlfriends and sisters. Mothers are invoked in insults to probe young men's associative links with femininity and expose their vulnerabilities. This produces heterosexual hierarchies between 'real' lads and those susceptible to 'feminine' sensibilities and capable of crying. During the research period sexist jokes, innuendoes and comments were frequently employed by young men at the expense of female pupils. Certain young women would be teased about many aspects of sexual activity, real or imagined, particularly 'doing business at the back of Goodman's'.[4] As other researchers have found, misogynistic labelling and a concern with female sexual reputations were key markers for the construction of young women's identities...The young women we spoke to were sensitive to the sexism embedded in these exchanges and were acutely aware of the gendered inequalities they must endure.

Hewitt found sexist and racist discourses could be simultaneously enacted in slanging matches through comments such as, 'Oh shut up you silly black cunt' (1986, p. 158). Gordon *et al.* in their study of Finnish and English schools found 'cussing' matches 'could be based on "otherness", and took place between different nationalities and ethnic groups' (1996, p. 12). These examples indicate how a racist orientation may be employed divisively within the insult to reduce an encounter to its most personal level. Indeed, it appeared that young men in our study could augment an insult by recourse to sexist, homophobic or racist discourses of power. Insults such as 'your mom's a dog' are then a slur on the sexual reputation of the mother, where the vagina becomes the focus of association for birth ('they know where they came from'), penetrative heterosexual intercourse and the insult.

Formulaic insults

Although mother insults were regularly employed during the highly charged showdown of a classroom 'cussing' match, at other moments young men drew upon these familiar codes to generate humour amongst friends out of school. However, the meanings of these insults were *transformed* in the contexts of friendship groups, and away from the intensity of classroom cultures, indicating that it was not the language *per se* that was immediately regarded as offensive. Within the male friendship group the telling of jokes and relating of insults is structured through the context of peers and situation. Schooling cultures are central to interpreting the shouting rituals of 'cussing' matches. However, outside school young men were able to decode mother insults differently according to the variable circumstances in which they deployed them. Walker and Goodson elaborate on the performative dynamics of humour and describe the relevance of interpersonal relationships:

> The nature of humour is complex because it resides not only in the logic and content of what is said, but in, the performance of the teller, in the relationship between the teller and the audience, and in the immediate context of the instance.
>
> (1977, p. 212)

The importance of context suggests that mother insults, as invoked for the public appraisal of masculinities, may take on different meanings. This goes some way to explaining how an insult during a 'cussing' match may be treated as offensive and capable of reducing males to tears, yet is bandied around between mates at another point under the guise of 'play'. Such examples of mother insults, nevertheless, remained highly misogynistic and often explicitly sexual in whatever contexts they occurred. A school student called Macca related two typically formulaic ritual insults[5] to us which were passed around within the male peer group and used as a resource for humour among friends: 'Your mom's been raped so many times she puts a padlock on her fanny. Your mom's got so many holes in her knickers you can play Connect Four.' Unlike other aspects of pupil humour (see Woods, 1990), such 'speech events' have a 'well articulated structure' (Labov, 1972, p. 334) and may be strategically employed at given moments. The insults described by Macca in situations outside school formed a style of banter that was taken far less personally than in the classroom context of the 'cussing' match where masculine identities were more visibly being conveyed. [. . .]

Labov describes how the structure of mother insults is defined precisely 'as against' middle-class adult sensibilities, and aims to violate social norms:

> Many sounds *are* obscene in the full sense of the word. The speaker uses as many 'bad' words and images as possible – that is, subject to taboo and moral reprimand in adult middle-class society...the meaning of the sound and the activity would be entirely lost without reference to these middle-class norms. Many sounds are 'good' because they are 'bad' – because the speakers know they would arouse disgust and revulsion among those committed to the 'good' standards of middle-class society.
>
> (Labov, 1972, p. 324)

Here, the act of transgression is itself treasured, where the rules and norms of adult middle-class society are inverted for shock value. According to Labov, middle-class norms act as a reference point through which the language of young men can be defined as abusive. The rationalism of bourgeois discourse can be disrupted by the 'vulgarity' celebrated by young men in school, where middle-class culture is central to the definition of what is acceptable. The ability of 'family name-calling' to violate 'adult' conventions is also referred to by Troyna and Hatcher (1992, p. 56). However, it is the contrast of sexual explicitness and elaborated structural codes that may appear an unusual combination for the language residing within pupil cultures. The misogynistic practice of mother insults are both a means of speaking the unspeakable and a way of contesting the boundaries of masculine competency within the peer group. In the following section we demonstrate how other competitive bodily practices are encoded through humour and used to demonstrate heterosexual masculine identities and hierarchies among males in school.

Punch-'n'-run

The object of punch-'n'-run is to hit an opponent and run off before he or she has time to retaliate. The punch-'n'-run game is usually initiated by young men, though some young women could be drawn into participation. The following is an example of mock fighting which we have termed punch-'n'-run. Here, a young woman, Tina, responds to the masculine physical gaming in school.

> I don't really like Darren that much now. He's always competitive ain't he? Have you seen him with Clive? Clive punched me in my arm and he punched me three times, and so Darren did. So I went [*demonstrating*] one-two-three!

The extract shows how punch-'n'-run may be a competitive intra-male contest to see who can deliver the most blows. Tina identifies Darren as 'competitive' and suggests the physical displays are partially about outdoing another peer, put simply, getting more punches in than Clive. Such continual, competitive jockeying for status within male peer groups leads Jordan (1995, p. 79) to suggest that 'many of the disadvantages as suffered by girls and women are the result of being caught in the crossfire in a long-standing battle between groups of men over the definition of masculinity'. Masculinity is performed through the supposedly humorous repetition of sequences such as punch-'n'-run. Punch-'n'-run is also structured around certain implicit conventions, where Tina tolerated Clive engaging in these interactions but disliked Darren's attempt to join in.

The ritual performed similar interpersonal functions as the 'back slap and chase' game that featured in Back's youth club research:

> Duelling play is a process whereby young people test out the boundaries of interpersonal relationships (i.e. how far play can be extended and pushed). These exchanges have greater significance than just play for play's sake. They not only mark the boundaries of tolerance within friendships but they also mark those who are included in the peer group – those who are 'alright' – and those who are excluded – 'wallies'.
>
> (1990, p. 10)

The formative styles and conventions are continually negotiated through the action of game playing. Punch-'n'-run offers a ritual for masculine bonding to be sure, yet it also provides a highly regulated sphere for physical contest. The significance of peer group relations is seen where Darren attempts to copy Clive's action in an attempt to mimic a desired masculinity. In this example Darren is trying to inhabit the masculine presence of Clive by replicating his actions. Tina is positioned as the foil for these transactions, yet her fighting response suggests a refusal to allow Darren to occupy a dominant masculinity in the way he desires, and can be seen as an assertion of her own identity.

The examples provide insights into the way male power is negotiated and contested through the bravado of ritualised humour and social exchanges in schools. Beynon (1989, p. 198), writing about masculinity and routine violence in schools, notes how certain forms of physical humour could be regarded as 'funny violence', becoming 'the boys' principle source of laughter, enjoyment and excitement'. Other researchers have documented the relationships between such types of competitive game-playing more generally, linking them to forms of masculinity and working-class occupational culture (Willis, 1977; Back, 1990; Hollands, 1990). [...]

The comments indicate the ways in which male violence is valorised through styles of humour which draw on verbal and physical game-play. The practice of gaming can also be a coercive technique exerted by certain male peer cultures to establish and maintain power over other subordinated masculine schooling cultures. The routines of 'cussing', banter and punching were used to substantiate male heterosexual identities by expelling 'femininity' from self on to others. This had the effect of creating heterosexual hierarchies within male cultures where 'macho' lads were seen as 'proper' boys and other males were subordinated. Physical and verbal gaming rituals are thus an important route for the performativity of masculine identities in schools.

Retelling ourselves – mythic events and heterosexual identities

Alongside the rituals of gaming, we found collective storytelling played a central role in framing classroom humour and consolidating versions of heterosexual masculinity. Certain events achieved a lasting appeal in school and could be reinvoked for the shared pleasure of mutual retelling. The various identifications made when relating certain events elevated these stories to mythic status; they were described as 'classics' and understood as key reference points for making sense of young men's time and place within the education system. The influence that these narratives bring to bear on the structuring of identity is explained by Delamont, who writes of the need to explore anecdote, reminiscence, urban legends and folklore within school contexts:

> The argument is that conventional ethnographers have focused too exclusively on rational accounts provided by pupils and teachers and have not spent enough energy unearthing the irrational fears and the fictional narratives that enliven the school day. Educational institutions are rich in contemporary folklore: cautionary tales, jokes, urban legends, atrocity stories, and so on.
>
> (1989, p. 191)

The popularity of mythic events can be seen in young men's constant readiness to resort to these narrative styles with much relish and little obvious connection with topics under discussion. The shared telling and remembrance affirmed links between the present and the past, and augmented heterosexual identities. As Delamont goes on to explain, analysing narrative forms and irrational investments may 'enrich our understanding of pupils' and teachers' culture' (1989, p. 191); we claim it can also enable us to explore the values embedded in masculine humour in school.

Paddy's story

The repetition of mythic events provides for moments of pleasure where collective investments in the humiliation of teachers have enduring comic status. During our time in school we heard several stories involving teachers having nervous break-downs, falling through trapdoors, having their flasks of coffee spat in, being chased by pupils and chasing pupils (Kehily, 1993; Kehily and Nayak, 1996). The comic narrations celebrate oppositional forms of behaviour in the classroom and emphasise pupil power in oppressive circumstances. Like flags being unfurled, these narratives were unfolded with pride and thrust down as markers of resistance, a symbolic victory against the odds.

The attraction of these stories to adolescent male culture can be seen in the rapid ease with which the tale is 'sparked'. In this example Paddy is spotted walking past the room, where an immediate link is made between Paddy as a person and an event in his past which is prioritised by pupils. Incredibly, the event occurred in another school so was not witnessed by the pupils in our research, yet its resonance for the male peer group informs us of the cult status of this story. The interview took place with a mixed group of girls and boys and displays a dramatic style of masculine resistance which appears to be enjoyed by most of the pupils. The mythic tale was repeatedly referred to, becoming a touchstone for pupil experience, while providing evidence of how male resistance to schooling can be fashioned and celebrated through humour. It is difficult within the written format to capture the flavour of the regional accents, the speed of delivery, intonation and excitement embedded in the dialogue, so these must be left to the reader's imagination.

Smithy: There's Paddy!
Jason: He's the one you want to question – Paddy.
All: [*laughter*] Watch him go red.
   Why what's he done?
Clive: He's a nutcase!
Samantha: He's a nutter! [*all laugh*]
Jason: You'll have to go and fetch him and watch him go red.
Clive: Ask him about his old school days.
[*Savage enters*]
Samantha: Savage, go and fetch Paddy.
Savage: Paddy's just beat me up! [*all laugh*]
Jason: Paddy's beat him up!
Samantha: Is he coming?
Jason: Watch his face. He's going red already! [*all laugh*]
Samantha: Oh, leave him. He's probably doing something for his own house group.
[*Swelling laughter*]
Smithy: What's he say?
[*Paddy enters*]
Clive: Ask him why he got expelled from his old school.
Jason: Say why d'yow git expelled, aye.
We don't wanna embarrass him.
[*increased laughter*]
Jason: [*loudly to Paddy*] Why d'yow git expelled from your last school?
[*all laugh*]
Samantha: Go on tell 'em!
Jason: Jus' tell 'em Paddy!
All: Tell 'em!
   You've said it before.
Smithy: They're curious.
Jason: Nothing gets said.
Samantha: Go on!
No, don't embarrass him.
Clive: Jus' say it Pad, go on.
Paddy: I made a cock outta clay an' give it to a nun!
[*Mass Laughter*]

Paddy's story, in keeping with previous aspects of male humour, can be understood as a 'verbal performance' structured through the social interplay of 'audience' and 'situation' (Volosinov, 1973). Here, the social act of storytelling is reliant upon recognition with others, as the group of pupils collaborate and interact as both actors and audience. Within the research dynamic we felt that the group were providing an audience for Paddy, staging a show for us (and one another) while watching our reactions. Watching Paddy, and watching us watching Paddy, generates great excitement in the school context. The research group mediated relations between ourselves and Paddy, presenting us as an interested party – 'they're curious' – and a confidential one – 'nothing gets said'. At the same time we are informed about Paddy that 'he's the one you want to question' and asked about 'fetching' him in. Our role as audience is central to the building excitement, where our comments about not wanting to embarrass Paddy serve to fuel the exhilaration. The references to being beaten up by Paddy, and the laughter this produces, refer to the punch-'n'-run gaming discussed earlier.

The celebratory fervour of the story stems from the violation of norms produced in the mythic event. Making a 'cock outta clay' and presenting it to a nun can be seen as an ultimate transgressive expression, with all its symbolic masculine overtones. Here, the cock as a symbol of phallic power has the ability to threaten and shock, a means through which Paddy can use a masculine discourse of power against female teachers in a Catholic school. The act of defiance is further exaggerated where a nun is said to be the recipient of the clay cock. The narrative humour is produced through seeing the nun as a symbol of passivity and purity, with Paddy's gesture of defiance crossing religious and sexual boundaries. The gendered juxtaposition of (male) cock and (female) nun is a symbolic moment of masculine resistance where the power of the teacher is subverted by the pupil. Walker and Goodson (1977) have suggested how oppression is fertile ground for humour and that its emergence in asymmetric relationships is evidence that power is rarely experienced in totality. As Valerie Walkerdine (1990) has illustrated, such transformations in the dynamics of power are possible through the multiple positions subjects can occupy in discourse. The multiple and contradictory subjectivities of teacher/nun/adult/female or pupil/adolescent/male are thus neither unitary, simplistic, or in any way straightforward. Consequently, Walkerdine indicates that not all acts of resistance against school authority have revolutionary effects; they may be 'reactionary' too, especially when we consider the dynamic of gender.

The pleasure in the mythic story derives from the various transgressive practices and the infringement of multiple boundaries: religious/sexual, teacher/pupil, male/female, public/private. The event brings each of these borders into sharp relief and reveals the complexities of power within school arenas. Paddy is ushered in by the pupil group for comic reasons, to tell his story and 'watch him go red'; he was immediately dispensed with after the performance. The group operate as supporting actors and provide the context for Paddy's delivery of the infamous one liner. Paddy's masculinity is continually appraised through the retellings of the narrative sequence and the collective 'remembrance' of his expulsion. In recounting the mythic sequence, pupils keep alive the notion of Paddy as 'mad' or 'a scream' and a 'nutter'. If the mythic event is to be believed, the celebratory humour conceals the tragic underside of Paddy's expulsion. However, we have been less interested in the 'facticity' of events and more concerned with the investments made by young men in particular incidents, and their desire continually to retell and relive the experience in the mythic imaginary. The narrative functions to consolidate Paddy's display of hyper-heterosexuality and the values of the group more generally.

The arthritic tongue

Although a main feature of the narratives is their anti-authoritarian structure, sexual stories concerning other pupils could become mythic events (Canaan, 1986). Here, sharp retorts and humorous barbed remarks could be used to question the heterosexual masculinity of other young men, Willis (1977) found intra-male conflict to be a means of bolstering working-class masculinities which were not simply fashioned against girls and women but also against conformist boys, the 'ear'oles'. We found that although clear hierarchies existed between those who saw themselves as 'lads', and those they labelled 'snobs',[6] peer group status was continually being reshuffled when young men engaged in quick-fare exchanges. This suggests the exhibition of a public performance of masculinity through the use of humorous devices. The following example illustrates the ways humour can be used to put down another male and at the same time consolidate the heterosexual masculinity of the teller and the rest of the group.

OK then Macca, tell us about Tom
Macca: OK, he was going out with this girl for, like, three months and he never did anything with her, like get off with her or anything. And she went to get off with him and he pulled away. So after this, this kid goes to him, 'You've got an arthritic tongue, that's why you've not got off with Sally'. A classic.

Mythic events suggest that pupils are engaged in processes of 'storying' where associative links are made between people and specific incidents. Through embellishment and repetition certain events acquire mythologised status in the eyes of pupils. The narrative concerning Tom and his legendary 'arthritic tongue' becomes 'a classic' in similar ways to the story of Paddy and the clay cock. The arthritic tongue narrative questions Tom's heterosexual masculine performance and his hesitance with Sally, 'he never did anything with her'. The use of a 'put-down' has the effect of asserting the status of the teller, which in turn consolidates the male peer group who impose their values upon the target male (Stebbins, 1980). The class cultural significance of this style of humour is discussed by Hollands (1990), who found that for working-class young men 'the definition of being male was shot through with the need to display sexual prowess and power'. This may further explain the admiration for Paddy as someone who was said to be expelled for sexual exhibition. The arthritic tongue narrative also reveals the various performative levels of masculinity: the need to perform sexually with Sally, the need to boast about the 'sexual performance' with other young men and the 'put-down' itself as a performative regulator of masculine behaviour.

The repetition of mythic stories and ritual game-play promotes group solidarity and shared male identity through 'othering' teachers, girls, women and those who fail to cultivate a hyper-masculinity. Lyman (1987) regards such masculine jocularity as part of a 'theatre of domination', pointing out that sexist jokes function to augment male bonding as 'nearly all jokes have an aggressive content, indeed shared aggression toward an outsider...may overcome internal tension and assert [group] solidarity' (p. 150). Perhaps this insider/outsider split can also be said to take place within the male subject, where critically putting down the sexual practices of a peer, or laughing at his sexual inexperience, may hide broader insecurities about relationships and the masculine pressure to 'perform'. As Freud (1905) postulates, this type of humour permits the forbidden to be expressed and indirectly articulates vulnerable feelings. From this perspective humour can be seen as a form of 'joke-work' which displaces sexual anxieties on to others through laughter, while relieving the self of embarrassment. Similarly, although Paddy has a reputation for being a 'nutcase', his embarrassment may suggest an uneasy relationship with the projected image of himself as the ultimate masculine performer. As Tom found out to his cost, uncertainties may exist within the male psyche when young men misrecognise themselves against the expectations of a hyper-masculinity. Sex/gender identities are stringently policed by male peer groups within school when Tom is humiliated and laughed at for gender inappropriate behaviour and Paddy is celebrated as school rebel for his phallic performance. The mythic events commemorate versions of masculinity that display sexual daring and an audacious resistance to authority. The repetition of these episodes through a storytelling format affirms hyper-heterosexual versions of masculinity and acts as regulatory reminders, and performative rehearsals, for the desirable behaviour of the male peer group.

Humour and sex/gender hierarchies

Researchers have commented on the ways in which male sexual power is consistently utilised by males against women and girls in school arenas (Griffin, 1982, 1985; Lees, 1986, 1993; Jones and Mahoney, 1989; Walkerdine, 1990). In this section we focus on the struggle to fashion dominant heterosexual masculinities through techniques of humour and joking. Here, young women and subordinate males can be seen as targets for comic displays which frequently blur the boundaries between humour and harassment. The competitive process of humour created and consolidated sex/gender hierarchies within pupil groups. Young women deconstructed the competitive workings of masculine performance in formal classroom situations. The young women we spoke with seemed to regard sexist practices as part of everyday life in a mixed comprehensive school (Jones, 1985), and responded to the tiresome routines of male banter in ambiguous ways. As in previous examples, 'play' and aggression become fused:

> Tina: Jason, he gets on my nerves he does. He used to be really quiet but now I prefer him being quiet, he's really loud. He'll come up behind yer and shout and bawl in yer ear. Or he'll say stupid little things, he keeps on and on and on. He says, 'Oi you! I got something to tell you'. He says, 'Give me three seconds, I'll be home in two' and stupid things like that to you.
>
> Samantha: You're sitting there doing yer work and he'll just shout in yer ear.
>
> Tina: Or do stupid little noises, makes me laugh some days though.
>
> Samantha: It ain't very often though! [*both laugh*]

Here, Samantha and Tina describe the use of male sexual power and their reactions to it. The harassment evoked in this passage ranges from bullying behaviour such as shouting and bawling, through to making 'stupid little noises' and implicitly sexual comments referring to heterosexual intercourse and orgasm. Although Samantha and Tina view Jason's behaviour as a nuisance ('he gets on my nerves he does'), they regard these encounters as commonplace practices to be humoured, while at other moments want to punch back. The laughter that Samantha and Tina enjoy at Jason's expense ('makes me laugh some days though/it ain't very often') suggests that young women may use humour subversively as a form of resistance to sexist practices (Skeggs, 1991). The young women suggest that the routines are repetitive and monotonous in their remark, 'he keeps on and on and on'. The interaction also traces Jason's arrival to the school as a new and insecure pupil to someone who now cultivates a masculinity that is 'really loud'. [...]

However, sexist interchanges were not the only resource used to locate heterosexual masculine identities. We found that homophobic humour and gestures were used by young men to enact a hyper-masculine identity and so consolidate their heterosexuality. The following extract is taken from an interview with a group of young women where the subject of homophobia arose:

> *In your class do you think that boys could be more homophobic or do you think that girls are?*
> Lucy: I think that boys are.
> Susan: Definitely.
> Lucy: Because they go 'STAY AWAY' [*demonstrates crucifix sign with fingers*] or something like.
> All: Yes.
> Susan: Like as if he's contagious.
> Amy: If they're all sitting together like that [*i.e. huddled up*], one of them will move away.

Homophobic humour is a means through which male exhibitionists are able outwardly to display a heterosexual masculinity. Male sexual power is in process between males where homophobias are performed through symbolic gestures and bodily practices. The homophobic performance suggests an instability of gender categories where masculinity is repeatedly struggled over within male peer groups. The combination of humour with homophobia becomes a technique for the display of heterosexual masculinities as independent, entirely 'unfeminine' and exclusively 'straight'. The crucifix performance is, then, an attempt to purvey a coherent masculinity by ridiculing others through questioning their gender and sexuality. In a doubly defining moment the homophobic performance consolidates the heterosexual masculinity of Self and the homosexual femininity of Other. Homophobic performances can be seen as an (impossible) attempt to convey a coherent heterosexual masculinity. These identities are sustained through fraught exhibition, where the highly dramatised performance is itself evidence of the insecurities and splittings within the male psyche (Nayak and Kehily, 1996). In keeping with Mac an Ghaill (1996), we found interconnections between homophobia and misogyny: 'heterosexual male students were involved in a double relationship, of traducing the 'other', including women and gays (external relations), while at the same time expelling femininity and homosexuality from within themselves (internal relations)' (Mac an Ghaill, 1996, p. 13).

This suggests that rituals such as the crucifix performance and mother insults are more about psychic processes of enactment where the 'other' within the self must be traduced. Here, homophobic humour is used to police the sex/gender identities of other students, as well as the self. The bodily performance of making a crucifix, shouting 'STAY AWAY' and moving away from other males is interconnected with psycho-sexual struggles and displacements. These internal anxieties suggest the fear that being gay is 'contagious' and needs warding off through humour and performance. According to Lyman (1987, p. 156), homophobic jokes are 'targeted at homosexuality, to draw an emotional line between the homosocial male bond and homosexual relationships'. This allows for the intimate closeness of male peer cultures to be sanctioned, without compromising on an overtly heterosexual group identity. Homophobic displays not only consolidate the identities of the heterosexist individual but speak to the wider hyper-masculinity of the peer group. In such exchanges masculinities are visibly performed, highlighting the frequently misogynistic and homophobic structure of these practices and the uncertainties that underlie these outbursts.

Young men who did not cultivate a hyper-masculinity were subject to homophobic abuse which had oppressive effects on their life in school.

> *Miles:*   It's a sort of stigma ain't it? A quiet person in a class would be called 'gay' or summat. I was for a time 'cos I was fairly quiet in the classroom and for a while everyone was callin' me gay...I think my grades have suffered 'cos of disruptive members of the class. They're not really interested in getting a qualification so it's, 'Well what can we do for a laugh today? Disrupt the history lesson or something like that'.

As Miles indicates, calling other young men gay is seen as a 'laugh'. It is used as a cultural axis for charting dominant and subordinate heterosexualities within male peer group culture. The oppressive effects of homophobic. humour are seen in Miles's articulation of the social stigma of being called 'gay' and his belief that his 'grades have suffered'. This style of humour is a technique for disciplining the enactment of heterosexual masculinities where, '[h]umour is a powerful device for celebrating one's own identity and for enhancing one's status, and for whipping others into shape' (Woods, 1990, p. 195). Walker and Goodson (1977) also identify a relationship between humour and power, to view joking as a 'social contract' since '[s]uccess or failure at telling jokes endangers status in the immediate context and so not surprisingly it is usually those with most power in the situation who tell most jokes' (p. 214). [...]

Conclusion: the last laugh?

The ethnographic evidence discussed in this paper suggests that humour is an *organising principle* in the lives of young men within school arenas. Humour was seen as a regulatory technique, structuring the performance of masculine identities. Young men who did not circumscribe to the hyper-heterosexual practice of masculinity were ridiculed through humorous rituals. Consequently, those who worked hard at school, or exposed sexual vulnerabilities in relationships with young women, were targets for banter and abuse. These examples revealed the *disciplining* effects of humour on sex/gender identities within the English education system. The development of 'cussing matches' and other rituals of abuse offered a practical means of testing male prowess that avoided the dangerous, and somewhat more determining, consequences of fights. In this sense, humour was *constitutive of* masculine identities in school: macho behaviour was mythologised in stories of defiance, some pupils could be seer as 'gay' for conforming to teacher authority, while others were regarded as sexually impotent with 'arthritic tongues' if they failed to perform sexually with girlfriends. Here, humour was a style for the perpetual display of 'hard' masculinity and also a means of displacing fears and uncertainties. Humorous interactions amongst young men were continually concerned with bodily practices: clay cocks, punch-'n'-run rituals, arthritic tongues, padlocked vaginas, sweaty armpits, antigay crucifixes. In these exchanges the disciplining process of heterosexuality occurs across the bodies of self and other. The rituals of humour involve the embodiment of heterosexuality where disciplinary techniques operate as an 'anatomy of power' (Foucault, 1977). Bodies are trained, indeed schooled, into heterosexual elaborations through the humorous techniques we have discussed.

The repetitive game-play and retelling of stories creates and affirms the values practised in working-class male peer group culture. Although humour is undoubtedly used by pupils as a working-class mode of resistance against the middle-class ethos of schooling authority, this can have oppressive effects on female teachers and pupils. This suggests a need to gender accounts of humour and nuance studies of working-class localities with women's perspectives. By addressing the ways in which comic routines may be used to consolidate heterosexual masculinities, we have drawn attention to the *conformist* dynamics of humour in English schools. This approach remains underdeveloped where class-based notions of 'humour as resistance' (Dubberley, 1993) are more readily recorded over the 'reactionary effects' (Walkerdine, 1990) of masculine display. A significant omission in this paper (and the literature more generally) is a careful study of young women's varied uses of humour and the types of fun that subordinate males engage in. An analysis of these styles may provide new understandings of school resistance, parody and subversion – for example, how young women resist male sexism, how camp humour can subvert machismo, how in-group banter among black students can be a challenge to racism. Certainly, the practices observed in this paper suggest that humour is used for positioning pupils within differing dominant and subordinate peer group sexual cultures. The exchanges could define those who belonged (operating as a form of male bonding) and those who did not (operating as a form of 'othering'). [...]

Notes

1   This project was initially funded by the East Midlands Health Authority. The authors take full responsibility for the views expressed here.
2   Quicke and Winter (1994) found examples of boys and girls using mother-insults in their study of year 8 pupils. Gordon *et al.* (1996, p. 12) claim: 'Cussing occurs between boys, between girls and between boys and girls' in schools in Finland.
3   Hewitt (1986, pp. 137–149) found that the ability to mix Creole with Standard English could be of further benefit in adolescent 'slanging matches' in South London.
4   A city centre store, mythologised as a site for prostitution.
5   For a full discussion of ritual insults see Labov (1972, pp. 297–353).
6   Pupils we spoke to described the 'snob' as being 'already clever', a 'creep' and someone who rarely got into trouble.

References

Askew, S. and Ross, C. (1988) *Boys Don't Cry: Boys and Sexism in Education* (Buckingham, Open University Press).

Back, L. (1990) *Racist Name Calling and Developing Anti-racist Initiatives in Youth Work*, Research Paper in Ethnic Relations No. 14, University of Warwick.

Beynon, J. (1989) 'A school for men': an ethnographic case study of routine violence in schooling, in: S. Walker and L. Barton (Eds) *Politics and the Processes of Schooling* (Milton Keynes, Open University Press).

Canaan, J.E. (1986) Why a 'slut' is a 'slut': cautionary tales of middle class teenage morality, in: H. Varanne (Ed.) *Symbolising America* (Lincoln, NG, University of Nebraska Press).

Connell, R. (1989) Cool guys, swots and wimps: the interplay of masculinity and education, *Oxford Review of Education*, 15, pp. 291–303.

Delamont, S. (1989) The nun in the toilet: urban legends and educational research, *Qualitative Studies in Education*, 2, pp. 191–202.

Dubberley, W.S. (1993) Humour as resistance, in: P. Woods and M. Hammersley (Eds) *Gender and Ethnicity in Schools: Ethnographic Accounts* (London, Routledge).

Finch, J. (1984) 'It's great to have someone to talk to': the ethics and politics of interviewing women, in: C. Bell and H. Roberts (Eds) *Social Researching* (London, Routledge & Kegan Paul).

Foucault, M. (1977) *Discipline and Punish: The Birth of the Prison* (London, Penguin).

Freud, S. (1905) *Jokes and their Relation to the Unconscious*, Pelican Freud Library, 6 (Harmondsworth, Penguin).

Gordon, T., Holland, J. and Lahelma, E. (1996) Nation Space: the construction of citizenship and difference in schools, paper presented at the *British Sociological Association Annual Conference*, 1–4 April, University of Reading.

Griffin, C. (1982) The good, the bad and the ugly: images of young women in the labour market, Centre for Contemporary Cultural Studies Stencilled Paper, No. 40, University of Birmingham.

Grfifin, C. (1985) *Typical Girls* (London, Routledge).

Harding, S. (Ed.) (1987) *Feminism and Methodology* (Bloomington, IN, Indiana University Press).

Haywood, C. (1996) 'Out of the curriculum': sex talking, talking sex, *Curriculum Studies*, 4, pp. 229–249.

Hewitt, R. (1986) *White Talk, Black Talk* (Cambridge, Cambridge University Press).

Hollands, R. (1990) *The Long Transition: Class, Culture and Youth Training* (London, Macmillan).

Hollway, W. (1989) *Subjectivity and Method in Psychology* (London, Sage).

Humphries, A. and Smith, P. (1984) Rough-and-tumble in preschool and playground, in: P. Smith (Ed.) *Play in Animals and Humans* (Oxford, Basil Blackwell).

Jones, C. (1985) Sexual tyranny: male violence in a mixed secondary school, in: G. Weiner (Ed.) *Just a Bunch of Girls* (Milton Keynes, Open University Press).

Jones, C. and Mahoney, P. (Eds) (1989) *Learning our Lines* (London, Women's Press).

Jordan, E. (1995) Fighting boys and fantasy play: the construction of masculinity in the early years of school, *Gender and Education*, 7, pp. 69–86.

Kehily, M.J. (1993) Tales we heard in school: sexuality and symbolic boundaries, unpublished M.Soc.Sci. thesis, Department of Cultural Studies, University of Birmingham.

Kehily, M.J. and Nayak, A. (1996) The Christmas kiss: sexuality, storytelling and schooling, *Curriculum Studies*, 4, pp. 211–227.

Labov, W. (1972) *Language in the Inner City: Studies in the Black English Vernacular* (Pennsylvania, PA, University of Pennsylvania Press).

Lees, S. (1986) *Losing Out* (London, Hutchinson).

Lees, S. (1993) *Sugar and Spice* (London, Penguin).

Lyman, P. (1987) The fraternal bond as a joking relationship: a case study of the role of sexist jokes in male group bonding, in: M. Kimmell (Ed.) *Changing Men* (London, Sage).

Mac an Ghaill, M. (1996) Deconstructing heterosexualities within school arenas, *Curriculum Studies*, 4, pp. 191–209.

Nayak, A. and Kehily, M.J. (1996) Playing it straight: masculirities, homophobias and schooling, *Journal of Gender Studies*. 5.2, pp. 211–230.

Phoenix, A. (1994) Practising feminist research: the intersection of gender and race in the research process, in: M. Maynard and J. Purvis (Eds) *Researching Women's Lives from a Feminist Perspective* (London, Taylor and Francis).

Quicke, J. and Winter, C. (1994) Pupils in control: sex talk as an educational resource, *Pastoral Care in Education*, 12, pp. 24–30.

Rhodes, P.J. (1994) Race of interviewer effects: a brief comment, *Sociology*, 28, pp. 547–558.

Skeggs, B. (1991) Challenging masculinity and using sexuality, *British Journal of Sociology of Education*, 12, pp. 127–137.

Stanley, L. and Wise, S. (1993) *Breaking Out Again* (London, Routledge).

Stebbins, R. (1980) The role of humour in teaching: strategy and self expression, in: P. Woods (Ed.) *Teacher Strategies* (London, Croom Helm).

Troyna, B. and Hatcher, R. (1992) *Racism in Children's Lives* (London, Routledge).

Volosinov, V.N. (1973) *Marxism and the Philosophy of Language* (London, Seminar Press).

Walker, R. and Goodson, I. (1977) Humour in the classroom, in: P. Woods and M. Hammersley (Eds) *School Experience* (London, Croom Helm).

Walkerdine, V. (1990) *Schoolgirl Fictions* (London, Verso).

Willis, P. (1976) The class significance of school counter culture, in: M. Hammersley and P. Woods (Eds) *The Process of Schooling* (London, Routledge).

Willis, P. (1977) *Learning to Labour* (Farnborough, Saxon House).

Woods, P. (1976) Having a laugh: an antidote to schooling, in: M. Hammersley and P. Woods (Eds) *The Process of Schooling* (London, Routledge).

Woods, P. (1990) *The Happiest Days? How Pupils Cope with School* (Lewes, Falmer Press).

GENDER-BLIND RACISM IN THE EXPERIENCE OF SCHOOLING AND IDENTITY FORMATION

Cecile Wright, Debbie Weekes and Alex McGlaughlin,
International Journal of Inclusive Education, 3, 4, 1999

Research on pupils' responses to schooling has been greatly influenced by work on resistance (Willis, 1977; Giroux, 1983), feminist research on female adolescents (McRobbie, 1978; Anyon, 1983; Davies, 1984) and the theorizing of 'race' and schooling (Wright, 1987a,b, 1992; Mac an Ghaill, 1988; Gillborn, 1990). Work has begun to detail the production of early masculinities through the exploration of male pupils' responses to school (Connell, 1989; Mac an Ghaill, 1995). School masculinities have also been linked with constructs of 'race' (Sewell, 1997). Thus, there now exists a plethora of research on both gendered and racialized processes of teacher/school stereotyping and pupils resistance and contestation in schools. These various pieces of research have provided important theoretical and empirical insights into the experiences of African-Caribbean and Asian pupils in school. However, in neglecting specific aspects of the interrelation of 'race' and gender in Black pupil identities, some theorists have only offered a partial view of racialized pupils' responses. The focus on 'race' and schooling, as with other research on Black subcultural forms, has too often concentrated on the experiences of black males, thus equating black identities and forms of resistance with masculinity (Mama, 1995; Weekes, 1996). Similarly, the current educational climate has high-lighted the increasing exclusion of African-Caribbean males from school, and focused on the anti-school attitudes of black male pupils. This entirely negates the important work that has shown black pupils' pro-, as well as anti-, school responses within education (Fuller, 1982; Furlong, 1984; Sewell, 1997)....

Important work is increasingly conducted on black masculinities in schooling, but research needs to build on that of Mirza (1992), Fuller (1982) and Riley (1985) to address how schools also produce black femininities. Feminist work in this area has tended to subsume the construct of 'race' within that of gender (McRobbie, 1978). Therefore, based on a study of school exclusions within five schools in a large education authority, this chapter explores the adaptations of both black male and female pupils to school, to teacher–pupil relationships and to the experience of school sanction.

The study

The data presented and discussed here are derived from a much broader ethnographic study of school exclusions conducted in a large local education authority in the Midlands.[1] The aims were to explore and document the nature and pattern of secondary school exclusions of pupils from ethnic groups in general and to identify the school processes which may lead to the exclusion of African-Caribbean pupils in particular.... In brief, the study involved surveying all secondary schools in one county education authority, to assess the overall pattern of exclusions; extensive interviews with pupils and staff in five representative secondary schools; and additional interviews with a small group of African-Caribbean male pupils who had experienced permanent exclusion from school.

The bulk of the research was conducted within the five selected schools, which varied according to their local authority status, the characteristics of the local catchment area and the nature of their pupil intake.... The schools were primarily selected according to the proportion of their pupils from ethnic backgrounds. Represented among the five selected for study were schools with low, average or higher than average proportions of African and African-Caribbean pupils.... A total of 62 pupils and 52 members of teaching staff were interviewed from the five schools in the research sample. Of these pupils, 25 were of African-Caribbean/mixed parentage. The pupils interviewed were from Years 9 and 10 only (age range 13–15 years). As far as possible, nine pupils from each year group and an even mix of African-Caribbean, Asian and white pupils were selected for interview. The pupils were recruited for interview by Heads of Year, with each pupil selected either having previously been excluded from school, or having experienced a number of school sanctions (i.e. being withdrawn from lessons, referred to on-site units or placed on report). Three of the nine pupils from each year were white, three Asian and three African-Caribbean. The educational abilities of the pupils varied. In addition to these pupils, 11 African-Caribbean young people and their parents were also interviewed. These young people had experienced permanent and fixed period exclusions from other schools in the local authority.

Testimonies are provided below from the pupils and senior teachers at two out of the five schools that participated in the research. These testimonies have been used to highlight that the nature of the school attended had a certain influence on the adaptations of pupils to schooling and education that equally affected the responses of teaching staff to issues surrounding black pupil behaviour. The majority of the pupil testimonies are derived from African-Caribbean pupils. The schools will simply be referred to as A and B. School A was situated in the middle of a fairly wealthy suburb in the city, and performed very well within the education authority in terms of GCSE A–C grades obtained. The majority of the pupil population was drawn from the immediate area and, therefore, many of the pupils came from professional families. There was a small but increasing African-Caribbean and Asian population, both in the area and the school. School A was under local authority control. School B was situated near a fairly large housing estate in the centre of the city. It would take excluded pupils from a nearby technology school and had a greater number of Black and Asian pupils than school A. There was a greater focus on 'race' as illustrated by a number of displays on the walls. School B had recently introduced a new exclusion policy and was also under local authority control. The testimonies provided here are not intended to be representative. Indeed the study as a whole can only offer a snapshot of the nature of school exclusions as experienced by the participating teachers, pupils and their parents over a particular period of time.

Gendering 'race'

In looking at the responses of both minority ethnic male and female pupils to schooling, the chapter builds upon the work of black feminists who have historically argued for the interrelation of 'race' and gender in the exploration of black experiences (Collins, 1990; Mama, 1995). There is much scope within the area of secondary education for black feminist analysis (Mirza, 1992). However, for some black feminists, the need to focus on interrelating gender and 'race' within education has meant rejecting the way that mainstream feminism has subsumed constructs of 'race' within those of gender when exploring female pupils (Bryan *et al.*, 1984). In view of this it has been argued that:

> Black women cannot afford to look at our experience of Britain's education system merely from our perspective as women: this would be to over-simplify the realities we face in the classroom. For Black schoolgirls, sexism has, it is true, played an insidious role in our lives. It has influenced our already limited career choices and has scarred our already tarnished self-image. But it is *racism* that has determined the schools we can attend and the quality of the education we receive in them.
>
> (Bryan *et al.*, 1984, p. 58)

These are important considerations when exploring the experiences of black female pupils' in schools, particularly in relation to the way they may experience teacher stereotyping. However, if black feminist perspectives are to be made integral to an analysis of black female and male experiences within education, the complex ways in which gender and race intersect for black pupils, require examination. This includes an acknowledgement that gender is not restricted to the exploration of femininity and, therefore, that sexism is not the only modality through which gender is experienced.

[. . .]

   Attempts to explain the differing adaptations of black male and female pupils to schooling have been rare. Mac an Ghaill's (1988) study of teacher pupil relations offered an analysis of the 'Black Sisters' – a group of high achieving African-Caribbean and Asian female students – and of the 'Rasta Heads' and 'Asian Warriors' who were male pupils at the school under study. Though that study provided a useful examination of gendered and racialized forms of pupil resistance, comparison was only made of the strategies adopted by the African-Caribbean and Asian males, since the 'Black Sisters' were older college students. But like the respondents in the work of Fuller (1982) and Mirza (1992), the 'Black Sisters' in Mac an Ghaill's (1988) study highlight the fact that strategies other than disaffection are open to black pupils. However, the experiences of the black female members of this group were not looked at explicitly. Other work has suggested that due to the prominence of female-headed households within many African-Caribbean families, and the participation of black women in the labour market, young black females acquire gendered identities which differ to those of both white females and black males (Phoenix, 1988). Such theorizing of gendered differences among black adolescents has been used to explain differing adaptations and rates of academic achievement (Woods, 1990). However, Mirza (1992) has criticized work which has attempted to explore the higher rates of academic achievement among African-Caribbean females, as often this work assumes that their motivation stems from their mothers' heightened commitment to occupational statuses, or, as in the work of Fuller (1982), suggests that black females wish to prove their self-worth both to parents and to black male peers. These theoretical assumptions position black women within the stereotype of the 'superwoman' and negate the experiences of black females in families that are not female-headed. They also fail adequately to theorize the experiences of black males, through suggesting that they have negative attitudes towards black female peers, or reducing them to the status of absent black fathers.

Research on black pupils' adaptations to schooling has, however, pointed towards aspects of community life upon which black pupils are seen to draw in their schooling experiences. The relationship between black pupils and black communities must be viewed as a complex process of negotiation with cultural forms. Black pupils (particularly male) may reject the forms of knowledge available within schools and instead draw on alternative knowledge sources situated within their communities (Sewell, 1997). Conversely, teachers within schools have been documented as reducing the behaviour of black pupils precisely to these cultural community forms (Mac an Ghaill, 1988). To be viewed as exhibiting these cultural community forms, for example, may well inhibit a young male's educational opportunities within school. As Sewell (1997) argues within his study of black masculinities, teachers would refer to the musical forms consumed by many of the black males as an explanation for their aggression and anti-school behaviour. Within the study on which this paper is based, teachers suggested they understood that the behaviour of some black pupils was related to their experiences of racial attacks and abuse within their communities. However, these processes of understanding the experiences of black pupils can often be read in pathological ways. The explanations offered by some teaching staff within our study indicated that they were attempting to understand, and hence counter, the difficulties that their pupils were experiencing. However, the link between a black pupil's unacceptable behaviour at school and the explanation provided for this behaviour by his/her teacher was often quite tenuous.... Here a white male teacher attempts to provide his own theory as to why black and white pupils may experience school differently.

> I have noticed that we have West Indian groups of lads, grouping together as Black kids and running around. I say running because they are ever so gregarious...that's a social thing as well, of course you get White kids but they don't seem to be [as] they...[black kids]'re always singing and dancing and they're much more physically expressive. Now that in itself makes them noticed more and they're really keen on developing an identity. And there's a special uniform that they wear and if they can help it, they'll get it into school...[I mean] even dreadlocks, that's fine, but when they're like walking around with scarves across their face, with all of them hidden. That's fine, that's brilliant. Come into the classroom, coats off and sit down but they'll bring it into the classroom. And we've got one or two of these groups with strong leaders who are actually coming out with the racist thing like 'it's because I'm black that you're doing this'. And that really irritates me because it's not, it's because they're not taking their bloody scarves off. So they're very racially aware as well. Now there's no doubt, no doubt that they get racial abuse outside school, in school and [their] parents have as well and you can see where they're coming from.
>
> (Mr Johnson, teacher, school A)

This teacher acknowledges that the experience of racial abuse plays a huge part in the construction of these young males' identities, but in his comments seems to reduce the definition of racism to the experience of racial name-calling, or attack. He fails to recognize the multifaceted forms that racism takes, in terms of being situated within institutional (schooling) practices and responses to black pupils. Additionally, though an understanding of the group's racialized background is expressed here, Mr Johnson suggests that the racial identities of these boys, and the signifiers associated with them (coats, scarves, etc.), prevented them from participating adequately in classroom interactions. It is also important to note that though the wearing of scarves was seen by this teacher to have particular cultural currency for young black males, the majority of pupils also wore scarves in similar ways. For the black pupils in this group, the cultural currency was more evident in their abilities to group together within a predominantly white setting. The coats and hats worn were indicative of wider styles worn by African-Caribbean, and increasingly Asian and white, adolescents, in their communities.

What is important from the teacher's quote is that the discussion of racial identity is restricted to that of black *males*. Within the same school, a friendship group of Year 10 black females also existed alongside the male groupings. The response of the teacher cited above to issues of 'race' and the adaptation to schooling of black pupils generally, appeared to begin with a discussion of black masculinity. The work on schooling masculinities, which is a rapidly developing area of research, has arisen at least partly in response to the readiness with which schools define troublesome behaviour both as masculine and as increasingly racialized.

Much of the black male pupil response documented within these studies, notes that reactions to schooling are based on the way that disaffection and disruption is equated with black masculinity (Mac an Ghaill, 1995; Sewell, 1997). Research has also drawn attention to the issue of black females responding in empathetic ways to the treatment they feel their African-Caribbean male peers experience within schools (Wright, 1985, 1987a,b; Mac an Ghaill, 1988). Additionally, Asian pupils often acknowledge the equating of African-Caribbean masculinity with disruption. They have also been shown to display identities that incorporate empathy for their peers (Mac an Ghaill, 1988; Gillborn, 1990).

The varying nature of these responses to schooling by racialized pupils needs to be explored. This will then provide a wider picture of black responses to the issue of school sanction and exclusion. In addition, the responses/behaviours of African-Caribbean and Asian students are examined in conjunction with the opinions of some of their senior teachers. [...] These accounts will illustrate that the issue of exclusion, and the environment and context within which it takes place, is fraught with tensions both for senior teachers and their pupils....

Racializing school exclusions

The concept of school exclusions has become heavily racialized over recent years. Research highlights the over representation of black pupils in exclusion statistics (Bourne *et al.*, 1994; Parsons *et al.*, 1995; OFSTED, 1996; Osler, 1997; Smith, 1998). Within the schools participating in the research, the issue of increasing exclusions of black pupils gave both teachers and pupils cause for great concern.... All head and senior teachers felt that school exclusion was an essential part of managing discipline and most would talk about the issue of increasing school exclusions in non-racial ways. However, the occurrence of fixed period exclusions in one particular school involved increasing numbers of black pupils, and though the discourse around the issue of exclusions was not racial, the representation of particular groups of pupils within the school's statistics clearly was. This was an issue that was clearly apparent to some of the black pupils interviewed, who felt that many of the sanctions available to the school were overused. However, where staff attempted to look at these issues in order to counter them, pupils rejected their efforts.

> A while back there was loads of tension between black students and the teachers. They even set up a...thing for black students where Mr Mills was there, and another teacher and he [headteacher] was like asking us why we was getting into so much trouble and stuff like this. And it happened once...and then they said 'oh this is going to happen every week'. Then the students were OK about it, well not OK about it, we were quite annoyed because it was just like black students.... He said it was going to happen every week, and we had one. And that was ages ago, and it's not happened again.... There was so much going on with black students that something had to be done.... The black students were getting into trouble, getting a bad reputation.... The popular black students, they seem to get in more trouble than everybody else, it's like...if you're black in this school, you've got to be quiet, like a good little black person, you can't be popular. You're not allowed to be popular, and that's why they were getting so much trouble.
>
> (Aaron, Year 10 pupil, school B)

The black pupils, whom Aaron speaks of, rejected being 'singled out' by the headteacher, yet wanted a forum within which they could discuss their experiences. The headteacher had racialized the issue of disruption and other pupils felt this negated his attempt to introduce 'discussions'. However, the headteacher felt that his efforts had had a positive effect on his pupils,...

> The number of black kids excluded has dropped right down. It will still be higher than the white pupils but again it's continued this term Who knows what the reason is for that? I'd like to believe that as a result of that meeting that black pupils feel we're concerned about them, that we don't want them to be excluded, whereas there might have been a perception before that that 'they want to get rid of the black kids, we're always being excluded'. I just didn't know whether that was true or not I was talking to [a senior teacher] and she thought the meeting was a very positive one but I think she felt it wouldn't be a good thing to give a sense of identity to a certain group of pupils who are selected out as being in danger of exclusion. Because it's a labelling process.
>
> (Headteacher school B)

The staff had felt the process of talking to the black pupils about the issue of discipline and exclusion had been positive. However, the advice given to the headteacher about the dangers of labelling a particular group of pupils illustrated that careful consideration had not been given to the exercise. The meeting itself, and changes in school behaviour policy had created tensions among some of the older black pupils, because of the way that discipline and school exclusion had seemingly become racialized:

> *Chantel*   Do you know how many black pupils he's [the headteacher]
> *(Year 10 pupil,* excluded? Seventeen last time I looked. I was the first black
> *school B):*   girl to be excluded. It was all boys and then we...it was like

we was putting up a stubborn way. If he spoke to us we would just walk off and kiss our teeth after him. He started excluding white people to style it out. He said 'we're going to kick all the clowns out'....

Researcher: How have you all reacted to that?

Chantel: Bad. Every time he speaks to us we don't listen to him. It makes us turn bad if you know what I mean. It like causes... [I mean] he calls everyone a clown and only excludes black people. He must think we'll react in a [certain] way to that. We're bound to react in a bad way.

In contrast, the headteacher spoke about his confusion as to why the need to exclude black pupils was continuing at the school, despite his attempts to address the issue, and failed to see that the pupils had perceived these attempts to be racially biased rather than helpful. Lines of communication had clearly broken down and conflict between staff and black pupils, often regardless of the racial background of the teacher, was invariably perceived to be racial by the pupils that we interviewed.

Differential experiences

Within this context of racialization it is possible to map out the differentiating responses of pupils to the threat of school exclusion. Chantel spoke of a response to the issue of exclusion that was not gender-specific. Indeed, some of the pupils in the study responded in a way that cut across their racial and gendered position. But for one of the young women interviewed, differences between male and female pupils were noted. Samantha, an African-Caribbean Year 10 pupil in school A, was also a member of a large group of students, who would often mix with the group of African-Caribbean males mentioned earlier by the teacher from school A. Her response to staff perceptions of her group and black pupils generally, was both one of concern and one that berated black male pupils for the way they would confront their teachers. Thus, she saw her response as different from those of her male peers.

Samantha (Year 10 pupil, school A): If someone starts on us, we'll start back....I think that's why the teachers have picked up on it. It's just got stupid now [because] if any little thing happens, 'it's those Year 10 girls'. Especially if there was a fight [and] all the black people are together...'cause some of them are black, some of the teachers are intimidated by that as well because it's a big group and maybe they don't know how to deal with it or whatever. So the first instance of [anything]...[they say] 'right get inside, something's going to happen', and that's the only way they can deal with it....And like with the boys as well, they're like half-caste and black. But they [boys] make it worse anyway cause, they just, they can't keep quiet, they just have to mouth off. They should just stand still and go 'hmm' [imitates raising eyebrows at imaginary teacher] and talk about it later.

Researcher: Is that what you do?

Samantha: That's the best way. Keep 'em sweet [imitates slowly nodding her head to imaginary teacher] and just like walk off.

Samantha realized that she was in a group that was viewed in a particular way by some staff. It is worth noting that the school had a small minority ethnic pupil population and many of these pupils were very close and spent much of their time with each other. Samantha also highlights that there are differential ways in which the African-Caribbean males and females respond to their construction as 'problematic'. Samantha felt it important to talk with her peers and family members about interactions with teachers, whereas she felt that the boys were too eager to confront teachers with their complaints. However if involved in a disagreement, she would also engage in verbal interchange with subject teachers. The head of year group that Samantha was in also commented on the behaviour of the group of girls with whom Samantha was friendly:

> Samantha is somebody who, at the moment, is giving me a lot of cause for concern. She's a bright girl. She's got a lot of potential. Causes an awful lot of problems with regard to friendships with other girls. Other girls can be at times quite intimidated and threatened by her. [She] has a little Mafia like friendship group around her, who when they move around school at times can make other children feel... [She] has been involved in fights at times. At the moment is against the system by being perpetually late...when challenged about it doesn't really understand why you are picking on her.
>
> (Mrs Frank, Head of Year, school A)

The group of young women who were part of Samantha's peer group had similar qualities to those of the young black and white women called the 'Posse' in Mac an Ghaill's (1995) study. Pupils often reacted to Samantha and her friends on the basis of their reputation for fighting in the school, and Samantha felt that because of this, if another pupil attempted to provoke her, teachers would think them to be the innocent party. It is of interest that Mac an Ghaill should view the group of young women in his study as adapting to schooling in masculine ways. Connolly's (1995) work on masculinity illustrated that white male peers would attempt to provoke African-Caribbean male pupils who had 'fighting' reputations, to challenge their masculinities. The ability to fight in school, therefore, has specific masculine connotations. However, to equate the behaviour of Samantha and her friends with masculinity, reinforces specific 'controlling images' of black women as 'non-feminine' (Collins, 1990). These racialized stereotypes interact with those held by teachers generally of young women who subvert traditional definitions of femininity, as documented in feminist theorizing (Davies, 1984). That the young black women in this peer group constructed themselves in ways that led to them being considered 'non-feminine' (they would integrate the wearing of exceptionally short skirts with big coats, trainers and scarves) situates the nature of their response.

Although the issue of school exclusion was not as heavily racialized in school A as it was in school B, some of the staff interviewed (such as Mr Johnson and Mrs Frank), felt that pupils grouping together ethnically was problematic... Within both schools, therefore, the ill feeling that emerged out of often racially charged classrooms and corridors made it difficult for staff to discuss issues with pupils. It is worth noting that only black female pupils commented on the difference in the ways that black male and female pupils would interact with staff. However, when the teachers were asked about the relationship they had with their pupils from an ethnic background, for the most part they would initially only mention African-Caribbean boys. Like Mr Johnson, another senior teacher

[Mr Peters] ... only talked about the black male pupils he had observed:

Mr Peters (teacher, school A):	We 've got some black kids, and they seem, not all, but a lot of them, to hang around with their own peers within a group. They have their own subculture. Try to bend the uniform so they can dress in whatever way and so when they're together, some of them don't perform as well as they should do, because, yet again, they want to be one of the boys. And they're bright, there's no problem in that respect, it's just they want to be different – that's understandable perhaps – but it does affect the way they learn. Perhaps they do see school differently to other people ... black lads, really
Researcher:	Lads more than the girls?
Mr Peters:	Oh yes. There's no problem with the girls at all. Year 7 lads will come in, they will see the Year 9 lads and want to be a member of that group.

Power and powerlessness

The black female pupil quoted above, who had developed a reputation equated with non-feminine behaviour, can be seen to derive relative forms of power from her position within the school. However, the nature of the power or powerlessness that pupils experienced as they attempted to respond to the racializing of sanctions and exclusion was to a certain extent mediated through their gendered positions. Their responses related to their status as pupils within school, viewed in relation to teachers and the school in general. But as Riddell (1989, p. 184) has argued, 'for many pupils, education is experienced as a form of repression', and the area of school sanctions made this power relationship even more evident. Many of the pupils in the study, regardless of their racial background, talked about the ways they attempted to subvert the traditional relationship of teacher as powerful, student as powerless. The responses of the African-Caribbean and Asian pupils showed their awareness that power was also mediated through particular gendered and racialized concerns. Therefore, it would be simplistic to assume that these pupils reacted against an unequal power differential without acknowledging the way that their own racial and gendered backgrounds affected their experiences. [. . .]

The racialized tension within school B had placed an increased focus on the use of exclusion by senior members of staff. Hence, the possibility of experiencing an exclusion here was perceived to be far greater by African-Caribbean pupils. Chantel talked above about her relationship with her headteacher. However, she also talked of a response where her interactions with staff made her feel powerless.

She's [teacher] got a big problem She said something racist to me. I can't remember the words but I reported it and [the headteacher] says 'you'll find that Miss Beverage is not racist because she is in the black bullying group'. Sometimes we just go in the [section 11] room and cry our eyes out. We just cry, because we report it, report it and no one does anything. So they wonder why we turn bad. [They say], 'the best thing to do with Chantel is to chuck her out before the lesson starts'. I go home and I feel like ... I've just started my period.

(Chantel, Year 10 pupil, school B)

Chantel's response to tensions within her school go beyond the interchanges between staff and pupils so often seen by teachers as pupil inability to take responsibility for their behaviour. Chantel's inability to persuade senior staff of her concerns is one mediated through both her racial background and her gendered position.

> Me and Donna were in assembly and this white boy was talking. Miss Beverage came up [to us] and said 'You two, out now!'. Me and Donna looked at each other and said 'What are you talking about?', and then she said we were talking and we didn't even say one word. Mr Mills [headteacher] sent us to his office, gave us a detention and everything. But we wouldn't go because we didn't do nothing and we didn't say anything. So anyway, they were saying that we were talking and everything and we just said 'what's your problem? What's your problem with black people?' and [Mr Mills] said 'Are you trying to say we are racist?' We says 'No. We're just standing up like fools saying it for no reason!' And Donna kissed her teeth. So he says 'Don't think I don't know what that means'...and he started shouting 'get out of this school, you are going to be excluded' [We said] '...we haven't done anything wrong'. Then Miss Beverage came out and we had two teachers shouting at us. We got punished. Donna got excluded and she had to apologize – for nothing, for nothing! Donna started crying when she walked out of his office because she was saying sorry for no reason
>
> (Chantel, Year 10 pupil, school B)

Both Donna and Chantel have reacted to their powerless status in the pupil–teacher/school relationship. It appears that the powerlessness, embedded within their inability to convince the two teachers that they had not in fact been talking in assembly, engenders an almost helpless feeling. They also avoid displaying this helplessness to the teachers who are sanctioning them. Chantel goes into a separate room, and Donna waited until she had left the headteacher's office. Thus, they attempt to extract power from the interactions with teachers at every available opportunity by verbally challenging decisions which they feel to be illegitimate.

In contrast, one Pakistani male pupil responded to his interactions with teachers by challenging the status of his teachers. Although Chantel and Donna, had challenged the decisions taken by generally teachers, Shrafid, below, challenged the authority of his teacher as an individual:

> You know these teachers, I think they're [like] normal people who walk around on the street.... When they haven't got white shirts, trousers on, some of 'em got suits on...some of' em have got glasses on, they're all the same to me....Outside school they're nothing. They're nothing at all. Inside school they're the teachers, but no teacher could hit me in this school, neither can they touch me. This teacher that touched me, he won't touch me again 'cause I'd break his fingers. Near the sports hall, he started poking me in my chest, like a dog, y'know. Whack, whack saying 'Don't you want to do PE?' I said 'sir, I'm grabbing your hands now, and I'm putting them back there where it belongs. Don't touch my chest, speak with your mouth, don't speak with your fingers'. [Then] he just walked away.
>
> (Shrafid, Year 10 pupil, school B)

Shrafid suggests that, as teachers are the same as other individuals outside of school, the status and power they confer upon themselves is illegitimate. Though he uses verbal interchange in a similar way to the other pupils, above, to effect his contesting of teacher status, he also implies a threat of physical violence. Embedded within Shrafid's response is an acknowledgement of the illegitimacy of the sports teacher's actions. Certain forms of physical contact by teachers as a form of school sanction are illegal within schools. Therefore, Shrafid cannot be rendered powerless to a teacher's response which is legally as well as personally constructed as illegitimate. Shrafid's response is not constructed through 'race' but rather the nature of teacher power. However, it also signifies a symbolic confrontation between the racialized background of the pupil and the teacher. This is particularly clear when this, and the other teacher–pupil interactions at school B, are set within the school's increased surveillance of black pupils through the threat of school exclusion.

Shrafid's ability to reject the status of teachers was related to his own greater status within his community and among his peers in the area in which he lived. Chantel and Donna also had varied status (and reputation) within the school. Outside of school, however, they were restricted to a certain extent by their gendered positions from engaging with others outside in the streets and communities (McRobbie, 1978, 1991). Nevertheless, it would be too simplistic to reduce the responses of Shrafid, Chantel and Donna to expressions of masculinity and femininity. The effect of power within their interactions structured various racial and gendered responses. Shrafid was not subject to similar racialized forms of teacher surveillance as Chantel and Donna due to his Pakistani background, which may have made it less restrictive for him to challenge his sports teacher. The racializing of the threat of school exclusion in this case related specifically to African-Caribbean pupils. [. . .]

Conclusion

This chapter has explored the differential responses of a small group of pupils to schooling. Though there were clearly some important gendered differences in the way black pupils adapted to school, the more prominent differentials and similarities were based on 'race'. For example, the greater surveillance of African-Caribbean pupils (both male and female) in both schools illustrated that the group was homogenized by teachers. Gendered differences were also evident. For example, Samantha's group of female peers was referred to as a 'particularly nasty group of girls'. Such a comment serves to underscore feminist theory, which points to the way in which female deviance is individualized and responded to on the basis of inappropriate femininity (Davies, 1984; Robinson, 1992). Regardless of this however, the gender of the group became subsumed within their presence as challenging African-Caribbean students. Thus, it is the way schools constructed blackness, which is the main issue here. As Back (1996, p. 178) has argued: 'racist common sense is not "gender blind". But equally, the experience of racisms is not always gender specific. In this way racist discourse differentiates between gendered black subjects and at the same time unifies them in racialized social groupings'. However, it was also noticeable that little reference was made to the black female groupings in school B, and that the headteacher there considered the African-Caribbean male pupils to pose specific discipline problems. Thus, the process of equating 'race' with disruption is not a simple linear development, it is based around the way that 'race' has historically been gendered in the image of the black male (Wallace, 1979; Mercer and Julien, 1988; hooks, 1991; Mama, 1995). Teachers and schools which racialize (and, hence, gender) notions of non-conformity, disruption and school sanction, contribute to the equating of 'race' with masculinity, which has important implications for theorizing how *all* pupils adapt to these processes. Clearly a black feminist perspective on this issue might interrogate the extent to which 'race' is the prominent feature in black pupil identities.

Note

1   Black refers to children who have at least one parent of African-Caribbean heritage.

References

Anyon, J. (1983) Intersections of gender and class: accommodation and resistance by work-ing class and affluent females to contradictory sex-role ideologies. In S. Walker and L. Burton (eds), *Gender, Class and Education* Lewes: Falmer).

Back, L. (1996) *New Ethnicities and Urban Culture: Racisms and Multiculture in Young Lives* (London: UCL Press).

Bourne, J., Bridges, L. and Searle, C. (1994) *Outcast England: How Schools Exclude Black children* (London: Institute of Race Relations).

Bryan, B., Dadzie, S. and Scafe, S. (1984) *Heart of the Race* (London: Virago).

Collins, P. (1990) *Black Feminist Thought* (New York: Routledge).

Connolly, P. (1995) Racism, masculine peer group relations and the schooling of African Caribbean infant boys. *British Journal of Sociology of Education*, 16, 75–92.

Davies, L. (1984) *Pupil Power: Deviance and Gender in Education* (Lewes: Falmer).

Fuller, M. (1982) Young, female and black. In E. Cashmore and B. Troyna (eds), *Blade Youth in Crisis* (London: Allen & Unwin).

Furlong, M. (1984) Inequality: gender, race and class. Unit 27, Course E205, *Conflict and Change in Education* (Milton Keynes: Open University Press).

Gillborn, D. (1990) *'Race' Ethnicity and Education: Teaching and Learning in Multi-ethnic Schools* (London: Unwin Hyman).

Giroux, H. (1983) *Theory and Resistance in Education: A Pedagogy for the Opposition* (London: Heineman).

hooks, B. (1991) *Yearning: Race, Gender and Cultural Politics* (London: Turnaround).

Mac an Ghaill, M. (1988) *Young, Gifted and Black* (Milton Keynes: Open University Press).

Mac an Ghaill, M. (1995) *The Making of Men: Masculinities, Sexualities and Schooling* (Milton Keynes: Open University Press).

Mama, A. (1995) *Beyond the Masks: Race, Gender and Subjectivity* (London: Routledge).

McRobbie, A. (1978) Working class girls and the culture of femininity. In Women's Study Group (eds), *Women Take Issue: Aspects of Women's Subordination* (Women's Study Group).

McRobbie, A. (1991) *Feminism and Youth Culture from 'Jackie' to 'Just Seventeen'* (London: Macmillan).

Mercer, K. and Julien, I. (1988) Race, sexual politics and black masculinity: A Dossier. In R. Chapman and J. Rutherford (eds), *Male Order: Unwrapping Masculinities* (London: Lawrence & Wishart), 97–164.

Mirza, H. (1992) *Young, Female and Black* (London: Routledge).

Office for Standards in Education (1996) *Exclusions from Secondary Schools 1995/6* (London: OFSTED).

Osler, A. (1997) *Exclusion from School and Racial Equality* (London: Commission for Racial Equality).

Parsons, C., Hailes, J., Howlett, K., Davies, A., Driscoll, P. and Ross, L. (1995) *National Survey of Local Education Authorities' Policies and Procedures for the Identification of, and Provision for, Children who are Out of School by Reason of Exclusion or Otherwise* (London: Department for Education).

Phoenix, A. (1988) Narrow definitions of culture: the case of early motherhood. In S. Westwood and P. Bhachu (eds), *Enterprising Women* (London: Routledge).

Riddell, S. (1989) Pupils, resistance and gender codes: a study of classroom encounters. *Gender and Education*, 1, 183–197.

Riley, K. (1985) Black girls speak for themselves. In G. Weiner (ed.), *Just a Bunch of Girls* (Milton Keynes: Open University Press), 63–76.

Robinson, K. (1992) Class-room discipline: power, resistance and gender. A look at teacher perspectives. *Gender and Education*, 4, 273–287.

Sewell, T. (1997) *Black Masculinities and Schooling: How Black Boys Survive Modern Schooling* (Stoke-on-Trent: Trentham).

Smith, R. (1998) *No Lessons Learnt: A Survey of School Exclusions* (London: Children's Society).

Wallace, M. (1979) *Black Macho and the Myth of the Superwoman* (London: John Calder).

Weekes, D. (1996) Discourses of blackness and the construction of black femininity. Paper presented to the British Psychological Society Annual Conference.

Willis, P. (1977) *Learning to Labour: How Working Class Kids get Working Class Jobs* (Aldershot: Saxon House).

Woods, P. (1990) *The Happiest Days? How Pupils Cope with Schools* (Lewes: Falmer).

Wright, C. (1985) School processes – an ethnographic study. In J. Eggleston, D. Dunn and M. Anjali (eds), *Education for Some: The Educational and Vocational Experiences of 15–18 Year Old Members of Minority Ethnic Groups* (Stoke-on-Trent: Trentham).

Wright, C. (1987a) Black students – white teachers. In B. Troyna (ed.), *Racial Inequality in Education* (London: Tavistock).

Wright, C. (1987b) The relations between teachers and Afro-Caribbean pupils: observing multi-racial classrooms. In G. Weiner and M. Arnot (eds), *Gender Under Scrutiny: New Inquiries in Education* (London: Hutchinson).

Wright, C. (1992) *Race Relations in the Primary School* (London: David Fulton).

PART 4

KNOWLEDGE AND PEDAGOGY

CHAPTER 12

BOYS DON'T WRITE ROMANCE

The construction of knowledge and social gender identities in English classrooms

Gabrielle Ivinson and Patricia Murphy, *Pedagogy,*
Culture and Society, 11, 1, 2003

Social and political context of the study

The chapter reports part of a wider study that has been investigating how schools in the United Kingdom have been reacting to the moral panic about boys 'under achievement', particularly in English. ... Local education authorities and schools have been obliged to respond to this by introducing ameliorative strategies to support boys' learning (Murphy and Ivinson, 2000). These strategies advocated at policy level treat boys and girls as homogeneous groups, and only differentiate between them in terms of achievement. We have been investigating the impact of some of these strategies, such as gendered seating (boy-girl-boy) and single sex teaching from a sociocultural perspective, in order to make visible the intended and unintended effects on students' access to subject knowledge of treating boys and girls in this way. [. . .]

The study

Monks Secondary School, where the comparative case study took place, had instigated what they called, 'The Year of the Boy'. The two English teachers in the study had employed different, but related ameliorative strategies that focused attention on the needs of low achieving boys and assumed for girls an unproblematic peer-tutoring role. In classroom A, all the average and high achieving boys had been placed together. In classroom B, the other boys in the year had been dispersed with mixed ability girls in a ratio of 2 : 1 girls to boys. Gendered seating (boy-girl-boy) was also introduced. Both teachers agreed to teach the same creative writing activity to their year 10 classes (students aged 14–15). This chapter describes how each setting influenced the way teachers using the same activity realised (recontextualised) subject knowledge.

Understanding learning and settings

Sociocultural perspectives view learning as a social practice that takes place within social settings. Learning involves 'understanding and participation in on-going activity' (Lave, 1996, p. 9) in social settings. Each learning instance involves a process of active appropriation that builds on what went on before. The process transforms participants and settings according to a dialectical relationship

(Vygotsky, 1978, 1986). Context, persons and worlds are inescapably flexible and changing (Lave, 1996, p. 5).

When Lave first elaborated situated learning through her notion of 'setting for activity' (Lave, 1988) she made a distinction between arena and setting. Arena signals an analytical focus that works at the level of the institution, and accounts for those aspects of a practice that endure before and after any one individual's experience. In her original example, which described the learning that takes place through the practice of shopping, supermarkets were arenas and shoppers' experiences within these were settings. The supermarket was outside the individual and yet encompassed the individual. Lave defined an arena as a 'physically, economically, politically and socially organised space-in-time' (Lave, 1988, p. 150). Setting was used to foreground subjective experiences within local contexts. For example, while searching for particular grocery items, some aisles in the supermarket will be salient to one shopper, while others pass relatively unnoticed. For the individual, the supermarket is experienced as a 'repeatedly experienced, personally ordered and edited version of the arena' (Lave, 1988), which is a setting.

When researching schools there has been difficulty in explaining how social forces penetrate classrooms and influence individual learning. The way that Lave conceptualises the relationship between arena and settings, that is that the latter is encompassed by the former, was further elaborated by Lave and Wenger (1991) who consider that there are 'common processes inherent in the production of changing persons and changing communities of practice' (Lave and Wenger, 1991, p. 55). This perspective therefore recognises that sociohistorical and political forces shape activities enacted in schools. When classrooms are viewed as social settings in which students participate, we can no longer omit what students bring to classrooms as a consequence of their participation in a myriad of other social contexts. What is learned, therefore, has to be viewed as appropriation that will be mediated by student's understanding and therefore, '...is likely to involve many peripheral features of which the teacher is unaware, but which collectively make sense to the learner' (Brown and Duguid, 1993, p. 11).

The social world of gender

We understand gender as a hegemonic social representation (Moscovici, 1976, 1984, 2001; Duveen and Lloyd, 1990; Lloyd and Duveen, 1992; Ivinson, 2002) that circulates as a set of ideas, social norms, conventions and associations within societies. Social representations of gender ensure that practices can become marked as masculine or feminine, and therefore entail legitimate ways to be a boy/man or a girl/woman. As individuals participate in social arenas and their practices, they develop social identities of which subject or gender identities are parts. Duveen elaborated social identities by referring to 'the transition from extended identities as children are incorporated into the social world through the actions of others, to internalised identities as children become independent actors in the field of gender' (Duveen, 2001, p. 264). As Fivush observes 'gender [thus] moves beyond knowing which behaviours are deemed appropriate for females and males to become a self-regulating system' (1998, p. 60): a system that needs to be understood as an evolving set of values and activities. Research suggests that as a consequence of this self-regulating process, boys and girls develop common sense knowledge, attitudes and interests that differ in significant respects. The common sense knowledge that is available to boys on the one hand, and girls on the other, has common characteristics (Browne and Ross, 1991;

Kimbell *et al.*, 1991; Davies and Brember, 1995; Murphy, 1996, 1997, 1999; White, 1996; Cooper and Dunne, 2000).

Within classroom settings, social representations such as gender are actively reconstructed through the activities of teachers and students; they are not given (Connell, 1987). Classroom settings therefore present students with an edited version of the gender arena. As students participate in classroom practice they experience gender as a range of social possibilities or constraints about what they can legitimately say, do, write and behave as a boy or as a girl, as they attempt to realise the skills, know-how and practices that make up subject knowledge. We focused on the interaction between individual student's knowledge about gender and their need to negotiate a social gender identity within the setting.

Activity within classroom settings, situated within matrices of other social contexts, can either reinforce or resist the social norms that are maintained in other social arenas. Hegemonic social representations of gender may be reinforced, challenged or transformed through classroom practice. We were interested in how students resolved and managed social gender identities that can become fractured and transformed as they encounter multiple arenas, such as families, peer groups, leisure activities and classrooms. We were concerned with how students' experiences of classroom settings facilitated or disallowed their participation in English (disciplinary) practices.

We consider the transformation of social identities to be the very foundation of learning. For example, the production of a creative writing text can be seen, at least in part, as the expression of a social gender identity (Penuel and Wertsch, 1995; Duveen, 2001) within a classroom setting. The individual trajectories in the final section of the chapter demonstrate a range of ways that students managed and expressed social gender identities in the production of subject knowledge.

Research stance

We restricted our field of enquiry by focusing on preselected activities presented in subject lessons. We insisted that the activity should form part of the usual English curriculum and of teachers' schemes of work. Accordingly, we were able to take advantage of naturalistic settings and at the same time create some structure in the design that was essential for comparative purposes. The activity had a history within the flow of English lessons and this ensured that it remained embedded in English classroom culture as students had been experiencing it up to that moment in their school career. It also had an outcome, our window into the expression of students' gender identities.

Method and design

The activity

Prior to observation teachers were asked to select an activity from their 'normal' practice that had an identifiable end product. The activity they chose was for students to write three different types of novel openings. These would be submitted as a piece of coursework for the continuous assessment component of the public examination in English at age 16. The activity was planned to cover three lessons. Both teachers agreed to teach the same three lessons to their classes.

We applied our methodology to two parallel English classroom settings with year 10 students (aged 14–15 years) in the same school. Setting A involved boys with average and above average achievements in the subject. Setting B involved a mixed ability group of girls and a group of boys judged to be 'low achievers' in the subject. In this setting gendered seating had been introduced as a strategy to improve the boys' participation and, therefore, their achievement. Thus, there were 'good' boys to be nurtured, and 'problem' boys to be controlled and changed. Alongside these characterisations of 'boys' is the characterisation of the 'successful' girl to be emulated.

Data collection

Conceptually, Lave's notion of a 'setting' required us to focus in our data collection on the embedded nature of classroom settings. Therefore, we consider teachers' pedagogic practice as forms of mediation that regulate the boundary between the classroom settings and the other settings that students negotiate in the course of a school day. The regularities that we observed as researchers allowed us to describe how teachers orchestrated settings and made subject knowledge visible.

We observed each of the three lessons in each setting.

- *Lesson 1.* This introduced students to literary techniques relating to different genres. Extracts from novel openings were read out in a whole-class forum from a booklet (an 'in-house' production) on creative writing. Exercises from the booklet were discussed in pairs and/or groups. Feedback from the group work was discussed in whole-class interaction.
- *Lesson 2.* The students undertook further exercises from the creative writing booklet. The focus was on individual work and so there was less group work than in lesson 1. Novel openings were drafted and read out in class. The teachers provided feedback and then students continued with their individual writing.
- *Lesson 3.* Most of the lesson was spent doing individual writing.

The data collection mapped out how the teachers orchestrated settings in each classroom. We employed non-participant classroom observation and used field notes to record:

- classroom layout;
- seating arrangements;
- movements around the classroom;
- peer group interaction;
- material culture;
- samples of classroom discourse.

Lesson 2 was video recorded and a sample of students was radio-miked to capture their discourse as they undertook the task. Teachers were interviewed before and after the series of lessons. Specific questions asked teachers about the purpose of the lessons, and what might institute successful and less successful creative writing.

Data were also collected from students to find out how they understood and experienced settings.

Having observed the lessons, four boys and four girls from the mixed setting, and four boys from the single sex setting were chosen in terms of teachers' judgements about their participation in the lessons and the quality of their work generally. Students were presented in individual interviews with stimulus material from the lessons and asked to explain what the teacher expected them to learn. They were also asked about their own texts, what they perceived to be successful writing and, separately, what they thought the teacher perceived to be successful writing. Interviews were audio recorded and transcribed in full. We collected and photocopied the English texts produced by each student in both classroom settings.

Analysing learning

In order to recognise and account for the influence of multiple participation frameworks in the construction of knowledge, we draw upon Rogoff's distinction between three planes of analysis (Rogoff, 1995). Rogoff (p. 141) distinguished three planes that she later termed lenses of analysis (Rogoff, 2001) that are mutually constituting and inseparable. These are community/institutional, interpersonal and personal. A 'plane' indicates a different grain of focus within sociocultural activity. Rogoff's three planes provide analytic distinctions, which allow cultural practices and representations to be investigated in local settings, while maintaining an awareness of the way local settings are embedded within wider sociocultural arenas. To understand the teachers' orchestration of settings we focus on the interpersonal plane. To understand how individual students experienced settings we re-adjust the analytical lens to the personal plane. Rogoff described this plane as the personal process by which, through engagement in activity, individuals change and 'become prepared for subsequent involvement in related activities' (Rogoff, 1995, p. 142). We first present findings from the interpersonal plane before turning to our investigation of the personal plane.

Interpersonal plane of analysis

We analysed field notes and video footage of classroom observation in order to describe differences and similarities in organisation, practice and discourse between the two classroom settings. We paid particular attention to aspects of teachers' everyday classroom practice in order to suggest how social, verbal and physical interactions mediate gender as a hegemonic social representation. We considered which students' work was legitimated and made visible through teachers' commendations of 'good' work. By comparing teachers' responses to boys and girls within and between settings, we were able to describe how gender was influencing the construction of subject knowledge.

Classroom A: 'all boys' setting

The boys in this group were not considered to have difficulties with English in contrast to the boys in classroom B. The boys sat in a horseshoe-shaped seating arrangement. There was no restriction on who sat next to whom. The boys sat in loose friendship groups at the beginning. During the first lesson a great deal of discussion was carried out in pairs and groups. The teacher asked boys to change seats three times to allow the possibility for paired work with a range of other boys. She told the boys this was a challenge for them commenting: 'I want you to work with everyone in this room'. This pattern of movement provided support for interaction between boys. The interaction was buoyant irrespective of which boys were paired or sat together.

During the first lesson the teacher worked through a booklet that contained the first paragraphs from novels in a range of genres. Teacher B used the same booklet. Teacher A asked questions of the boys about atmosphere, character and description. During these sessions boys replied to the teacher readily and noisily. They seemed to vie for her attention. There were no lulls or quiet periods. There was no identifiable pattern to how she chose boys to answer her Questions. No group of boys dominated in this session.

Following the introductory exercises boys were asked to draft a novel opening in a genre of their choice. They were asked to discuss their ideas with the boy beside them and were told they would be required to read their novel opening to the class. At the end of the time limit the teacher asked every boy in turn to read out his novel opening. When a boy was about to read the teacher moved so that she was standing in front of him. She often bent her head forwards as if indicating that she was listening intently. While the boy was speaking she insisted on complete silence, and she did not turn away or speak to anyone else. She responded to each boy's contribution with a positive and often a complimentary comment. Her manner seemed to suggest that each boy's contribution was special and that every boy was equal. The boys' openings covered a range of content: horror, war, crime, adventure, science fiction and fantasy, involving humour and action. The teacher allowed all these reconstructions to be made visible and gave value to them equally.

Throughout that and subsequent lessons boys received an almost equal amount of attention from the teacher. Every boy spoke during the course of the first two lessons. It was clear that the teacher was not selecting one individual in preference to another in seeking responses. Some boys did try to speak more than other boys and interrupted. The teacher had a difficult job keeping order so that she could listen to each boy's contribution.

Classroom B: mixed with gendered seating

Students in the mixed setting were allocated places to sit by the teacher. They sat in groups and in a horseshoe-shape in a boy-girl-boy sequence. In general, no boy sat beside another boy, although a few girls sat beside each other. They had been allocated places according to the alphabetic order of their second names. Students remained in the same places throughout the sequence of lessons.

The gendered seating produced a different range of possibilities for interaction in comparison to classroom A. The class was instructed to consider the variety of novel openings. Teacher B asked similar question to teacher A about atmosphere, characterisation and style. Students put their hands up to answer and there was no obvious pattern to the way they were chosen to respond. The atmosphere was subdued in comparison to classroom A and the teacher did not need to use any techniques to control or quieten the class. Some students were visibly ill at ease in their places, although some groups and pairs were not.

When students came to draft their first novel openings they were directed to discuss their ideas with their immediate neighbours. For some students, the gendered seating strategy was empowering and altered their perceived status in the subject culture. The boys were 'low' achievers in English, yet some found their ideas being validated by the girls seated around them during group discussions. For others, the seating arrangement kept them from participating more fully. Thus, the intention to influence boys' performance had an immediate impact on some girls. We observed a number of boys and a number of girls who failed to interact with their neighbour, even when the teacher instructed them to undertake small group or paired discussion. The teacher's instruction to 'Talk to the person beside you', was ineffective in overcoming some students' discomfort at having to discuss ideas with an unfamiliar boy or girl. This meant that some students engaged in lively exchanges, while others remained completely silent. In this setting, Keiko (a girl), for example, worked in isolation throughout all three lessons.

While the students were preparing their first draft, the teacher circulated around the class and read their first attempts. When she came to ask for volunteers to read out she had already decided which selected students would be chosen in contrast to teacher A. The majority of students chosen to read were high achieving girls and many had drafted Romance novel openings. By choosing the writing of high achieving girls the teacher was making visible what she considered to be a successful reconstruction of English knowledge as a piece of creative writing. The content and style that was legitimated differed from that legitimated by teacher A and the range was narrower. Throughout the three lessons there was uneven treatment of students in the setting.

Summary of the teachers' orchestration of settings

In setting A the teacher's even-handed approach meant that it was not easy to differentiate what she considered successful and less successful reconstructions. Through her response to boys' texts and her practices that supported boys' preferred ways of interacting, the teacher realised a subject culture that was congruent with and not in conflict with boys' common sense ways of knowing. The teacher's manner suggested that every idea the 'high achieving' boys had to offer was valued, and no one genre emerged as high status knowledge. It seemed that each boy had an equal right to the semi-public classroom space.

No boy read out a novel opening in the Romance genre in the single sex boys' setting. The teacher did not discuss the Romance genre with the boys as a possible writing style. In this way she seemed to legitimise the implicit consensus that boys were not expected to reconstruct English in the form of Romance and, therefore, it did not acquire a high status. In contrast, the teacher in setting B, through her practices and responses to students' work, orchestrated an emerging subject culture in which the Romance genre emerged as a model of high status subject knowledge in English: a genre gender marked as 'feminine'.

In classroom A the teacher consciously used practices to support all students' participation. In classroom B the teacher consciously regulated students' participation in order to shape the emergent subject culture. Her practices were in conflict with boys' preferred ways of interacting. The seating arrangements and lack of movement limited the opportunities for students to participate compared with classroom A.

Students' experience of setting A

In classroom A boys spoke at length of the way rituals of masculinity were recognised and reacted to within the peer group. Competing for the teachers' attention and challenging other boys' ideas were key characteristics that they spoke about. There was a general recognition that one had to appear as independent and autonomous, and if possible to have good ideas. The boys considered that their male peers judged ideas as a measure of masculinity. Male peer group culture maintained and amplified hegemonic masculinity through the ways boys policed other boys' behaviour, practices and texts.

We asked the boys in classroom A why no boys had written in the Romance genre. We wished to explore this absence. James, from the single sex classroom, spoke about the vulnerability that boys would feel if they revealed personal concerns through their writing:

> *James:* I don't know, I think its harder to write about real things because if you were writing about them, then if people read them they would like know what your thoughts were about, things that were actually happening to you. But whereas if it is just a fantasy thing it is not going to really reveal anything unless you want to reveal it through it, so you could like choose what does not really matter.

The potential cost to a boy's reputation within the peer group culture of producing a piece of 'Romance' was high. James's comments demonstrated that certain practices were constantly and actively excluded as legitimate practice for boys by boys. In this sense, setting A supported an emergent subject culture that did not suppress the influence of the male peer group as the primary audience for draft productions. Boys policed the range of legitimate ways of being, ways of writing and ways of doing things. The reasons given by James, which was substantiated in interviews with other boys, was to avoid becoming vulnerable, being exposed or letting anyone know what you were really like.

Students in the mixed classroom spoke, during interviews, of the setting in - gender terms. The higher ratio of girls to boys was perceived by some boys to exaggerate the gender marking of the subject culture. Some boys spoke about having to defend their views against a dominant 'girl culture'. However the dominant 'girl culture' provided some boys with opportunities for reconstructing English in ways that they reported would not have been possible in the 'all boys' class.

Boys and girls recognised that Romance was a high status reconstruction of English knowledge. Boys and girls agreed that girls in general, were good at writing romance and boys were not. We explored with the girls their understanding of the writing conventions required to produce a piece of Romance. Girls spoke about the importance of description, feelings, emotions, authenticity and making the story believable to the audience. They contrasted this to writing that was 'just plain'. Jane explained why boys do not write Romance:

> *Jane:* They like rough play, fighting and stuff like that. Whereas girls like dressing up and playing with dolls because of that...and with boys, they like fighting and stuff, things that are rough and exciting and horrors and glory. I know that one boy wrote Romance and he got into trouble.

Tom's comment showed how this view of boys became translated into 'being hard'. His use of the word 'supposed' indicates the knowledge he has about gender that he brought to his writing:

> *Tom:* Well we don't really tend to think about Romance and stuff like that because like the way its *supposed to be* [our emphasis], is we are supposed to be all hard and all that.

Katie suggested too that boys would be into the rough and tumble, rather than the 'lovey dovey' stuff:

Katie: for boys because its like love and lovey dovey stuff and 1 don't think boys are too interested in things like that. It is more of a girls' book, more like a girlie sort of thing that girls would sit down and read and a boy would read like a horror story or something like that.

Jane, Tom and Katie elaborated the interaction between the social representation of gender and of knowledge. The Romance genre was associated with a dedicated femininity. Katie recognised the kinds of writing that were socially acceptable for boys and for girls, and she brought this knowledge about gender to the activity.

Lawrence from the same class explained why boys do not write that 'kind of stuff':

Lawrence: I think it is because they [boys] have no interest or if they did like some of it but they are embarrassed of what their friends will say and of what other girls might say they are like.

We asked who made him feel embarrassed, the teacher, the girls or the other boys?

Lawrence: I think it would be a mixture of both – because if you write something that is not good and it is bad but he's tried it as a Romantic novel and it is pretty bad and the girls think it is bad then they are going to think that he did not have any clue at all about relationships, and the boys are going to crack up at him and they are just going to really, really embarrass him.

Lawrence suggested that the problem for boys in writing Romance was that peers would be able to judge whether or not they had experienced what they were writing about. Lawrence pinpointed the element of authenticity as the problematic area, a point reiterated frequently by boys.

Summary remarks

It emerged from students' interviews that they had common sense understandings of boys' and girls' ways of knowing and acting. As we mentioned before these are brought into settings by students, and shape their experience of the setting and their reconstructions of social representations of gender that manifest themselves in behaviour, practice, texts and social identities. In classroom A boys joked with each other, vied for the teacher's attention and challenged each other's ideas. When creating their first drafts some boys constructed them specifically for the audience of peers rather than for the teacher. In classroom B, we saw boys straining in their seats to communicate with other boys across the classroom. Yet, we also observed boys settle into effective working relationships with girls. In interviews, students confirmed our observation that some boys tried to use the girls beside them to work for them by repeating the teacher's instructions or explaining the activity. We were struck by the variety of relationships that developed in classroom B.

We identified several characteristics in students' reconstructions of English associated with boys as a group and girls as a group. The topics that boys and girls chose to write about, and the styles of writing, as well as ways of behaving were three such characteristics. The genres that boys tended to choose to write in were science fiction, crime, horror, war, humour and action-orientated, whereas for girls' we noted the dominance of the Romance genre, although this was not used exclusively by girls or by all girls. Boys stated that they tended to prefer what we have called 'self-masking' styles of writing. These styles dealt with emotion and 'real life situations' through distancing mechanisms. These allowed some boys to manage their identities within the male peer culture and protected them from exposing their social identity in the female peer culture. For girls exposing their emotions and feelings was associated with success in the subject, culture and accepted behaviour within the male and female peer culture. As Tom observed 'it is different for girls... there isn't the same pressure on them to be kind of hard'.

We consider the characteristic manifestations that we have identified to be the products of social pressure that students encounter in a range of social arenas, and which classroom settings either disrupt or reinforce. To understand the process that leads to these resolutions for individuals and how the settings mediate this process we move next to the personal plane.

Personal plane of analysis

To investigate how individual students' resolved the tensions that emerged between values anchored in different social contexts, we focused on how students censored their own and others writing at different phases of production. We investigated their perceptions of audience and the impact of this on the process of self-censorship. We present stories from four students, one from setting A and three from setting B.

Steven: from deformed bananas to serious writing

Steven, from setting A, said that for the work to be read out in class he had deliberately chosen a story that would appeal to the other boys because it was so ridiculous and therefore would ensure laughter:

> *Steven:* Yeah I wanted to get a reaction from somebody who was reading it you know... You understand that well when someone says 'Oh that's really good' or somebody's laughing... you know.

The story involved a banana that had no friends because it was deformed, The other boys in the class laughed out loud as he read out his first draft. Steven managed his identity as a popular boy within the boys' class by reconstructing text that reflected characteristics of hegemonic social representations of masculinity. The text was intended to be humorous, it showed daring, which reflected the 'rich taking' that is so often identified in research as a hegemonic masculine trait. The device of the 'banana' also provided the essential distancing between the private and the public Steven. Although Steven said that he had deliberately played to the audience of boys there was a serious side to the story:

> *Steven:*   Yeah – it was more sort of controversial type you know…and it was about a deformed banana…and nobody would have [anything to do with it].

Although Steven said that he was, 'playing around with it', the playing around had the potential to become an exploration of an emotional state that underpinned the construction of the story, that of 'rejection'. However, Steven did not take the emotional exploration any further because his intention had been to maintain his identity as a popular boy. He abandoned the story, in part, because he said the teacher did not think it was particularly brilliant. Later in the interview he described characteristics of his writing style in general:

> *Steven:*   But its like writing about something that would not happen normally – it would be, it would be like putting on a different pair of shoes if you know what I mean…experiencing something that would normally happen so trying to make it more interesting I suppose…I like writing stories I mean I quite like its just like imagining what you are doing in your head you know and its just like you train yourself in a different scenario.

His description of a writing technique that he calls, to 'train yourself in a different scenario' was also the one he had employed when he wrote the 'deformed banana' story. Although many boys described a similar technique, it was hidden from the teacher.

Steven demonstrated through his self-censorship of his texts that he was able to differentiate between the audience of peers and audience of teacher and eventually the examination board. He rejected the 'banana' text for his examination coursework folder, and selected instead a science fiction story, a crime story and a diary extract of a scientist as novel openings. Steven knew that these were suitable topics for boys to write about. Steven can be seen as a sophisticated social actor within the 'all boys' classroom setting. He was able to reconstruct English in a form that would be considered high status by the teacher and that preserved his social gender identity as a popular boy. In his interview he showed a detailed awareness of the principle features of the Romance genre, but he also recognised the danger to his standing as a popular boy if he had written a romance. As Duveen observes 'Membership in particular social categories provides individuals with both a social location and a value relative to other socially categorized individuals. These are among the most basic prerequisites for participation in social life' (Duveen, 1997, p. 21). We could note two things about Steven's writing. First, by complying with representations of gender appropriate texts he was excluded from exploring other genres. Hence, there were constraints imposed on his access to the subject culture. In developing texts to maintain his gender identity in the peer group he was learning about how to analyse and create texts to produce particular effects – effects that remained invisible to the teacher and therefore unrecognised in her reconstruction of the subject culture.

Josie writes romance

Josie was one of the 'higher achieving girls' in the mixed class and her mother was a poet. She was one of the girls chosen by the teacher in the mixed class to read out the draft of her first novel opening, which was titled 'Love Train'. Later she submitted the final draft of this text for assessment. During the interview she described in detail how she had drawn on the film 'Titanic' to reconstruct her Romance story:

> *Josie:* Yeah that's the eye contact comes between the two but she's actually (well instead of Jack), instead of him feeling what he was obviously feeling by the look she actually saw, she was feeling what he was feeling and not him.

In the mixed class, boys and girls mentioned Josie's novel opening as a good piece of writing. When we asked if she was pleased with her work she spoke about having read her Romance to her mum:

> *Josie:* And – yeah I was happy because I read them out to my Mum and she thought, the first one which is called 'Love Train' – She thought it was very good, so very good.
> *R:* Tell me what she liked about it?
> *Josie:* She just liked the feel of what 1 was writing, she is a great romantic herself it was a bit like the Titanic 1 suppose, except that it was on a train instead and it was right at the beginning where she sees him on the balcony.

Josie experienced no tension between the reconstruction of feminine marked English knowledge, and her social gender identity maintained in society, in school and in her home. The classroom setting had made Romance visible as a legitimate realisation of English and Josie had her texts validated across a range of in-school and out-of-school settings. She received an 'A' grade for her assessed work. Like Steven, Josie's compliance limited the range of genres she engaged with, but to an even greater degree. The high status accorded to emotive responses also meant that her engagement in a limited style of writing was treated as unproblematic for her learning and for her understanding of the English subject culture. Success for Josie limited her access to English.

Adam from romance to war stories

Adam's presence in setting B identified him as a 'low' achiever in English, and in our observations influenced his participation in the setting and the emergent subject culture. At one point in the first lesson he called out to the teacher, 'I don't write'. However, after the section in the lesson when students had been asked to read out drafts, we noticed that Adam suddenly started to write. In interview Adam explained that he was 'actually getting into it' suggesting that the ameliorating strategy was having its intended effect.

Adam started to experiment with the Romance genre after he had heard the pieces that the girls had read out. During the lesson, while he was writing, the teacher came and read what he had written, Adam told us later: 'The teacher read it and said, "Make sure it doesn't get into an X-rated sort of thing" because it was actually starting to get a bit rough in there with the writing so...' We mentioned this to the teacher afterwards and she suggested that Adam had started to write Romance because he had found out that he could write 'naughty things'. However, during the same lesson Katie was chosen to read out her Romance novel opening, which the teacher described during feedback as 'A rather steamy Mills and Boon piece [popular romantic fiction]'. The students did not interpret this as a negative comment as the writing met the conventions of the genre that the teacher had also praised. Adam recognised the model of high status English constructed by the teacher's practice. He said, 'Katie's was pretty good because in hers she described how she thought she was being watched by a man...and she was writing stuff like, "I could feel his eyes against my body...burning through my skin" and stuff like that.'

Adam's writing was about an event in a romance, but not the authentic feelings and emotions typically considered romantic. Consequently, Adam did not reconstruct romance in the style that was conventionally recognised. Instead, it was action-orientated and included humour. The story recounted an event when Tom, Adam's friend, invited his girlfriend, Anna around purportedly to play scrabble. Tom managed to dispose of the scrabble board in order to initiate other activities with Anna. For someone with limited experience of the written Romance genre and no experience of reconstructing it, this was a starting point that could be developed with the support of the teacher and other students. This support was not forthcoming. Katie handed in her piece of Romance text as part of her assessed coursework. Adam did not. Consequently, through his engagement with the English task, Adam came to a renewed understanding that certain practices were not legitimate for boys. In interview, Adam explained that boys prefer action and horror writing to Romance:

> *Adam:* Cause action is more masculine – you don't see really an action film or a martial arts film with a lady if you know what I mean. In Romance it is more the ladies and their feelings of relationships and stuff...they are not going to do the action stuff.

Because the classroom setting in the mixed class made Romance visible, a space was opened up for boys to experiment with writing Romance. We have argued that the requirements of the Romance genre are in conflict with hegemonic masculinity, so Adam's draft can be interpreted as a brave move and his reconstruction of Romance according to masculine writing characteristics was understandable. His reconstruction of English through a genre that was marked by peers and society as feminine suggests that Adam was on the verge of crossing a boundary into a new way of writing. According to sociocultural perspectives, such crossings may entail a change in identity that, if successful, is the very foundation of learning and, therefore, the very process that teachers need to support. In order to overcome the tension that boys are likely to experience when they experiment with Romance, teachers have to provide a setting where crossing boundaries is legitimate and safe to counteract prevailing social forces.

This is extremely challenging and makes considerable demands on teachers to first understand learning in this way and second to be able to practice in the way that such a view of learning entails. In our view the teacher had neither and projected a social representation of masculinity onto the 'low ability' boys that made it essential for her to police and maintain the boundary for Adam by steering him away from femininely marked writing practices. She extended to Adam a hegemonic masculine identity wherein it was only possible to reconstruct Romance as pornography. Adam had no option in this setting, if he wished to succeed, to forgo his text and to fall back and comply with this extended identity. For his submitted coursework Adam produced gender appropriate texts such as a war story and a crime story.

Martin: a rejected Romance 'a bit close to the bone'

After students in the mixed classroom had handed in their final texts for assessment, the teacher tore up one of Martin's three submitted pieces and gave him a grade based on the remaining two pieces only. We found out about the incident from a range of sources: from the teacher, from a number of students from the mixed class that we interviewed and from Martin himself. The teacher told us that the piece of writing verged on the pornographic. She had consulted with two other English colleagues to check that her reaction to the text was justified. She had taken Martin aside outside the classroom and had told him that his Romance novel opening was unacceptable.

Martin did not experiment with Romance in the classroom setting. He explained that he had been a bit stuck for a third novel opening and that his mum had suggested Romance. He had asked her for a book to help him with the writing style and she had lent him one of her Jackie Collins's novels. He submitted the piece, as coursework after his mum had read it and told him it was 'a bit close to the bone'. Therefore, in out-of-school settings Martin encountered a reconstruction of the Romance genre as a legitimate writing form, from which he modelled his piece. In school he showed his work to a few students, all girls. He described the way they commented 'Oh this bit is really good' or 'Oh this bit is too extreme'. From these reactions he said he thought of changing the piece, but not rejecting it 'I just handed it in praying that it would be quite good but well you all have your own opinions about that'. It was the teachers who censored Martin's text and through them he found out that his reconstruction of Romance was not a legitimate realisation in the schooled English subject culture. Reports from other students and from Martin himself stressed that he had not intended to be provocative. Martin said that there were far worse bits in the novel and that he had attempted to tone them down a bit.

Martin, in interview, revealed that he recognised masculine and feminine interpretations of Romance and understood both. He did not accept for himself, however, the constraints of a hegemonic masculine interpretation. Josie defended Martin during her interview. She objected to the teacher's reactions. She described Martin as a boy who preferred to talk to the girls in the class, rather than to the boys. Martin also told us of the bullying he had received and of his separation from the male peer culture as a consequence, and how he valued female company.

We could see that Martin was able to maintain an emancipated social gender identity outside school and with some of the girls in the mixed classroom. He, more than Adam was positioned in the setting to take risks and experiment with the genre in the space the teacher had created for Romance by making it visible and high status. His Romance text was an expression of his emancipated gender identity. However what he hoped might be a good piece of work was not even worthy of a grade. The teacher's reaction created a boundary that prevented his identity from being maintained within the setting. The teacher's intent was to maintain the subject culture and her actions were to reject the work but in so doing she rejected Martin's creative/expressive identity and limited the opportunities available to him to learn.

Adam was left with an extended identity that made sense to him in terms of what was legitimate behaviour for him to succeed in the subject although this limited the access to the subject culture allowed to him. The same identity was extended to Martin, it represented him and located him socially in particular ways, ways that were in conflict with his emancipated gender identity. He was left still searching for understanding of the subject culture armed only with the knowledge and the associated fear that, in his own words, he must not 'go overboard', be 'too extreme' or 'over the top'.

Concluding remarks

In our research we were concerned to challenge essentialist generalisations and recommendations about pedagogy. We have argued that a sociocultural approach, in particular the concept of a setting as orchestrated by teachers and experienced by students embedded in the institutional and social arena of school, provides a way of analysing learning and understanding pedagogy. A way that helps to understand how gender as hegemonic social representations mediates learning. Teachers need insights into this mediation process to understand students' decisions about their subject knowledge reconstructions and the role that they play in these.

The orchestration of essentialist pedagogic strategies heightened awareness of gender of the teachers in the study. We found that teachers projected social representations of gender onto boys and girls, and then onto high and low achieving boys differently. This manifested itself first through the orchestration of the setting, such that high achieving boys in setting A were granted autonomy and all their ideas were accepted equally. We suggest that the teacher colluded in this because the social representation of high achieving boys conforms to an association that links the mind, rationality and the intellect with masculinity (Walkerdine, 1988).

We found that both teachers focused on their interpretations of students' attributes (as male – female, high – low achievers) and not on the texts they were producing. When students' presented the ideas they had produced through draft and final copies of written text, teachers reacted to high and low achieving boys differently. High achieving boys received praise irrespective of the content and style of their writing. The teacher in setting A did not question Steven about his deformed banana reconstruction. By reacting to the boy and not the text, she failed to recognise the hidden writing technique that we have called 'self-masking' and therefore did not realise that Steven was on the verge of exploring the difficult emotion of rejection. Had she interpreted his text according to the conventions of English that include skills of description, characterisation and plot, she could have shifted the frame from rituals of masculinity to rituals of writing. Had she achieved this she could nave helped Steven to escape the constraints of having to perform hegemonic masculinity and given him permission to be, in public, the person who explored emotions and fictional scenarios in private. This would have provided one instance of pedagogic strategy that would have shifted the production of hegemonic masculinity in the modern gender order (Connell, 1995).

'Low achieving boys' represent an opposite form of masculinity to high achieving boys, one associated with the body. The gendered seating was a part of the teacher's orchestration intended to 'control' the low achieving boys physically. When boys in setting B chose Romance as a genre, they wrote according to 'masculine' writing characteristics. The teacher interpreted their ideas as a form of out-of-control sexuality. She read their texts not in terms of their skills in producing stories, but as manifestations of attributes and intentions associated with 'bad masculinity'. It is important to recognise that, through their actions, these boys were not performing 'oppositional masculinity' (Willis, 1977; Connell, 1995). Instead, the teacher extended (Duveen, 2001) a bad masculine identity to them, simply because they had been placed by the school in classroom B, rather than in classroom A. Neither Martin nor Adam was able to articulate why the teacher had reacted to their texts as 'pornographic'. However, they expressed vague thoughts about having 'gone over the top', 'been too extreme' and of 'getting a bit rough'. Each of these phrases relates to issues of masculinity and not issues about writing techniques. Both boys read the teacher's reaction as a reflection on their character and not of their skills in writing. They were given no tools or techniques to produce the kinds of writing that teachers value so highly at GCSE level.

Teacher B used the girls to provide a model of good writing. Instead she could have articulated the techniques that make up successful writing at that level, and then drawn on a range of students' texts to demonstrate to what extent each measured up to her model. In this way all kinds of text can be used for pedagogic purposes. Girls were being used to control boys physically too and therefore, they were constrained in movement of ideas and we noted this in the isolation of individual girls throughout the three lessons. Girls were also used by the teacher in the production of ideas to support her reconstruction of English. Consequently the opportunities made available for them to learn in the setting were constrained, as they could not explore topics and genres that were marked as 'masculine' according to hegemonic social representations of gender. They were also being encouraged to use a writing technique we labelled as 'self-exposing'. This technique though valued at this level is increasingly devalued in the assessment of the subject culture in the later phases of education.

Strategies that have been motivated by a heightened awareness to gender and are not backed up by research into how students learn are in danger of reproducing hegemonic social representations of gender. Furthermore, classroom settings orchestrated in this way police the boundary between classrooms and other social contexts in conservative ways that exclude ways of being, acting and writing that cross gender boundaries.... [a]meliorative strategies are effective when they build on the cultural capital and know-how that students bring with them into classrooms. However, educational policies need to hand back autonomy to teachers in order to allow them to build on students' know-how through pedagogic guidance that is based on (disciplinary) subject orientated skills and tools, and not on policing attributes of boys or of girls.

References

Brown, J.S. and Duguid, P. (1993) Stolen Knowledge, *Educational Technology*, March.

Browne, N. and Ross, C. (1991) Girls' Stuff, Boys' Stuff: young children talking and playing, in N. Browne (Ed.) *Science and Technology in the Early Years*. Buckingham: Open University Press.

Connell, R.W. (1987) *Gender and Power. Society, the Person and Sexual Politics*. Cambridge: Polity Press.

Connell, R.W. (1995) *Masculinities*. Cambridge: Polity Press.

Cooper, B. and Dunne, A. (2000) *Assessing Children's Mathematical Knowledge*. Buckingham: Open University Press.

Davies, J. and Brember, I. (1995) Attitudes to Schools and the Curriculum in Year 2, Year 4 and Year 6: changes over four years, paper presented at the European Conference on Educational Research, Bath, 14–17 September.

Duveen, G. (1997) Psychological Development as a Social Process, in L. Smith, J. Dockrell and P. Tomlinson (Eds) *Piaget, Vygotsky and Beyond*. London: Routledge.

Duveen, G. (2001) Representations, Identities, Resistance, in K. Deaux and G. Philogène (Eds) *Representations of the Social*. Oxford: Blackwell.

Duveen, G. and Lloyd, B. (1990) Introduction, in G. Duveen and B. Lloyd (Eds) *Social Representations and the Development of Knowledge*. Cambridge: Cambridge University Press.

Fivush, R. (1998) On Interest, Gender and Personal Narrative: how children construct self-understanding, in L. Hoffmann, A. Krapp, K.A. Renninger and J. Baumert (Eds) *Interest and Learning*. Emory University: IPN.

Ivinson, G. (2002) Instructional and Regulative Discourses: a comparative case study of two classroom settings designed to ameliorate boys' under achievement in English, paper presented at the Basil Bernstein Symposium, University of Cape Town, 17–19 July.

Kimbell, R., Stables, K., Wheller, T., Wosniak, A. and Kelly, V. (1991) *The Assessment of Performance in Design and Technology*. London: School Examinations and Assessment Authority.

Lave, J. (1988) *Cognition in Practice*. Cambridge: Cambridge University Press.

Lave, J. (1996) Introduction, in S. Chaiklin and J. Lave (Eds) *Understanding Practice: Perspectives on Activity and Context*. Cambridge: Cambridge University Press.

Lave, J. and Wenger, E. (1991) *Situated Learning Legitimate Peripheral Participation*. Cambridge: Cambridge University Press.

Lloyd, B. and Duveen, G. (1992) *Gender Identities and Education: The Impact of Starting School*. Hemel Hempstead: Harvester Wheatsheaf.

Moscovici, S. (1976) *La Psychanalyse, son image et son public*, 2nd edn. Paris: Presses Universitaires de France.

Moscovici, S. (1984) The Phenomenon of Social Representations, in R.M. Farr and S. Moscovici (Eds) *Social Representations*. Cambridge: Cambridge University Press.

Moscovici, S. (2001) *Social Representations: Explorations in Social Psychology*. New York: New York University Press.

Murphy, P. (1996) A Review of Science Achievement – the IEA studies, Special Edition, *Assessment in Education*, 3(2), pp. 213–232.

Murphy, P. (1997) Gender Differences – Message for Science Learning, in A. Burgen (Ed.) *Growing up with Science*. Cambridge: Jessica Kingsley.

Murphy, P. (1999) Supporting Collaborative Learning: A Gender Dimension, in P.Murphy (Ed.) *Learners, Learning and Assessment*. London: Paul Chapman in association with Open University Press.

Murphy, P. and Ivinson. G. (2000) Boys Don't Do Romance: some unintended consequences of national policy for boys' literacy development in England, paper presented at the American Conference on Literacy, New Orleans, USA, April 24–28.

Penuel, W.R. and Wertsch, J.V. (1995) Vygotsky and Identity Formation: a Sociocultural Approach, *Educational Psychologist*, 30(2), pp. 83–92.

Rogoff, B. (1995) Observing Sociocultural Activity on Three Planes: Participatory Appropriation, Guided Participation, and Apprenticeship, in J.V. Wertsch, P. Del Rio and A. Alvarez (Eds) *Sociocultural Studies of Mind*. Cambridge: Cambridge University Press.

Rogoff, B. (2001) Key Note Paper, presented at International Conference on Communication, Problem-Solving and Learning, University of Strathclyde, Glasgow, Scotland, June 25–29.

Vygotsky L.S. (1978) *Mind in Society: The Development of Higher Psychological Processes*. Cambridge: Harvard University Press.

Vygotsky L.S. (1986) *Thought and Language*, trans. A. Kozulin. Cambridge: MIT Press. (Original work published 1934.)

Walkerdine. V. (1988) *The Mastery of Reason*. London: Routledge.

White, J. (1996) Research on English and the Teaching of Girls, in P.F. Murphy and C.V. Gipps (Eds) *Equity in the Classroom: Towards Effective Pedagogy for Boys and Girls*. London: Falmer Press and UNESCO Publishing.

Willis, P. (1977) *Learning to Labour. How Working Class Kids Get Work Class Jobs*. Farnborough: Saxon House.

CHAPTER 13

BEYOND THE BIRDS AND THE BEES

Constituting a discourse of erotics in sexuality education

Louisa Allen, *Gender and Education*, 16, 2, 2004

Introduction

There are few sex education programmes which embrace the idea that positive experiences of sexual desire and pleasure are integral to young people's sexual health and well-being. More generally, as Aggleton and Campbell (2000) notes, sex education equates young people's sexual health with the absence of sexually transmitted infections and the avoidance of unintended pregnancies. This observation is supported by a tradition of feminist research that identifies the way in which much sex education denies that young people are sexual subjects (Jackson, 1978; Wolpe, 1987; Lenskyj, 1990; Lees, 1994). Fine's work has made an important contribution here in documenting a 'missing discourse of desire', that positively acknowledges and incorporates young women's sexual desire within sex education (Fine, 1988). While it has been established that positive and empowering discourses of desire and pleasure are 'missing' from sex education, arguments about why their inclusion is important are less well articulated (Gagnon and Simon, 1973). Subsequently, this chapter explores the benefits of including these discourses within sexuality education for young women and men's sexual health and well-being.[1] [. . .]

This chapter does not detail the finer points of how a discourse of erotics might be worked into sexuality curricula. How this might occur is largely dependent on contextual factors such as policy governing the teaching of sexuality, teacher training and class composition (age, ethnicity, etc). Discourses are 'an interrelated 'system of statements which cohere around common meanings and values [that] are a product of social factors, of power and practices, rather than an individual's set of ideas' (Hollway, cited in Gavey, 1992, p. 327). Their social complexity and production within a particular historical moment and geographical space mean that what constitutes a discourse of erotics will vary across programmes. Instead, this chapter highlights some potential benefits of opening up discursive space within our communications with young people about sexual pleasure and desire. This does not mean that young people have to, or will necessarily seize upon these spaces, but that they are no longer denied them because they are 'missing' from some sex education programmes.

The chapter begins the process of constituting such a discourse by drawing on empirical research with 17- to 19-year-olds. This work documents the experiences and conceptualizations of desire and pleasure specific to a group of young

New Zealanders and may or may not be the kind of information included in a curriculum which comprised a discourse of erotics. The aim of presenting these findings is to constitute young people as sexual subjects with the capacity for, and right to, positive experiences of sexual desire and pleasure. It is also a means of drawing upon the knowledge and resources of young people themselves, so that this discourse is constituted through their own experiences of 'erotics'. By using this contextual information as a starting point, this discourse is more likely to tap into what is relevant and interesting for young people.

Findings are derived from a larger study involving 515 self identified (hetero)sexuals[2] which explored the relationships between young people's sexual knowledge, subjectivities and practices. This investigation was framed by an interest in understanding what is conceptualized as a 'gap' between what young people learn in sexuality education and what occurs in practice. Diverse exploratory methods were used to collect data about desire and pleasure ranging from individual and couple interviews[3] to questionnaires,[4] focus groups[5] and 'Pleasure Sheets'. These sheets asked subjects who were sexually active at the time of the research, to indicate what sexual practices they found pleasurable and why. The purpose of a multiple method approach was to provide research contexts that could generate different types of narratives about (hetero)sexualities. While data from the interviews and focus groups have been explored in detail elsewhere (Allen, 2002a,b, 2003) material from the 'Pleasure Sheets' and questionnaire relating to a discourse of erotics is focused on here.

A diversity of narratives was sought through the sample composition which consisted of various ethnic groups and youth at school or in job training programmes in the community.[6] As all participants were volunteers the research findings cannot be generalized to the wider youth population. They are instead weighted towards those who were at school, Pakeha,[7] young women and (hetero)sexual. With these limitations in mind this work can only make a small contribution to the constitution of a discourse of erotics. It can not for example offer what should be integral to any discourse of erotics and that is conceptualizations of pleasure and desire from gay, lesbian, bisexual, transgender,[8] takataapui[9] and intersex[10] youth. It is hoped however, that it will open spaces for others to enter this conversation to build and integrate this discourse for positive effect within sexuality education.

Given the (hetero)sexual exclusivity of the research sample and the importance of incorporating sexual diversity within any discourse of erotics, this constraint warrants special mention. It can be said that, while the desires of young (hetero)sexuals, especially young women, have been missing from sexuality education, any acknowledgement of the mere existence of lesbian, gay, bisexual, transgender and intersex (LGBTI) identities are a gaping omission in many programmes. In those instances when homosexuality does surface, it is often associated with gay men and the dangers of contracting HIV. Burgeoning empirical evidence indicates that sex education has traditionally ignored young LGBTI's needs for knowledge and affirmation of their sexual identities, to considerable detriment for some (Epstein, 1994; Quinlivan, 1996; Vincent and Ballard, 1997; Hillier *et al.*, 1998). In order that a discourse of erotics does not contribute to heteronormalizing techniques that render heterosexuality as 'normal' and 'homosexuality' as 'deviance', it will need to tap into young LGBTI's experiences of desire and pleasure. Work in this area is already being undertaken by Ussher and Mooney Somers (2000), who have examined young lesbian women's negotiation and interpretation of initial experiences of sexual desire.

To establish the context for a discussion about the benefits of including a discourse of erotics within sexuality education, the following section briefly outlines how the embodiment of desire and pleasure have been 'missing' from programmes.

'The birds and the bees': de-eroticized sex education

Much has been written about the purpose(s) of sex education and how at any historical moment these are mediated by public discourses that constitute social and economic phenomena as 'problems' to be addressed (Diorio, 1985; Reiss, 1993). This has meant that since its inception in the Western world, sex education has been variously perceived as a tool for curbing rising rates of sexually transmitted infections, 'promiscuity', 'sexual deviance' and or the 'negative' effects of unintended pregnancy (Thomson, 1994; Thorogood, 2000). As a result of this concentration on curtailing various 'social problems', the positive exploration of desire and pleasure as part of sexuality has often been ignored or sidelined. In fact, the pursuit of desire and pleasure outside of marriage has generally been perceived as a core factor contributing to these problems. Subsequently, sex education's messages have often sought to quell sexual desire and underplay sexual pleasure in an endeavour to discourage seemingly inappropriate quests for either.

Attention to sexual desire and pleasure have been diverted in sexuality education through the constitution of sexual intercourse as synonymous with reproduction (Thorogood, 2000). In this way (hetero)sexual intercourse is legitimated by the procurement of children rather than the quenching of desires (Diorio and Munro, 2000; Scholer, 2002). In learning about 'how sperm fertilizes egg' the potential reproductive effects of intercourse are given precedence over the embodied sensual experiences of those engaging in this activity (Gilbert, 1996). By failing to mention the possible pleasurable corporeal effects of sexual intercourse, the only inducement to engage in this activity is the production of children. A further consequence of equating sexual activity with reproduction is a construction of sexuality that is fundamentally (hetero)sexual and ultimately defined in terms of men's penetration of women. As Thorogood explains:

> Sex education in this model, therefore, becomes concerned with contraception, and by implication hetero-sex, fertile sex and childbearing. This of course marginalizes all other forms of sexuality and defines them as against the 'norm' of monogamous, heterosexual, married fertile and penetrative sex.
>
> (Thorogood, 2000, p. 433)

Another means by which positive explorations of desire and pleasure have been precluded from sex education is the way involvement in sexual activity is constituted as 'dangerous'. This connection is created through prioritizing the potential negative consequences of sexual activity over the positive. For example, by concentrating on the acquisition of sexually transmissible infections, or the threat of physical violence and abuse and not mentioning the corporeal and emotional pleasures of sexual activity. An often cited example here are the images of genitalia covered in angry pustules to which many students in sexuality education have been exposed (Gilbert, 1996). These have served to impress upon young people the potential risks of engaging in sexual activity and ultimately to frighten them out of this behaviour. Treating sexuality as exclusively a 'risky business' has not only fostered a missing discourse of erotics in sexuality education but communicated a one sided view which omits the possible pleasurable benefits of such activity.

A final example of how a discourse of erotics has been missing from much sexuality education is the way some students have been taught about the (sexual) body. Rather than being portrayed as a pleasurable element of subjectivity which is sense bestowing and responsive, bodies are often represented as desexualized and desensitized. Evidence of this is seen in the medicalized images of genitalia, purposefully labeled 'Reproductive Organs' with which students are presented. Instead of pictures of actual bodies, images are often diagrammatic with emphasis placed on an internal view of organs as if the body had been dissected. This concentration on internal organs rather than the more sexualized external contours of bodies, serves to draw our attention away from its sensuality and place it firmly on its (reproductive) function. Similarly, bodies are constructed as desensitized in that their capacity for desire and pleasure is often ignored, so that the penis is rarely shown as erect and the clitoris sometimes left unlabelled. The definitive effect of these representations is to de-eroticize the body and disassociate it from embodied feelings of desire and pleasure.

Benefits of including a discourse of erotics in sexuality education

Power can be seen to operate in the way sexuality education serves as a 'disciplinary technique' for the production of particular subjected and practiced bodies (Foucault, 1980). According to Foucault (1981) this occurs because sexuality has been 'deployed' as a domain of regulation and social control and sexuality education is one of the many sites in which this regulation is discursively produced. Referring to how the disciplinary power of sexuality education is exercised Wagener explains that:

> Particularly since the early decades of the twentieth century, curriculum technologies, such as those that clearly define, categorize, examine, evaluate, distinguish, and standardize appropriate and inappropriate behaviour, have enabled pedagogical practices, including those found in sexuality education, to participate in the multiple ways in which lives of school students are governed.
>
> (Wagener, 1998, p. 145)

In the Foucauldian sense, this regulation of subjects is possible because of power's essentially positive nature and ability to produce certain behaviours, attitudes and desires from them. In the context of sexuality education, this means that the institutionally sanctioned power of discourses contained within these programmes engender a micro-management of subject's sexual practices. This effect of power is gendered in that dominant discourses within sexuality education produce different subject positions for young women and men to take up. In terms of a missing discourse of erotics then, there are varying consequences for young women and men's sexual subjectivities and ultimately their experience of sexual well-being.

The silence around a discourse of erotics within sexuality education has particular ramifications for young women. This is because access to such discourses are generally more difficult for them, as they are already socially constituted as possessing lower levels of sexual desire and being able to experience sexual pleasure less easily than young men (Allen, 2003). This means that young women are often cast as the passive recipients of active male desires, a subject position sexuality education (re)produces through the absence of a discourse of erotics.

Without exploring the possible benefits of sexual activity in terms of pleasurable sensation, sexuality education fails to provide young women with a standard against which to make decisions about engaging (or not) in this activity (Bollerud *et al.*, 1990; Warr, 2001). In fact, it suggests that sexual activity will not be pleasurable for them and subsequently denies them a subject position from which they might make an active choice. Without acknowledging young women as sexually desiring subjects and revealing the possibility sexual activity might have pleasurable, corporeal outcomes, sexuality education fails to convey a sense of personal empowerment and entitlement for young women. As others have noted (Holland *et al.*, 1991; Lees, 1993; Stewart, 1999), this has important repercussions for young women's sense of being able to initiate safer sex in relationships.

If there is no acknowledgement that young women's bodies can have strong pleasurable physiological responses during sexual activity and that these are 'normal' and positive outcomes, then the possibility of this being their experience may be reduced. This might be explained by the way that discursive constructions can be seen to have 'real effects' because in post-structural terms, language constitutes meaning and possibilities for practice (Weedon, 1987). So for instance, it is not that women's bodies are in some way essentially less easily pleasured than young men's, but that language constitutes our experience of them as such. The reality of this is seen in numerous studies which document young women's dissatisfaction and disillusionment with (hetero)sexual practices (Thompson 1990; Thomson and Scott, 1991; Hillier *et al.*, 1999). Given that the experience of sexual pleasure can have physical and mental health benefits, any omission to convey this to young women may potentially have negative effects for their sexual well-being.

It might be argued that young men's (hetero)sexual desire and pleasure are given more space in some sexuality education programmes. This occurs in the form of information about 'wet dreams' and 'erections' which are often framed in a heteronormative discourse of 'growing up' and becoming interested in 'the opposite sex'. However such discourses around 'awakening male sexuality' also have a regulatory effect in their prescriptions of 'normal' and 'expected' (hetero)sexuality. Allusions to male (hetero)sexual desire in the absence of equivalent references for young women, constitute young men's sexuality as predatory. This offers a standard against which young men might measure their sexuality as appropriately masculine and discover themselves 'sub-standard' if their experiences do not conform. Thus while sexuality education is more likely to provide a discourse of (hetero)sexual desire for young men, it offers them limited ways of being masculine sexual subjects. So that young men may be able to express their sexuality in a broader range of ways (including homosexual desire), it is necessary that any discourse of erotics enables them to move beyond the constraints of hegemonic masculinity (Connell, 1995).

There is another argument for why the inclusion of a discourse of erotics is important for young men. The larger project from which this chapter is derived collected data about young people's sources of sexual knowledge. These findings revealed that almost three quarters of young men in the sample had consulted pornographic magazines and rated this information 'very useful'.[11] It might be seen that in the absence of a discourse of erotics in sexuality education many young men may seek such information in other contexts and find it most overtly available within pornography. Anti-pornography feminists have written prolifically about the effects of pornography and the way it can be seen to exploit and objectify women (see Coward, 1987, p. 307). Mainstream pornography is a key way by which hegemonic male sexual subjectivities are constituted and this construction is deleterious for sexual equality. As Jackson and Scott have argued, pornography:

> ....helps to circulate and perpetuate particular versions of these narratives such as the mythology of women as sexually available, deriving pleasure from being dominated and possessed and a model of masculinity validated through sexual mastery over women. A man does not rape as a direct reaction to a pornographic stimulus; rather pornography contributes to the cultural construction of a particular form of masculinity and sexual desire which make rape possible.
>
> (Jackson and Scott, 1996, p. 23)

Pornography as a source of information about (hetero)sexual desire and pleasure arguably can reproduce oppressive male sexual subjectivities that sustain inequitable sexual politics (Dworkin, 1981). By neglecting to include a discourse of erotics that incorporates (hetero)sexual desire and pleasure in a positive, empowering and gender equitable manner, sexuality education offers no alternative discourses with which to contest mainstream pornography. Without these, most young (hetero)sexual men will only have access to discourses of pornography that not only limit their own experience of sexual desire and pleasure, but those of their partners also.

The current study also indicates that including a discourse of erotics may have other positive effects for both genders. For sexuality education that fails to meet the needs and interests of young people, the inclusion of such a discourse may bring these programmes closer to young people's own concerns. While this argument has been explored in detail elsewhere (Allen, 2001) it is briefly reiterated here. I have argued that the concept of a 'gap' between knowledge gleaned from sexuality education and young people's actual sexual practices does not acknowledge young people's own conceptualizations of their sexual knowledge. The 'logic' underlying the conceptualization of this 'gap' is that what is learned in sexuality education is deemed necessary for sexual practice, a notion which many young people in my research did not share. What these young women and men's narratives indicated, was that to them being sexually knowledgeable meant being knowledgeable about a discourse of erotics. While 'erotics' means 'of, concerning, or arousing sexual desire or giving sexual pleasure' (Sinclair, 1995) for subjects in this sample it also comprised details about how to instigate or manage interaction that involved or might lead to sexual activity. For example, how to ask someone on a date or how to physically engage in sexual activity. This kind of knowledge was given precedence over more 'official' discourses about for example, safer sex and was identified by young people in the research as missing from sexuality education. Including a discourse of erotics in sexuality education would not only acknowledge these young people's own conceptualizations of sexual knowledge, but bring its teachings closer to their own interests and concerns.

First steps: building a discourse of erotics around young people

What follows makes a limited contribution to laying the empirical foundations for a discourse of erotics within sexuality education. It is offered alongside other evolving work from feminists, masculinities and queer theorists who have sought to explore young women's and men's sexual subjectivities and practices

(Holland *et al.*, 1994; Tolman, 1994; Quinlivan, 1996; Wight, 1996; Hillier *et al.*, 1998; Stewart, 1999). While I have traversed young (hetero)sexual women's and men's embodied experiences of desire and pleasure elsewhere, here I concentrate on those practices seen to elicit this pleasure and what it is about them which produces this.

Documenting such practices is a political act aimed at recognizing young people as sexual subjects. In doing this it is acknowledged that seeking and expressing desire and pleasure can be a legitimate aspect of young people's sexual health. This objective supports the assertion by the Pan American Health Organization and World Association for Sexology that 'erotic pleasure is a positive, rewarding, health promoting and basic human need' (Pan American Health Organization and World Health Organization, 2000, p. 25). Collecting such data also endeavours to answer recommendations for the promotion of sexual health made by these organizations. These include calls for the:

- Need for knowledge about the body, as related to sexual response and pleasure.
- Need of recognition of the value of sexual pleasure enjoyed throughout life in safe and responsible manners within a values framework respectful of the rights of others.
- Need to foster the practice and enjoyment of consensual, non-exploitative, honest, mutually pleasurable sexual relationships.

In presenting these data, my intention is not to provide a prescription of what 17- to 19-year-olds should or could find pleasurable and desirable about sexual activity. Because all discourses have regulatory effects, a discourse of erotics would need to be integrated into programmes so as not to cast sexual desire and pleasure as normative and imply their absence signifies deficiency. Rather than producing its meanings as mandatory, the effect of incorporating such a discourse is to make young people's access to it possible and legitimate within school environments, so they might gain in the ways outlined above. It would therefore include the right of young people to not want to experience desire and pleasure.

The following data provides insights into a group of 17- to 19-year-olds experiences of sexual pleasure and desire. These findings are not representative of the youth population as a whole or of young (hetero)sexuals generally, but instead are bound by these individual's experience of what is pleasurable and desired. In many ways these practices/feelings are constituted through dominant discourses about appropriately gendered pleasures/desires, and therefore do not encompass all the possible sexual pleasures young people might experience. In terms of constituting a discourse of erotics, it is not so much the specifics of sexual practice that is useful here, but the fact that such data reveals young people as sexual subjects.

Data on what might be constituted as a discourse of 'erotics' could be found in the 'Pleasure Sheet' completed by six couples who participated in the couple interviews. While one partner was with me during an individual interview, the other filled out a sheet naming particular sexual activities they had engaged in during their present and previous relationships and whether or not they had found these pleasurable. The activities ranged from hugging/kissing, mutual masturbation, to anal sex and sharing sexual fantasies. Space was also provided for subjects to indicate any activities not specified (however only one subject utilized this). From these sheets the most common sexual activities engaged in were hugging, kissing, sexual intercourse, oral sex, mutual masturbation, sexual touching and sharing sexual fantasies. Although not referred to by other subjects, one young woman who had been in her relationship for 9.5 months added that she also enjoyed 'talking dirty'. The least practiced activity was 'anal sex' with only one young woman having engaged in this during a previous relationship. This echoes findings from an Australian study of 18 to 19-year-olds, where only 5% of (hetero)sexual couples reported this practice (Rodden *et al.*, 1996). Most of the activities were found to be pleasurable by all subjects, although two young men indicated that they did not find giving a partner oral sex so.

Information which might constitute a discourse of erotics could also be found in response to questions posed in an anonymous written questionnaire. In order to establish whether young people found sexual activity pleasurable or not, subjects were asked to 'agree' or 'disagree' with the statement that 'sexual activity is pleasurable'. This statement was one of 15 items aimed at determining young people's attitudes towards sexual activity. In an attempt to disrupt the conflation of sexual activity with sexual intercourse, subjects were provided with the explanation that 'sexually active means engaging in petting and/or sexual intercourse with a partner'. Of those who responded to this question 92% of young women and 94% of young men agreed that sexual activity was pleasurable. This indicates a resounding majority of young people in this study had lived experience of (or if they were not sexually active thought that this activity could be) pleasurable.

Another open ended question was designed to determine what young people found pleasurable about sexual activity and asked subjects to complete the sentence, 'What I find pleasurable about sexual activity is...'. Only those who described themselves as having been sexually active with a partner answered this question. In accordance with the definition of 'sexual activity' above, 89% of subjects categorized themselves as sexually active. Answers revealed an interesting array of corporeal and emotional pleasures derived from (hetero)-sexual activity which could be coded into a series of themes displayed in the table below.

The most consistently mentioned answers could be coded under the general heading 'pleasure and enjoyment' and made reference to a sense of this activity being simply 'fun' and 'enjoyable' or as one young man described it 'exhilerating' [*sic*]. The following is a sample of answers representative of those provided by subjects for this question. Original grammar and spelling has been preserved.

> Enjoying being with my partner. (Female, At School, 17 years)

> I love the fun of it. Very exciting. (Male, Not at School, 17 years)

> That I can have fun and do what I want to do in a fun manor. (Female, At School, 17 years)

> You get enjoyment from both sides. (Female, At School, 17 years)

> The level of enjoyment I get from it. (Male, At School, 18 years)

As this question was posed within the context of an anonymous questionnaire there was not an opportunity to define exactly what subjects found 'fun' and 'exciting' about this activity. However other answers to this question discussed

Table 12.1 What I find pleasurable about sexual activity is...

What young people find pleasurable about sexual activity	% Young women *() = N	% Young men *() = N	Total *() = N
Activities other than sex	(24) 12.4	(16) 17.0	(40) 13.9
Desiring someone	(2) 1.0	(2) 4.2	(4) 1.3
Being desired	(16) 8.2	(4) 4.3	(20) 6.9
Being in control	(5) 2.6	(3) 3.2	(8) 2.8
Positive feelings associated with body	(41) 21.1	(27) 28.7	(68) 23.6
Learning/experimentation	(10) 5.2	(2) 2.1	(12) 4.2
This activity being mutual	(20) 10.3	(0) 0.0	(20) 6.9
Experience of pleasure/enjoyment	(70) 36.1	(41) 43.6	(111) 38.5
Pleasurableness of emotional intimacy	(13) 6.7	(13) 13.8	(26) 9.0
Relief/relaxation	(4) 2.1	(2) 2.1	(6) 2.1
Togetherness/closeness	(67) 34.5	(18) 19.1	(85) 29.5
Touching someone else	(11) 5.7	(4) 4.3	(15) 5.2
Way of increasing emotional intimacy	(20) 10.3	(4) 4.3	(24) 8.3

Note
Pertains to the number of mentions young people made of these themes. One answer could potentially contain more than one theme.
N = 336, Female = 214, Male = 122

below give some additional insights here. There were no significant differences between young women and men's answers to this question, suggesting that the fact this activity could be fun and enjoyable was an equally relevant pleasure for both.

The feeling of 'togetherness and closeness' which sexual activity can generate was another popular specification for both genders. This 'togetherness' was expressed in terms of the way physical proximity incited a pleasurable mix of corporeal and emotional sensation. These statements were differentiated from others that could be categorized under the theme 'pleasurableness of emotional intimacy' in that they made specific reference to the way physical closeness increased emotional bonds. This can be seen in the statements below where being physically close to a partner evokes pleasurable emotional feelings.

> Feeling you get when you are close to them. (Male, At School, 17 years)
>
> Being close to someone I love. (Female, Not at School, 18 years)
>
> The feeling of being so close to someone. (Male, At School, 17 years)
>
> The feeling of closeness and affection between two people. (Female, Not at School, 18 years)
>
> The intimacy and the feeling and the bond afterwards. (Female, Not at School, 19 years)

There was a significant gender difference in responses here, however, with more young women than young men reporting this (sig. 007). These responses generally drew upon dominant discourses of (hetero)sexuality where young women are constituted as having greater investment in the emotional benefits of relationships, while young men are perceived to be more concerned with its corporeal benefits (Duncombe and Marsden, 1993). Holland *et al.*'s research has revealed how sexuality is a central site in men's struggles to become successfully masculine and this involves a disengagement with so-called feminine concern with emotion (Holland *et al.*, 1993). The expression of young women's sexuality, by contrast, is regulated by their need to manage their sexual reputations (Holland *et al.*, 1991; Thomson and Scott, 1991; Lees, 1993). Displaying too much interest in the physical pleasures of relationships (without emotional investment) puts young women in danger of being a 'slut' and gaining a negative sexual reputation. Given these disciplinary features regulating young women and men's (hetero)sexualities, it may not be surprising that more young women than men wrote about 'togetherness and closeness' being a pleasure gleaned from sexual activity.

Answers which indicated what young people rated as the third most pleasurable thing about sexual activity were coded under the heading 'positive feelings associated with the body'. These expressions of pleasure were grounded in bodily sensations which produced a positive and enjoyable corporeal experience. This acknowledgement of pleasurable corporeal feeling was evident in the following statements.

> The feeling of having my partner inside my body. (Female, At School, 17 years)

> The closeness involved and the feeling of naked skin together. (Female, Not at School, 19 years)

> The feeling of the penis going in and out of me and him touching me all over and feeling me. (Female, Not at School, 17 years)

> My partner's body against mine. (Male, Not at School, 18 years)

> Feeling, kissing, staring, hugging. (Male, Not at School, 17 years)

> Slow touching, and getting hot/sweaty. (Male, At School, 18 years)

The differences between the number of young women and men who named positive feelings associated with the body as pleasurable were not significant. However, as the Table 12.1 indicates when these themes were ranked by gender, young men named 'positive feelings associated with the body' as the second most pleasurable aspect of sexual activity, while for young women this came third after 'togetherness and closeness'. While positive emotional benefits featured in young people's answers to this question (as seen in the themes of 'increasing emotional intimacy' and 'pleasurableness of emotional intimacy') on their own these did not rate as highly as pleasures of the 'flesh'. I think that some caution might be exercised in reading these results as young people finding the physical benefits of sexual activity more pleasurable than their emotional advantages. In responses to this question, it was difficult to distinguish whether subjects were referring to the emotional or physical pleasures of sexual activity, because in many of their answers these seemed inextricably entwined. This is clearly seen in the first two themes of 'pleasure and enjoyment' and 'togetherness/closeness', which may be indeterminately derived from physical/emotional sources.

One particularly interesting result is that a significant gender difference was found in answers which described 'emotional intimacy' as being a pleasurable aspect of sexual activity. In a manner that appears to disrupt dominant (hetero)sexual subjectivities, more young men than young women indicated they found this pleasurable. This finding might be explained by the fact that the sample was comprised of volunteers and as is common in sexuality research fewer young men offered to participate (Ehrhardt, 1997). Lower numbers of male volunteers might be attributed to the fact that discussing sexuality in a research context is not appropriately masculine and therefore participation is less appealing for young men. This means that those young men who do volunteer may be more flexible in revealing what they find pleasurable about sexual activity when this does not conform to dominant discourses of male (hetero)sexuality.

[. . .]

Exploring how young people expressed their desires was the focus of another survey question. The intention here was to disclose how sexual desires were given expression in a relationship with a well known partner. In response to, 'How would you express your sexual desires to a partner you knew well' subjects could tick one of the following options:

(a) By telling them.
(b) By showing them what I like and want.
(c) By telling and showing them what I like.
(d) I don't express my sexual desires to my partner.

The majority of subjects indicated they would both 'tell and show' their desires to a partner with the next preferred method being to simply 'tell them'. A significant gender difference was found here with more young women indicating they would do this. The fact that young women would take an additional step and physically act on their desire, by showing a partner what they liked, is an interesting contravention of dominant notions of female sexual passivity. As Kenway reveals, young women's sexual subjectivities are the result of a mutable set of resistances and accommodations which depend upon contextual factors and access to power (Kenway, 1997, p. 65). That showing someone what they liked is less likely to be an option that young men adopt may be a result of increasing education around sexual harassment and prohibitions around 'touch', especially men touching women (Jones, 2001). The influence of these messages might also be seen in the fact that significantly more young men than women disclosed that they 'do not express their desires to their partners.

Closing thoughts

The central aim of this chapter has been to outline the benefits of including a discourse of erotics within sexuality education and imply how these might be gendered. In support of these arguments, another objective has been to provide some empirical foundations for the creation of such a discourse in sexuality education.

Previous research has revealed how desire and pleasure have been missing from sexuality education and this chapter has sought to discuss and build on these findings. It has done this by exploring what gendered consequences this has for young people's sexual well-being. I have argued that by not acknowledging and positively incorporating young women's desires and pleasures into sexuality education, there may be a failure to communicate a sense of personal empowerment and sexual entitlement to them. For young men, the lack of a positive reconfiguration of desire and pleasure in sexuality programmes, suggests that their sexual experiences are confined by expressions of hegemonic male (hetero)sexuality. Given that dominant subject positions of male (hetero)sexuality 'require young men to exercise power over women', such discourses not only limit any alternative expression of male sexualities (including homosexuality) but are also disempowering for their partners.

A further argument in support of including a discourse of erotics within sexuality education is that it provides a means of contesting competing discourses of 'erotica' within mainstream pornography. Such pornography offers denigrating portrayals of women as the objects of male desire rather than the subjects of their own. It is therefore important that young people have easy access to more positive and equitable erotic discourses of (hetero)sexuality. Similarly, there is evidence to suggest that including such a discourse would not only acknowledge young people's own conceptualization of sexual knowledge, but bring sexuality education's messages in closer alignment with their interests and concerns.

On the basis of these arguments it is believed that the inclusion of a discourse of erotics within sexuality education could contribute to the sexual health and well-being of young people, especially those who choose to engage in sexual activity in relationships.

Notes

1　Since the inception of the *Health and physical education curriculum* (1999) in New Zealand 'sex education' has officially undergone a name change to 'sexuality education'. It is stated in this curriculum that 'sex education, generally refers only to the physical dimension of sexuality education' while 'sexuality education' is believed to be a more holistic and inclusive term which covers all aspects of sexuality (Ministry of Education, 1999, p. 38).

2　'Hetero' is bracketed in an attempt to decentre the notion of (hetero)sexual experience as the 'norm'.

3　Six couple interviews were conducted with young people who were in a relationship at the time of the research. These were directly followed by individual interviews with each partner.

4　411 questionnaires were completed asking young people about their sexual subjectivities, knowledge and practices.

5　17 Focus groups were conducted by the researcher in both mixed and single gender group contexts. In 10 of these groups subjects were 'At School' while the rest of the groups were comprised of young people who were no longer at school.

6　16.3% Maori, 16.3% Pacific Islands, 9.1% Asian, 57.4% Pakeha (see note 7), 1% Other.

7　Pakeha is a term commonly used in New Zealand to denote non-Maori New Zealanders of European descent.

8　An umbrella definition to describe anyone who transgresses normative gender categories.

9　In New Zealand the 'Maori Gay, Lesbian, Bi-sexual and Transgender community have adopted this word to identify as being Maori and queer' (Definition from the New Zealand AIDS Foundation, Takataapui Pamphlet).

10　Intersex refers to 'people born with an anatomy that someone decided is not standard for male or female'. More specifically this means someone 'born with sex chromosomes, external genitalia, or an internal reproductive system that is not considered 'standard' for either male or female' (Intersex Society of North America, 2002 as sighted at http://www.isna.org/drupal).

11 By contrast 74.5% of young women had never consulted pornographic magazines as a source of information. Of those who had, only 3% reported finding them very useful. It is possible this is because a discourse of erotics can be accessed from other sources such as women's magazines.

References

Aggleton, P. and Campbell, C. (2000) Working with young people – towards an agenda for sexual health, *Sexual and Relationship Therapy*, 15, 283–296.

Allen, L. (2001) Closing sex education's knowledge/practice gap: the reconceptualization of young people's sexual knowledge, *Sex Education*, 1, 109-122.

Allen, L. (2002a) 'As far as sex goes, I don't really think about my body': young men's corporeal experiences of (hetero)sexual pleasure in: H. Worth, A. Paris and L. Allen (Eds) *The life of Brian: Kiwi masculinities, sexualities and health* (Dunedin, Otago University Press), 215–236.

Allen, L. (2002b) Exploring young women's narratives of (hetero)sexual pleasure through a spectrum of embodiment, *Women's Studies Journal*, 18, 45–67.

Allen, L. (2003) Girls want sex, boys want love: young people negotiating (hetero)sex, *Sexualities*, 6.

Bollerud, K., Christopherson, S. and Frank, S. (1990) Girls' sexual choices: looking for what is right, in C. Gilligan, N. Lyons and T. Hamner (eds) *Making connections: The relational worlds of adolescent girls at the Emma Willard School* (Cambridge MA, Harvard University Press).

Connell, R. (1995) *Masculinities* (Cambridge, Polity Press).

Coward, R. (1987) Sexual violence and sexuality, feminist review, in: *Sexuality: a reader* (Virago, London).

Diorio, J. (1985) Contraception, copulation, domination, and the theoretical barrenness of sex education literature, *Educational Theory*, 35, 239–254.

Diorio, J. and Munro, J. (2000) Doing harm in the name of protection: menstruation as a topic for sex education. *Gender and Education*, 12, 347–365.

Duncombe, J. and Marsden, D. (1993) Love and intimacy: the gender division of emotion and 'emotion work', *Sociology*, 27, 221–241.

Dworkin, A. (1981) *Pornography: men possessing women* (London, Women's Press).

Ehrhardt, A. (1997) Gender, in J. Bancroft (ed) *Researching sexual behaviour: methodological issues* (Indiana, Indiana University Press).

Epstein, D. (1994) *Challenging lesbian and gay inequalities in education* (Milton Keynes, Open University Press).

Fine, M. (1988) Sexuality, schooling and adolescent females: the missing discourse of desire, *Harvard Educational Review*, 58, 29–51.

Foucault, M. (1980) in: C. Gordon (Ed.) *Power/knowledge: selected interviews and other writings 1972-1977* (New York, Pantheon).

Foucault, M. (1981) *The history of sexuality. Volume 1: an introduction* (Harmondsworth, Penguin) (Original work published 1976).

Gagnon, J. and Simon, W. (1973) *Sexual conduct: the social sources of human sexuality* (Chicago, Aldine).

Gavey, N. (1992) Technologies and effects of heterosexual coercion, *Feminism and Psychology*, 2, 325–351.

Gilbert, J. (1996) The sex education component of school science programmes as a 'micro-technology' of power, *Women's Studies Journal*, 12, 37–58.

Hillier, L., Dempsey, D., Harrison, L., Beale, L., Matthews, L. and Rosenthal, D. (1998) *Writing themselves in: a national report on the sexuality, health and well-being of same-sex attracted young people*. Monograph series 7 (Australian Research Centre in Sex, Health and Society, National Centre in HIV Social Research, La Trobe University).

Hillier, L., Harrison, L. and Bowditch, K. (1999) Never-ending love and blowing your load: the meanings of sex to rural youth, *Sexualities*, 2, 69–88.

Holland, J., Ramazanoglu, C., Scott, S., Sharpe, S. and Thomson, R. (1991) Between embarrassment and trust: young women and the diversity of condom use, in: P. Aggleton, G. Hart and P. Davies (Eds) *AIDS: responses, interventions and care* (London, Falmer Press).

Holland, J., Ramazanoglu, C. and Sharpe, S. (1993) *Wimp or gladiator: contradictions in acquiring masculine sexuality.* WRAP (MEAP) paper 9 (London, Tufnell Press).

Holland, J., Ramazanoglu, C., Sharpe, S. and Thomson, R. (1994) Power and desire: the embodiment of female sexuality, *Feminist Review*, 46, 21–38.

Jackson, S. (1978) How to make babies: sexism in sex education *Women's Studies International Quarterly*, 1, 341–352.

Jackson, S. and Scott, S. (1996) (Eds) *Feminism and sexuality: a reader* (Edinburgh, Edinburgh University Press).

Jones, A. (Ed.) (2001) *Touchy subject: teachers touching children* (Dunedin, Otago University Press).

Kenway, J. and Willis, S. (1997) *Answering back: girls, boys and feminism in schools* (Sydney, Allen and Unwin).

Lees, S. (1993) *Sugar and spice: sexuality and adolescent girls* (Harmondsworth, Penguin).

Lees, S. (1994) Talking about sex in sexuality education, *Gender and Education*, 6, 281–292.

Lenskyj, H. (1990) Beyond plumbing and prevention, *Gender and Education Journal*, 2, 217–231.

Pan American Health Organization and World Health Organization (2000) Promotion of sexual health, recommendations for action, proceedings of a regional consultation convened by the Pan American Health Organization, World Health Organization in collaboration with the World Association for Sexology, Antigua, Guatemala.

Quinlivan, K. (1996) Claiming an identity they taught me to despise: lesbian students respond to the regulation of same sex desire, *Women's Studies Journal*, 12, 99–114.

Reiss, M. (1993) What are the aims of school sex education? *Cambridge Journal of Education*, 23, 125–136.

Rodden, P., Crawford, J, Kippax, S. and French, J. (1996) Sexual practice and understandings of safe sex: assessing change among 18 to 19-year-old Australian Tertiary students, 1988-1994, *Australian and New Zealand Journal of Public Health*, 20, 643–649.

Scholer, A. (2002) Sexuality in the science classroom: one teacher's methods in a college biology course, *Sex Education*, 2, 75–86.

Sinclair, J. (1995) *Collins English dictionary* (Glasgow, HarperCollins).

Stewart, F. (1999) Femininities in flux? Young women, heterosexuality and (safe) sex, *Sexualities*, 2, 275–290.

Thompson, S. (1990) Putting a big thing into a little hole: teenage girls' accounts of sexual initiation, *Journal of Sex Research*, 27, 341–361.

Thomson, R. (1994) Moral rhetoric and public health pragmatism: the recent politics of sex education, *Feminist Review*, 48, 40–60.

Thomson, R. and Scott, S. (1991) *Learning about sex: young women and the social construction of sexual identity.* WRAP Paper 4 (London, Tufnell Press).

Thorogood, N. (2000) Sex education as disciplinary technique: policy and practice in England and Wales, *Sexualities*, 3, 425–438.

Tolman, D. (1994) Doing desire: adolescent girls' struggles for/with sexuality, *Gender and Society*, 8, 324–342.

Ussher, J. and Mooney-Somers, J. (2000) Negotiating desire and sexual subjectivity: narratives of young lesbian avengers, *Sexualities*, 3, 183–200.

Vincent, K. and Ballard, K. (1997) Living on the margins: lesbian experience in secondary schools, *New Zealand Journal of Educational Studies*, 32, 147–161.

Wagener, J. (1998) The construction of the body through sex education discourse practices, in: T. Popkewitz and M. Brennan (Eds) *Foucault's challenge: discourse, knowledge and power in education* (Columbia, Teachers College Press).

Warr, D. (2001) The importance of love and understanding: speculation on romance in safe sex health promotion, *Women's Studies International Forum*, 24, 241–252.

Weedon, C. (1987) *Feminist practice and post-structuralist theory* (Oxford, Blackwell).

Wight, D. (1996) Beyond the predatory male: the diversity of young Glaswegian Men's discourses to describe heterosexual relationships, in: L. Adkins and V. Merchant (Eds) *Sexualizing the social: power and the organization of sexuality* (London, MacMillan).

Wolpe, A. (1987) Sex in schools: back to the future, *Feminist Review*, 27, 37–47.

CHAPTER 14

POWER, BODIES AND IDENTITY

How different forms of physical education construct varying masculinities and femininities in secondary schools

Carrie Paechter, *Sex Education*, 3, 1, 2003

Sex education, especially education about what it means to have a gendered body, is not confined to the obvious arenas such as personal, social and health education, or biology lessons, but takes place across a number of school sites. In this chapter I focus on physical education (PE) as an important site in which students learn about the gendered nature of their embodiment. I examine how different ways of using bodies in PE, sport and fitness-based activities construct particular heterosexual masculinities and femininities, and thereby demonstrate the importance of PE to the less overt forms of school sex and sexuality education.

In secondary schools in particular, physical education lessons are an important arena for the displaying and acting out of masculinity and femininity, particularly those forms which could be described as hypermasculine and hyperfeminine.[1] In this chapter, I want to explore to what extent this is related to the ways bodies are used in PE lessons. I want to consider how the particular types of bodily use exemplified in PE, sports and fitness activities construct particular forms of masculinity and femininity within the activities themselves, and whether there is anything we can do to alter this situation.

PE is compulsory in state schools in England from ages 5–16, and schools are expected to aspire to providing two hours physical activity per week for all students (Department for Education and Employment, 1999). The National Curriculum for PE in England (Department for Education and Employment, 1999) specifies both the knowledge and skills students are expected to acquire at each of four 'key stages' (ages 5–7, 8–10, 11–13 and 14–16) and the 'contexts, activities, areas of study and range of experiences' (Department for Education and Employment, 1999, p. 12) through which these should be taught. At all levels the knowledge, skills and understanding element comprises four broad components: acquiring and developing skills; selecting and applying skills, tactics and compositional ideas; evaluating and improving performance; and knowledge and understanding of fitness and health (Department for Education and Employment, 1999). Students in the lower secondary age range (Key Stage 3) are expected to undertake games activities and at least three out of dance, gymnastics, swimming and water safety, athletics, and outdoor and adventurous activities; at least one of these three should be dance or gymnastic activities. For those aged 14–16 (Key Stage 4), learning is expected to take place through two out of six activity areas: dance, games, gymnastics, swimming and water safety, athletics, and outdoor and adventurous activities.

Much PE, in the UK at least, remains gender segregated,[2] allowing masculine and feminine cultures to flourish and be reflected in the activities carried out and the kinds of students who dominate the lessons. This is particularly the case in classes consisting only of boys and young men, who use prowess at sport and their developing muscular strength as a way of establishing and developing not only a physically based heterosexual hypermasculinity but also a social pecking-order in which those who are successful dominate, often to the point of bullying, those who are less so. [...]

Performing gender in secondary school PE

Within schools, the performance of gender, particularly of masculinity, is closely bound up with PE's position as the subject that focuses most directly on the body, both as an instrument and as an object of knowledge. Femininity is also performed in relation to PE, but largely in opposition to, rather than through physical activity. PE is concerned not just with the direct education and training of the body itself, but with the education of students about health and fitness. Thus, in PE lessons, the body is explicitly used, displayed and talked about. Bodily presentation and display are also important aspects of the performance of masculinity and femininity; this means that in PE teaching spaces and in the associated areas such as communal changing rooms and showers, claims (both physical and social) to dominant forms of heterosexual masculinity and femininity can be established and/or challenged. In these areas, students' gendered bodies and behaviours are both scrutinised and disciplined by their peer group, with public and negative labelling for those unwilling or unable to conform to group norms.

Because of the importance of the body in PE, and the association of sports and sporting prowess with hegemonic masculinities (Epstein *et al.*, 2001; Fitzclarence and Hickey, 2001),[3] PE lessons become an important arena for acting out such hypermasculinities and femininities, as well as for policing the behaviour of the peer group. In this context, those boys who are not good at or dislike physical activities and sport, or who enjoy those forms, such as dance, associated with femininity, stand out particularly strongly (Gard, 2001). Parker (1996) notes that, partly because of the larger amount of space available, including less closely supervised areas such as changing rooms, PE lessons can be an important site for acts of violence and aggression aimed at establishing and consolidating the dominance of hypermasculine young men. This was combined, in the school he studied, with the stigmatisation, as less than masculine, of those boys who were not particularly successful at school sport:

> Just as violence was utilised within physical education at Coleridge, as means by which the 'Hard Boys' could threaten, intimidate and dominate their 'Victims', so questions surrounding the sex/gender identities of pupils were raised by this group in order that their own masculine status might be reinforced, and that of others trivialised. What is more, the sporting inadequacies of a selection of 'Victims' and 'Conformists' provided the 'Hard Boys' with ample opportunity to ridicule certain individuals in terms of their inability to adhere to the masculine norms in play.
>
> (Parker, 1996, p. 148)

The relationship of girls and femininity to PE is more complex, partly because the agenda is at least partially set by the boys. Boys and young men clearly do not expect girls to have an interest in the subject; Nespor points out, for example, that even prepubescent boys use talking about sports as a marker of exclusive masculinity that denies any knowledge that girls might possess:

> A public preoccupation with sports was an assertion that a boy was a member of an indisputably male domain, an assertion made plausible by the continuing dominance of men's sports in the popular media and by the boys' refusal to talk with girls about sports, even when girls knew demonstrably more about the subject than the boys did.
>
> (Nespor, 1997, p. 147)

Thus an interest in sports is excluded for girls by their male peer-group, and there is evidence that this pressure on girls to distance themselves from PE and sports persists well into early adulthood. Furthermore, being good at PE, because it calls stereotypically heterosexual femininity into question, brings with it the implication that a young woman may not be fully or exclusively heterosexual; sporty young women are often assumed to be lesbians and can be subject to homophobic abuse as a result (Lenskyj, 1987; Dewar, 1990; Griffin, 1992; Sparkes, 1994). This means that for girls who like and are good at physical activities, it is important to demonstrate femininity through other means, such as the ways in which they dress and behave outside of sporting arenas (Dewar, 1990; Nelson, 1996).[4]

For many girls, however, femininity is demonstrated by a resistance to PE and sports, though there are some specifically feminine-labelled activities, such as aerobics and keep-fit, that are considered acceptable and practised outside of school. Scraton (1992) notes that before the introduction of the National Curriculum, such opportunities were commonly provided for older girls in English schools in an attempt to retain their interests; these activities, however, provided little physical challenge for girls, and were justified as 'an activity which won't mess up their hair or make them too sweaty' (Scraton, 1992, p. 107). The use of the body as a strong and powerful instrument runs counter to dominant notions of femininity, and adolescent girls, struggling to work out what it means to be women, may find this contradiction too much to deal with and therefore avoid the more physically taxing forms of PE; the failure of some PE departments, despite the requirements of the National Curriculum, to provide challenging activities for girls (Scraton, 1992; Curtner-Smith, 1999) colludes with this stance. The subject also involves elements of bodily display, often with the compulsory wearing of skimpy and body-revealing clothing, at a time when girls are particularly conscious of their developing bodies and resistant to having them observed. There is also some evidence that some PE arenas, such as mixed swimming galas and athletics meetings, can be occasions for sexual harassment of girls by boys (Scraton, 1992, 1993). The construction of some forms of PE, such as dance, as feminine, suitable for girls but not boys (Talbot, 1993), while giving girls a form of physical activity with which they are more likely to feel comfortable, at the same time reinforces the masculine image of more mainstream aspects of PE and makes it more likely that young women will construct and demonstrate their femininity in opposition to these.

Frank's typology of bodily usage

Because of the importance of the body to the knowledge base and practices of PE, different forms of bodily usage construct and are constructed through PE, sports and health and fitness practices both inside and outside of school. By taking part in the various forms of these we enact particular bodily types and forms. In the rest of this chapter I am going to describe and explain one particular typology of bodily forms and usages, that of Arthur W. Frank (1991, 1995), and then consider the extent to which these can be mapped onto particular forms of PE, sport and fitness-based activities. This mapping draws attention to how hypermasculine and hyperfeminine notions of how the body can be used have become instantiated in particular traditions and forms of PE, sport and fitness practices.

Frank (1991) emphasises both the corporeal nature of the body and its importance in carrying out actions that take place within discourses and institutions. 'Thus what I am calling "the body" is constituted in the intersection of an equilateral triangle the points of which are *institutions, discourses,* and *corporeality*' (p. 49). Within the complex configurations of discourses and institutions, he argues, bodies are used purposefully by the consciousness within them; 'the progression to the self must be through the body as consciousness of itself' (p. 50). This self-consciousness of the body is greatest when it encounters resistance. Hence, Frank proposes that there are four questions which the body must ask itself as it undertakes action in relationship to some object. These questions then provide the four continua within which types of body usage may be conceptualised (p. 51).

The first of these questions is that of *control,* of the predictability of performance. The second relates to *desire,* 'whether the body is lacking or producing' (p. 51); Frank argues that this problem is made particularly acute by consumer culture. Third comes the question of the body's *relation to others,* in particular as 'monadic, or closed in upon itself, or as dyadic, existing in relation of mutual constitution with others' (p. 52). Finally, there is the dimension of *self-relatedness:* does 'the body consciousness associate itself with its own being, particularly its surface, or dissociate itself from that corporeality?' (p. 52). The ways in which these questions are dealt with produces four ideal types of bodily activity, as can be seen in Figure 13.1.

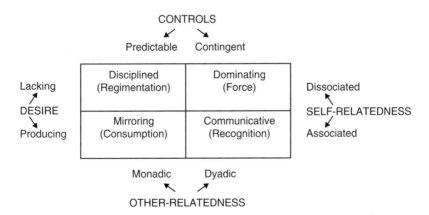

Figure 13.1 A typology of bodily use in action (from Frank, 1991, p. 54).

These four ideal types of body use represent four different resolutions of the questions of *control*, *desire*, *self-relatedness* and *other-relatedness* into different media of activity, which are their modes of action. It should be emphasised at this point that they are ideal types, and that real bodies move between different forms of activity, and thus different ways of experiencing and using the body. They also represent extreme points of intersecting continua, and some of the examples Frank uses to illustrate them, though based on historical accounts, demonstrate very extreme forms of human behaviour and approaches to the body. These ideal types are a useful heuristic, however, for exploring and understanding ways in which the body relates to discourses and institutions, and, in the specific case I am discussing here, how masculinity and femininity can be constructed through particular forms of physical activity.

The disciplined body

For the disciplined body the most important action-problem is that of control (Frank, 1995). It deals with this problem through regimentation; by following the regime it makes itself predictable. In doing so, it is dissociated from itself; this allows, for example, extreme ascetics to follow difficult regimes, because the body is seen as separate, as something to be overcome.[5] With regard to desire, the disciplined body sees itself as lacking, and attempts to remedy this lack by regimentation. To sustain the discipline of the regimen, however, the sense of lack must remain conscious, and the disciplined body tends to deal with this by placing itself in some kind of hierarchy in which it remains subordinated; military or monastic regimes are clear examples of this. Frank (1991) argues that when this happens 'subordination is a medium and outcome of lack. The lack justifies the subordination, which in turn reproduces the lack' (p. 55). Finally, the disciplined body, though part of a regimented group, is monadic in its relation to others; it is focused inwards towards itself and its performance of the regimen, not outwards towards the group.

The mirroring body

The mirroring body defines itself in acts of consumption and achieves predictability by mirroring what is around it. It seeks predictability of appearance, fearing disfigurement (Frank, 1995), and concerns itself with bodily surface, with its outward appearance. Frank (1995) argues that the mirroring body-self is almost compulsively associated with its body as a surface, with a primary focus on the visual. As its name suggests, it is essentially narcissistic, bound up in the details of its own surface, and unable to relate to others except as objects of consumption. It is uninterested in the interior of itself or of others, concerned entirely with surface forms. Frank (1991) notes, for example, that cosmetic surgery is one instantiation of the mirroring body, focusing as it does on the body's outward appearance rather than its inner condition. For the mirroring body, the lack of desire must remain unconscious, and this is achieved by the constant production of superficial desires through consumption (Shilling, 1993). Its narcissism means that the mirroring body is monadic in its relation to others, seeing that which is outside itself only in terms of how it can be consumed or used.

The dominating body

For the dominating body the most important body question is the sense of a lack of desire; which manifests itself as anxiety and fear. In order to overcome this lack, rather than turning in on itself, it displaces this anxiety and fear onto others, and turns to the subordination of these others, who may be seen as subhuman (Frank, 1991). It is dissociated from itself in order both to punish and to absorb punishment, and is pre-eminently a warrior body, 'which can only exist with itself by dominating' (Frank, 1991, p. 73). Frank further argues that the dominating body is fascinated by death and images of death, and that 'ultimately the soldier male's hatred is of life itself, as productive and contingent' (p. 76). It will be clear from this description that the dominating body is associated with masculinity, and indeed Frank points out that 'dominating bodies are, at least in the literature, exclusively male bodies. Hence it is impossible to consider the dominating body without also questioning the construction of the masculine body' (p. 69).[6]

The communicative body

The final form of bodily use in Frank's typology, and the only one of which he speaks positively, is also, in his view, more of a future possibility than a current actuality, though he does suggest that it may be found in some feminist dance forms and in some relationships between carers and those they care for. The communicative body, for Frank, represents an ethical ideal for bodies; it is how all our bodies should be and should act. Unlike the other three, the communicative body accepts its contingency not as something to be feared or controlled, but as part of the fundamental contingency of life, seeing it as a possibility rather than a problem. It is fully associated with both itself and others, and is productive of desire, which is for dyadic expression, not, as with the mirroring body, for monadic consumption (Frank, 1991). Frank suggests strongly that because of the unpredictability of women's periodicity and reproductive capacity, combined with what he sees as the other-relatedness of female desire (he argues that male sexuality is at least initially monadic), it is easier for female bodies to be communicative than for male; women, he suggests, are able to deal with dyadic other-relatedness without moving into domination. Thus the communicative body, if and when it exists, is for him strongly associated with femininity. I have serious reservations about this position, which seems at the very least to verge on biological essentialism, but will not discuss them here. It is important to understand, however, that I am not taking the position that female bodies or feminine bodily usage is necessarily communicative; indeed, I will argue later that stereotypical feminine forms of PE and fitness activities are much more closely associated with the mirroring body.

Bodily use, PE, sports and fitness practices

Given Frank's typology, how might we try to map it onto the different forms of PE, sporting and fitness activity available to young people inside and outside of schools, and what insights might this give us into the construction and sustaining of different forms of masculinity and femininity through these activities? The mapping is not altogether straightforward; we do not have a simple one-to-one correspondence between Frank's partially gendered bodily usages and the gendered forms of PE and sports. Although all activities are to some degree hybrids of at least two of the bodily usage types, I would contend that a partial mapping remains possible, and that this can give us some insights into how PE, fitness practice and sport invite and support particular forms of masculinity and femininity as part of their practices.

PE is one of the most strongly and overtly gendered school subjects. In UK secondary schools it is largely taught in gender-segregated groups, and attempts, both in the UK and elsewhere, to introduce and support mixed PE teaching have been at most only partially successful (Scraton, 1993; Kenway *et al.*, 1998). This overt gender divide within the subject not only has its origins in but remains reinforced by longstanding separate male and female PE traditions, in terms of training, orientation and activities; male PE, which has origins in military drill, is focused around competitive games and Olympic gymnastics, while female PE has its roots in educational and artistic gymnastics with an emphasis on movement and dance (Fletcher, 1984; Paechter, 2000). The training of PE teachers has itself only relatively recently become co-educational, so that some of those currently teaching it have themselves studied it in single-sex institutions or groups, not only at school but as student teachers, and are likely as a result to have limited expertise in those activities traditionally carried out by groups of the other gender. There is some evidence that this segregation has persisted beyond the introduction of coeducational PE colleges, due to the de facto exclusion of young women from full participation in traditionally male sports and the resistance of young men to the learning of rhythmic gymnastics and dance (Flintoff, 1993). Consequently, it seems reasonable to suggest that many PE activities remain strongly gendered in the minds of both staff and students.

PE and the disciplined body

The disciplined body is most closely associated with the origins of the male PE tradition in the drill sessions introduced into elementary schools in the UK around 1870 in an attempt to improve the supply of healthy military recruits (Fletcher, 1984). Military drill is in many ways the archetypal activity of the disciplined body; the body is subject to the command of a superior outside of itself and is expected to obey instantly and unthinkingly. The body thus becomes an automaton, subject to an outside authority and moving to a regular drumbeat or command (Foucault, 1977). Comparatively little of this form remains in PE or leisure-based sports and fitness activities today, although Lesko (2000) and Fitzclarence and Hickey (2001) point out that male athletes and sportsmen at all levels are expected to discipline their bodies to ignore pain so that they can carry on playing even when injured. However, although the male PE tradition in the UK originally had a strong link with disciplined bodily use, it would be fair to say that drill-based activities are now not often found outside of military training establishments and institutions modelled on these. It could be argued, however, that drill lingers on in some forms of circuit training, in which participants move from activity to activity at set times and to the sound of a whistle. It is interesting to note that Scraton (1992) found that some schools used such activity as a punishment for groups of girls who had misbehaved in more feminine-marked PE activities. Such an activity seemed to be construed as something teenage girls were bound to dislike, despite many being observed by Scraton to enjoy these sessions. This underlines the masculine marking of such forms of PE.

PE and the dominating body

Current forms of PE and sports which are both masculine marked and fall strongly into the male PE tradition, however, particularly competitive team games, seem to have a predominantly dominating body usage. This is particularly noticeable in those masculine arenas (e.g. male US high school teams, and at professional level) in which winning is seen as all-important. Rees (1997) argues, for example, that in the US winning at team games (not just participation, as is traditionally the case in the UK) is seen as building character, and that team games have historically been considered as instilling 'manly' characteristics. Such characteristics reflect those of the dominating body, which is dissociated not only from others but from itself, trained neither to feel its own pain nor to empathise with that of others. Sporting activities are also an important terrain for the demonstration of masculine prowess (Wright, 1996; Fitzclarence and Hickey, 2001), again reflecting the warrior as the paradigmatic instantiation of the dominating body. The sports-related focus on overcoming the opposition is a central characteristic of the dominating body, which can only deal with its own lack through the domination and subjugation of others. Although it remains the case (in the UK at least) that most students taking part in team games have as their main motivation the experience of playing in a team and for fun (Penney and Evans, 1994), it is undeniable that the main and overt purpose of competitive games is precisely that, competition, with the ultimate aim of victory over one's opponent(s). This is reflected, for example, in the language of the English National Curriculum for PE, where even children under seven are expected to learn 'simple tactics for attacking and defending' (Department for Education and Employment, 1999, p. 17). Furthermore, some of the competitive games played in the US, Australia and the UK (American football, Australian rules football, rugby, for example) have violent aspects which, in some cases, require participants to wear what amounts to forms of body armour; this emphasises the similarities to traditional battlefield structures, where the subjugation of the opposing force is paramount (Fitzclarence and Hickey, 2001). Finally, the competitive and dominating activity of the dominating body is, at its extremes, characterised as all-encompassing. Frank (1991) quotes one of the Freikorps soldiers studied by Theweleit (1987) as saying that:

> The only real thing was fighting. (You couldn't be a man without fighting, and being a man was the only way of being alive.) When there is no more fighting, no more being a man, life ceases and everything (the man, the world) becomes a pulp.
>
> (Theweleit, 1987, quoted in Frank, 1991, p. 71)

If we replace the word 'fighting' with 'football' do we not have the world-view of many young men in British society – albeit that their participation is at least in part vicarious, as spectators rather than players? This suggests that, taken to extremes (as it is for a significant number of men in British and, it is likely, US and Australian society), the overwhelmingly hypermasculine dominating body is constructed in and through participation, both as player and spectator, in competitive team sports, both inside and outside of school.

PE, fitness practices and the mirroring body

The mirroring body is stereotypically feminine in orientation, and this is reflected in many of the PE and fitness practices that are associated with it. The female PE tradition, with its origins in the Swedish Ling system of gymnastics, originally focused on outward manifestations of female health such as movement and posture (Fletcher, 1984); these practices seem therefore clearly to be those of the mirroring body, though the drill-like approach of the early years provide some elements of the disciplined body. This was later displaced by a form of educational gymnastics associated with Laban, which blurred the line between gymnastics and dance, and, in Australia, with artistic gymnastics (Wright, 1996). These too, as does dance, focus on the body as an object of display, as something to be looked upon, whether by itself or by others, and suggest a move further towards the ideal type of the mirroring body. Work in this area, however, gradually became more problem-solving and child-centred. While retaining their monadic nature, with each individual largely working alone with their own body, such practices in theory move away from the body surface and towards a greater self-relatedness that accepts bodily difference and imperfection. Scraton (1992) suggests, however, that the practice of female PE retains a focus on outward forms, particularly 'feminine grace, poise, finesse and flexibility' (p. 96) and an emphasis on an end goal of looking good for others rather than developing strength and fitness for their own sakes.

> In each school the case study observations noted an emphasis on 'standards' of appearance, presentation and specific 'ladylike' behaviour. For girls and young women, physical education reinforces one primary objective of the 'physical'; to look good for others with a central concern for personal appearance.
>
> (Scraton, 1992, p. 101)

Other fitness practices fall very clearly into the ideal type of the mirroring body, and it is interesting to note that not only are these activities not rejected by girls and young women, but that the overwhelming majority of those taking part are female. Such activities were a common feature of provision for older girls in England before the introduction of the National Curriculum for PE (Scraton, 1992), and may remain so in many schools despite their lack of fit with the statutory curriculum (Curtner-Smith, 1999). Aerobics and fitness classes are almost entirely the province of women, and their aim is at least as much the shaping of the outward form of the body as its inner health and wellbeing. This is in some cases even reflected in the language used; classes are advertised as 'legs, bums and tums' with the obvious connotation that they are designed to 'improve' the outward appearance of these supposedly 'problem' areas of the female anatomy. The spatial layout of aerobics studios (and many gymnasia) is also literally mirroring, with enormous mirrors so that the bodies of the practitioners are permanently on display both to themselves and to others.

In many ways, the ultimate physical practice within the use paradigm of the mirroring body is that of body-building. This also has a number of elements which are both transgressive and at the same time reinforcing of the stereotypes of both masculinity and femininity. While body-building practices are not encouraged or taught in school, they are becoming more popular among teenage boys. Here, the look of the body is pre-eminent, designed for visual consumption, and the body is explicitly 'pumped up' into artificial poses that show the musculature to best advantage. It is the only masculine-associated fitness activity for which the mirroring body is the paradigmatic form of use, and it is interesting that this mirroring nature, this strong element of display, is itself transgressive of heterosexual masculinity; it is usually women's bodies that are on display, not men's. It is only the display of large amounts of muscle that distinguishes male body-building competitions from beauty contests (male body-builders even remove their body hair). At the same time, female body-builders are considered sufficiently transgressive of stereotypical femininity for there to be a requirement of explicitly displayed heterosexual femininity in competitions; in order to preserve the 'feminine' look despite their supremely muscular bodies they are expected to compete in full make-up and with bouffant hair, and those whose breasts have shrunk as a result of diet and exercise may feel compelled to have implants to preserve the illusion of femininity (Johnston, 1996).

> ... By tacking breasts onto female muscle, the female bodybuilder might be seen to make a particularly forceful move towards reinscribing herself within the site of the male gaze and male fetishism.
>
> (Coles, 1994–1995, p. 69)

Once again, it is not the body as a whole that is at issue here, but the surface features of a body produced by and for consumption. That the breasts have been lost to exercise is immaterial; they have to be reinstated so that the body as a whole can appear as expected for a claim of femininity.

Aspects of the mirroring body, then, map onto particular forms of PE and other health, fitness and exercise practices, to construct stereotypical forms of femininity, along with a transgressive but rapidly reinscribed heterosexual femininity and a transgressively heterosexual masculinity 'saved' from its transgression by the very visible outward forms of male muscle. Or, to put it another way, these PE, health and fitness practices construct a version of femininity that is closely bound up with particular forms of body display. Like the hypermasculinities constructed through competitive sporting practices, these femininities are extreme and stereotypical, even in the initially transgressive form of the female bodybuilder.

Conclusion

The mapping of some forms of PE, sports and fitness activities onto gendered forms of bodily usage suggests that PE, sports and fitness practices as currently constructed support the development and perpetuation of gendered forms of bodily usage. The dominance of competitive sport (in popular culture, though less than heretofore in the official PE curriculum (Department for Education and Employment, 1999)) and monadic, surface-focused fitness practices discourage the development and use of open, communicative bodily practices and forms. Such practices and forms might, because of their empathetic other-relatedness, cut across and undercut stereotypical notions of masculinity and femininity (Gard, 2001). How we might move towards such practices within school PE is not clear, however. Frank (1991) suggests that experimental and feminist dance practices may be one way through which the communicative body could be realised. However, dance has such historically and stereotypically feminine connotations, particularly within the traditional PE curriculum, that this is unlikely to be a way forward in practice, though Gard (2001) suggests that it is for precisely this reason that dance could be a fertile area for challenging dominant constructions of masculinity. It may be that the co-operative nature of some outdoor adventure activities, if they can be prevented from becoming arenas for displays of masculine prowess, may give some possibilities for using PE to encourage more open, communicative and connective body practices and break the stranglehold that gender stereotypes have on the more traditional forms of PE and sport. What is certain, is that unless we can find a way to cut through the gendering of these traditions to a more communicative, gender-neutral or gender-transgressive way of encouraging children and young people to use their bodies, they and we will remain stuck in gender stereotyped bodily usages that are disempowering to all concerned.

Notes

1 Buchbinder (1994) relates hypermasculinity to 'excessive maleness' and 'machismo' (p. 1); I treat it similarly as an exaggerated form of stereotypical masculinity, focusing on physical prowess, sexual conquest, hardness and the image of extreme rationality. Hyperfemininity is its counterpart in the feminine, emphasising and exaggerating stereotypical forms of femininity such as softness, helplessness, sexual subordination combined with bodily display, and a strong focus on the home and homemaking.
2 Gender segregation is neither encouraged nor discouraged in the National Curriculum for PE.
3 This association is not exclusively heterosexual within wider society; the sexualised display of the strong male body is an important theme in some forms of homoerotic imagery. Within schools, however, physical prowess is strongly and exclusively associated with heterosexual masculinities; terms of homophobic abuse are used against those boys who dislike or perform badly at PE and sport. In consequence, in this chapter I will focus on the heterosexually-marked aspects of sports-based hypermasculinities.
4 Due to racialised images of femininity, this pressure appears, at least in the UK, to apply less to girls and young women of African-Caribbean descent.
5 Although I shall argue that the forms of PE associated with the disciplined body are predominantly masculine, it seems likely that one instantiation of the disciplined body is the overwhelmingly female affliction of anorexia nervosa. The bodily forms are not necessarily associated of themselves with masculinity or femininity, though Frank clearly regards the dominating and communicative bodies as primarily attributes of males and females, respectively.
6 Frank appears to see masculinity and femininity as unproblematically heterosexual.

References

Buchbinder, D. (1994) *Masculinities and Identities* (Melbourne, Melbourne University Press).

Coles, F. (1994–1995) Feminine charms and outrageous arms, *Trouble and Strife*, 29/30, pp. 67–72.

Curtner-Smith, M.D. (1999) The more things change the more they stay the same: factors influencing teachers' interpretations and delivery of National Curriculum Physical Education, *Sport, Education and Society*, 4, pp. 75–97.

Department for Education and Employment (1999) *Physical Education* (London, Department for Education and Employment/Qualifications and Curriculum Authority).

Dewar, A. (1990) Oppression and privilege in physical education: struggles in the negotiation of gender in a university programme, in: D. Kirk and R. Tinning (Eds) *Physical Education, Curriculum and Culture* (Basingstoke, Falmer Press).

Epstein, D., Kehily, M., Mac an Ghaill, M. and Redman, P. (2001) Boys and girls come out to play: making masculinities and femininities in school playgrounds, *Men and Masculinities*, 4, pp. 158–172.

Fitzclarence, L. and Hickey, C. (2001) Real footballers don't eat quiche: old narratives in new times, *Men and Masculinities*, 4, pp. 118–139.

Fletcher, S. (1984) *Women First* (London, The Althone Press).

Flintoff, A. (1993) Gender, physical education and initial teacher education, in: J. Evans (Ed.) *Equality, Education and Physical Education* (London, Falmer Press).

Foucault, M. (1977) *Discipline and Punish* (London, Penguin).

Frank, A.W. (1991) For a sociology of the body: an analytical review, in: M. Featherstone, M. Hepworth and B.S. Turner (Eds) *The Body: social process and cultural theory* (London, Sage Publications).

Frank, A.W. (1995) *The Wounded Storyteller: body, illness and ethics* (Chicago, IL, University of Chicago Press).

Gard, M. (2001) Dancing around the 'problem' of boys and dance, *Discourse*, 22, pp. 213–225.

Griffin, P. (1992) Changing the game: homophobia, sexism and lesbians in sport, *Quest*, 44, pp. 251–265.

Johnston, L. (1996) Flexing femininity: female body-builders refiguring 'the body', *Gender, Place and Culture*, 3, pp. 327–340.

Kenway, J., Willis, S., Blackmore, J. and Rennie, L. (1998) *Answering Back: girls, boys and feminism in schools* (London, Routledge).

Lenskyj, H. (1987) Female sexuality and women's sport, *Women's Studies International Forum*, 10, pp. 381–386.

Lesko, N. (2000) Preparing to Teach (crossed out) Coach: tracking the gendered relations of dominance, on and off the football field, in: N. Lesko (Ed.) *Masculinities at School* (Thousand Oaks, CA, Sage Publications).

Nelson, M.B. (1996) *The Stronger Women Get, the More Men Love Football* (London, The Women's Press).

Nespor, J. (1997) *Tangled up in School* (Mahwah, NJ, Lawrence Erlbaum Associates).

Paechter, C.F. (2000) *Changing School Subjects: power, gender and curriculum* (Buckingham, Open University Press).

Parker, A. (1996) The construction of masculinity within boys' physical education, *Gender and Education*, 8, pp. 141–157.

Penney, D. and Evans, J. (1994) It's just not (and not just) cricket, *British Journal of Physical Education*, 25, pp. 9–12.

Rees, C.R. (1997) Still building American character: sport and the physical education curriculum, *The Curriculum Journal*, 8, pp. 199–212.

Scraton, S. (1992) *Shaping Up to Womanhood: gender and girls' physical education* (Buckingham, Buckingham University Press).

Scraton, S. (1993) Equality, coeducation and physical education, in: J. Evans (Ed.) *Equality, Education and Physical Education* (London, Falmer Press).

Shilling, C. (1993) *The Body and Social Theory* (London, Sage Publications).

Sparkes, A.C. (1994) Self, silence and invisibility as a beginning teacher: a life history of lesbian experience, *British Journal of Sociology of Education*, 15, pp. 93–118.

Talbot, M. (1993) A gendered physical education: equality and sexism, in: J. Evans (Ed.) *Equality, Education and Physical Education* (London. Falmer Press).

Theweleit, K. (1987) *Male Fantasies, Volume 1: women, floods, bodies, history* (Minneapolis, MN, University of Minnesota Press).

Wright, J. (1996) Mapping the discourses of physical education: articulating a female tradition, *Journal of Curriculum Studies*, 28, pp. 331–351.

CHAPTER 15

MASCULINITY, VIOLENCE AND SCHOOLING
Challenging 'poisonous pedagogies'

Jane Kenway and Lindsay Fitzclarence, *Gender and Education*, 9, 1, 1997

Introduction

Violence is one of the major social problems of our times and so should be one of the major issues in current debates about education. As people have become more aware of the extent and consequences of domestic violence, childhood sexual abuse, sexual harassment, homophobia and racial vilification, our understanding of violence has become more nuanced and the definition of violence has widened. It is increasingly understood that violence occurs along a continuum and involves physical, sexual, verbal and emotional abuses of power at individual, group and social structural levels. Kelly (1987) argues that violence involves 'a continuous series of elements or events that pass into one another and cannot be readily distinguished' but that, nonetheless, these different events 'have a basic common character' (1987, p. 48). Our particular focus in this chapter is on physical violence (sexual and other assault and homicide). However, the backdrop to our understanding is the Kelly continuum. In this context of understanding many social institutions and cultural forms have become implicated in discussions about both the causes of violence and its prevention. One such institution is the school.

There are several bodies of research literature which support the following contentions: that violence is widespread in schools, that most often such violence is perpetrated by males and can thus be understood as a violent expression of certain types of masculinity, that schools are implicated in the making of masculinities and that consequently they can be involved in the unmaking of the types of masculinity which are implicated in violence. It is increasingly accepted that schools have an important role to play in the prevention of violence. However, the connections between the matters noted and the exact role of the school with regard to the prevention of violence and how it might best be carried out are not at all clear. These are the difficult issues which we will begin to address.

Violence and masculinity, marginality, sexuality, intimacy and age

[. . .] It is now fairly well understood that the social, cultural and psychic construction of masculinity is related to violence and that some kinds of masculinity are more directly associated with violent behaviour than are others. It is less well understood that particular types of masculinity are related to particular types of violence. Which masculinity is most associated with such physical violence as sexual and other assault and homicide and what are its key features? Answers to this question must be placed in the context of our current understandings of the construction of masculinity itself and its relationship to the politics of gender between males and females and between males alone. [. . .]

The most convincing discussions of the construction of masculinities, and it is difficult to go past Connell (1995) here, make the following points. They argue firstly that masculine identities are not static but historically and spatially situated and evolving. They arise through an individual's interaction with both the dynamisms and contradictions within and between immediate situations and broader social structures – gender regimes and gender orders. It is this under-standing which allows Connell to talk about masculinity as a life *project* involving the making and remaking of identity and meaning. It also allows us to understand the social and psychic complexity and fragility of masculinity. An appreciation of such complexity and fragility is essential to an understanding of male violence.

Although there are many masculinities, these can be clustered on the basis of general social, cultural and institutional patterns of power and meaning and are built in relationship to each other. Connell (1995, ch. 3) calls these *hegemonic, subordinate, complicitous and marginal*. The concept 'hegemonic masculinity' is now widely used in discussions of masculinity and refers to those dominant and dominating forms of masculinity which claim the highest status and exercise the greatest influence and authority. It structures dominance and subordinate relations across and between the sexes and legitimates the broad structure of power known as patriarchy. Hegemonic masculinity makes its claims and asserts its authority through many cultural and institutional practices – particularly the global image media and the state, and although it does not necessarily involve physical violence it is often underwritten by the threat of such violence. Subordinate masculinity stands in direct opposition to hegemonic masculinity and is both repressed and oppressed by it. Indeed, as Connell (1995, p. 79) says, it is 'expelled from the circle' of masculine legitimacy. Gay masculinities feature in this category. Also represented are any forms which draw most elements of their core identity from beyond the core of the hegemonic. Any major attachment to 'the feminine' is likely to propel its owner into this category and to subject him to various forms of violence. Hegemonic masculinity is the standard-bearer of what it means to be a 'real' man or boy and many males draw inspiration from its cultural library of resources. Nonetheless, few men can live up to its rigorous standards. Many may try and many may not, but either way, according to Connell, they benefit from the '*patriarchal dividend*; the advantage men in general gain from the overall subordi-nation of women...without the tensions or risks of being the front line troops of patriarchy' (1995, p. 79). In this sense, he says, in the politics of gender, they are complicitous with hegemonic forms of masculinity even if they fail to live up to and do not draw moral inspiration from its imperatives.

Connell (1995, p. 80) says that these masculinity dynamics are 'internal to the gender order. The interplay of gender with other structures such as class and race creates further relationships between masculinities'. In order to explain the dynamics going on here he argues that there are masculinities associated with the dominant and subordinate or *marginal* races and classes. He further notes that these marginalised masculinities, which are associated with subordinate social groupings, may draw both inspiration and legitimacy from hegemonic forms but only wield structural power to the extent that they are *authorised* by the dominant class/race. Thus, while marginal masculinities may not be marginal within their own patch, they are unlikely to exert power beyond it without some sort of sponsorship by and only within the tolerance limits of the dominant. In summary, what we see here is the ebb and flow of masculinities in concert and contest.

It is commonly accepted that masculinities cannot be fully understood without attending to their relationship to femininities within the broader scope of patriarchy. It is therefore important to identify the sorts of femininities which unwittingly underwrite hegemonic masculinity. The literature suggests that this particular version of femininity involves compliance and service, subservience and self-sacrifice and constant accommodating to the needs and desires of males. This indicates that anti violence education is not a boys' only matter.

The emphasis on the fragile and fluid nature of masculinities in the context of dynamic power politics between males and females and between males points to the uncertainty of settlements about what constitutes masculinity in a given person, time and place and between and within groups. It also suggests that some masculinities may be more 'at risk' than others. Such settlements are challenged both intentionally and unintentionally by an array of life forces. The social movements associated with feminism, gay and lesbian movements and anti racism are amongst such forces, but so too are other and perhaps bigger historical sweeps associated with such major economic and cultural shifts as post-modernity. In turn this means that many masculinities are constantly on the offensive and the defensive and in need of regular maintenance, renewal, repair and adjustment (Kenway, 1995). Nonetheless, when insecure, masculinity is likely to 'lash back', to reinvent itself and to try to shore up either its old or new foundations. [. . .]

Predictably and in very general terms it is the characteristics most associated with hegemonic masculinity which are most likely to be articulated with violence, but not in the obvious way that simplistic discussions of 'macho values' might suggest. At this stage of Western history, hegemonic masculinity mobilises around physical strength, adventurousness, emotional neutrality, certainty, control, assertiveness, self-reliance, individuality, competitiveness, instrumental skills, public knowledge, discipline, reason, objectivity and rationality. It distances itself from physical weakness, expressive skills, private knowledge, creativity, emotion, dependency, subjectivity, irrationality, co-operation and empathetic, compassionate, nurturant and certain affiliative behaviours. In other words it distances itself from the feminine and considers the feminine less worthy. Violent males draw selectively from this repertoire, exaggerate, distort and glorify these values, attributes and behaviours and blend them into potent combinations. For example, rather than distance themselves from the feminine they might avoid and even fear it; rather than look down upon the feminine they might hold it in contempt and despise it; rather than consider women and children their inferior, they may regard them as less than human and more as objects and possessions to be used and discarded at will. To take some more quick examples, assertiveness may be exaggerated to become aggression, physical strength to toughness associated with physically beating others, bravery to bravado and cruelty, adventurousness to extreme risk-taking, self-discipline to disciplining others as well, self-reliance to isolation – preferably from above, emotional neutrality to emotional repression on the one hand and to extremes of rage and shame on the other, competitiveness to hostility, rationality to the rationalisation of violence, sexual potency to control over and contempt for women's bodies and so on.

Violent cultures, be they in the family, the school, the locker room, the pub, the workplace or the street, draw from, distort and exaggerate discourses from the discursive field of hegemonic masculinity. Nonetheless, their emotional underbelly remains characterised by identity uncertainty, anxiety and fear; with unfortunate consequences. The consequences involve what Miller (1987a) labels a complicated psycho dynamic mechanism of splitting off from uncomfortable feelings and of projecting such feelings on to an externalised object or other person. Such splitting and displacement are key features of violence. Miller (1987b, pp. 88–89) uses the notion of the *vicious circle of contempt* to explain how emotions that cause discomfort are projected on to others. She describes the process thus: 'Contempt for those who are smaller and weaker thus is the best defence against a break-through of one's own feelings of helplessness: it is an expression of this split-off weakness.' Let us now consider some more specific examples of violence – male to male, male to female and adult male to child.

Male/male violence

The literature on boys and schooling is replete with examples of school boy tribalism and tribal rivalry. It shows that groups develop a distinctive style either in line with or against the criteria mentioned above. Boy groups offer their members peer friendship, pleasure and pride, identity development, excitement and status resources and goals. However, there is often a price to pay for both the individual and the group.

In and out of school life for many adolescent boys is characterised by constant attempts to sort out identity issues and dominance relations (Weisfeld, 1994, p. 56). Dominance performances and contests occur at the individual and the group level, may revolve around issues of toughness, athletic ability, strength, popularity with girls, sexual achievements, risk-taking, fearlessness and fighting prowess. These will often include harassing girls, teachers and other boys, particularly those identified as 'gay'. Sexual harassment and homophobic violence can be seen to arise from the gender politics, hetero/sexist politics (Epstein, 1996) and the fear of the feminine noted above. Such performances are directed towards reputation, towards being seen as strong, cool and in control and towards saving face, avoiding humiliation. Often dominance displays will involve a calculated rejection of school achievement and an anti-authority stance.

Male dominance/subordination relations are often worked out through the use of legitimate (sport) and illegitimate (brawling, bashing) physical violence. Again, such violence is premised on beliefs about the importance of aggressive and violent acts for gaining and maintaining status, reputation and resources in the male group, to sustain a sense of masculine identity and as a form of 'self' protection. Studies of violent older boys in the school and in out of school gangs show that much time is spent seeking respect and striving for positional power which is recognised by the group. However, power here is unstable and those who achieve positional power must work hard to sustain it. As a consequence, such groups often are characterised by intense male to male competition for dominance. Taking risks and fighting over drugs, territory, honour, girls, perceived insults, and ethnic tension can readily transform into assaults and homicides when access to alcohol, drugs and weapons is readily available and involved (Goldstein, 1994).

The boys and men from racial and class minorities who subscribe to the beliefs about violence outlined above and who use various forms of violence to demonstrate their power and potency may find that it pays off in group leadership, popularity, pride, friendship and excitement and other resources which may not be available to them in other settings outside, say, the group or gang. Indeed, there is an argument which suggests that it is the groups of boys who are most marginalised by society and by the school who are most prone to violence and who subscribe to such values and who, paradoxically, are victims of such values. They are Connell's 'shock-troops'; those who do the dirty work of patriarchy.

The argument goes that for boys who are in poverty, from racial and ethnic minority cultures, who are educationally disadvantaged, homeless, unemployed, risky and violent behaviour provides almost the only way of obtaining status and cultural resources. In other words, physical violence may well be most pronounced among those who have more to gain and little to lose (in the short term at least), most likely to occur amongst those outside the mainstream of education, employment and stable relationships. Such behaviour provides 'an opportunity to exercise personal power under conditions of minimal structural power...a mode of influence of last resort' (Archer, 1994, p. 317). What we see in these examples is the consequences for individuals of belonging to groups with less structural power and status and the ways in which a lack of power and status at the structural level can result in the exercise of violence at the individual and group level. What we also see are the consequences of the failure of society and its institutions to integrate all its members. This is not to suggest that males from other social groupings are non-violent, rather it is to offer an explanation for the relatively high levels of violence among disadvantaged groups. [. . .]

Male/female violence

Violence by males against females most commonly takes the form of rape and sexual assault, domestic violence and verbal and physical harassment. Most violence against women and girls occurs within relationships of one sort or another. Intimate relations and settings are more likely to result in violence than are stranger relations and public spaces, although clearly violence erupts there too. Even so there is overwhelming evidence to show that verbal and physical harassment, teasing and taunting relating to sexuality or gender against girls and women is rife in schools. Most boys either engage in this or comply with it.

The literature indicates that the males who are most likely to resort to serious physical violence against females subscribe to traditional and patriarchal views of male power and supremacy, traditional gender roles and to the view that violence is an acceptable way of resolving conflict. They believe that men are superior to women and have natural rights over them and natural dues from them. These include the following: the male's right to regard the woman as property and legitimately to control her through violence; the belief that it is legitimate to use physical violence when the rights and dues are not fulfilled and to resolve interpersonal conflict through the use of violence. When the male's status or power is threatened in some way, violence is regarded as an appropriate way of restoring the right and proper order – of keeping women in a subservient position. In this view the male's sense of his masculine identity is caught up in the exercise of power over women through violence.

Sex and sexuality are a key feature of this scenario. Misogyny easily translates into sexual violence. Denigrating women and girls legitimates such violence and allows violent males selectively to interpret their own behaviour around, for example, 'only joking' motifs and to ignore the feelings of others. Violent males' reputations may be based on obtaining sexual access to women but their self-worth is often caught up in the sexual dominance and exploitation of women. Callous sexual attitudes are a common feature of the conversation of young males in schools, as are conceptions of sexual violence as manly – this is how 'real men' treat women (Wood, 1984). Belonging to a sexually exploitative peer group is more than likely to predispose a young man towards violence against girls and women. There are many generally accepted social beliefs which develop a cultural tolerance of rape and other sorts of violence against women and girls. These are called *rape myths* and prepare the male for his rape or harassment activities through a cultural library of excuses to forgive his misdemeanours.

There is a literature which argues that males and females have different orientations to aggression and violence. This suggests that to males, violence is instrumental to obtaining tangible or abstract benefits. As Anne Campbell (1993, p. 11) says:

> men see aggression as a means of exerting control over other people when they fell the need to reclaim power and self esteem. Women see aggression as a temporary loss of control caused by overwhelming pressure and resulting in guilt.

To women violence represents an emotion and not coping rather than an exercise of power. This literature also suggests that men and women have different orientations to intimacy. It suggests that men who subscribe to traditional versions of masculinity find intimacy terrifying as it represents the feminine values about which they are so fearful. It 'makes' them feel vulnerable and puts their sense of control at risk. For women, intimacy is more the natural order of things and they find it difficult to understand and deal with such men's distancing behaviour with regard to it. When one brings these understandings to the issues of violence between males and females in relationships we see a fundamental clash of styles and understandings with explosive potential. Further, as Jenkins (1990, p. 37) argues:

> males have an exaggerated sense of entitlement and status in relation to females and children, an avoidance of social and emotional responsibility and a reliance on others (especially females) to take social and emotional responsibilities.

Adult male/child violence

Childhood sexual abuse/assault is more difficult to explain than the other forms of violence discussed above. Nonetheless it is not too difficult to extrapolate from those values associated with violence against females – particularly those associated with entitlement and emotional irresponsibility. Most cases involve adult males aged between 35 and 40 years of age; however, as Andrews (1994) reports, they have no agreed profile. Even so, many have cognitive distortions about the acceptability of their behaviour, which often has traumatic consequences for survivors leading to severe psychological problems and next generation offences. This inter-generational process is well explored and explained by Alice Miller, formerly a practising psychoanalyst for over 20 years and currently a strong critic of both psychoanalytic theories and methods.

Miller's (1987a,b, 1990) basic thesis is that from generation to generation the practices of child-rearing privilege the needs of adults over those of children. Based on her many years of counselling, she argues that this often involves various forms of abuse – some obvious, some not so. Either way, the processes involved are aimed at breaking the will of the child in order that he or she can be controlled. Miller argues that when children are abused in this way they are 'trained' to be abusive and that as a result they learn, subconsciously, how to 'train' others in turn. Miller calls this process *poisonous pedagogy*. She observes that the effects of this abuse are destined to be repeated by victims at a later time in their lives unless they have had an opportunity to acknowledge what has happened and to work through the associated feelings. The absence of such a conscious acknowledgement of the powerful feelings associated with abuse leads, she says, to the ongoing return of repressed anxieties and frustrations and this can sometimes lead to violent and destructive behaviours. Such behaviour is often rationalised in the perpetrator's mind and thus made 'legitimate'. This in turn leads to further repressions, and to the cyclical repetition of the behaviour. In order for a person to break out of the cycle and avoid violent and abusive behaviour, he/she has to be able both to acknowledge the situation and to understand and integrate anger/fear/frustration as part of him/herself.

'Schooling the violent imagination'[1]

What does all of this imply about school education? Here are the hard truths as we see them based on our preceding analysis. If schools implicitly subscribe to and endorse hegemonic versions of masculinity, particularly in their more exaggerated forms, then they are complicit in the production of violence. If they fear 'the feminine' and avoid and discourage empathetic, compassionate, nurturant and affiliative behaviours and emotional responsibility and instead favour heavy-handed discipline and control then they are complicit. If they seek to operate only at the level of rationality and if they rationalise violence then they are complicit. If they are structured in such a way as to endorse the culture of male entitlement and indicate that the needs of males are more important than those of females then they are complicit. If they are repressive in their adult/child relations and do not offer adolescent students in particular opportunities to develop wise judgements and to exercise their autonomy in responsible ways then they are complicit. If they operate in such a way as to marginalise and stigmatise certain groups of students then they are complicit. [. . .]

It is our view that interventions which do not attend to all these matters will be limited in their effects and conversely that whatever schools do to address the issue of violence must attend to them (Fitzclarence *et al.*, 1995). However, how schools might best do this is not at all clear. We do not know as much as we need to know about schooling and violence, let alone about making gender and related matters central components of educational challenges to it. That aside, the main difficulty in all of this is firstly that *gender, age and marginality* are central structuring features of school cultures and education systems, and secondly that *emotional neutrality and hyper-rationality* are core structuring values. Hence, to attend to the matters mentioned is to go right to the heart of school culture (Fitzclarence, 1995).

Attending to school culture is not a popular approach in anti-violence programmes in schools. Most approaches draw their insights from psychology. This has meant that they have concentrated on the personal and interpersonal and the small scale. The dominant tendency here has been to individualise and pathologise and indeed infantilise the violence which occurs within schools and/or to blame the peer group, family and/or the media for violence both in schools and beyond. Such approaches have not encouraged schools to see themselves as amongst the many institutions which are complicit in the production of violent behaviour. More recently however, the focus has shifted, at least in some quarters.

This shift has resulted from insights developed in educational sociology and feminism. According to this view, the school is not the innocent victim of isolated incidents of violence, neither is it the safe haven for victims of outside violence; violence is embedded in its culture and power relationships. In many obvious and subtle ways schools model permit and shape violent attitudes and behaviours, they encourage students to accept that certain levels and orders of violence are normal and natural. This means that violence often goes unrecognised and unaddressed. This set of perspectives has encouraged 'whole school' approaches to addressing violence at the level of administration and curriculum (see Salisbury and Jackson, 1996).

This general approach provides a necessary corrective to those which focus on the psychology of the individual or group. Clearly, an adequate understanding of patterns of violence in schools requires a holistic perspective. However, it is not clear to us that even the sociocultural or the psychological perspectives *together* offer such a perspective. As we have implied throughout; it is not a matter of putting the big picture alongside the small, it is a matter of seeing how each is represented in the other. It is also our view that the sociocultural perspective does not attend sufficiently to what we have identified above as the central components of violence. Indeed, we would go so far as to say that some of the approaches contribute to the very problems that they seek to eradicate. How could this possibly be? Some examples from the research into gender reform and education in schools by one of us will serve to illustrate the point. Further details of the research are provided in Kenway *et al.* (1997) so suffice it to say that case, cameo and survey data were gathered in many schools which were selected because they were undertaking some sort of gender reform. The schools ranged over various types and locations and included students of different social and cultural catchments. This choice of example is apt as gender reform should be a central component of anti violence programmes.

We categorised strategies for gender reform in our research schools into two broad camps, one which demonstrated elements of authoritarianism and the other, elements of therapy. In the first instance the tendency was to ignore altogether the world of feelings and to resort to highly rationalistic and even authoritarian policies and pedagogies. Hyper-rationalistic solutions were offered to deeply emotive issues. In many cases these subverted their intentions and alienated many students and staff. Alternatively, when they did attend to such matters, it was often the case that the approach was more therapeutic than educational. Ensuring that students and colleagues enjoyed themselves and/or felt good about their gender became more important than helping them to become critical, informed and skilled advocates for a better world. Usually for the people on the receiving end, either too much or too little was demanded and at stake. In both cases gender reform in our schools was a heady emotional cocktail. The feelings which were mobilised included discomfort, uncertainty, inadequacy, defensiveness, anxiety, envy, insecurity, stress, anger, resentment, rejection, contempt, fear, grief, loss, pain, blame, shame, betrayal, and abandonment. They also included feelings of pleasure, courage, yearning, security, strength, comfort, amusement, delight, connectedness, excitement, gratification and even gusto, but, to be honest, less often. As a result the effects of gender reform were not easy to predict (Kenway *et al.*, 1996). Nonetheless, on the basis of this research it is possible to make some points which pertain to anti-violence education.

This research suggests that approaches which preach rather than teach and which are destructive rather than deconstructive and reconstructive do not work. Adolescents do not like to be told and they particularly do not like to have the things they do and value criticised by older generations. Peer relations are generally considered far more important than teacher–student relations. The implication here is that a socially critical/deconstructive *negotiated* curriculum is preferable; one which guides and encourages students both to discover their own truths about gender, marginality and age and violence and to develop their own responsible preventative practices. This should be a curriculum which is oriented towards action. It should treat students as agents of rather than passive recipients of anti-violence reform. There is another implication here about discipline. As we indicated above, repressive practices help to produce violence and also prevent victims/survivors from addressing its consequences for them as individuals.

Equally counter-productive in our research schools were approaches which failed to recognise that adolescence is a time at which young people are shaping up their identities in the context of individual, and indeed economic and cultural uncertainty and instability. Destabilising gender can be very disruptive, particularly for those who have invested heavily in particular types of masculinity or femininity. This has implications for those anti-violence programmes which seek to encourage students to rewrite their gender identity through pedagogies which attend to the emotions. Arguably, it has particular implications for those boys who fear 'the feminine' and who see no worthwhile investment in emotional reworking; indeed, who may well see such work as risky in the context of the pecking order of schoolboy culture. Clearly a *pedagogy of the emotions* needs to be carefully thought through. It must attend to the ways in which the big picture is represented in students' emotional worlds and it also must help them develop the 'emotional intelligence' (Goleman, 1996) to understand the implications of their emotions for the ways they behave. We will offer some suggestions for such a pedagogy shortly.

A final point to be made about the sociocultural perspective is that despite its sociological insights, this set of approaches generally fails to attend to one set of school practices which is particularly complicit in producing violence. We refer to the relations of power between adults and children, a particular feature of schooling, and particularly to the verbal, emotional and sometimes physical violence associated with certain disciplinary practices. Such understandings of violence are likely to make teachers and policy-makers uncomfortable. But let us take a closer look to see why.

Poisonous pedagogy

Alice Miller's work offers new insights into the relationship between schools and violence. Generally, her ideas suggest that mass education, with its penchant for order and control and for privileging the rational and the instrumental over the relational and affective provides a fertile seed-bed for advancing the culture of violence through 'poisonous pedagogy'. Sendak commenting on Miller's (1987a) work says 'She makes chillingly clear to the many what has been recognised only by the few: the extraordinary pain and psychological suffering inflicted on children under the guise of conventional child rearing practices.' Miller's studies raise questions about the dominant idea that teacher–student relationships are based principally on care. The idea of breaking the will of the child by force or by connivance in order that he or she can be controlled is no stranger to education, which is structured around the power relationships between adults and children. Indeed, school organisation depends upon such control and almost invariably the needs of the organisation and the teachers take precedence over those of the child. In a sense then, schools repeat the poisonous pedagogies that many children have been exposed to in the home.

Miller's ideas also question the extent to which it is wise for schools to move down the late twentieth-century path of increasingly rational curriculum development encouraged by our economically rationalist curriculum policy-makers. Let us consider this issue a little more closely.

The structures and discourses of contemporary education are built on a foundation of rationality. Built into the organisation of learning is an overwhelming faith in the orderly pattern of human affairs. This extends from the dominant ideas about intelligence through to methods for teaching particular subjects. This faith is also reflected in approaches to violence. Take two examples. Some schools have relied on pedagogies of authority in an attempt to control 'outbreaks of violence'. Strict codes of behaviour have been enforced inspired by the regimes of discipline used in industry and the military. Other schools have used counselling methods designed to effect conflict resolution via approaches involving 'talking through the problems'. While apparently different, this draws on the same underlying faith in rationality. However, when it comes to issues of violence, this faith in human rationality becomes unstable (Fitzclarence, 1992).

For Scheff and Retzinger (1991) any adequate interpretation of patterns of violence involves a consideration of complex emotional responses such as shame, rage, alienation, humiliation and repression and revenge. However, such a lexicon is hardly the conceptual material of 'rational' education discourses. Indeed it is alien to them. Nonetheless, the absence of an adequate pedagogy of the emotions has serious consequences. Miller's ideas imply that the replacement of the expressive and creative aspects of the curriculum with instrumental, cognitive-based regimes may actually *reduce* the capacity of education to break what Miller (1987a) describes as the 'vicious circle of contempt' which characterises inter-generational patterns of violence. To ignore the emotional world of schooling and of students and teachers is to contribute to the repressions which recycle and legitimate violence.

Miller's work thus raises doubts about professional development and a curriculum on violence which only appeals to people's rationality and which assumes that teachers and students have rational control over their behaviours. Her work points to the probability that such reforms on violence are likely to touch deep psychic sensitivities and investments, particularly for certain students and teachers; victims, survivors, perpetrators and those who are complicit and in different ways draw on the patriarchal dividend. It thus casts some doubt on those reforms which overlook the powerful role of emotion in the teaching/learning process and suggests that we may well rely too heavily on students' and teachers' goodwill and rationality in attempts to effect change. The challenge here, then, is to work with and through the emotions and to look to other fields of inquiry which may help us to do this. This quest has led us to turn to therapy for ideas; not, we stress, to the sort of self-absorbed, ahistorical and culturally decontextualised therapy which Connell (1995, pp. 206–212) critiques as 'masculinity therapy', in what he scathingly describes as 'Books about Men'. Instead we have turned to narrative therapy in order to explore its implications for pedagogy.

Narrative therapy and its implications for anti-violence pedagogy

In an attempt to get beyond the limitations of social and psychological theories that are not sensitive enough to the reflexive and dynamic nature of humanity and social life, White and Epston (1990) have turned to narrative and have developed narrative therapy in their counselling practice at the Dulwich Centre in South Australia. They use the 'story' metaphor to explore the perpetual process of identity construction through meaning making. Their following statement explains this perspective:

> In striving to make sense of life, persons face the task of arranging their experiences of events in sequences across time in such a way as to arrive at a coherent account of themselves and the world around them. Specific experiences of events of the past and present, and those that are predicted to occur in the future, must be connected in a lineal sequence to develop this account. This account can be referred to as a story or self narrative.
>
> (White and Epston, 1990, p. 10)

According to White (1992, p. 123), people live and shape their lives by stories. These stories, he argues, 'have real, not imagined effects'; they 'provide the structure of life'.

Narrative therapy offers individuals and groups a means for remaking the dominant story-lines which have governed their lives. It encourages them to search for alternative stories – to search for accounts that contradict or resist the dominant individual and socio-cultural stories through which their lives have been constructed and through which they have constructed their lives. This involves a process of 'externalising' the problem with its attendant feelings through the use of story and also of identifying critical moments which tell a different story. Through such a process it becomes possible for the dominant narrative to be resisted. White refers to such moments as 'unique outcomes'. He describes these moments when an invitation to retell the dominant story of a particular problem is resisted and a new meaning is established. In the case of perpetrators of violence, this process also encourages them to accept responsibility for their actions and for the consequences of previous behaviours. In turn, this becomes a process of shaping a new and alternative story-line through which to rebuild identity and relationships. The following example is derived from an exchange between a therapist and a violent offender. It highlights the start of a restorying process designed to facilitate new action.

> Can you remember a time when you took action to stop/prevent violence yourself? Can you remember a time when you made a stand against your own violence and did not expect your partner to do it for you? How did you do it?
>
> (Jenkins, 1990, p. 87)

In our view there are several advantages to be gained in using ideas drawn from narrative therapy to address the problems of violence in schools. First, as Kehily and Nayak (Chapter 10 this volume) vividly demonstrate, storying is a key feature of schooling and of students' and teachers' ways of making meaning about their place in schools. Second, the indeterminate nature of storytelling suggests that collective and individual stories and identities are fluid and can therefore be rewritten or retold – albeit not easily. For both perpetrators and victims of violence, alternative stories point to the possibility of changing direction. To make the link to violence in education more concrete, consider the following self-narrative of Adam from one of the research schools referred to earlier.

> I have been harassed at eleven schools now. At every school I have been to I have been the ten pound weakling. Like, I am the only kid I know with backwards elbows! And, like, because in my job in the school I deal with the locker grills and all that. I get harassed guaranteed at least every morning. They just feel like throwing rocks at me, pushing me around, shoving me, throwing me into walls.

Adam's story is one of a good humoured victim. But what might it look like if he rewrote it and himself as a courageous survivor and emphasised the strengths he has had to draw on to maintain his sense of humour? A word of caution is necessary here. This is not to suggest that tangible, material practices can be simply thought or talked out of existence. Adam's story makes clear that stories of violence represent harsh realities. It is to say, however, that he is able to see himself differently in this context.

A third advantage of the narrative approach is that it enables a person's experience to be considered within wider frameworks of meaning. It encourages them to consider the impact on their lives and relationships of wider cultural and social power relations. For example, a personal story can be linked to a more general cultural story. This helps to develop an appreciation of the ways in which a person is situated within the dominant story-lines of a culture or a society. Let us take some other examples of this process. The following 'story' of 15 year-old Colin contains some identifiable socio-cultural themes.

> Being big is great. [Laughter] No, I just walk down the road and people dodge out of your way, 'cause they think I'm going to hit them. Sometimes I do if they get too close to me. So they let me go first, unless there's a girl, I let her go first. It's better than being one of those school kids that keep getting pushed around you see. I save the rest of them, so when they get pushed around, I just grab the other kid and smack him against the wall or something.

The story-lines represented in Colin's self-narration have widespread currency. 'Big is best' and 'take control by force and fear' are cultural themes that apply in the world of business and in law enforcement systems. Quite possibly Colin has modelled his behaviour on one of the current stock of independent law enforcers depicted in Steven Segal or Sylvester Stall one warrior movies. This next example shows how a teacher of a single-sex class of 'tough' boys and two members of that class formed an alliance around exaggerated hegemonic masculinity. In commenting on his relationship with the class, the teacher Mr Kennedy notes that:

> When I'm there and I'm relaxed I'm also one of the boys. You know if you had an inexperienced man or an effeminate man or a bloke who's too academically inclined or something like that, then that might not work. You might end up with a 'them and me' situation. [. . .]

What has narrative therapy to offer in these instances? At a minimum it would help Colin and Mr Kennedy to identify the entitlement story-lines they are living their lives by and would also invite them to search for others that are more socially and emotionally responsible. Let us consider further the implications of narrative therapy for school's anti-violence education programmes.

While narrative therapy has been pioneered by therapists working primarily outside of the education system, the possibility of adaptations for work in school is now being recognised – but not of course by the hyper-rationalists who drive school systems. At this stage the suggestions for pedagogy which we think have the most potential are those developed and employed by Sydney's *Men Against Sexual Assault Group* (MENSA). Their approach also builds on the strengths but avoid the weaknesses of the authoritarian and the therapeutic approaches we outlined earlier. It also operates outside of the rationalist frameworks which we mentioned earlier and seeks to work with and through the anxieties of young males in particular. Without going into detail, in an environment characterised by respect and support rather than by blaming and shaming, it explores with students their experiences of violence and encourages them to identify the dominant narratives which have shaped such violence (rape myths, for example) and to unpack the cultural library of excuses which are used to justify it. However, this approach does not stop there. It then assists students to find some positive counter-narratives; to draw out and upon alternative sources of strength and status and to build new communities of support for alternative ways of being male and female. Witness the following example.

David Denborough's (1996) work on narrative therapy has been used in working with male students in a programme designed to address emerging problems in junior secondary schools. The process, designed to address issues of sexual harassment/violence and by implication power relations and contested identities, demonstrates a whole-class approach for working through issues that are clearly embedded in the dynamics of society more generally. The process includes mapping experiences of violence, naming the effects, inviting an articulation of the need to change and naming a counter plot. In more specific detail the approach which Denborough advocates can be summarised as follows:

- Beginnings – considering notions of respectful practice; a game of sex and lies; addressing the climate.
- Mapping the extent of the violence in their lives.
- Eliciting an articulated invitation to discuss these ideas.
- Identifying the gendered nature of violence. Identifying messages and beliefs about the dominant masculinity and exploring why it is that men are the ones who are violent in the vast majority of instances. Looking at some key gendered messages and how boys are encouraged and coerced into positioning themselves within them.
- Naming this dominant plot, for examples 'being tough'.
- Mapping the effects of this dominant plot on different social groupings.
- Inviting an articulation of the need for change.
- Finding exceptions – exploring what it means to exist in terms of hope and in terms of what it says about them.
- Naming the counter-plot.
- Asking for an articulation that moving towards this counter-plot, a plot of resistance, would be a good thing (for men, women – hetero- and homosexual, young people, children).

- Building on exceptions: building on strengths – exploring how they did it; building on histories – instances in the past that would support thinking of themselves in this new way; building communities of support – who supported them, how they could find other support.
- Reflecting on strengths: what it says about them; what significant others would think.
- Broadening the responsibility – taking their suggestions as to how they could be supported in their attempts to move towards 'being themselves', by staff, the school, families, and the local community.

The approach outlined here is part of a layered pedagogy. This involves discussions at a number of different levels in the school and including parents and community members. Of particular relevance is the focus on developing respectful dialogue between boys and girls.

> We need to work with our boys *and* our girls – together. They have much to learn from each other, we have much to learn from all of them. The potential for programs in which boys and girls listen to one another's experiences, and develop strategies to work together against out-dated notions of gender, are perhaps the most exciting of all.
>
> (Denborough, 1996, p. 26)

As we see it, the goal of anti-violence education is a future in which males and females, males and males and adults and children can live alongside each other in safe, secure, stable, respectful and harmonious ways and in relationships of mutual life-enhancing respect.

Note

1 This title is taken from Schostak (1986).

References

Andrews, B. (1994) Family violence in a social context: factors relating to male abuse of children, in: J. Archer (Ed.) *Male Violence*, pp. 195–210 (London, Routledge).

Archer, J. (1994) Power and male violence, in: J. Archer (Ed.) *Male Violence*, pp. 310–332 (London, Routledge).

Campbell, A. (1993) *Out of Control* (London, Pandora).

Connell, R.W. (1995) *Masculinities* (Sydney, Allen & Unwin).

Denborough, D. (1996) Step by step: developing respectful and effective ways of working with young men to reduce violence, in: C. Mckean, M. Carey and C. White *Men's Ways of Being*, pp. 91–117 (Denver, CO, Westview Press).

Epstein, D. (1996) Keeping them in their place: hetero/sexist harassment, gender and the enforcement of heterosexuality, in: J. Holland and L. Adkins (Eds) *Sex, Sensibility and the Gendered Body* (London, Macmillan.).

Fitzclarence, L. (1992) *Shame: The Emotional Straw that Breaks More than Backs*, paper presented at the *Australian Association for Research in Education Conference*, November, Deakin University, Geelong.

Fitzclarence, L. (1995) Education's shadow? Towards an understanding of violence in schools, *Australian Journal of Education*, 39 pp. 22–40.

Fitzclarence, L. With Warren, C. and Laskey, L. (1995) Schools, sexuality and violence: a case for changing direction, in: L. Laskey and C. Beavis *Schooling and Sexualities: Teaching for Positive Sexuality* (Geelong, Deakin University Centre for Education and Change).

Goldstein, A.P. (1994) Delinquent gangs, in: J. Archer, (Ed.) *Male Violence*, pp. 37–105 (London, Routledge).

Goleman, D. (1996) *Emotional Intelligence: Why it can Matter More than I.Q.* (Bloomsbury Publishing, Lonon, UK).

Jenkins, A. (1990) *Invitations to Responsibility* (Adelaide, Dulwich Centre Publications).

Kehily, M.J. and Nayak, A. (Chapter 10 this volume) Narrative of Oppression: pupil cultures and story telling forms, unpublished paper, CEDAR, University of Warwick.

Kelly, L. (1987) The continuum of sexual violence, in: J. Hanmer and M. Maynard (Eds) *Women, Violence and Social Control*, pp. 46–61 (London, Macmillan).

Kenway, J. (1995) Masculinity – under siege, on the defensive, and under reconstruction, *Discourse*, 16, pp. 59–81.

Kenway, J., Blackmore, J. and Willis S. (1996) Beyond feminist authoritarianism and therapy in the curriculum? *Curriculum Perspectives*, 16, pp. 1–12.

Kenway, J., Willis, S., Blackmore, J. and Rennie, L. (1997) *Answering Back, Remaking Girls and Boys in Schools* (Sydney, Alien and Unwin).

Miller, A. (1987a) *For Your Own Good: The Roots of Violence in Child-Rearing* (London, Virago Press).

Miller, A. (1987b) *The Drama of Being a Child* (London, Virago Press).

Miller, A. (1990) *For Your Own Good: Hidden Cruelty in Child-Rearing and the Roots of Violence* (New York, The Noonday Press).

Salisbury, J. and Jackson, D. (1996) *Challenging Macho Values: Practical Ways of Working with Adolescent Boys* (London, Falmer Press).

Scheff, T. and Retzinger, S. (1991) *Emotions and Violence* (Lexington, M.A, Lexington Books).

Schostak, J. (1986) *Schooling the Violent Imagination*, (London, Routledge and Kegan Paul).

Weisfeld, G. (1994) Aggression and dominance in the social world of adolescent boys, in: J. Archer, (Ed.) *Male Violence*, pp. 12–70 (London, Routledge).

White, M. and Epston, D. (1990) *Narrative Means to Therapeutic Ends* (New York, London, W.W. Norton & Co.)

White, M. (1992) Deconstraction and therapy, in: D. Epston and M. White *Experience, Contradiction Narrative and Imagination; selected papers of David Epston and Michael White, 1989–1991* (Adelaide, Dulwich Centre Publications).

Wood, J. (1984) Groping towards sexism: boys' sex talk, in: A. McRobbie. and M. Nava (Eds) *Gender and Generation* (Basingstoke, Macmillan).

PART 5

REFLEXIVITY AND RISK

WORKING OUT INTIMACY
Young people and friendship in an age of reflexivity

Julie McLeod, *Discourse: Studies in the Cultural Politics of Education*, 23, 2, 2002

> Our cultural habitat has become saturated with narratives of relationships from the most intense to the most trivial, with lovers, with workmates, with friends. Through the intense focus on biographies, personalities and minutiae of the lives of the famous and not so famous, in the press, on the television and in the cinema, a new culture of the self has taken shape.
>
> (Rose, 1999, p. 91)

This chapter examines young people's experiences of and reflections on friendship in the light of recent analyses of the destabilisation of gender norms and an intensified focus on the self as a project in the making. The perception and formation of the self as a reflexive and self-conscious biography has been identified by theorists such as Ulrich Beck (1992) and Anthony Giddens (1991) as a defining feature of modernity. The self, they argue, has become a project to be produced and reflected upon: choice biographies replace prescribed roles and futures (Beck, 1992, p. 135; Beck and Beck-Gernsheim, 1995).

Analytic attention is focused upon the decisions and reflexivity of the agent whose traditional and once inherited roles (of gender, of family, of class identity) and codes of conduct are dissolving (Adkins, 2000, p. 261). Beck argues that such 'detraditionalisations happen in a *social surge of individualisation*' (Beck, 1992, p. 87). Individualisation refers paradoxically both to 'individualism' and the obligation 'to standardize your own existence' in line with the imperatives of the labour market and governmental agencies (Beck and Beck-Gernsheim, 1995, p. 7). This double process involves an increasing tendency to self-monitoring, so that 'we are, not what we are, but what we make of ourselves' (Giddens, 1991, p. 75). In such accounts of reflexivity and detraditionalisation, contemporary gender identities and relations become emblematic, representing in a kind of idealised form the possibilities of a self cut loose from tradition and required to make itself anew.

It is beyond the scope of these introductory comments to fully discuss how or whether the reflexive modernisation thesis overstates the extent of the detraditionalisation of gender norms (but see Adkins, 2000; McNay, 2000, pp. 40–42; Thomson and Holland, 2001). Older forms of femininity and masculinity can be reinscribed in new ways (Kenway and Kelly, 2000) and conventional patterns and gender-based inequalities exist alongside evidence of changed expectations. Feminist transformation has not been as comprehensive as some might hope or fear. Nevertheless, feminism has produced some demonstrable changes in the life course of certain groups of women. For example, in Australia there have been overall increases in rates of women's participation in education and the labour force, an increase in the average age at which women have their first child, and a decrease in the average number of children per family. Feminism has also generated significant changes in how many women and men perceive themselves and imagine their futures. It is also the case that a range of feminisms has emphasised the 'construction' of gender (as opposed to essential or biological or fixed natures) and the concept of individualisation captures elements of that orientation. The situated and uneven effects of feminism are important matters to debate. However, my concern in this chapter is with analysing how gender difference and feminist and gender change are manifest in interpersonal relations: how do young people negotiate relationships with others and themselves in an era marked by feminism and an emphasised attention to 'relationship narratives' and self-understanding?

This discussion draws on a longitudinal, interview-based study of Australian secondary school students ('The 12 to 18 Project'[1]). Young people's friendship experiences and attitudes to the self are examined in terms of the broader theoretical concerns noted above. I consider the ways in which these abstract frameworks and characterisations of modernity and the self can help illuminate how young people today, in very different locations, mediate interpersonal relationships. I argue that the cultural meanings of intimacy and friendship are being reconfigured in the wake of feminism and the predominance of psychotherapeutic ways of constituting and knowing the self. This has consequences for the production of gendered subjectivities and for how young women and men represent and imagine their present and future selves. I discuss examples of how gender is being rearticulated in new yet familiar ways and note some persistent tensions in desires for connection and community versus autonomy and freedom. In terms of that dilemma, the work of Carol Gilligan is briefly revisited, particularly her account of gender differences in orientations to autonomy and connection. Finally, I consider the influence of class, locational and schooling differences on dispositions to friendship and the interpersonal, looking at what could also be interpreted as the effects of particular social fields on the formation of habitus (Bourdieu and Wacquant, 1992) and emotional dispositions. I elaborate this through a discussion of the 'relationship orientations' of two white Anglo-Australian young men.

Affect, relationships and the self

Capacities for friendship and intimacy have operated discursively as key markers of gender difference. Historically, women and girls have been aligned with the affective, and juxtaposed to the properly human and rational (Walkerdine, 1988). But these binaries are changing. Much of early second-wave feminism sought not only to acknowledge but also to celebrate women's apparently distinctive ways of being, knowing and feeling. In education, claims that women have a distinctive voice, morality, style of learning and a predisposition for 'care concern and connection' underpinned the emergence of genderinclusive and girl-friendly schooling throughout the 1980s and onwards. These educational reforms drew on notions of feminine ways of knowing, and of women's natural inclination for cooperative interpersonal relations and 'conversational' based learning – views whose lineage was both conventional stereotypes of femininity and forms of object-relations psychology (McLeod, 1998).

The growth of the men's movement and the question of 'What about the boys?' have also focused attention on emotions and gender difference. One of the qualities boys appear to lack and men want to reclaim is the experience of being in touch with their feelings, of being expressive and able to forge close bonds with one another (e.g. Morton, 1997; Hickey *et al.*, 1998). In other words, the desire now is for men and boys to be able to conduct their personal and social relations with the kind of emotional openness said to characterise women's personal and social interactions. Educational programmes designed to assist boys often target the development of their social, emotional and communication skills: for example the recent *Australian Parliamentary Inquiry into the Education of Boys* (2000) called for a focus on strategies to improve 'socialisation skills in the early and middle years of schooling'. In the current educational and social climate, then, emotional competence and openness are represented neither negatively nor as signifying feminine excess or pathology. Instead they are regarded as part of the desired repertoire of masculinity, a feature of a 'healthy' well-rounded identity and as competencies capable of generating cultural change.

One such change identified by Giddens is the 'democratization of the private sphere' (1992, p. 185). Feminism has prompted many women, he argues, to explore the 'potentialities of the "pure relationship," a relationship of sexual and emotional equality which is explosive in its connotations for pre-existing forms of gender power' (1992, p. 2; Giddens, 1991). 'The transformation of intimacy,' he suggests, 'presses for psychic as well as social change and such change, going "from the bottom up", could potentially ramify through other, more public institutions' (1992, p. 182). In short, for Giddens, the 'possibility of intimacy means the promise of democracy' (1992, p. 188). Giddens's discussion of intimacy – as redemption, as change agent – both points to and is part of a substantial body of research (much of it feminist inspired) addressing intimacy and the affective dimensions of social life. Lois McNay suggests that 'Intimate relations may be understood as becoming increasingly unbounded and having variable effects across different fields.' Following the work of Nicklas Luhman, she notes that the 'demand for intensive, intimate relations traditionally confined to the female domestic arena has spilled over into other areas of social life' (McNay, 2000, p. 71). There is a strong field of research broadly characterised as the 'sociology of emotions' (e.g. Stephenson *et al.*, 1996), as well as discussion of the place of emotion in public and political life: from politicians crying in public to philosophical debate about evoking compassion as a political strategy in struggles for social justice (Spelman, 1997). A recent issue of the journal *Critical Inquiry* (1998) explored the topic of 'Intimacy', and the affective dimensions of feminism are also receiving critical attention (Ahmed *et al.*, 2000). In schools and in teacher education programmes, there is growing attention to the idea of 'emotional literacy', a focus evident in a range of curriculum initiatives, including Howard Gardner's 'multiple intelligences' and his categories of 'intrapersonal' and 'interpersonal intelligence' (Gardner, 1993). Current attention to the practices and experiences of friendship is an element of this broader orientation to intimacy and the 'emotions'.

While Giddens optimistically declares the redemptive emotional transformations wrought by feminism, a more pessimistic assessment of the emotional wounds inflicted by feminism coexists alongside this. This pessimism can be found in concerns about men being emotionally awkward, a condition exacerbated by feminism because it has destabilised gender roles, making men more vulnerable. Elements of this discourse, as I have suggested, fuel anxious debates about the disadvantages boys experience in education. A different assessment of the attention to the 'personal', but one also less celebratory than Giddens's, is proposed by Nikolas Rose. He argues that the intense focus on intimacy and personal relationships represents a new form of subjectification (in the Foucauldian sense of regulation of the self), not, as Giddens suggests, more democratic and feminist-friendly ways of being. Rose argues that in current times, psychological knowledges and techniques structure the way in which we understand and know ourselves and mediate our social and personal experiences. Autonomous individuals know and conduct themselves through these psychotherapeutic lenses and discourses – they constitute the contemporary form of government of the self and of others. There is an emphasised process of scrutinising relationships – those of and with other people, as well as the project of 'relating to' oneself – leading to a 'new culture of the self' (Rose, 1999, p. 91).

> The individual is to adopt a new relation to his or her self in the everyday world, in which the self itself is to be an object of knowledge and autonomy is to be achieved through a continual enterprise of self-improvement through the application of a rational knowledge and technique...Hence the norm of autonomy produces an intense and continuous self-scrutiny, self-dissatisfaction and self-evaluation in terms of the vocabularies and explanations of [psycho-therapeutic] expertise.
>
> (Rose, 1999, p. 93)

Rose's analysis contrasts to emancipatory conceptions of intimacy, indicating the incitements to young people to understand and represent themselves in terms of therapeutic 'relationship' narratives. What is missing, however, from Rose's persuasive argument is much sense of what that incitement to the personal, to make oneself a biographical project, is gendered, or indeed differentiated according to other identity categories. In cultures saturated with knowledge of gender difference, and particularly the feminisation of affect and 'relationships', such therapeutic techniques of the self are going to resonate differently for girls and boys.

In what follows, I discuss aspects of the gendered dimensions of contemporary cultures of the self, and point to examples of the iteration and reiteration of gender through friendship and relationship discourses. In some instances, gender is transforming; in others it is recoded and reworked along familiar binaries. This dual process of detraditionalisation and retraditionalisation of gender has been explored by others, especially in terms of women's and men's relation to the economic. In an analysis of women, work and 'post-occupational reflexivity' Lisa Adkins argues that

> reflexive modernity, while certainly signalling new modes of interaction, involves not a simple detachment or disembedding of individuals from social categories such as those of class and gender, but also re-embedding process in circuits and networks in which new, yet traditional – re-traditionalised – rules, norms, and expectations are at issue.
>
> (Adkins, 2000, p. 260)

Kenway and Kelly (2000) underline the effects of economic restructuring and globalisation on local patterns of class and gender identities for young people engaged in vocational education and training, arguing that this has produced 'enduring gender issues, new gender issues and new manifestations of old issues' (Kenway and Kelly, 2000). In the remaining discussion, I explore some of the connections between generalised theories of modernity, gender and the self, and observations from a qualitative study of young people growing up today.

Changing patterns of gender difference

In 1993, Lyn Yates and I began an interview-based longitudinal study of students progressing through secondary schools in Australia, Students were interviewed twice each year of their secondary schooling and twice in their first year after leaving school: interviews were completed with most students at the end of 2000 (Yates and McLeod, 1996; McLeod, 2000; Yates, 2000). They attended four different schools in country and metropolitan areas: an elite coeducational private school, a metropolitan state school in a middle-class suburb, a former technical school and a relatively traditional 'academic' high school. We have been examining both changing patterns over time among students from different schools and developments within individual students over the course of their secondary years. Comparisons are developed that are synchronic – across different groups of students at the same age level – and diachronic – developments and changes in individuals and cohorts over time. In interviews, three themes in particular have been explored: the development of gendered subjectivity; young people's changing engagements with and attitudes to school; and students' thinking about their future. In relation to extending understandings of gender subjectivity today, I consider young people's reflection on friendship and relationships.

Friendship is part of the web of social practices that mediate and constitute gender identities. In an important ethnographic study of friendship, Valerie Hey has argued that

> The so-called private, marginal realm of schoolgirl friendships is a significant place where the 'social' is indexed. It is between and amongst girls as friends that identities are variously practised, appropriated, resisted and negotiated.
>
> (Hey, 1997, p. 30)

A related argument is developed by Barrie Thorne in her study of interactions among primary school students and 'the fluctuating significance of gender in the ongoing scenes of social life' (Thorne, 1993, p. 61). Numerous ethnographic and other qualitative studies of young people and friendship, often drawing on critical traditions within cultural studies, have elaborated the political and subcultural significance of friendship practices among school children (e.g. Nilan, 1992; Griffiths, 1995; Hey, 1997). This includes studies of popularity, friendship cliques, tension in friendships, bullying and processes of inclusion and exclusion (Eder, 1985; Giordano, 1995; Tulloch, 1995; Leckie, 1997). Many such studies point to gendered patterns in friendship, suggesting that while friendship is important for both girls and boys, there are differences in its conduct: 'Women's friendships are a sharing of themselves, men's more a sharing of activities' (Hartley, 1994, p. 5). And in our longitudinal study there were strong indications that girls and boys understood friendship in similar ways.

Sam:	Girls often gossip and keep secrets. A lot and the boys are always the ones trying to find out I suppose. Well that's not always the case but … girls have girls' talk …
Laurie:	Boys talk about …
Sam:	Boys talk about cricket and footy and girls talk about, I don't know, relationships and who they're going out with and who they're going to ring tonight … I don't know. It's the sort of impression I get.

Laurie: That's being a bit sexist though.
Sam: Yea, I know.

For both girls and boys, from very different schools and backgrounds, friendship is a central part of their experience of growing up and of being at school. In Years 7 and 8 students frequently described seeing friends as one of the best things about school: 'Like if you don't have friends then you don't really have anything in school,' says Angela (Yr 7, 94a.) Narelle responds, 'I mean the only reason I come to school is because of my friends' (Yr 8, HC. 95b).

There was an equally strong sense across the four schools that girls and boys reacted differently to friendship troubles. For boys, the reaction was often to look beyond the immediate upset and focus more single-mindedly on school work and looking to a future and a world of work away from school (McLeod and Yates, 1998; McLeod, 2000). In Year 7, Sanath, from an ethnic-minority background and relatively new to Australia, was finding it hard to make friends and to work out the patterns of social relations at his school. But he was determined not to let his social isolation and uncertainty distract him from his schoolwork. Instead, he reported spending his lunchtimes sitting by himself under a tree memorising the distance between the planets because he believed that this would help him to fulfil his long-term aim to study science at university. It also gave him legitimate means to observe from a safe distance the interpersonal and social protocols of the school setting, and to become more familiar with the cultural codes of the playground. Retreating to study, then, was a resourceful response to being alone. (When older he sometimes linked his social isolation at school to ethnic and cultural difference, but he also continued to represent it as a consequence of his individual personality.)

For girls, in contrast, friendship troubles tend to be all-consuming traumas, and it is difficult for them to focus on schoolwork or other issues. For many girls, especially in junior and middle school, there is an intense preoccupation with being a good friend and displaying the right qualities of friendship: trust, honesty, loyalty. There was also an intense preoccupation with what counts as betrayal, and with processes of inclusion and exclusion. When asked towards the end of secondary school about high and low points, many girls continued to identify earlier friendship problems as vivid and unhappy memories, even though they tended not to have the same intense anxiety about friends at that older age.

Alongside these traditional gender patterns there are signs of changes emerging in how young women and men negotiate friends and relationships and these, in turn, signal rearticulations of femininity and masculinity. It is possible here only to illustrate some of these tendencies via two examples, and to raise some questions for further investigation. First, I briefly discuss the autonomy/connection dilemma in relation to young women; and second, I outline how two young men from different socioeconomic backgrounds and locations navigate relationship discourses and constitute themselves in 'cultures of the self'. I address issues concerning both binary gender difference (between male and female), and differences within gender (in this case, among young men). On the one hand, it is clear that analyses of gender difference can subsume other determining social differences and that we need to be mindful of the dangers and blindnesses of this binary, and the constitutive effects of other 'differences'. On the other hand, asking questions about gender difference of universalising theories of, for example, the self, modernity or morality remains a priority and a key task of feminist enquiry.

Connection and autonomy

The work of Carol Gilligan and colleagues engaged in the Harvard Projects on Women's Psychology and Girls' Development examines the manifestations of gender difference in moral and emotional development. Emerging from object-relations and developmental psychology, this work ascribes gender differences to the nature of the early relationship between mother and infant. While both boys and girls initially identify with the mother, the process of individuation is different. Girls can remain identified with the mother, a relationship that predisposes them to certain emotional traits such as a concern and empathy for others and interdependence. Boys, in contrast, need to separate from the mother, and this predisposes them to autonomy, detachment and objectivity (Gilligan, 1977, 1982).

However, Gilligan argues, as girls grow up they experience a conflict between desires for autonomy and desires for connection (e.g. Gilligan *et al.*, 1990; Taylor *et al.*, 1997).

> Adolescence poses problems of connection for girls coming of age in Western culture, and girls are tempted or encouraged to solve these problems by excluding themselves or excluding others – that is, by being a good woman or by being selfish. [. . .] for girls to remain responsible to themselves they must resist the conventions of feminine goodness; to remain responsible to others, they must resist the values placed on self-sufficiency and independence in North American culture.
>
> (Gilligan *et al.*, 1990, pp. 9–10)

Similar tensions were apparent in our study – a juggling of the desire for personal freedom and success and a compelling sense of emotional responsibility. This tension was most pronounced among middle-class girls and those who attended the elite college, all of whom were Anglo-European. For example, a girl in Year 9 at the elite college was very worried about her mathematics teacher, feared that she was not doing very well in the subject and was falling behind. She had had the same teacher for three years and felt she was not learning much from him – he did not explain things in a way she could understand. But when we asked her if she or her parents had considered seeing whether she could be in another class, she said of the teacher 'he's the sort of person that would be upset if he thought you didn't understand'. In other words, she was taking responsibility for not hurting his feelings, even if it undermined her own chances of doing well. Elsewhere, we have discussed girls' immersion in the intricacies and demands of emotional life alongside their striking narratives and fantasies of escape and adventure (McLeod and Yates, 1998). These suggest that young women today continue to negotiate tensions between desires for personal autonomy and a sense of obligation to and responsibility for others. But the psychological explanations proposed by Gilligan capture only part of the scenario. [. . .]

In Western countries such as Australia, feminism has obviously had a profound impact on contemporary gender relations and on schooling, and this is an important context for understanding the aspirations and desires of the young women in our study. At the elite college, for example, there was an overt commitment to equal opportunity and equity feminism: it was a prominent feature of its niche marketing. Rather than the tension between autonomy and connection being seen as the result of either feminine psychosexual development, or lack of self-confidence or of ambition, or in the case of the US the influence of individualism (though this is significant), it is also perhaps the possibilities for personal success and public achievement opened up and emphasised by feminist reform that has heightened the connection/autonomy dilemma for young women. In other words, women are torn between obligation and autonomy, not simply as a consequence of a North American sensibility of individualism, but also because of the effects of feminism and a culture that incites us to remake ourselves.[2]

Feminists inside and outside of education have often praised girls' and women's intrinsic capacity for friendship and affective relations. Significant educational reforms have been based on such presumptions. Care, conversation and connection have been thought of as unassailable virtues, as self-evidently good for girls, and for boys, if only they were not so thwarted by detachment and autonomy. But the desire for intimacy can engulf girls, and dominate their experience of schooling, especially in the junior and middle school years. Here we have a dilemma for feminism. On the one hand, feminism expects and rewards girls for being affective and sensitive, and, on the other, it demands that they succeed at school and in the world beyond. These twin imperatives thus exacerbate and produce new dimensions to, rather than obviate the autonomy/connection conflict for girls. In one sense femininity is being detraditionalised through the opening up of a wider range of possibilities for girls. In another sense, femininity is being rearticulated as ideally integrating and embodying both conventionally feminine and masculine aspirations. The ideal person embraces both emotional openness and ambitions for autonomy: girls can do and be anything.

Relationship narratives, the quest for self-improvement and the 'norm of autonomy' resonate differently for men and women because of the traditional positioning of femininity in service of the other. This remains the case even when both men and women are constituted through, in Rose's terms, a psychotherapeutic culture of the self (Rose, 1999). For the young women in our study, a sense of obligation to others continues to complicate desires for autonomy, success and adventure, but only in part because of the legacy of discourses of gender difference. It is also complicated because a concern with relationships and self-knowledge, linked to both feminism and modernity's project of the self, is becoming normative for both men and women. It is perceived as socially transformative in the sense outlined by Giddens, and in the sense espoused by educators who wish to improve boys' social and emotional skills, or who attribute special capacities to girls. In the following section I outline how two young Anglo-Australian men articulate their sense of self and relation to others in this changing social and emotional context.

Rearticulating masculinity through relationship narratives

Mark attended an ex-technical school in a working-class area of a large country town. At the end of primary school he described himself as 'helpful' and as a good friend. As he grows up, he continues to understand himself in this way: standing by his mates is important for him, a matter of honour and pride. He hopes his friends know that 'I'd do anything for 'em if they needed to and that. If it was in limits. I'd stick by them' (Yr 9, BSCM.96a). He enjoys recreational shooting, has a thought-out opposition to restrictive gun laws and disdains authority (particularly teachers and the police) but respects his 'bosses'. He holds strong populist-conservative political views...and expresses 'chivalrous'/patriarchal attitudes to women and girls: 'I wouldn't hit a girl, unless if she was trying to kill me or something...if...a girl hit me or something, I'd just keep walking. I wouldn't hit a girl. It's wrong' (Yr 9, 96a), but throughout school, girls occupy a marginal place compared with the world of his mates. 'Work and social life' are important to him, and the things that matter most are 'Getting a job. Friends, family, school at the start' (Yr 11, 98b). He spends most of his time out of school and at the weekends 'with his mates' 'shooting' and 'mucking around with cars'.

He imagines a conventional future – the nuclear family and a male breadwinner in regular work. In his final year of school, he sees himself in a few years time as having 'Oh steady job. My own house. Oh and quite a few years, settle down, have a family, I suppose' (Yr 12, 99a). But it is not a scenario he appears to have actively determined. It is expressed more as the unfolding of a perceived inevitable future. In many respects, then, Mark continues to embody a relatively traditional form of country-town white working-class masculinity. His identity is tied up in sport, cars, his mates and manual or trade work; he describes himself as 'easygoing' and the future, from his point of view, is unproblematic: he will 'take things as they come' (Yr 12, 99a).

In his senior years of school Mark, began a traineeship in engineering and welding, undertaking some subjects at school, others at a local college of Technical and Further Education (TAFE) and spending two days a week working in a truck-building factory on welding. In our last interview with him, he was struggling to complete the formal requirements of the course and had effectively left school. A large part of the attraction of the traineeship was that it placed him among work-mates who treated him as an adult. Throughout his schooling he is impatient to move beyond that infantilising domain, which stands in the way of his entering manhood.

> You go to work they treat you like an adult, at [TAFE] they treat you like an adult but here they just treat you like a kid really, a little child...

> Yeah I feel a lot older, in the workplace. They all know I'm a lot younger but they all treat me like one of the adults. Except like telling me what to do. If we are doing a job and something goes wrong, like I put in my input about it too, like what I think should happen, instead of sitting back and not allowed to say anything.

The decline of the manufacturing sector, the growth in rural and youth unemployment, a restructured labour market (Kenway and Kelly, 2000), and its attendant ideas of the 'flexible workforce' combine to produce for young men such as Mark a possible future of insecure, limited or no paid work. In such an economic context, 'mates' and interpersonal relationships become increasingly important and in a sense occupy the space once filled by the sociality and purposefulness of paid work. Mark's work experiences are also depicted in terms of his positive and affirming interactions with workmates. For another young man, in the same town and school and similarly on the margins of the labour market, the local athletics club provided a forum for connection and regular commitment. Significantly, while masculinity is an overtly marked aspect of identity, in Australia whiteness as an ethnicity, and particularly Anglo-Australian whiteness, remains largely an unmarked aspect of identity, 'invisible' yet dominant (Hage, 1998; Luke and

Carrington, 2000). Mark, for example, understands himself as a young male adult (engaged in relatively traditional male pursuits), and within a national discourse as being 'an Australian', but he would not see himself as 'having an ethnicity'.

With us Mark appears uncomfortable reflecting on his emotional life and on what he thinks about himself. He does not seem familiar with the modes of self-scrutiny discussed by Rose (1999), and nor does he understand himself within the discourse of 'choice biography': he takes things as they come. He presumes a traditional masculine experience and role – the expectation of work, of being a breadwinner, and of settling down with a family – despite the changed economic and social circumstance he inhabits. On the one hand. Mark appears to embody a relatively traditional, even an emphasised and intransigent form of white, provincial, working-class masculinity. Being with his mates is linked with a repertoire of masculine activities and values that appear relatively unchanged by a 'transformation of intimacy' and feminism. On the other hand, his marginal connection to the labour market and the pleasure he derives from his relations with friends and workmates point to a retraditionalised masculinity that is anchored not in paid work, but in relationships.

While Tim embodies a different kind of masculinity, it is also one rearticulated in terms of relationship narratives. He attends an 'arty' government school in a middle-class suburb of a large city. The school has a reputation for being tolerant and socially inclusive and has a number of programmes for 'at risk' students, such as a breakfast club for homeless students, and an extensive pupil welfare and support programme. Students tell us that it accepts 'difficult' students who have been expelled from other schools. Positive social and interpersonal relations among students and between students and teachers are actively promoted. Students talk positively about the care they receive at the school, and of the personal approach of the teachers: at the end of their secondary schooling, all students regarded this as an important part of their schooling experience. Tim thinks 'it's a good school in a lot of ways like the attitudes of the teachers, like they don't push you a whole lot, but they, most of the teachers you know, care about your education and don't really treat you like some sort of number really' (Yr 9, 97b).

> It wasn't a disciplinarian sort of school...developing sort of the alternative side as opposed to your disciplinarian go ahead and succeed in life sort of thing...[how he saw private schools]...as far as looking outside the square seeing how other people live, um you know, seeing a wider variety of people I think you get to know at state school, i think yeah I learnt a lot from my time at [. . .], probably brought me down to earth made me I don't know, maybe less arrogant or something.

The school promised a 'second chance' for all, another chance to remake yourself, to not mindlessly conform but to work out your own goals and values. It encouraged a therapeutic approach to students' problems; talking through issues, visiting the counsellor, self-understanding. The school also encouraged political awareness of difference: 'That's one of the good things about it. Sort of accepting you and stuff. Um, yeah, generally sort of, yeah, you know it's not cool to be racist and stuff like sexist, so they're pretty nice sort of people' (Yr 10, 97b).

All the students we interviewed at this school were shaped by this ethos. They emphasised a desire to sort out what they really wanted to do, to not rush into decisions, to question the *status quo*, and to attend to things that really mattered to them – this orientation was particularly apparent in the senior years (Yates and McLeod, 2000). Tim embodied the habitus of the school in a very striking way. Towards the end of secondary school he is preoccupied with working out what he wants to do, but with a focus on working on his emotional well-being, on sorting himself out – self-discovery – rather than planning strategically for his immediate future. Tim and several other students speak of the possibilities of self-improvement as self-knowledge: 'I think you should live by your own sort of, set your own sort of standards and morals and ethics and stuff, and live by that' (Yr 10, 97b).

He has a romantic view of the quest for self-knowledge, from drugs to overseas travel; thinks he might be an artist.

> I don't want to have a meat and 3 veg sort of life, if you know what I mean…I don't want to be your ordinary sort of person that lives in a house with two kids and a wife and stuff. I sort of want to, I want to like experience other things, experiment with things.
>
> (Yr 9, 96b)

> I've got loads of stupid ideas going through my head, but, things like moving away to, you know travelling around a lot. I don't really like the idea of being settled in one place, I like to move around a lot. And, um, I don't want to have a boring life, I want to, I want to, you know, make something of my life and not just something, you know, uninteresting.
>
> (Yr 10, 97a)

At 18, he has returned from an overseas student exchange but is not motivated to return to secondary school in Australia to complete Year 12, since he is not sure it is the right thing for him to do. He is unable to commit to a particular job, even a part-time casual one – he just has to find himself. He is immersed in understanding and making the self: 'choice biography' produces overwhelming indecision and inertia.

> I really haven't found any direction at all, yet really, don't know exactly what I want to do, I'd like to write, I'd like to travel, I know I want to travel in my life, that's for sure, that's a priority for me to get out and see different things, but haven't really found my direction in life, in terms of career, don't know what I'm going to do.

The schools' pedagogic and pastoral care strategies and Tim's orientation to understanding the personal are psychotherapeutic in the sense discussed by Rose (1999). They constitute a culture of the self that privileges self-knowledge and 'relationships' and requires endless self-monitoring. This represents a particular form of government of the self, and suggests how an emphasised attention to relationships and the 'personal' is being rearticulated as normative for both women and men.

In these two examples, we see traditional forms of masculinity alongside retradition-alised and more therapeutic forms. In one sense, this assessment appears consistent with the youth research literature on 'normal or traditional biographies' and 'choice biographies': that is, young people who pursue a relatively traditional pattern of transition through school and work and anticipate conventional gender roles, and young people who, in Giddens's sense, pursue a detraditionalised pathway and emphasise choice and flexibility in their imagined futures (du Bois-Reymond, 1998; Dwyer *et al.*, 1998; Collins *et al.*, 2000). Such categorisations can convey a sense of the broad patterns of difference in young people's identity and future making. However, in such typological thinking there arc dangers of reifying biographies as categories, and of concentrating attention on the extent to which young people's lives conform to the available categories of identity. I have been trying to keep in focus the different social context and the ambivalence and dynamics of individual biographies alongside a sense of the emerging and dominant characteristics of different kinds of biographies and subject positions. (The longitudinal, comparative and relatively small-scale design of the 'The 12 to 18 Project' is intended to allow us to observe closely the contours of individual biographies in relation to larger social patterns and changes.) Further, I have been arguing and trying to illustrate some of the ways in which either kind of biography (choice or traditional) is formed in the context of 'cultures of the self'. I have also tried to suggest another dimension to the 'choice biography'; to see choice as not simply an empowering moment of opportunity, but also as a form of subjectification that, in its relentless self-scrutiny, can have its own 'reflexivity dangers'. In the case of Mark, friendship and relationships with his mates are clearly important, and are likely to become more so. At the same time, his self-identity remains linked to getting work, being independent and a traditional future as a breadwinner. He has a confidence in who he is which is not shared by Tim. Instead Tim's sense of self is characterised by intense reflexivity and by the task of sorting himself out – in relation to others and to his true self – independently of the world of work. Tim's work is his biographical project – an emblematic subject of modernity.

Concluding comments

> In a post-traditional order, the narrative of the self has in fact continually to be reworked, and life-style practices brought continually into line with it, if the individual is to combine personal autonomy with a sense of ontological security.
>
> (Giddens, 1992, p. 75)

Friendship and interpersonal relations are practices for the playing out and policing of gender identities (Thorne, 1993) and they are important registers of the social, as Valerie Hey has argued (1997). The incitement to be reflexive, to be 'up close and personal', is powerful but it does not interpellate all young people in the same way. For young women, the demand for intimacy is mediated by a historical alignment of femininity with the affective, and this is linked to a perceived dilemma of choice between autonomy and connection, both prized goals of different forms of feminism. This is not to argue that it remains a dilemma for all young women, and in the examples I discussed it was particularly apparent for white Australian middle-class girls at both the government schools and the elite private college. Through the examples of two young men, I have indicated how intimacy and the personal are experienced and articulated in diverse ways, and I have argued that such orientations are as much mediated by class, region and school ethos as by embedded (traditional) gender difference. Mark and Tim are both ethnic-majority (i.e. white): but it is usually only in interviews that directly address topics of ethnicity or racism that they (and most of the other Anglo-Australian participants) talk about these issues or describe themselves as 'Australian' (Mark) or 'white' (Tim) (McLeod and Yates, 2003). There clearly needs to be more research on friendship patterns and emotional orientations among different groups of ethnic-minority students, between ethnic-minority and ethnic-majority students and on how these are mediated by gender, class, region and schooling (see Allard, 2002). In an educational climate marked by a concern with boys' emotional literacy, we also need more research that goes beyond simply reiterating the cliches of gender difference and emotions, and looks instead to how and why particular patterns of interpersonal conduct and self-reflection are sustained or are changing.

Giddens speaks optimistically of the possibilities afforded by the transformation of intimacy and the project of making the self. Rose locates the focus on relationships and quest for the 'personal' as representing new forms of governing the self. Feminism is not the emancipatory engine here, nor does the possibility of intimacy mean the promise of democracy. For Rose, turning the self into a biographical project is understood not as a guarantee of autonomy or of ontological security, but rather as an artefact of the predominance of psychotherapeutic knowledges. They represent a particular set of strategies in the history of practices of freedom and practices of the self. I have attempted to bring together elements of these two different lines of argument to examine some of the socially specific and local ways in which young women and men are negotiating relationships. This has been prompted in part by a desire to understand how broad, universalising theories of modernity, gender and the self translate to particular settings, regions, schools and different groups of young people. It is not a matter of seeing whether young people 'fit' the theories or biography categories, but more a matter of trying to understand the relation of culturally specific and day-to-day experiences to the theorisation of large-scale social and historical trends. In many respects Giddens's discussion of feminism and intimacy and the related analyses of the detraditionalisation of gender are utopian and overstated. However, the concepts of individualisation and reflexivity and Rose's analysis of relationship narratives within a culture of the self do, I hope I have shown, help us to see and think in new ways about intimacy, friendship and the rearticulation of gender being worked out in the lives of actual young people today.

Notes

1 The Project has been jointly conducted by Lyn Yates (University of Technology Sydney) and Julie McLeod (Deakin University). It began at the end of 1993, interviewing students in grade 6, and continued through to 2000, by when most of the students had either finished or left school. Students were interviewed twice a year through each year of their secondary schooling. There are more than 350 interviews with 26 main students, as well as interviews with their friends. The Project has been supported by funding from the Australian Research Council, La Trobe University, Deakin University and the University of Technology Sydney.

2 In making this argument, I do not wish to suggest that there is no connection between North American individualism and the political and philosophical underpinnings of different forms of 'first' and 'second' wave feminism. Rather, I am wanting to emphasise the significance of feminism *per se* in governing identities, an argument that does not preclude the congruence between feminism and individualism; and I am also wanting to make an argument that is not so US-centric.

References

Adkins, L. (2000) Objects of innovation: post-occupational reflexivity and re-traditionalisations of gender, in: S. Ahmed, J. Kilb, C. Lury, M. McNeil and B. Skeggs (Eds) *Transformations: Thinking Through Feminism* (London, Routledge).

Ahmed, S., Kilby, J., Lury, C., McNeil, M. and Skeggs, B. (Eds) (2000) *Transformations: Thinking Through Feminism* (London, Routledge).

Allard A.C. (2002) ' "Aussies" and "wogs" and "group in-between": year 10 students' constructions of cross-cultural friendships', *Discourse: Studies in the Cultural Politics of Ecucation*, 23, 2, pp. 193–209.

Australian Parliamentary Inquiry into the Education of Boys (2000) Standing Committee on Employment, Education and Workplace Relations, www.aph.gov.au/house/committee/eewr/

Beck, U. (1992) *Risk Society: Towards a New Modernity*, trans. M. Ritter (London, Sage).

Beck, U. and Beck-Gernsheim, E. (1995) *The Normal Chaos of Love*, trans. M. Ritter and J. Weibel (Cambridge, Polity Press).

Bourdieu, P. and Wacquant, L.J.D. (1992) *An Invitation to Reflexive Sociology* (Chicago, University of Chicago Press).

Collins, C., Kenway, J. and McLeod, J. (2000) *Factors Influencing the Educational Performance of Males and Females in School and Their Initial Destinations after Leaving School* (Canberra, Department of Education, Training and Youth Affairs, AGPS).

Critical Inquiry (1998) Issue on 'Intimacy', 24(2).

Du Bois-Reymond, M. (1998) I don't want to commit myself yet; young people's life concepts, *Journal of Youth Studies*, 1(1), pp. 63–79.

Dwyer, P., Harwood, A. and Tyler, D. (1998) *Life Patterns, Choices, Careers: 1991–1998* (Melbourne, Youth Research Centre, Faculty of Education, University of Melbourne).

Eder, D. (1985) The cycle of popularity: interpersonal relations among female adolescents, *Sociology of Education*, 58, July, pp. 154–165.

Gardner, H. (1993) *Frames of Mind: The Theory of Multiple Intelligence* (New York, Basic Books).

Giddens, A. (1991) *Modernity and Self-Identity: Self and Society in the Late Modern Age*, (Cambridge, Polity Press).

Giddens, A. (1992) *Transformations of Intimacy: Sexuality, Love and Eroticism in Modern societies* (Stanford, Stanford University Press).

Gilligan, C. (1977) In a different voice: women's conception of self and morality, *Harvard Education Review*, 47(4), pp. 481–517.

Gilligan, C. (1982) *In a Different Voice: Psychological Theory and Women's Development* (Cambridge, Harvard University Press).

Gilligan, C., Lyons, N. and Hanmer, T, (Eds) (1990) *Making Connections: The Relational Worlds of Adolescent Girls at Emma Willard School* (Cambridge, MA, Harvard University Press).

Giordano, P. (1995) The wider circle of friends in adolescence, *American Journal of Sociology*, 101(3), pp. 661–697.

Griffiths, V. (1995) *Adolescent Girls and Their Friends: A Feminist Ethnography* (Aldershot, UK, Avebury).

Hage, G. (1998) *White Nation: Fantasies of White Supremacy in a Multicultural Society* (Sydney, Pluto Press).

Hartley, R. (1994) Young adults and friendship, *Family Matters*, 39, December, pp. 4–7.

Hey, V. (1997) *The Company Site Keeps: An Ethnography of 'Girls' Friendship* (Buckingham, UK, Open University Press).

Hickey, C., Fitzclarence, L. and Matthews, R. (Eds) (1998) *Where the Boys Are? Gender sport and masculinity* (Deakin Centre for Education, Deakin University, Geelong).

Kenway, J. and Kelly, P. (2000) Local/global labour markets and the restructuring of gender, schooling and work, in: N. Stromquist and K. Monkham (Eds) *Globalisation and Education* (Lanham, MD, Rowman and Littlefield).

Leckie, B. (1997) Girls' bullying behaviours and peer relationships: the double-edged sword of exclusion and rejection. Paper presented at the annual conference of the Australian Association for Research in Education, Brisbane.

Luke, C. and Carrington, V. (2000) Race matters, *Journal of Intercultural Studies*, 21(1), pp. 5–24.

McLeod, J. (1998) The promise of freedom and the regulation of gender – feminist pedagogy in the 1970s, *Gender and Education*, 10(4), pp. 431–445.

McLeod, J. (2000) Subjectivity and schooling in a longitudinal study of secondary students, *British Journal of Sociology of Education*, 23, pp. 501–521.

McLeod, J. and Yates, L. (1998) How do young people today think about self, work and futures? *Family Matters*, 49, pp. 28–33.

McLeod, J. and Yates, L. (2003) Who is 'us'? Students negotiating discourses of racism and national identification in Australia, *Race, Ethnicity and Education*, 6, pp. 29–49.

McNay, L. (2000) *Gender and Agency; Reconfiguring the Subject in Feminist Social Theory* (Cambridge, Polity Press).

Morton, T. (1997) *Altered Males: The Man Question* (Sydney, Allen and Unwin).

Nilan, P. (1992) Kazzies, DBTs and Tryhards: categorisations of style in adolescent girls' talk, *British Journal of Sociology of Education*, 13(2), pp. 201–214.

Rose, N. (1999) *Powers of Freedom: Reframing Political Thought* (Cambridge, Cambridge University Press).

Spelman, E.V. (1997) The heady political life of compassion, in: M.L. Shanley and U. Naryan (Eds) *Reconstructing Political Theory* (Cambridge, Polity Press).

Stephenson, N., Kippax, S. and Crawford, J. (1996) You and I and she: memory-work and the construction of self, in: S. Wilkinson (Ed.) *Feminist Social Psychologies: International Perspectives* (Buckingham, UK, Open University Press), pp. 182–200.

Taylor, J., McLean, G. and Sullivan, A. (1997) *Between Voice and Silence: Women and Girls, Race and Relationship* (Cambridge, MA, Harvard University Press).

Thomson, R. and Holland, J. (2001) Imagined adulthood: resources, plans and contradictions. Paper presented at the 'Gender and Education' conference, Institute of Education, University of London, 4–6 April.

Thorne, B. (1993) *Gender Play: Girls, Boys and School* (Buckingham, Open University Press).

Tulloch, M. (1995) Gender differences in bullying experiences and attitudes to social relationships in high school students, *Australian Journal of Education*, 39(3), pp. 279–293.

Walkerdine, V. (1988) *Mastery of Reason: Cognitive Development and the Production of Rationality* (London. Routledge).

Yates, L, (2000) Representing 'class' in qualitative research, in: J. McLeod and K. Malone (Eds) *Researching Youth* (Hobart, Australian Clearinghouse on Youth Studies).

Yates, L. and McLeod, J. (1996) And how would you describe yourself? Researcher and researched in a qualitative longitudinal study of secondary school students, *Australian Journal of Education*, 40(1), pp. 88–103.

Yates, L. and McLeod, J. (2000) Social justice and the middle, *Australian Education Researcher*, 27(3), pp. 59–77.

CHAPTER 17

UNEASY HYBRIDS

Psychosocial aspects of becoming educationally successful for working-class young women

Helen Lucey, June Melody and Valerie Walkerdine,
Gender and Education, 15, 3, 2003

That young women today can 'have it all' is an idea that had its seeds sown in the 1960s but really took root and established itself in the 1980s. It has turned out to be a particularly seductive and tenacious idea, surviving in the face of strong feminist critique and overwhelming evidence that shows the persistence of gendered inequalities. Nevertheless, from the power-dressed female executive of the 1980s, through the kick-ass and clever 'girl power' of the millennial years, modern stories of transformed contemporary femininity have, in some quarters, been unrelentingly celebratory. Discourses of endless possibility for *all* girls circulate freely, although tempered and regulated by the kind of meritocratic principles that can explain any failure to 'achieve' and to 'have' as a personal one.

Drawing on the longitudinal study *Project 4:21 Transitions to Womanhood*, which focused on two groups of girls, both born in the 1970s and studied over a 17-year period, this chapter will concentrate on two of those 'success' stories of the 1990s – two working-class young women who, though coming from families where there was no history of educational achievement, nevertheless did well in school and gained enough examinations to study on undergraduate courses (for a full analysis see Walkerdine *et al.*, 2001). This process of educational success and of social mobility involves crossing borders of social class, gender and ethnicity, of negotiation between competing subjectivities as other spaces, other possibilities are opened up.

We examine the notion of hybridity, as put forward by cultural theorists in relation to new forms of ethnic subjectivities (Bhabha, 1984; Gilroy, 1993; Hall, 1993), and argue that while it is a useful concept in exploring more fully the multiple layers of experience of subjects in a context of shifting economic and social relations and adds another dimension to theories of fragmentation (Bradley, 1996), there are, however, no easy hybrids. We demonstrate how the uneasiness of hybridity in terms of social mobility through educational achievement for young women from the working classes stems partly from the difficulties of negotiating the emotions, negative as well as positive, that are aroused when aspiration and success mean becoming and being profoundly different to your family and peer group.

Even though working-class and black families have often been negatively implicated in the educational failure of their children, we do not want to abstract these young women from their families (Walkerdine and Lucey, 1989). The challenge for us is to refute those models whose explanatory power lies in pathologising any family practices not immediately recognisable as middle class and instead work towards theorisations which are able to take on board the significance of family practices in a different way. [. . .]

Unquestioned in contemporary social and educational policy is the notion that upward social mobility is the desired outcome of social improvement. This is an implicit assumption that runs through all variations of the discourse of 'social capital' embraced by New Labour (Coleman, 1988; Fukuyama, 1999; Putnam, 2000). However, discourses of social mobility and social capital tend to hold denials: of the losses that are fundamental to and unavoidable in change, even when those changes are desired; of the enormous amount of psychological work involved in transformation; and of the costs of that work. However, these inherent tensions are not commented on in policy debates (Thomson *et al.*, 2003). This silence/absence in the discourse creates obstacles to exploring the ways in which the hybridisation of working-class feminine subjects through educational success, with its promise of social mobility, can provoke as many difficult feelings in families, such as anxiety and ambivalence, as it can positive ones, such as pride, excitement and love. By refusing to pay attention to them we are in danger of denying crucial aspects of our experience (Tokarczyk and Fay, 1995; Reay, 1997; Plummer, 2000). We wish to stress here that anxiety, ambivalence and the psychic mechanisms developed to defend against them are by no means the sole province of the working classes, and we have discussed their powerful articulation and effects in professional middle-class families elsewhere (Lucey and Reay, 2000, 2002; Walkerdine *et al.*, 2001). We should not be afraid to look at the darker side of our experience, to confront the shadows cast by ambivalence. We will therefore explore some of the emotional dynamics in the working-class girls' families that have helped to sustain their success; the kinds of psychic defences that are produced to deal with difficult and contradictory feelings that educational success and failure so acutely, though often unconsciously, provoke for working-class people.

Hybridity

The concept of 'hybridity' was first developed to identify and understand new patterns of ethnic identity in a 'post-colonial' context of globalisation, shifting forms of international relations and processes of migration (Bhabha, 1984, 1990, 1996; Gilroy, 1993). Hybrid cultures are transmitted and transformed within new locations and contexts, creating new forms or developing old forms in new ways. In these changing environments we see the emergence of multi-ethnic, multilayered identities; what Modood calls 'hyphenated' 'identities' (Modood, 1992).

Bhabha, who developed the notion of hybridity in relation to conditions of political inequity and oppression, views it as holding positive possibilities. He stresses the constant 'negotiation of discursive doubleness' in hybridity, but is at pains to point out that by 'doubleness' he does not mean the same as binarism or duality. For Bhabha, 'the hybrid strategy or discourse opens up a space of negotiation where power is unequal but its articulation may be equivocal. Such negotiation is neither assimilation nor collaboration' (1996, p. 58) but an opportunity to take up and develop a critical stance towards hierarchy. Closely allied to the concept of hybridity are notions of 'border existences', 'liminality' (Grossberg, 1996, p. 91) and a 'third space' (Bhabha, 1990) to describe and map the existence of the hybrid.

[. . .] Adkins wonders whether hybridity is s good enough concept to capture the complexities of 'current refashionings of gender' (Adkins, 2001, p. 12). In the context of changing work practices, it has been argued that there is a hybridisation and reversal of workplace gender identities (see Adkins, 1995, for a review) where men are required to adopt more 'feminine' attitudes and skills associated with the service industries. Ironically, at the same time, 'These changes involve the performance of new forms of femininity, a distancing from variants traditionally perceived as normative and the adoption of qualities previously viewed as masculine' (Reay, 2001, p. 163). [. . .]

These kinds of transformations in the economy require a new kind of feminine subject – one who is capable of understanding herself as an autonomous agent, the producer of her present and her future, an inventor and constant reinventor of the person she may be or become. Some theorists emphasise the liberating opportunities presented by these shifts; chances for us all to break free from the old constraints of gender, class and community (Giddens, 1991; Beck, 1992). Discourses which describe young women's lives through narratives of 'wanting', 'getting' and 'having' abound, but far fewer accounts are able or willing to engage with the complex losses which the new sociality brings.

The construction and maintenance of a self is a constant struggle 'won only provisionally and always entailing expenditure of considerable amounts of psychological energy' (Frosh, 1991, p. 187). It is clear that for many of the young women of our research the speed of societal change and the instabilities of the social world are turned inward to be experienced as instabilities of the self. This inner turmoil is particularly intense for educationally successful girls and young women. How, then, do working-class girls and young women inhabit the phantasmatic spaces accorded to them of the complex subject positions through which they are regulated? How are they supposed to remake themselves as workers and as women in the new sociality? In particular, how do working-class girls who succeed in education manage to negotiate hybrid subjectivities, or other kinds of self-invention and regulation?

Project 4:21 transitions to womanhood

Project 4:21 is a longitudinal study of two groups of working-class and middle-class girls and young women who were born in the 1970s and who grew up through a turbulent period of British history. One group of 30 middle-class and working-class girls, born in 1972/73, was studied when they were four years old, at home with their mothers and at nursery school (Tizard and Hughes, 1984) and then in school when they were 10 years old (Walkerdine and Lucey, 1989). Another smaller group of girls, born in 1978, also took part in the study when they were six years old. Ten years later we followed up both groups when they were 16 and 21 years old.[1]

Of the 21 working-class young women who took part in the last phase of Project 4:21, only five (27%) had stayed on past compulsory schooling to A level and were applying to study, were already studying or had completed courses of study at higher education level. This was compared to 15 (93%) of the middle-class young women. In the following section we focus on two of these working-class young women: Holly, a 'mixed-race' 21 year-old who lives with her partner and their two children, and Nicky, a single, white 21 year-old. Both lived in large towns within an hour's train journey to London. We are using the particularities of their biographies to highlight not only their uniqueness, but also to pick out and trace the threads of similarity that run through and across the narratives of the educationally successful working-class young women.

Into the family

The inseparability of home and school in the success and failure of working-class children has long been taken as read. Although this is also the case for the production of middle-class educational success, middle-class families are discursively positioned in a positive way and they are not subject to the kind of pathologisations which historically inform regulative and interventionist educational policies aimed at raising the achievement of working-class children (Finch, 1984; David, 1993; Vincent and Warren, 1999). While we wanted to retain the significance of the family in explanations of educational achievement, we felt that we were in danger of becoming trapped by available discourses which we felt to be inadequate on two counts. First, a deficit model underpins conceptions of working-class families. That is, since middle-class children do vastly better in school than working-class children, the everyday practices of working-class families must somehow be lacking that which ensures success in middle-class families. Policies and initiatives designed to improve working-class children's educational performance have focused on precisely those interior spaces of family interaction; spaces that have been inevitably pathologised when set against the obsessively 'normalised' interior family spaces of the middle classes. Furthermore, this serves to push responsibility further and further into the family and away from considerations of sociality (Vincent and Warren, 1999).

Second, existing sociological work which attempts to theories connections between the individual and society (between agency and structure) is limited by an unwillingness to work with the notion of unconscious processes. In addition to this, traditional sociology invests much in an individual/society dualism (Henriques *et al.*, 1997) so that the social and the psychic are understood as twin but opposite poles or forces. The psychoanalytically informed post-structuralism that guides our work assumes what Althusser (1969) called a position of 'absolute interiority' between the subject and the social.

While the educational pathways from primary school to university for the vast majority of the middle-class girls were so smooth and similar it was almost as if they were on educational 'conveyor belts', there were contradictions and anomalies at every turn when we looked at the production of working-class educational success. Although we could not come up with any convenient typologies of the successful working-class girl, we can point to some complex trends in this subgroup. Powerfully present in all of their narratives was the notion of 'independence', and an identification of themselves as 'strong and independent', a self-identification which, throughout their narratives, is closely linked to their parents' struggle and the desire for 'escape'.

Nicky

Nicky, a white working-class 21 year-old young woman, was in the last year of her undergraduate course. She hoped to continue her studies to Master's level. When she was 10 years old Nicky's primary school teacher described her as 'a steady, competent little worker...she's quietly motivated, she's not one of these that makes a great fuss about anything' (Walkerdine and Lucey, 1989). This resonates clearly with the adolescent Nicky, who quietly got on with her work and never made a fuss about being bullied because she did not want to worry her parents and because she wanted 'to try and sort things out for myself'. 'Never asking for anything' and 'never making a fuss' were common themes in these young women's narratives and in their parents' descriptions of them.

Nicky went to a mixed comprehensive which she describes as 'very rough' and which she 'couldn't wait' to leave. After achieving two As, two Bs, four Cs and one D at General Certificate of Secondary Education (GCSE), she went on to study science A levels at the local further education college. Having firmly decided that she wanted to go to university, which she describes as her 'big aim in life', she was also aware that competition was tough and she needed no get good A level results. Feminist accounts have highlighted how even the most basic information about the education system is simply not available to working-class children (Plummer, 2000). Even those young women who were considered 'bright', who were able to apply themselves at school and whose parents wanted them to do well educationally were given little advice on how to move into higher education.

> Well I talked to my parents about it, but my parents never went to college or anything, they finished school early, so. They always wanted me to get a good education, but they weren't able to give much practical advice...I had to make them on my own, and when I actually applied for my university degree, I didn't really know what I wanted to do at the time, apart from science. So I was a bit in the dark.

When Nicky didn't get the grades she needed to get into university she took a year out. This wasn't a gap year characterised by the kind of travel and 'experience' (often through paid or voluntary work overseas) which many of the middle-class young women describe. Instead Nicky took an Open University course to get the entrance qualifications she needed and worked in a shop in order to save enough money so that she would not have to ask her parents for any when she began her undergraduate studies.

Unlike the professional middle-class parents, who have a wealth of knowledge about higher education, as well as providing considerable financial support and stability, the working-class girls know that the only path to university is likely to be a lonely one. For some parents who attempted to provide the kind of continuity between home and school which was so firmly in place in the middle-class families, this meant going back to school themselves. Most working-class parents, however, whose own experiences of schooling were characterised by failure, only felt able to help their children in the early primary school years. It is probably difficult for some to imagine the complex emotions caught up in that relationship, of a parent who feels inadequate to help their child, especially as they progress through education. The parent may feel shame and the child equally shame and anger and pain. This is lived as psychic but it is produced socially and needs to be understood as profoundly psychosocial.

> I mean they've always been there. I knew they would have helped me if they were able to, and they did, sort of, like when I got my prospectus for university, they sat down and went through them with me and I sort of told them what I was looking for, and they tried to help me out that way. But apart from that there wasn't really much practical advice they could give, 'cos they hadn't been in the same situation themselves. They've been good.

Drawing on their longitudinal study of young people, Thomson *et al.* (2003) look at the relationship between resources, location, families, ability and ambition in the educational biographies of working-class young women. They maintain that 'theories of individualisation tend to underplay the importance of relationships and forms of reciprocity and obligation that are embedded within them for understanding the identities and practices in which individuals engage' (p. 44). Working-class girls like Nicky have found great inner resources in order to achieve their goals, but their unwillingness to seek help from parents, to never 'make a fuss about anything' also speaks of a massive psychic defence. Such defences are necessary to cope with the pain of family deprivation and poverty. It is not uncommon for working-class women who have gone through higher education to speak of the fact that their parents went without in order that the children might have something, often continually throughout their childhood (Walkerdine, 1996). [. . .]

Oppositions between play and hard work are not so stark in the middle-class families, where going to university is often a rite of passage that most family members have undertaken. For them, there is an expectation that student life should be both a time of serious study and a youthful sabbatical in which to experience and experiment with the new. In contrast, the working-class young women at or planning to go to university often encountered negative perceptions of students from wider family.

> My uncle... He's very biased about a lot of things and one of them is students so he doesn't believe I do anything at university except go out and get drunk....a lot of people in my family just think I'm playing at things. I'm going nowhere and that I just don't have what it takes to hold down a job. And that has been the view from a few of my uncles and aunts and one or two of my cousins and I've just given up trying to explain it.
>
> (Nicky)

Working-class young women, however, have on some level introjected the notion that students do indeed do what they want, which is usually taken to mean that they do very little. And indeed, the young women are enjoying themselves at university; they are having fun and doing what they want; they do not have the kinds of responsibilities that their parents had when they were the same age, and they are looking forward to a better life than their parents had. Not only this, but there is guilt in the knowledge that their parents are supporting something which is having an unforeseen consequence in pushing them further apart from one another. 'Survival guilt' is a common experience amongst people who have survived a great trauma or genocide, for example, when others died. While the families of these young women have not perished, of course, there is a sense in which their new lives as upwardly mobile women have been produced on the back of the sometimes self-imposed deprivations of their parents.

While parents give the strong message that this better life is exactly what they want for their children, envy is sometimes aroused, an emotion with such negative connotations that few will give voice to it. Nicky's mother says, 'I must admit I get jealous sometimes, you know, and thinking, Cor I wish we'd had the chance to do that when we were younger'. Whether envy and anger are spoken or not, the knowledge that they are being given a chance that their parents (or siblings) never had is embedded in the experience of educational success for working-class children. The recognition that one might be the object of others' envy may not exist on a conscious, rational level, precisely because it is so irrational to think that a parent with whom we share a loving relationship could harbour such negative feelings towards us. However, on an unconscious level, the fear that this envy may cause us to be the target of parents' aggressive feelings continues to operate and may in turn provoke our awn aggression. In an object relations model (Klein, 1959), aggression towards the parent (typically the mother) can be notoriously difficult for the child to express or even acknowledge because of intense fears that the parent will retaliate by an equally aggressive rejection of the child.

Holly

Holly, a mixed-race 21 year-old, had two young children of her own and lived with her partner who was the children's father. For her, being strong and independent and not having to rely on other people is articulated through a powerful identification with her mother, who escaped a violent relationship with their father to bring Holly and her siblings up alone.

> I don't know, I think my mum's like a really strong woman and I think she's made us – like all of us are really strong and independent and we can just stand by ourselves, we don't need anybody else. And I think it's the way she's brought us up, so that we don't need to rely on other people.

The idea for Holly that life is a struggle, that, as her mother told her, 'we're gonna have to work twice as hard as anybody else' because she is 'mixed race', together with a reliance on the self and a strong identification with her mother is the emotional and discursive mix which has driven her educational career. Mirza argues that a preoccupation with subculture, in particular 1980s subcultures of resistance, had a major effect on the study of black women. What emerged in this work was a core romantic idea that young black women were motivated mostly by and through an identification with strong black mothers. For Holly, the overlapping discursive categories of 'strong woman' and 'black woman', while there may indeed be mythical aspects to them (Mirza, 1992), have nevertheless been ones that are complexly meaningful to her. A recurring theme throughout her narrative is her mother's strength in having to do everything for and by herself and she consistently identifies with this. For herself, Holly has constructed a coherent self-identity as a 'strong black mother' even though her own mother is white.

Recent debates on cultural identity have stressed, variously, the fluidity, fragmentation and multiplicity of subjectivity in these postmodern and post-colonial times (Donald and Rattansi, 1992). Post-structuralist and feminist accounts of ethnicity question the fixed binary of black/white in previous models of race and racism, partly by paying attention to the ways in which differences such as those articulated around culture, gender, social class and locality are articulated (Blair and Holland, 1995; Brah, 1996). A further move towards breaking down those dualisms has been the critical examination of white ethnicities (Rattansi, 1993; Back, 1995; Nayak, 2001).

Holly's narrative articulates the uneasy hybrid position of the mixed-race girl, the pain as well as pleasure in the occupation of 'liminal' spaces, the borderlands of black/white where racism is also fluid and breaches boundaries. She was required to walk a very thin and fluid line in relation to her colour identity, particularly when she moved school at age 11. At this time she transferred from a predominantly white primary school where: 'I was getting beaten up, called nigger, coolie you know, and they didn't see me as white at all. 'Cos me and my sister were the only black kids in the whole of the school.' She then moved to a much more racially mixed secondary school, where, in order to fit in, she was required to perform a completely different kind of racial identification.

> I can remember everybody used to call me white girl because I'd grown up in…and we went to an all white school, I'd become like whitified, you know what I mean? So when I started the school I was very white, but they didn't like that because I wasn't being black enough. So then I went for a good few years trying to be as black as I could be, do you know what I mean? Talking in slang and just really hard and beating up white girls just for being white girls you know.

Holly highlights clearly that identifications are rarely straightforward and much more likely to be cross-cut by contradictory dis-identifications. Her shifting subjectivity could only be played out at school, while careful a attempts were made to protect her white mother from her rejection of whiteness. Holly had to perform major feats of binary demarcations: between home and school, black and white, conformity and resistance. For instance, she managed to be both rebellious *and* resistant to the school's culture at a public level, while privately conforming to the demands and discipline of academic work.

> Well I was quite smart actually, because I was doing all this at school, so that's probably why the teachers thought I wouldn't get anything, but then I'd go home and study. So I was having all the fun in the day and then I'd go home and do my work. I wasn't that stupid not to do any work.
>
> (Holly)

These were painful years for Holly, partly because of the ambivalence she clearly held, but was unable to acknowledge, towards her mother as a white woman. Perhaps she was also disowning a part of herself; her own whiteness – no wonder when it is this aspect of her subjectivity that is most problematic to and denied by others: white people only see her blackness and black people want to attack her whiteness:

> but it's a case of if I'm walking down the street, I'm seen as black, I'm not seen as being white, if I'd committed a crime it's just another black person committing the crime. Not a white person, but people can't seem to see that.
>
> And I think also because I was like suffering abuse from black people as well for being part white, so I was like getting it from all directions.

The development of 'racial', ethnic and class identities depends upon processes of inclusion and exclusion:

> the positing of boundaries in relation to who can and cannot belong according to certain parameters which are extremely heterogeneous, ranging from the credentials of being born in the right place, conforming to cultural or other symbolic practices, language, and very centrally behaving in sexually appropriate ways.
>
> (Anthias and Yuval-Davies, 1992, p. 4)

Discussions of hybridisation stress fluidity and the possibilities contained in liminal spaces. What is less explored in those debases, but arises continually in the stories of our subjects, is that the creation of hybrid subjectivities also involves the construction and the constant policing of internal and external 'boundaries', where competing and conflictual people, behaviour, identifications and ideas must be kept apart. Holly kept her hatred of white girls away from her mother, whom she loved, through a series of complex emotional defences such as denial, projection and splitting. Object relations theory suggests ways in which boundaries are constructed, separating the 'good' and the 'bad' (Winnicott, 1957; Klein, 1959), 'the stereotypical representations of others which inform social practices of exclusion and inclusion but which, at the same time, define the self' (Sibley, 1995, p. 5). Internal demarcations are shored up and articulated through the development of external boundaries which help to keep things, people, emotions, activities in their 'proper' place. Psychoanalytically informed approaches, for instance, those drawing on the work of the psychiatrist Franz Fanon, have revealed how racial or ethnic identities are formed in a relational dynamic of power, fear and desire (Fanon, 1969). While we may desperately want to banish troublesome aspects of our own identities, this is no easy task. We are not only deeply attached to them, but also psychologically dependent on them; 'It is for this reason that what is socially peripheral is so frequently symbolically central' (Stallybrass and White, 1986).

> So this process of rejection is not a neat, clinical method of expulsion. Like a shadow cast by a moving figure, the sublimated identity is ever present in the act of subjectivity, operating in the dark margins of the unconscious.
>
> (Nayak, 2001, p. 142)

Belonging and escape

Nicky and Holly both state that they have 'always wanted to go to university'. This desire certainly seems to be connected to their determination to embark and remain on their educational journeys and to actively divert, if not halt, the process of social reproduction. As Nicky says:

> I've always wanted to go to 'uni'. I don't know why. I have to do a bit better for myself. 'Cos a lot of people my own age in my family, a bit younger, a bit older or, all they've done is, well a lot of them have dropped out of school early and gone and got themselves a job that's got absolutely no prospects to it, like working in a Burger Bar or something. And I just did not want that for myself. I couldn't see myself spending the rest of my life stuck in a Burger Bar. I just knew I had to get out and do something a bit better.

It is interesting to note that Holly was the only young woman who was able to sustain her educational career despite twice becoming pregnant in the middle of her studies: she had her first child during her A levels and her second child while she was studying for her first degree. But for Holly who, ironically, was the most highly qualified young woman in the entire sample at this point in her life, the spectre of such poverty and racial pathologisation had in part, at least, provoked and promoted the kind of motivation needed to stay on educational course and not, as she says, 'be another case of another black girl being on social security'.

All of the working-class young women who have done well at school share a fantasy of escape in their drive towards higher education, one which can be closely connected to their parents' explicitly articulated wish for their children to have better lives than they did. One mother says, 'All we want is for our children to do better than we did. I think that's what everyone wants'. Indeed, Holly expresses the same thing when she talks of her own educational career, and hopes for her children when she says she 'just want[s] things to be better for them'. But this is not what everyone wants or needs: it is not a desire articulated by the middle-class parents. For these working-class families, higher education and the possibilities it offers of entrance into a profession represents escape from the grinding facts of ordinary working-class life. These working-class mothers and fathers do not want their daughters to have to do the kinds of work they have to do: boring, repetitive, dirty and hard, with little pay, status or security. As Pilling (1990) suggests, working-class parents' desires and dreams of a better life for their children act as a powerful engine which drives their positive motivation towards education and helps to maintain them on the path to higher education. But the provenance of this motivation means that other, equally powerful messages are transferred in the emotional interchange between working-class parent and child. For the middle-class families, educational success is the theme around which the reproduction of social class position revolves (Walkerdine *et al.*, 2001; Lucey and Reay, 2002). Within this scenario, what is aimed at is to become like your parents in the sense of having the same kind of career as them, the same levels of income, material comfort and lifestyle. For the working-class daughters of aspirational parents, the message is quite different; it is clearly about *not* becoming like them and it is this which is central to both their daughters' drive to higher education and the deep ambivalences which beset some of them. They are, as Caroline Knowles observes in the context of her discussion on 'race, identities and lives', 'caught in the dynamic of belonging and escape' (1999, p. 128).

In order to improve on their parents' lives they have had to differentiate themselves from those who did not or could not improve (Skeggs, 1997, p. 82; Thomson *et al.*, 2003). Wanting something different, something more than your parents, not only implies that there is something wrong with your parents' life, but that there is something wrong with *them*. This kind of dis-identification with one's parents and family can engender a deep sense of shame – itself so shameful that it must be psychically regulated through repressive mechanisms.

Perhaps most importantly, and which we think explains why so many of the working-class young women give up, these dis-identifications with their parents mean that the leaving involved in going to university and perhaps becoming a professional hits on a very deep level. These are separations on a grand scale which the middle-class young women simply do not have to tackle. Of course, psychic separation from parents is an issue for everyone to a greater or lesser extent. But for able working-class girls who do well at school, what is so clearly at stake is the loss of identity, control, status (within the family perhaps), the community, belonging, safety: all major ego losses, any one of which can unconsciously consti- tute a threat to our very survival. Nicky made a very clear and conscious decision to 'get away' to a university far from her home town. Perhaps less conscious was her decision to go to one in a city where there were strong family connections. Her rational choices about which university offered her the best course, had the best reputation, facilities etc. may have been powerfully informed by her unconscious desire to put in place some bridges between her old and new world. Holly, like Nicky, articulates clear, conscious desires for independence and escape, and yet by becoming a teenage mother, not once, but twice, both at crucial junctions on her educational pathway, she did the very thing guaranteed to keep her close to and dependent on her mother. We could therefore view teenage motherhood as a complex attempt to maintain present status in the face of overwhelming change and loss.

Going it alone

As Nicky points out, nobody seems to know anything that can help her and she has no financial resources to fall back on if she gets into debt. In this view, nobody is psychically or economically there to help her: there is no strong bounded autonomous ego (as in the picture painted of the normal middle-class, four year-old, *pace* Walkerdine and Lucey, 1989), but a painful separation which wards off the anger, the pain and loneliness with a defence that she needs no one, can do it all by herself. Actually, underneath all this pain may be a powerful anger that her parents have nothing to give her, or a fear that there is nothing to stop her falling apart other than her 'outer armour' (Trevithick, 1988).

The going alone protects her and them from the pain and the anger. Freud posited that we are all in a state of conflict with our loved ones as we try to reconcile the love we feel for them with our sense of disappointment and resulting anger over their inevitable failings. It is this conflict which lies at the heart of ambivalence and the reason why it can be very hard, even impossible, to accept such a conflict. Unconsciously, we may 'substitute a conflict within themselves for a conflict with the other' (Hoggett, 2001, p. 46). At times like these, when parts of ourselves are at war with other parts, we are clearly not unitary subjects – we may even be actively engaged in a destructive relationship towards other parts. Anger directed against the external world, but which remains unspeakable, is turned upon the self, turned inwards with its full and destructive force, to produce self-denigration, feelings of worthlessness, blame and accusation.

It would be easy to argue that such defences are pathological, and we could muster many a theory to sing a song of inadequate parenting. But in our view, such analyses would be wildly wrong. The defences Nicky and Holly exhibit are the very things that ensure that they get to and succeed in higher education. The double bind is that they may have aspects that are harmful to them emotionally but they are also essential to them practically. Just as it is completely inappropriate to assume that working-class copies of middle-class family practices would make for educational success, so it is equally inappropriate to assume that working-class psychic processes should, in the best of all worlds, mirror those of the middle classes. As Pheterson (1993) argues, systems of domination bring their own defences to dominator and dominated. We might argue further that the kind of dissociation which allows Nicky and Holly to succeed is a way of coping with the terrifying differences in practices, subject positions, modes of discourse, performance and regulation which the two worlds provide. This kind of split and fragmented subjectivity in this analysis is necessary to cross the divide. Whether a new position, that of hybrid, is formed in the process is no simple matter, either psychically or socially. It would be all too easy to suggest that these two worlds that Nicky and Holly keep so defensively apart could be easily integrated for them. This is not to say that they could not be integrated with a great deal of hard emotional work. But to suggest otherwise would be to deny the massive social inequalities which are at their foundation.

Conclusion

Liberal discourses ask, 'what can we do to make working-class children succeed at school?' and focus on pedagogy and practice, of teachers and parents, particularly mothers. The Left is, in the meantime, hooked on theories of reproduction. None of these frameworks can really address how or why some working-class children succeed. The more recent 'conformist' literature on working-class children who do well at school is replete with problems, with the 'conformist' category set up as an opposition to the 'resistance' literature (e.g. Willis, 1977). We are advocating an understanding of working-class girls' success as not a simple conformity at all, but then neither could it be understood as an easy rebellion or resistance. Why some girls would long for something different and be able to make this happen through what is an emotionally and socially terrifying shift while others feel safer staying within the well-understood and maintained practices of school failure is a question which demands to be asked, but is not the question which is usually addressed within the educational literature.

The twin shafts of education and professional status on which many strands of middle-class subjectivity rest mean that the children of the professional middle classes receive strong messages from early childhood that it is their destiny to go to university and become professionals, a destiny which is pushed hard and has its own real constraints and costs (Lucey and Reay, 2002). This is certainly not the destiny of the working-class girls, nor is it presented as such by those who have achieved examination success at school. Is this why so many of them give up, even when they have a relatively sure footing on that path (see Walkerdine *et at.*, 2001)? Because it is not the working-class girls' destiny, the motivation to remain on that path must be generated from within. There are no structural reasons why they should succeed and therefore they have to rely on their own inner resources. However, we also wish to stress that, should that success be achieved by the working-class girl, the hopes and aspirations of her and her parents become intertwined with the pain of separation and therefore loss and shift of identity (Reay, 1997). The girls who have not done so well at school at least do not have to face the difficulties that choice can bring. How, then, do any working-class girls at all succeed in education when they are regulated to be produced as 'docile subjects' who in the present 'government of freedom' must remake themselves as autonomous, reflexive subjects? We argue that the regulation is double-edged. It is precisely the strong boundaries between work and play which are crucial for understanding the production of a subject who is capable of recognising the absolute separation of home and school (Walkerdine, 1991) and coping with it psychically by complex defences. These very inner resources which are necessary to success can also be self-destructive and this contradiction needs to be understood in order to assist children and adults in this transition.

There are no easy hybrids. Hybridity may be a cultural and social fact but it is never lived easily in a psychic economy. Not only are working-class girls who do well at school and go on to higher education moving into intellectual and occupational spheres traditionally seen to be masculine, they are also moving out of their class sphere, beyond the wildest dreams of anyone in their families, into clean, professional, interesting jobs. Just moving into the intellectual domain is a massive shift for them, requiring a complete internal and external 'makeover', where complex unconscious defences, put in place as protection, can also act as 'deep obstacles to the exercise of choice, and to the fulfilment of consciously held goals' (Rustin, 1991, p. 23). It is not just worthwhile but essential to explore these psychosocial processes if we are serious about the project of equality in education. Without a consideration of the psychodynamic processes involved, the deep and enduring failure of the majority of working-class girls and boys will continue unabated.

Note

1   The majority of the young women were white, though there was one Afro-Caribbean, one Asian and one 'mixed-race' young woman in the overall sample. A subsidiary sample of six black and Asian 21 year-old young women was added to the original sample.

References

Adkins, L. (1995) *Gendered Work: Sexuality, Family and the Labour Market* (Buckingham, Open University Press).

Adkins, L. (2001) Cultural feminisation: 'money, sex and power' for (wo)men, *Signs*, 26, pp. 31–57.

Althusser, L. (1969) *For Marx* (London, New Left Books).

Anthias, F. and Yuval-Davies, N. (1992) *Racialized Boundaries: Race, Nation, Gender, Colour and Class and the Anti-Racist Struggle* (London, Routledge).

Back, L. (1995) *New Ethnicities and Urban Culture* (London, UCL Press).

Beck, U. (1992) *Risk Society: Towards a New Modernity* (London, Sage).

Bhabha, H. (1984) The other question: the stereotype and colonial discourse, *Screen*, 24, pp. 18–36.

Bhabha, H. (1990) The third space, in: J. Rutherford (Ed.) *Identity* (London, Lawrence and Wishart).

Bhabha, H. (1996) Cultures in-between, in: S. Hall and P. du Gay (Eds) *Questions of Cultural Identity* (London, Sage).

Blair, M. and Holland, J. (Eds) (1995) *Identity and Diversity* (Clevedon, Multilingual Matters).

Bradley, H. (1996) *Fractured Identities: Changing Patterns if Inequality* (Cambridge, Polity Press).

Brah, A. (1996) *Cartographies of Diaspora: Contesting Identities* (London, Routledge).

Coleman, J. (1988) Social capital in the creation of human capital, *American Journal of Sociology*, 94, pp. 95–120.

David, M.E. (1993) *Parents, Gender and Education Reform* (Cambridge, Polity Press).

Donald, J. and Rattansi, A. (Eds) (1992) *'Race', Culture and Difference* (London, Sage).

Fanon, F. (1969) *Black Skin, White Mask* (Harmondsworth, Penguin).

Finch, J. (1984) *Education as Social Policy* (London, Longman).

Frosh, S. (1991) *Identity Crisis: Modernity, Psychoanalysis and the Self* (London, Macmillan).

Fukuyama, F. (1999) *Trust: The Social Virtues and the Creation of Prosperity* (London, Penguin).

Giddens, A (1991) *Modernity and Self Identity: Self and Society in the Late Modern Age* (Cambridge, Polity Press).

Gilroy, P. (1993) *The Black Atlantic* (London, Verso).

Grossberg, L. (1996) Identity and cultural studies – is that all there is?, in: S. Hall and P. du Gays, *Questions of Cultural Identity* (London, Sage).

Hall, S. (1993) New ethnicities, in: J. Donald and A. Rattansi (Eds) *'Race', Culture and Difference* (London, Sage).

Henriques, J., Hollway, W., Urwin, C., Venn, C. and Walkerdine, V. (1997) *Changing the Subject: Psychology, Social Regulation and Subjectivity*, 2nd edn (London, Routledge).

Hoggett, P. (2001) Agency, rationality and social policy, *Journal of Social Policy*, 30, pp. 37–56.

Klein, M. (1959) Our adult world and its roots in infancy, in: M. Klein, *Envy and Gratitude and Other Works; 1946–1963* (London, Virago Press).

Knowles, C. (1999) Race, identities and lives, *Sociological Review*, 47, pp. 111–135.

Lucey, H. and Reay, D. (2000) Social class and the psyche, *Soundings*, 15, pp. 139–154.

Lucey, H. and Reay, D. (2002) Carrying the beacon of excellence: social class differentiation and anxiety at a time of transition, *Journal of Educational Policy*, 17, pp. 321–336.

Mirza, H. (1992) *Young, Female and Black* (London, Routledge).

Modood, T. (1992) *Not Easy Being British* (Stoke-on-Trent, Trentham Books).

Nayak, A. (2001) Ice white and ordinary, in: B. Francis and C. Skelton (Eds) *Investigating Gender: Contemporary Perspectives in Education* (Buckingham, Open University Press).

Pheterson, G. (1993) Historical and material determinants of psychodynamic development, in: J. Adleman, and G. Enguidanos (Eds) *Racism in the Lives of Women in New York* (New York, Haworth Press).

Pilling, D. (1990) *Escape from Disadvantage* (London, Falmer Press).

Plummer, G. (2000) *Failing Working-class Girls* (Stoke-on-Trent, Trentham Books).

Putnam, R. (2000) *Bowling Alone: The Collapse and Revival of American Community* (Boston, MA, Simon and Schuster).

Rattansi. A. (1993) Changing the subject? Racism, culture and education, in: Donald J. and Rattansi A. (Eds) *'Race', Culture and Difference* (London, Sage).

Reay, D. (1997) The double bind of the working class feminist academic: the success of failure or the failure of success?, in: P. Mahony and C. Zmroczek (Eds) *Class Matters: Working Class Women's Perspectives on Social Class* (London, Taylor and Francis).

Reay, D. (2001) The paradox of contemporary femininities, in: B. Francis and C. Skelton (Eds) *Investigating Gender: Contemporary Perspectives in Education* (Buckingham, Open University Press).

Rustin, M. (1991) *The Good Society and the Inner World: psychoanalysis, politics and culture* (Verso, New York).

Sibley, D. (1995) *Geographies of Exclusion* (London, Routledge).

Skeggs, B. (1997) *Formations of Class and Gender* (London, Sage).

Stallybrass, P. and White, A. (1986) *The Politics and Poetics of Transgression* (London, Methuen).

Thomson, R., Henderson, S. and Holland, J. (2003) Making the most of what you've got? Resources, values and inequalities in young women's transitions to adulthood, *Educational Review*, 55, pp. 33–46.

Tizard, B. and Hughes, M. (1984) *Young Children Learning* (London, Fontana).

Tokarczyk, M. and Fay, E. (Eds) (1995) *Working Class Women in the Academy: Labourers in the Knowledge Factory* (Amherst, MA, University of Massachusetts Press).

Trevithick, P. (1988) Unconsciousness raising with working-class women, in: S. Krzowski and P. Land (Eds) *In Our Experience* (London, The Women's Press).

Vincent, C. and Warren, S. (1999) Becoming a 'better' parent? Motherhood, education and transition, *British Journal of Sociology of Education*, 19, pp. 177–193.

Walkerdine, V. (1991) *Schoolgirl Fictions* (London, Verso).

Walkerdine, V. (1996) *Daddy's Girl: Young Girls and Popular Culture* (London, Macmillan).

Walkerdine, V, and Lucey, H. (1989) *Democracy in the Kitchen: Regulating Mothers and Socialising Daughters* (London, Virago).

Walkerdine, V., Lucey, H. and Melody, J. (2001) *Growing up Girl: Psychosocial Explorations of Gender and Class* (Basingstoke, Palgrave).

Willis, P. (1977) *Learning to Labour* (Farnborough, Saxon House).

Winnicott, D.W. (1957) *The Child and the Family: First Relationships* (London, Tavistock).

CHAPTER 18

NOMADIC SUBJECTS
Young black women in Britain

Maria Tamboukou, Stephen Ball, *Discourse: Studies in the Cultural Politics of Education*, 23, 3, 2002

Introduction

This chapter reads the fragmented life stories of four young black women – Amma, Delisha, Kaliegh and Rena – living in London, at a transitional point of their lives, when they are making decisions about their post-compulsory education.[1]

We think that one of the striking themes of the interviews with these young women is their various attempts to take control of and remake their identities; to resist and escape from pre-formed racial, local and gendered identities with which they were confronted and in which they were positioned within schools, colleges and neighbourhoods. While they are not in any crude sense rejecting their ethnicity, they are rejecting essentialism and seem in some ways 'subjects in transit' (Braidotti, 1994, p. 10). As Britzman (1995) argues, they experience a complex and shifting spectrum of feelings, thoughts, desires and commitments towards social structures within which they must operate, an amalgam of thought and emotion. We will therefore argue that the concept of the nomad, which was first elaborated in the collective texts of Deleuze and Guattari (1983, 1988) is a useful tool to theorize the multifarious ways that these black young women try out places for themselves in the post-compulsory educational terrain and ultimately negotiate subject positions and make life investments. Nomadism, we suggest, is a trail we can follow to explore how these black young women are attempting to 'find the words concepts and ideas, with which to say who they are' (Davies, 1990, p. 345).

[. . .] In such a project of 'appraising concepts as possibilities of future thinking' (Colebrook, 2000, p. 5), the role of the data is both illustrative and as raw material for working upon and thinking about nomadism. Nomadism provides one way of thinking about these stories and we are not suggesting a perfect fit at each point in the discussion between the stories and the concepts in play. We do not use nomadism as a closely defined framework in which to locate these four black young women. What we are attempting to do is to draw a map of connections rather than of localizing points, since in the Deleuzian project to connect is to work with other possibilities, 'making visible problems for which there exists no programme, no plan, no "collective agency"' (Rajchman, 2000, p. 8). Furthermore, we do not want to individualize the individuals. We want to try to move beyond the impulse to represent their actuality. As Rajchman has suggested, we should make the 'passing from a representational to an experimental role, freeing the social imagination from the representation of anything given, prior, original' (2000, p. 101). Rather we take these young women to be 'tellers of experience', whose telling is 'constrained, partial and determined' (Britzman, 1995, p. 232), but prefigurative of discourses and histories.

As it has been argued, 'invention is a creative process in which one of a myriad possible constructions is made out of the stuff available' (Thomas, 1998, p. 146). In this vein, exploring nomadic aspects of subjectivity in the interviews of the young black women is one of a number of possible constructions that can be made using the data of the interviews with them. What the young black women said and did in the interviews is no more and no less than what they said and did (Thomas, 1998, p. 145). The interviews called upon them to give accounts of themselves as moral subjects and called up ideas of themselves that they were cumulatively taking up. The interviews were spaced over a four-year period but remain snapshots of a process of self-making. Moreover, the interviews have invited answers to certain questions which can only make certain configurations in the myriad of possible connections that can emerge from what these young black women think and do about themselves. In employing 'nomadism' to explore the construction of the self of young black women we do not want to make any claim to totality, neither do we have any intention to excavate hidden layers of truth or track down any psychological drives of nomadism. As it has been suggested, 'what is important about nomadism is its ability to stand as a figuration of an *other* mode of thought, not its content as such' (Buchanan, 2000, p. 117). In this light while we will trace nomadic lines in the lives of these young black women, we will not attempt to label them as 'nomads'. Neither do we want to suggest that being a nomad is perhaps an alternative mode of being in postmodernity. We do not intend to replace one kind of essence with another. Far from being advocates of a nomadic existence, we will argue that the notion of nomadic subjectivities is a useful interpretational device – a lens through which the experiences of these young women can be viewed. In looking at fragments of their life trajectories, we move beyond existing analytical frameworks to gain a different view of the unpredictable decisions these young black women make and of the unforeseen directions they seem to take. Having rejected the quest of how 'correct' or 'faithful' nomadism is as a concept, we are exploring instead how it can be used to work out some of the difficulties that arise when dealing with these lives, both in living them and also in thinking about and representing them. We therefore attempt to map the events of the women's thinking, speaking and acting on a different 'plateau' of thought, which, while keeping its connections to existing modes of thought, follows at the same time 'lines of flight' towards other unknown or yet 'unthought' planes. Nomadism we suggest, enables such 'flights' generating questions beyond determinations of identity, essentialism, emancipation and representation. In tracing connections of the theoretical trails of nomadism, we draw on the Foucauldian conception of subjectivities as a set of practices and technologies of the self.[2]

Of nomadic thinking, or to think is to experiment[3]

[. . .] In tracing the various spirals that revolve around the notion of nomadic subjects, Braidotti regards it as 'a suitable theoretical figuration for contemporary subjectivity' (1994, p. 1). Nomadism starts by acknowledging the bodily roots of subjectivity at the same time, however, that it rejects essentialism. As the nominal concept of nomadism suggests, nomadic subjects are subjects in transition. They are not characterized by homelessness, but by their ability to recreate their homes everywhere. 'The nomad has a territory; distributes himself in a smooth space; occupies, inhabits, holds that space' (Deleuze and Guattari, 1988, p. 380). However, this territory, the nomad's home, is a 'smooth', open space, 'one that is indefinite and noncommunicating' (Deleuze and Guattari, 1988, p. 380); it is not 'striated by walls, enclosures and roads between enclosures' (Deleuze and Guattari, 1988, p. 381). Distributed in a smooth space, the nomadic identity is not permanent. It is constituted by continuous shifts and changes, which have their cycles of repetition and recurrence. The nomad is not unified, but is not completely devoid of unity either. The nomad passes through, connects, circulates, moves on; she or he makes connections and keeps coming back: '[she or he] follows customary paths; goes from one place to another; is not ignorant of points...Although these points "determine paths", they are strictly subordinated to the paths they determine' (Deleuze and Guattari, 1988, p. 380). It is, however, in passing between these points that the nomad enjoys the autonomy of an independent, self-directed life. The life of the nomad is the going between, 'the intermezzo' (Deleuze and Guattari, 1988, p. 380). Nomadic subjects cannot be integrated into established social structures, and react critically to the discourses and practices that have set the conditions of their existence in this world. In this light Braidotti sees 'nomadic consciousness as a form of political resistance to hegemonic and exclusionary views of subjectivity' (1994, p. 23) and relates it to the Foucauldian notion of counter-memory that has the possibility of 'enacting a rebellion of subjugated knowledges' (1994, p. 25). It has to be remembered here, however, that resistance is not taken as the reverse of a top-down configuration of power. In the *History of Sexuality*, Foucault defines power as dependent on resistance: 'Where there is power, there is a resistance, and yet, or rather consequently, this resistance is never in a position of exteriority, in relation to power' (1990, p. 95).[4] Foucault has therefore pointed to terrains of local resistance, while Deleuze has used the notion of molecular revolutions (Braidotti, 1991, p. 126), and it is in this context that nomadic consciousness as a form of political resistance is delineated. [. . .]

A first reading of the young women's interviews does not reveal much in the way of such mobile tendencies in any pragmatic sense. On the contrary, the diagram of their lives seems arboreal rather than rhizomatic; these young women seem to be deeply rooted in the context of a triangle that is designated by their family, their local school/college and their community. As suggested by Mann (1998, p. 46), family context and interpersonal relations are often a key feature of how the young women make sense of their lives: 'I chose Hammersmith...My sister went there, and they were doing a scheme for like black students.' This is how Amma explains her choice of a further education (FE) college. What the young women choose, or what they decide to do, typically rests upon the fragmented hearsay and personal recommendations they collect from people around them – family and/or friends. They rely on 'real life' experiences, what Ball and Vincent (1998, p. 434) call 'hot knowledge' rather than the 'systematic' guidance the career officers and teachers are supposed to offer them at school. Family pressures and expectations are particularly evident in choices and decision making. As has been noted in sociological work on careership (Hodkinson and Sparkes, 1997, p. 33), the decisions of the young women are influenced by emotional bonding rather than a simple, rational and systematic examination of what is on, offer and what they want to do. We have, however, the paradox that although the young women seem to be prioritising relationships referring to their family, family support is frequently presented as misleading: 'I think, I should have talked to a lot more people rather than leaning on what my sister said, or what her friends said, you know…I left my choices late and very limited,' admits Amma, in one of her later interviews, as she looks back to the decisions she has already made and regrets her choice.…In making decisions about their lives, the young women seem to circulate in a network of freedoms and limitations. In grappling with a variety of real and/or virtual choices they sometimes respond to 'coercive invitations' (McLaren, 1996, p. 279), but they may also interrogate and even resist the constraints and expectations they confront (as we shall see). The young women are constantly avoiding the simplicities of 'cultural scripts' they voice, regrets about what they have done or might have done with their lives, and are making nomadic choices. They move from one point to another as a pragmatic consequence of not being able to accommodate themselves in striated educational spaces. Their 'careership' is marked by false starts, new beginnings, hiatuses and interruptions. Their decision making is social rather than individual, exploratory rather than definitive.[5]

As it has been noted elsewhere, beyond the family circle young women 'articulate, comprehend and shape their lives in relation to public narratives' (cited in Mann, 1998, p. 46) and populist themes. In doing this, they are sometimes confronted by powerful and seductive racial and gender stereotypes and social conventions. Delisha admires and fears the conventional aspects of family life:

> most of my family…earn a decent wage, they live in a decent house they have got a car, they have got their kids…I don't really want to be doing it but most of my family are secretaries…in the long run that's where it leads, house, car, mortgage, kids.

Rena, who is from a Gujarati family, is contemplating the prospect of an early marriage as likely to block her aspiration of a business career in hairdressing: 'I want a salon but I don't see it actually happening…I don't see my mother-in-law and father-in-law actually letting me do that.' Amma struggles with the idea of a black culture and identity:[6]

> There is a certain kind of stereotype within black people that they think of black people, so to be a black person from one black person's perspective, you listen to R&B music, you wear like kind of clothes, you have your hair a certain way…it is like you are somebody else, you are not really, really black, you know. Really silly, but when I was younger I honestly felt that I wasn't all black.

Amma seems not to recognize, to know herself in terms of the identities and positions available to her within the discursive practices of her immediate collectivities. She would appear to 'speak for herself'; that is, as someone 'who accepts responsibility for their actions, that is as one who is recognizably separate from any particular collective, and thus as one who can be said to be have agency' (Davis, 1990, p. 343). Here, Amma's agency is articulated as her will to become different from what she is or what she is expected to be. Similarly, Kaliegh is struggling towards some sense of identity and purpose over and against ubiquitous racist stereotypes and her experience of life on 'the estates'. This involves her in distancing herself from 'other' black students who are 'not like her'; 'I don't want to be seen in that way.' In Davies's terms, Kaliegh becomes 'agentic' (1990) by attempting to distance herself from her compulsory community. However, this type of 'discursive agency' is parodic, unstable and fragile. It is a shuttle to take her from one point to another, a nomad's tent to shelter her anxieties; it is definitely not the type of a hard core agency that will enable her to permanently recognize herself and her position in the world. Here, there are also some parallels with Fordham's (1996) analysis of the 'liquidating of the black self'. Fordham represents young women like Kaliegh and the others here as engaged in an ultimately pointless ' "pretending" that the social reality they experience everyday is not real' (1996, p. 330). While we would not want to subscribe entirely to Fordham's uncompromising essentialism, it is clear that these young black women are invited to inhabit subject positions that have been created by dominant social structures and hegemonic discourses and they are asked to regulate their own desires and behaviours accordingly. Thus, what first emerges from the interviews are acute feelings of entrapment, both physical and discursive, but there is also a sense of rebellion and agency and there are attempts to distance themselves from conventional identities, which are not as simple nor as pointless as an 'appropriation of the image of (an)other' (Fordham, 1996, p. 330). Rather they appear like moves to the outside of image.

Locating entrapment

One prime striated space within which young women feel confined is their own bodies. Delisha admits that 'I always want to lose weight. Every other week I am on a diet because the clothes look so nice on those models and when you bring them home, I know that they can't make you look like the models.' Rena gets 'really pissed-off' because 'when we go out on Sunday night I can't wear anything as short as that, I haven't got the body for it...I suppose it is my own fault the way I look', but also 'I think why do boys just look at the figure and it annoys me' and 'I don't care what everyone else wears.' McDowell regards the body as the most 'immediate place, location or site of the individual', further arguing that the ways bodies are gazed upon depends on the specific spaces and/or places they are situated (1999, p. 34). Feminist theorists have been particularly concerned with the implications and effects of the diet culture and the various ways they discipline women's bodies.[7] As Rena suggests above, women are expected to take responsibility for their bodily self. Examining the interlocking symptoms of anorexia nervosa and bulimia, Susan Bordo has pointed out that 'these disorders reflect and call our attention to some of the central ills of our culture – from our historical disdain for the body, to our modern fears of loss of control over our futures, to the disquieting meaning of contemporary beauty ideals' (1988, p. 88). It is perhaps interesting here to note how Delisha attempts to surpass the constraints of the 'good-for-models-clothes' by suggesting that 'they should make the clothes a little bit bigger...but still tight'. At this point, Delisha does not altogether reject the female fashion stereotypes, yet she seems willing to depart from some of their strict limitations. While traditional forms of femininity have value for her, she shows an awareness of the 'unbearable heaviness' (no pun intended) of the female image she has to adopt, and suggests alternatives. In a way she attempts to play the system by inflecting the norms that regulate the space a 'beautiful' female body is allowed to occupy, broadening thus her chances of being, if not beautiful, at least 'in the beautiful'.

The young women also convey a sense of entrapment in the ways that they describe their future employment prospects. As noted already, Delisha dreads the idea of 'ending up in one of those office jobs', while she has already embarked on an IT course in a local college though she hates the course and resents her decision of going there: 'I am not enjoying it at all, I hate it.' However, she finds it very difficult to escape the computer career, since this is a 'steady job' which safeguards a 'decent' life. Kaliegh is quite uncertain about the kind of job she will be able to get after finishing at college: 'I don't know what job I can get after... Of course you can be a manager but it's like how are you going to get there.' Kaliegh seems to be convinced that more is involved in getting a good job than simply gathering qualifications: 'You have to work your way to the top, you can't get straight there.' She also knows that not all courses can 'get you a job'. Thus while she 'wouldn't mind being a social worker', she believes that it is not easy to find a job after college. She eventually decided against college and found a job in a newspaper office.

The ambivalence surrounding the women's future employment prospects deeply influences their educational choices. On the one hand, there is the stability of some 'decent' jobs and life patterns that are envisioned by their families rather than the career advisors, who more or less appear to be useless or indifferent: 'I seen the woman [career officer] once and she gave me a list of the colleges. She couldn't even really explain to me what all of them were about. She just gave me a list and that was it basically.' On the other hand, however, there are various fantasies that, although rarely spoken out, shake the existing certainties and destabilize the grounds on which decisions must be taken. Delisha sees her future self engaged to 'a very wealthy man', the 'some day my prince will come' imaginary discourse. This fantasy, however, strangely coexists with plans of becoming a businesswoman and even taking up photography as a career. Delisha forcefully articulates her desire for 'a man', money and artistic creation. She has access to multiple femininities and can imagine herself located in a variety of subject positions. In Davies's (1990, p. 360) terms, she has access 'to recognized/recognizable discursive practices, in which a range of alternative ways of seeing and being are available, such that the positionings one currently finds oneself in are not experienced as inevitable'. Her dreams give a glimpse of the complex ways young women construct various self-images, drawing on a matrix of contradicting discourses (McLaren, 1996). Indeed there is here much movement and interweaving of discourses and contexts. This complexity becomes even more striking if we consider the detail that for Delisha there are also the counter-claims and possibilities of a criminal career: 'I know what is going on... I have seen everything, I have seen every type of illegal thing.' What emerges here is a very different, very dangerous and obviously very transgressive type of nomadism; outside law and correction, a move across the boundaries of 'legitimate' identities. It is from 'the ouside' of the state, 'the neoprimitive tribes of society' that Delisha speaks here, the terrain of 'the local mechanisms of bands, margins, minorities, which continue to affirm the rights of segmentary societies in opposition to the organs of State power' (Deleuze and Guattari, 1988, p. 360). Her 'community' offers both temptation and warning: 'my area... the people I know, the things that I have seen' have influenced her 'not to do the things that they are doing', although she admits that she sometimes succumbs to temptation, rendering the boundaries even more ambiguous. Such a risky and improbable interweaving of patterns of subjectivities is indicative of 'the hesitant voices of participants who [keep] refashioning new identities and investments as they [are] lived and rearranged in language'

(Britzman, 1995, p. 232). As Britzman has further pointed out, these data 'challenge a unitary and coherent narrative about experience' (p. 232).

Thus, the young women appear either indecisive, or unable to 'choose' and they are continuously changing their mind about where to go and what to do. They often interrogate the existence of choices. When she is asked about the choices people of her age have, Kaliegh says,

> I don't think they have a wide choice, it is not even a choice really. It is either one or the other because the other colleges if you went to them then I know you will be coming out with no better marks than you got already. So, I think you have just got a choice of staying on at school really, and St Faith's College or the other one, because the other one is new and it hasn't got a reputation.

The choice in question is neither a sum of subjective intentions, nor the expression of a collective programme. It is rather about an incapacity to choose and perhaps even to think. However, Deleuze and Guattari point to the fact that 'thought operates on the basis of a central breakdown, that it lives solely by its own incapacity to take on form' (Deleuze and Guattari, 1988, p. 378). Therefore not only does Kaliegh not see any real difference among the colleges she can choose from, but, in the light of nomadism, she seems able and prepared to 'recreate her home/school everywhere'. In grappling with real or imaginary choices the young black women are involved in negotiations and they often adopt contradictory strategies as they make choices in the triangle of school–home–friends. Within their narratives, they become nomadic. 'Their language moves backwards and forwards between the perspectives of home and peer group' (Mann, 1998, p. 52), but beyond these is their 'dreaming of elsewhere'. It is here interesting to note that, from the experience of nomadism, the young women occasionally perceive their indecisiveness and their consequent continuous shifts as a negative aspect of their life, as a vice to be avoided. In criticizing the way her friends make their decisions, Kaliegh notes that 'I think they help me because they say what they want to be, and change their minds every minute, and I hear it and say to myself Do I want to be that? and I say No, like that to myself.' Kaliegh seems here to resist the nomadic aspect of her situation. 'Changing her mind every minute' cannot help her settle down and becomes a source of anxiety and ontological insecurity. Organizing some sort of meaningful activity is occasionally necessary, especially when the subject in question is grappling to find a place for herself within a system with clear aims and strategies.

'Struggling to win some space' for themselves, the young women construct scenarios that can accommodate and give coherence to their otherwise fragmentary and contradictory life decisions and actions. These scenarios are made up of a bewildering array of actions and events, which serve to rationalize their actions and attitudes and compose a sustained narrative of themselves. In a way, they 'gain some time and then perhaps denounce or wait' (Deleuze and Guattari, 1988, p. 378). In these narratives they construct accounts of their struggles against expectation. In hers, Delisha, is a complex anti-heroine. She describes how she came to be excluded from her first FE college as a result of an incident in the library: 'Okay, there was a certain incident... I saw her one day in the library and picked up a chair and threw it and it hit her.' She recounts the situation of her HIV girlfriend to explain her celibacy; and the scenario of the boy who 'stopped' her from 'mugging'. What all these scenarios have in common is the emergence of an incident that creates a rupture with her previous way of life and opens up a nomadic passage to a different mode of being.

Nonetheless, the young women feel restricted within the boundaries of their local community, their educational milieu and the surrounding neighbourhood. In this case, entrapment is occasionally expressed as the fear of 'the gaze'. Women's sense of alienation from the everyday spaces of their lives is related to a fear, that they are always watched and evaluated. As it has been argued, this threat of being the object of the other's gaze is of critical importance in the objectification of the female self (Rose, 1993, p. 146). Thus, Kaliegh does not want to stay to the sixth form of her old school: 'I just don't like this school that much. Too many bad people, just because of how people look and everything they just judge you.' Sometimes the frustration of being watched is extended in the social places of the girls' community. Here is Delisha explaining the difficulties she encounters when she goes out dancing: 'If you are walking past a group of girls, yes, especially black girls and you look better than them, they look at you and will watch you all night. It is just them watching you, watching your every move.' What is striking here is that the disciplinary gaze Delisha so forcefully portrays is a female gaze upon female bodies. Delisha's narratives revolve around racial stereotypes. She feels more relaxed when she goes out dancing to places where 'there is more white people', who are themselves 'more relaxed', while 'black people are more tense', particularly boys who 'think that they are too bad'. Amma makes a similar point about her first college: 'Black students really know how to get to each other and they really knew how to get to me...every time I see a lot of black students I feel, "Okay, am I going to be able to learn here?"' Kaliegh is also fearful of the 'racial gaze'. She describes her sister being threatened by other black girls: 'She just said "Well, if you don't like the way I look, why are you looking at me anyway?"....basically when she walked past, snide comments!' Kaliegh does not 'want to go to a school that is all black people because, you know, a lot of them just do not work and we all get a bad name'. Rena talks about how she 'gets the looks from the Asian guys when she is with white students in her college canteen'.

Delisha also speaks of herself within the discursive constraints of gender stereotypes: she describes herself as 'more feminine' now that she has 'calmed down' and is not so 'outspoken' and she explains that she has a lot of male friends, because she feels she cannot bear the continuous intimacy of young women's company:

> women are more bitchy you know. Like with my male friends, I can go about my business. With girls, I could just stay with them all the time and they want to be with you all the time. With boys they are less demanding as friends you know...girls are more dependent.

Like Delisha, Kaliegh admits that 'it is easier to mix with boys than it is with girls'. Rena's narrative is equally enmeshed in racial and gender stereotypes. Although herself Asian, she dislikes Burbley College because 'it is like Asian people that go there' and what she finds particularly problematic is that 'it was really bitchiness between girls'.

There are often fears of confinement within their communities. Kaliegh does not want to go to a college that is 'too close' to where she lives: 'I live in Streetley, I know everyone on the way round and I don't want to know people, I don't want to know too many people, because they will distract me from work. So, if I know people, I end up talking to them in lessons and I wouldn't learn hardly anything.' In the same way, Amma does not want to go to a college with 'too many black people' around her 'sometimes black people you know can stop you from doing your work and it really depends upon the black person'. While entangled herself within racial stereotypes, at this point Amma resists the essentialist connection of blackness with laziness. Thus, she also chooses to distance herself from educational places with 'too many black people', to displace herself. As it has been commented, the nomad in Deleuze and Guattari's texts embodies 'the practice of shifting location, vectors of deterritorialization' (Kaplan, 1996, p. 89).

The young women further feel restricted and entrapped within their local colleges because of gossip and rumours going around about their sexuality. Delisha was in fact expelled from her college after being involved in a violent incident with another girl who was spreading those rumours (as described above), while Rena says that 'I wouldn't go with anyone from college, everyone knows about it and you think bloody hell.' When she hangs out with white girls from her college, which is inevitable because she is the only Asian girl on her hairdressing course, she 'gets the looks from the Asian guys' and feels intimidated.

The stories of these young women can, then, be read within a register and lexicon of entrapment but, we will argue, not merely that. They can also be read as 'escape attempts'. They contain possible ways out, ways of being different, other places in which to be. In other words, the stories are richly contradictory.

Escape attempts: the becoming thought of the young women[8]

For these young women, studying is often considered as an oppression itself (Mann, 1998, p. 55). There are often tensions between 'knowing what they have to do' and actually 'doing it'. Nonetheless, they seem to conceptualize education and information as a route of escape. Rena regards herself as good at what she does but she also admits being lazy and she does not know why. Kaliegh knows that she 'will get higher money for higher qualifications' and that 'whatever I can get good grades in I can always take it further'. Her family are clearly urging her to get more education so as to avoid 'a dead-end job'. This is how Delisha describes her imaginary 'different self': 'I would have studied more, I would have stayed in the first school I went to in the first place.' Distraction and laziness are recurring themes in the young women's narratives which seem to hinder their progress, since they restrict their access to information. [. . .]

Amma blames herself for not being able to get the information she needed to make a 'sensible' decision. She regrets not having widened her circle of informants, because she thinks that talking 'with a lot more people' would have given her more ideas and options. For her, as was the case for the vast majority of students interviewed in the main study (Ball *et al.*, 2000), it is social relations and personal communication, and not some systematic use of the advice of the careers advisor, that can make the difference. She is certainly far less advantaged than Kaliegh, who had the support of both her parents, and especially her mother, in gathering information about the educational options available to her, but who strikingly remains ambivalent about what she wants to do: 'I am not sure whether I want to go there, I might just stay on here.' And later on: 'A levels, I am not sure whether I want to do them any more. I want to do advanced GNVQ or something like that,' and when she is asked about the subjects she wants to do, she simply has not got a clue, but 'it would have to be something I enjoy'. Kaliegh may have been helped by her mother, but she also accepts a great deal of pressure from her, to 'make up her mind', since she is running out of time. However, the young black women sometimes seem to escape the discourse of the possibility of choice and at times see behind the masquerade of the 'wide range of possibilities' the career officers are supposed to present them. Delisha says that she would never go to a career centre because 'they [careers officers] just really draw an outline of what you want to do and you can go to a library and get a book like that instead of making the appointment. They don't really make that much difference.' Sometimes the young women even decide to reject advice altogether and draw on their own resources: 'It is just my own experience and I just build on myself, I don't follow nobody. I make my own choices and it is up to me, if I fail it is up to me, I done it, you know.' The young women's talk is imbued with a strong sense of what (Rose, 1993, p. 400) calls 'responsibilitisation', but this also reflects again Davies's (1990, p. 360) notion of agency, as the young women 'make the relevant choices, carry them through and accept the moral responsibility for doing so'. In making her choices, Delisha becomes here a temporal actor, moving along unstable and shifting positions. Like Lyotard's postmodern subject, she finds herself at 'nodal points of specific communication circuits' (cited in Kaplan, 1996, p. 16) and can therefore be seen as 'a construction of multiple locations':

> A self does not amount to much, but no self is an island; each exists in a fabric of relations, that is now more complex and mobile than ever before...one is always located at a post through which various kinds of messages pass. No one, not even the least privileged among us is ever entirely powerless over the messages that traverse and position [him] at the post of sender, addressee or referent.
>
> (Cited in Kaplan, 1996, p. 16)

In the past, Delisha escaped her gendered identity by becoming a bully at school, although she 'never used to pick on girls, just boys and sixth formers'. Here again, she speaks from 'the exteriority' of what escapes schooling as an organ of the state, mixing as we have already seen with 'tribes wandering or hanging about' (Deleuze and Guattari, 1988, p. 360). Her attitude and her particular choice of boys as her victims are in stark contradiction to her later views about her preference for male friends and her views about women being 'bitchy'. Perhaps, as she moves through adolescence, her gendered identity inflates and absorbs her previous subversive acts. Her thought, coming from a 'body charged with electricity' (Deleuze and Guattari, 1988, p. 378), seems to move to other planes, where she can more easily accommodate the contradictions already arising from the gendered positions she adopts. [. . .]

The young women's narratives suggest that they have internalized contradictory discourses that ultimately constrain their agency in complicated ways. They have also absorbed the thematic structure of the family and their locality, while at the same time knowingly negotiating their way around these themes and discourses. In general the young women are seeking to reconcile their educational choices with contradictions in their lives and at times when social frameworks are highly unstable and constantly shifting. It is therefore not surprising that there are often contradictions in their discourses. Here experience is lived as 'disorderly, discontinuous and chaotic'. At the end of her interview Delisha wishes she *could* change although she started the interview with the assertion that she *has* changed as a person. She describes her family as 'secretaries', only to expose a number of 'delinquencies' among them later on. Kaliegh talks about 'too many options' but 'not even a choice'. As she explains how much she and her sister have been influenced by their mother's hate for Muslims, she reaches a point of utter contradiction where she admits that although she is an anti-Muslim and 'we [she and her sister] go "Oh, we hate them, hate them"', she actually has Muslim friends and ultimately she reaches the conclusion that it all depends on how individual Muslims are brought up by their parents. The young women's identities are built and rebuilt with small and contradictory details (Britzman, 1995, p. 234). They are confident and insecure, certain and ambivalent, goal-oriented and aimless. What is ever present in their identities is the uncertainty of identity and indeed a tendency to move beyond it.

Moving off, becoming a nomad

A feeling of living in existential transit is a theme that occasionally appears in the young women's narratives, especially at the point where they see their school life end and new routes ahead of them. Despite the various difficulties that they experience, this transitional phase at the end of compulsory schooling opens up space for the emergence of imaginary discourses of change: 'It feels great. You know when you can't wait for it to end, you know come on, I have been here for so many years I just want it to hurry up and go.' However, fears of being entrapped again are openly expressed: 'It will be just great to leave, I can't wait, but the thing is I might be coming back.' It is against these fears that Kaliegh's imaginary discourses are articulated. In six months' time she hopes to be 'in a college some-where, that is as far as I know at the moment'. At times the young women seem to oscillate between the fear of the unknown and their wish to leave the local context of their college. Thus, although Kaliegh is not so keen on the idea of staying on in the sixth form of her old school – 'I don't want to stay in this school. I want to meet new people' – she thinks that knowing the teachers is an advantage she will have to bear seriously in mind: 'I think I would learn better from the same teachers.' Money is also a serious hindrance to trying new things, far away from their localities: 'I am going to try and find out where could I go, basically if I wanted to go somewhere further out would I be able to get a grant or whatever,' says Kaliegh considering further opportunities beyond her local sixth form college. All of this is very different from the vivid 'imagined futures' and material security of their middle class counterparts (see Ball *et al.*, 2000). They are constrained by the limits of their imaginations but in a sense are freer in not having to live up to their imaginings as their middle class peers are expected to do (Ball *et al.*, 2000). What remains as 'a consequence', or 'a factual necessity', is that in the end the young black women will have to depart. How they will move in between points of perhaps already established or decided paths is, however, the nomadic experience, which fills them with images of free and autonomous moving.

Space is important in the imaginary discourses of the young women. Speaking about her future college, Amma expresses her interest in the 'physical buildings and the vibes of the place'. Sometimes, however, space, as a place of dreams and possibilities, seems to open up beyond their present educational and local environ-ment. Rena talks about wanting to 'travel and do artistic stuff' – make-up work for Indian films. Amma travelled to the USA for one week, with a dance troupe, as assistant to the producer: 'on the films you see, especially black people you feel a connection…in a way you kind of feel, not that you are going to find your roots, but you are going to find out more about you'. Delisha sees her future in a place of her own, enjoying life and seeing 'nice things'. Travelling is for her part of a 'fantasy future'. It is quite striking that when she talks about her journeys to the Caribbean, she does not regard it as a real displacement, since she has never stayed 'in a hotel'. In Delisha's narrative, the hotel symbolises a place of transit, where stability is shaken, but only temporarily, perhaps as long as the stay itself lasts. Staying in a hotel may also be an indicator of having entered a different kind of lifestyle. Whatever its subtext, the hotel functions here as a transitional place, enabling Delisha to detach herself from home, 'as a place of escape, yet as a home-away-from-home...as a transit-place for women able to use it' (Morris, cited in Wolff, 1995, p. 122). Braidotti has expressed her special attachment to 'places of transit,...in between zones, where all ties are suspended and time stretched to a sort of continuous present' and has further defined them as 'oases of non belonging, spaces of detachment, no (wo)man's land' (1994, pp. 18–19). Braidotti refers here to real places of transit, like stations and airport lounges, which she associates with sources of artistic creation for women. We think, however, that the metaphor of transit can be used to stress women's experiences of existential fluidity in real and/or imagined spaces. As it has been argued, 'the notion of feminine identity as relational, fluid, without clear boundaries seems more congruent with the perpetual mobility of travel than is the presumed solidity and objectivity of masculine identity' (Wolff, 1998, p. 124). On the other hand, in using travel metaphors to explore aspects of female subjectivity, we are aware of Kaplan's (1996) critical comment that the imaginary discourses of travel have been associated with the existential expansion of the white bourgeois Western man. Developing on this line of criticism, Morris has argued that

> there is a very powerful cultural link – one particularly dear to a masculinist tradition inscribing 'home' as the site both of frustrating containment (home as dull) and of truth to be rediscovered (home as real). The stifling home is the place from which the voyage begins and to which, in the end, it returns...The tourist leaving and returning to the blank space of the domus is, and will remain, a sexually in-different 'him'.
>
> (Cited in Wolff, 1995, p. 122)

[. . .] What the young women want to avoid is being stopped or hindered from going beyond the limits of their local communities. As Grossberg (in Wolff, 1995) points out in the opening extract, in taking nomadic positions the young women are attempting to 'win some space' within their local context, but at the same time open up their place and go beyond their locality. The racial and gender stereotypes that fill their narratives are reverberating hegemonic discourses in their culture that the young women use to designate the social setting within which they feel constrained and inhibited. In a Deleuzian sense, the young women somehow want to become 'other' than what they are, and to do this they want to depart from where they are, create a distance between themselves and their surrounding communities, without, however, feeling utterly excluded from where they 'belong'. Amma talks very positively about her second college, which had, compared with her first, a mixed ethnic population: 'I don't know how to explain it, it was just a feeling of "I have found my place", you know.' As Braidotti lucidly notes in the above quotation, being a nomad involves shifting subject positions that allow oneself to be active in one's community without being obliged to accept the conventions of this very community to which one belongs. Being 'in' but not 'of' it, perhaps? Therefore, as it has been indicated, the figure of the nomad can track a path through a seemingly illogical space without succumbing to nation-state and/or bourgeois organization and mastery; the nomad represents a subject position that offers an idealized model of movement based on perpetual displacement (Kaplan, 1996, p. 66). This ability to continually depart from wherever one is creates possibilities for resisting hegemonic discourses that dictate 'the manner of being' you should be because of your gender, race, class, sexual preferences or nationality. Amma, regarded as a failure by her school, is now contemplating going to university; but as she peruses the brochures she looks 'for the kind of cultural, ethnic things they have going on, because...I want to feel comfortable'. The nomads will have to negotiate the terms of their organic connection to their community without fixing themselves anywhere permanently. As noted above they want to 'blur boundaries' rather than 'burn bridges'. By distancing themselves from where they stand they do not want to reject their place, but rather leave it temporarily and open it, and themselves, to new possibilities of being. As Rajchman suggests, it is about how 'to invent an "at home" of a very different kind, no longer given in the opposition of "lived space" to "abstract space" and requiring a different idea of what territories and borders are' (Rajchman, 2000, p. 94). McDowell has used the term 'global localism' to describe the possibility for the openness of place and has suggested that 'For all people...whether geographically stable or mobile, most social relations take place locally, in a place, but a place which is open to ideas and messages, to visitors and migrants, to tastes, foods, goods and experiences to a previously unprecedented extent' (McDowell, 1996, p. 38). Or perhaps this is an example of what Appadurai (1990), Bhabha (1990) and Hall (1991) call a 'third space', a space between 'indoors' and 'outdoors', or between convention and fantasy. In the project of nomadism, learning to be 'at home' in such transitional spaces is 'to see oneself as native prior to the identifying territories of family, clan or nation' (Rajchman, 2000, p. 95), a wandering self in nomadic cycles of one's life.

Therefore, in working with Braidotti's definition of nomadism, as related to the young women here, the idea of rejecting permanency rather than rejecting identity seems useful in cartographing the variety of ways young black women use to construct themselves. The young women, as nomadic subjects, are perhaps struggling against fixity and unity, looking and hoping for some kind of more flexible, dislocated identities. This may mean giving up a sense of a clear and predictable future, of a 'normal biography' (Du Bois-Reymond, 1998, p. 741), of cultural scripts, and accepting uncertainty, instability and risk, and thus fear. This may also relate to what Bourdieu (1986, p. 370) calls a denial of attachment to the local field, an attempt to evade the traces of local classification, 'a sort of dream of local trying, a desperate effort to defy the gravity of the local field'. In this light, the young women are neither 'persons to blame, nor heroes of resistance' (Britzman, 1995, p. 233). Nonetheless, perhaps, we can see them as attempting to speak outside or beyond the positions available within the collectivities to which they belong. They have access to and are able to mobilize a 'different' set of discursive practices (Davies, 1990, p. 991). Seen as a discursive practice, their agency is constructed along three axes: first, as their will to become different from what they are; second, as an attempt to distance themselves from where they belong; and third, as their ability to make specific choices. In other words, they are enabled to speak outside of the positions made available to them within their immediate social collectivities; to 'speak for themselves' and thus take themselves up, 'think' and 'do', differently. The question of agency has here been raised on a Deleuzian plane of thought, 'in terms of minorities, and the manner in which they insert "becomings" into the official histories of majorities' (Rajchman, 2000, p. 121). In exploring their nomadic passages, we have sketched out a cartography of various subject positions that the young black women inhabit, not in a permanent manner, but rather moving around them. We have argued that, in travelling around unstable and contradictory subject positions, these young black women have been trying to recreate patterns of their existence and imagine new relations to the world surrounding them. However, since their travels lack a specific starting or end point, their movement is difficult to trace and it thus remains ambivalent and not quite real.

However, Pfeil has argued that 'just as the vision of the boundlessly dispersed self is caught up within the fear of distortion, the flip side of the ease of "breaking" and "staying open" is the terror of contingency from which all possibilities of eventful significance have been drained' (1988 p. 386). Maybe Braidotti has underplayed this flip side and this is a point we have to consider when we confront the many fears, uncertainties and contradictions to be found in the young black women's narratives, which drive them through continuous shifts and changes that sometimes exhaust them and restrict their 'pragmatic' mobility. Nonetheless, even when they ultimately choose to remain local, they reject essentialism, open their localism to global messages and construct themselves within a culturally and historically specific context. [. . .]

Notes

1 This chapter draws on a study of the post-compulsory experiences of a cohort of young people from an inner London comprehensive school, Northwark Park, and the nearby Pupil Referral Unit (PRU). Pupil Referral Units provide education and support for young people who cannot attend mainstream school; they may be school phobic, they may have been permanently excluded from schooling, etc. The study involved the tracking of a group of 59 students (42 from the school and 17 from the PRU) from their last year of compulsory schooling through three additional years of post-16 education, training and social relations. The cohort was deliberately chosen for its diversity, i.e. ethnicity, class and gender as well as post-16 careers. The local post-16 education market extends over an inner-city/suburban setting based around the Northwark area of London (see Gewirtz *et al.*, 1995) and is defined in terms of the expressed interests and choices of this cohort of Year 11 young people. This local, lived market encompasses several different, small local education authorities (LEAs) that organize their schools' provision in different ways. The main players in the market for these young people are two 11–18 secondary schools, five Further Education (FE) colleges, a tertiary college, a denominational sixth form college and two Technical Educational Colleges (TEC). Three other FE colleges, another sixth form college, and an 11–18 denominational school impinge upon the margins of this market. A sample of the main groups of actors in this market – providers, that is, those offering education, training or employment; intermediaries, that is those offering advice or support, including teachers, careers officers and parents; and consumers or choosers, that is the young people themselves and their families – was interviewed (see Ball *et al.*, 1999a,b; Macrae and Maguire, 1999).

2 In his discussion of ethics, in relation to the formation of the self, Foucault focused his analyses on the 'technologies of the self', a set of practices that 'permit individuals to effect...a certain number of operations on their own bodies, and souls, thoughts and ways of being so as to transform themselves, in order to attain a certain state of happiness, purity, wisdom, perfection or immortality' (Foucault, 1988, p. 18). According to Foucault, these self-technologies were integrated with various types of

attitudes, rendered difficult to recognise and set apart from everyday experiences (Foucault 1990, p. 45).

3   John Rajchman argues that in Deleuzian thought 'to think is to experiment and not, in the first palce to judge' (2000, p. 5).

4   Resistance is immediately bound to freedom as it is unfolded in four different theses in Foucault's thought: first, the understanding that freedom is not the same as liberation; second, the view that freedom is a matter of concrete struggles for situated values; third, a recognition of the historical contingency of freedom; and fourth, the acceptance that there is no necessary end point in the struggle for freedom. (See Tamboukou, 1999, p. 33.)

5   Pignatelli argues that 'agency is an agonistic, daring enterprise marked by uncertainty, resolved and trail' (1993, p. 421).

6   We could note that Foucault's project of freedom rests upon the risks involved in a refusal of 'what we are' (Foucault, 1983, p. 216) – a refusal to base one's actions upon a fixed identity.

7   Bordo notes that 90% of anorexics are women (1988, p. 100).

8   '…the becoming-woman of the thinker, the becoming-thought of the woman' (Deleuze and Guattari, 1988, p. 378).

References

Appadurai, A. (1990) Disjunctive and difference in the global cultural economy, in: M. Featherstone (Ed.) *Global Culture: Nationalism, Globalization and Modernity* (London, Sage).

Ball, S.J. and Vincent, C. (1998) 'I heard it on the grapevine': 'hot' knowledge and school choice, *British Journal of Sociology of Education*, 19(3), pp. 377–400.

Ball, S.J., Macrae, S. and Maguire, M. (1999a) Young lives, diverse choices and imagined futures in an education and training market, *International Journal of Inclusive Education*, 3(3), pp. 195–224.

Ball, S.J., Maguire, M.M. and Macrae, S. (1999b) Young lives at risk in the 'futures' market: some policy concerns from on-going research, in: F. Coffield (Ed.) *Speaking Truth to Power* (Bristol, Policy Press).

Ball, S.J., Maguire, M.M. and Macrae, S. (2000) *Choice, Pathways and Transitions Post-16: New Youth and New Economies in the Global City* (London, Falmer Press).

Bhabha, H.K. (Ed.) (1990) *Nation and Narration* (London, New York, Routledge).

Bordo, S. (1988) Anorexia nervosa: psychopathology as the crystallization of culture, in: I. Diamond and L. Quinby (Eds) *Feminism and Foucault: Reflections on Resistance* (Boston, MA, Northeastern University Press).

Bourdieu, P. (1986) *Distinction: A Social Critique of the Judgement of Taste* (London, Routledge).

Braidotti, R. (1991) *Patterns of Dissonance: A Study of Women in Contemporary Philosophy* (Oxford, Polity Press).

Braidotti, R. (1994) *Nomadic Subjects* (New York, Columbia University Press).

Britzman, D. (1995) 'The question of belief': writing poststructural ethnography, *Qualitative Studies in Education*, 8(3), pp. 229–238.

Buchanan, I. (2000) *Deleuzism, A Metacommentary* (Edinburgh, Edinburgh University Press).

Colebrook, C. (2000) 'Introduction', in: I. Buchanan and C. Colebrook. (Eds) *Deleuze and Feminist Theory* (Edinburgh, Edinburgh University Press).

Davies, B. (1990) Agency as a form of discursive practice. A classroom scene observed, *British Journal of Sociology of Education*, 11(3), pp. 341–361.

Deleuze, G. and Guattari, F. (1983) *Anti-Oedipus: Capitalism and Schizophrenia*, trans. R. Hurley, M. Seem and H.R. Lane (Minneapolis, MN, University of Minnesota Press).

Deleuze, G. and Guattari, F. (1988) *A Thousand Plateaus: Capitalism and Schizophrenia*, trans. B. Massumi (London, Athlone Press).

Du Bois-Reymond, M. (1998) 'I don't want to commit myself yet': young people's life concepts, *Journal of Youth Studies*, 1(1), pp. 63–79.

Fordham, S. (1996) *Blacked Out* (Chicago, IL, University of Chicago Press).

Foucault, M. (1983) On the genealogy of ethics: an overview of work in progress, in: H. Dreyfus and P. Rabinow (Eds) *Michel Foucault: Beyond Structuralism and Hermeneutics* (Chicago, IL, University of Chicago Press).

Foucault, M. (1988) Technologies of the self, in: L. Martin, H. Gutman and P. Hutton (Eds) *Technologies of the Self* (London, Tavistock).

Foucault, M. (1990) *The Care of Self The History of Sexuality*, Vol. 3 (Harmondsworth, Penguin).

Gewirtz, S., Ball, S. and Bowe, R. (1995) *Markets, Choice and Equity in Education* (Buckingham, Open University Press).

Hall, S. (1991) The local and the global: globalisation and ethnicity, in: A. King (Ed.) *Culture, Globalisation and the World-System* (London, Macmillan).

Hodkinson, P. and Sparkes, A. (1997) Careership: a sociological theory of career decision making, *British Journal of Sociology of Education*, 18(1), pp. 29–44.

Kaplan, C. (1996) *Questions of Travel: Postmodern Discourses of Displacement* (London, Duke University Press).

McDowell, L. (1996) Spatializing feminism, geographic perspectives, in: N. Duncan (Ed.) *Body space: Destabilizing Geographies of Gender and Sexuality* (London, Routledge) 28–44.

McDowell, L. (1999) *Gender, Identity and Place: Understanding Feminist Geographies* (Cambridge, Polity Press).

McLaren, A.T. (1996) Coercive invitations: how young women in school make sense of mothering and waged labour, *British Journal of Sociology of Education*, 17(3), pp. 279–298.

Macrae, S. and Maguire, M. (1999) All change, no change: gendered regimes in the post-16 market, in: S. Rlddell & J. Salisbury (Eds) *Gender Equality Policies and Educational Reforms in the United Kingdom* (London, Routledge).

Mann, C. (1998) Adolescent girls reflect on educational choices, in: M. Erben (Ed.) *Biography and Education: A Reader* (London, Falmer Press).

Pignatelli, F. (1993) What can I do? Foucault on freedom and the question of teacher agency, *Educational Theory*, 43(4), pp. 411–432.

Pfeil, F. (1988) Postmodernism as a 'structure of feeling', in; L. Grossburg and C. Nelson (Eds) *Marxism and the Interpretation of Culture* (London, Macmillan).

Rajchman, J. (2000) *The Deleuze Connections* (London, MIT Press).

Rose, G. (1993) *Feminism and Geography. The Limits of Geographical Knowledge* (Cambridge, Polity Press).

Tamboukou, M. (1999) Writing genealogies: an exploration of Foucault's strategies for doing research, *Discourse*, 20(2), pp. 201–218.

Thomas, G. (1998) The myth of rational research, *British Educational Research Journal*, 24(2), pp. 141–161.

Wolff, J. (1995) *Resident Alien: Feminist Cultural Criticism* (Cambridge, Polity Press).

CHAPTER 19

CITIZENSHIP AND THE SELF-MADE GIRL

Anita Harris, *Future Girl: Young Women in the Twenty First Century*, Routledge, 2004

...If youth citizenship is constructed around responsibilities rather than rights, highly managed forms of participation, and consumption, young women are differently and specifically affected by these new constructions. Some young women are seriously marginalized by their inability to secure economic independence, and this in turn prevents them from enacting citizenship. It is more likely to be members of this group who are perceived as a problem for society, who are more at-risk of civic disengagement, and who are depicted as needing guidance and education for social responsibility and participation. They are least likely to have the resources to enjoy the benefits of market choice and consumer citizenship. For others, the transferral of the responsibility for social rights onto the individual has been reasonably unproblematic, as they are able to be supported in all ways by their family and social milieu. This group is most likely to be depicted as showing the way for future models of citizenship, participating in local communities, and forging harmonious intercultural connections. They are also those most able to exercise consumer rights and freedom of choice in the marketplace. Ideas about the can-dos as well as the at-risks thus also operate in the domain of youth citizenship. For both the most disadvantaged and the most privileged, the intertwining of discourses about youth citizenship and individual responsibility is equally powerful, but it has very different effects.

These discourses, which in turn inform policy, may well be out of step with the reality of young women's lives and the possibilities that actually exist for them to enact citizenship. As suggested by political theorists Jet Bussemaker and Rian Voet, "Policy makers are full of good intentions as they relate to preparing girls for full citizenship, but have scant regard for the concrete details with which these girls are confronted in their everyday life."[1] As with labor market success, all young women are depicted as leading the way forward for youth citizenship: they are forging their nations, becoming responsible self-made citizens, and are expected to either lead a revival in youth participation in the polity or make successes of themselves without state intervention. However, this representation both relies upon and conceals deep divisions between young women. In this chapter, I look more closely at these images of young women taking responsibility for social rights, acting as "ambassadresses" and leaders, as the new global citizens, and as those best able to blend consumer choice into citizenship duties. New models of youth citizenship depend upon young women to make real these vastly changed notions of rights, belonging, and participation. However, many young women are excluded from active citizenship at the same time. How can these profoundly different experiences coexist, and what does it mean for the future of young womanhood as the new model for citizenship?

Social rights and the self-made girl

One of the most significant ways young women are invested in is as symbols of economic independence in insecure times. Young women are constructed as those most able to succeed financially during periods of economic uncertainty and change. This kind of economic independence, which does not rely on the state and is bound up with a narrative of self-discipline and motivation, has become the key to a new kind of transition to citizenship for youth. Ironically, it is only when young people are able to give up their expectation that the state will fulfill their social rights that they are admitted to full citizenship. Along with the view that young women are best able to adapt and succeed in a world without economic certainties and safety nets is the idea that they are taking personal responsibility for their social rights and, in fact, will become self-made. This means that they will take the initiative in establishing themselves as financially autonomous. As political theorist Ruth Lister (1997) notes, women have traditionally been excluded from citizenship because they have been denied access to the public sphere and to economic independence. Today, young women are not only encouraged to take their places in the public world of work, but they are also expected to do this through their personal competencies and from a sense of their responsibilities to their social world, rather than through support structures framed around their state-protected rights to financial autonomy. The narrative organizing young women's relationship to citizenship as economic independence is not about social rights to livelihood, but about personal responsibility, self-starting, and not "sponging" off the state or the community. It is this kind of young woman who is held up as the ideal citizen for our times.

Work and the citizen mother

Work and personal responsibility for one's social rights are linked here to young women's capacity to make good choices that will maximize their participation. Young women are constituted primarily as workers in this new formulation, and the work/family balance is a matter for personal negotiation. As Van Drenth (1998) argues, at the same time that young women are expected to have and care for children at some stage, their key responsibility as citizens is to work. The good citizen mother is one who figures out this dilemma herself, through private means of support and in ways that do not involve the state excessively. Motherhood is still a requirement of can-do girls, as long as it is deferred long enough for a good job to be established first. Policies such as the Girls' Memo indicate how citizenship is awarded to young women who will combine work and motherhood in ways that demonstrate a commitment to independent economic standing.

Such policies demonstrate the constitution of what McRobbie describes as

> a population of "good girls" who will do well at school, go on to get good jobs and from then on juggle the demands of home and work alike but with more help from government than has ever been the case in the past.[2]

It is important to note that these "good girls," or what I am describing as "citizen mothers," are entitled to state support in the form of temporary baby bonuses or maternity leave as a reward for appropriate participation in the workforce. Thus it is not the case that motherhood is completely unsupported by the state; rather, it is only women who enact motherhood in the correct ways, that is, juggled with a good job at a later stage in their career, who will be approved of and assisted. As Michelle Fine notes,[3] with US welfare reform, this takes shape in a clever piece of class-inspired ideological reversal: middle-class mothers are told it is important to stay home for the sake of best-practice child rearing, while poor women are required to leave their children with nonexistent day care so they can work menial jobs.

For this reason, it is the young mother who is a bad citizen, in that she threatens to depend on state resources to secure her social rights. On account of her youth, she is unlikely to have established a career for herself prior to having a child, which consequently defies the new citizenship order of things. She can be represented as the exact opposite of the citizen mothers, in spite of considerable evidence that young motherhood increases commitment to education, training, and employment; improves self-esteem and confidence; enhances interest and involvement in civic life; and is better for a woman's and baby's health than a later-life pregnancy.[4] While there are also many difficulties associated with mothering at a young age, most of these are related to poverty.[5] The point is that the values and commitments that are supposedly important in the new citizenship are frequently held by young mothers. The key difference is that the socioeconomic circumstances of many of these young women necessitate government support. This situation does not sit with new efforts to make women responsible for their social rights and for balancing work and family with minimal assistance.

Young mothers problematize the notion that it is necessarily preferable for women to pursue work now and worry about motherhood later. Their presence brings into view the absence of industrial and family policy, as well as appropriate social values, that would enable a real balance between work and parenting. Their difficulties in finding appropriate and satisfying work that can help them fulfill their family responsibilities make apparent that this work may simply not exist. Consequently, young mothers are held up as examples of bad citizens who drain state resources; good girls are those who establish financial independence and become citizen mothers at times and in ways that better suit the state and the economy.

The girl entrepreneur

Another interesting example of this emphasis on making oneself is the phenomenon of the girl entrepreneur. Social theorist Nikolas Rose argues that the concept of "enterprise" has become a rationale for new structures of citizenship, writing that "individuals are to become, as it were, entrepreneurs of themselves, shaping their own lives through the choices they make among the forms of life available to them."[6] For young women, making oneself is also connected to making money for oneself. Entrepreneurship is not simply a metaphor for the choice biographer, but a practical scheme offered to young women to ensure economic self-sufficiency. The girl entrepreneur is the ultimate self-inventing young woman who represents a fantasy of achievement accomplished by good ideas, hard work, and self-confidence. McRobbie suggests that "the coupling of youthful femininity with money and success" has become common. She notes that in popular media, such as magazines, "A favourite feature is...the enormous earning power of a small handful of glamorous young women."[7] This fantasy of young women striking it rich through pluck and determination is supported through the cultivation of entrepreneurship among young women, which in turn contributes to a notion of self-starting citizenship. Susan Hopkins suggests that now, "The empowered female role model is...framed in the language of enterprise and opportunism."[8]

There has been an increase in both government-funded and corporate ventures that aim to get young people, and especially young women, educated for economic autonomy and involved in their communities by developing a commercial idea. Such entrepreneur programs and competitions, very popular in the United States, Canada, and Australia and expanding into the United Kingdom and Europe, generally operate by inviting young women to develop a business idea or plan, for which they can receive start-up funding or undergo the training scheme on offer. Programs have catchy titles such as Independent Means, Girls' Biz, Mind Your Own Business, and Mother and Daughter Entrepreneurs in Teams (MADE-IT). The Australis Self-Made Girl competition, one example of these programs, is an initiative of the teen cosmetics brand Australis, but it is sponsored by three separate government bodies, the Young Women's Christian Association, two young women's magazines, a bank, a tampon brand, and a car company. Like most of the other girl entrepreneur contests, this program aims to encourage and reward young women who are self-starters, who want to make something of themselves, and who can be role models for others. This kind of young woman is held up as an example to others of how they can be whoever they want to be and contribute to their communities. Typically, this involves forging a successful business that guarantees economic independence. [. . .]

The nongovernment United States-based *Girlstart* website, which claims to provide resources to help girls become "smart from the start" with regard to job opportunities, for example, offers a list of inspiring young businesswomen who run their own companies and "do it all." Similarly, three "girl entrepreneurs" who have businesses selling everyday products (earrings, handbags, and lipstick) are highlighted on the US Government Department of Health and Human Services *Girl Power!* website. *Girl Power!* is a national public education campaign that promotes policies to "help encourage and motivate 9–13 year-old girls to make the most of their lives," with entrepreneurship falling clearly within this mission. The US government also emphasizes the importance of introducing girls to entrepreneurship through programs in the Office of Women's Business Ownership.

The can-do qualities of being smart, having power, and making the most of one's abilities and opportunities have become folded into economic self-made success. By implication, any young woman can achieve if she is determined enough. In this respect, the DIY ethic is applied to money-making opportunities but underscores notions of the social rights of citizenship as young women's personal responsibility. [. . .]

Entrepreneur camps for young women aged thirteen to nineteen are another popular way to "empower girls to envision themselves as entrepreneurs," in the words of *Entrepreneur magazine*.[9] NGOs such as the Girl Scouts Association, universities, small businesses, professional associations, private foundations, and government-funded programs all run these kinds of camps. They aim to teach young women how to develop business ideas and plans, how to network, and how to promote their businesses to attract capital. The University of North Florida's camp provides young women with an "etiquette luncheon," a "business fashion show," and a "mocktail party." Columbia College in South Carolina gives campgoers the opportunity to "present a business plan to a panel of real lenders." Independent Means Inc., a private company operating in Australia and the United States, offers girls both Camp Startup and Summer Stock in which to conduct business and investment training. These programs are intended to encourage girls to imagine themselves as adult players in the market, to build their confidence to "do it yourself," to learn about economic independence, and to develop leadership skills. In this we can see notions about good youth citizenship dovetailing with marketization, consumption, and narratives of self-invention.

Thus entrepreneur schemes for young women are not just represented as holiday programs or leisure activities. Embedded within their framework is the construction of young women as makers of their own economic success. Business ventures are no longer the province of the lucky, the well funded, or older men. It is ordinary, determined young women who are the contemporary exemplars of the successful, modern-day entrepreneur. This image is linked back into meanings of youth citizenship both through the implication that social rights are a personal concern and the promotion of young women as those best able to embody the self-starting citizen. Young women are the money makers of the future. It is no surprise that the UK civics education curriculum uses the girls' entrepreneur camps as a prime example of youth citizenship for students to discuss. Nor is it unusual to see the San Francisco think tank, the Institute for Global Futures, imagine the ideal future digital entrepreneur, driving digital capitalism for this century, as a young girl.

Leadership

The proliferation of leadership programs for young women also speaks to the importance placed on them as self-made symbols for new forms of citizenship. While many of these programs draw on the language of self-empowerment and confidence also found in entrepreneurship and self-esteem movements, they are focused on developing young women's leadership abilities for the global good. The notion that girls are the world's future leaders is elaborated through campaigns such as the YWCA's "Power to Change: Commitment to Leadership of Women and Girls," a global fund-raising effort to sustain leadership development of young women. Young women are hereby imagined not only as the future, but as the most appropriate future leaders of a global citizenry. The World YWCA president, Jane Lee Wolfe, claims on the organization's website that "women are the last great resource to be developed."[10] Young women in particular are the focus of this $25 million plan, and Wolfe's resource metaphor alludes to a kind of use value of girls that has been previously unrecognized. At the same time, the opportunity to "give women and girls the chance to learn, lead and change the world" must be more attractive to potential investors than the more mundane and yet enduring issues of young women's more basic needs for health, safety, food, and appropriate work.

Leadership is reduced to the realm of the professional. Becoming a good leader means establishing economic literacy, networking, and discovering one's own power to realize ambitions. Young women are imagined to be constrained by their personal limitations in developing the right skills or taking advantage of opportunities. Once these individual barriers are removed, they will be able to accomplish their aims and become ethical leaders. In this example, *leadership* is fundamentally an equivalent term for *contemporary youth citizenship*. Economic self-sufficiency, self-belief, and role-modeling are all intrinsic to the new ways young women are supposed to position themselves as citizens. . . .

When limitations on young women's success are acknowledged, these are generally depicted as low self-esteem and lack of confidence. Consequently, various programs and strategies exist to encourage them to develop leadership skills and learn about independence. Clubs and community programs for young women sometimes utilize outdoor education, personal empowerment workshops, and "survival camps" to overcome their personal obstacles of low confidence and to encourage them to become leaders in their communities. The significance and purpose of cultivating leadership among young women is linked to their capacity to be good citizens. Young women thus need to be guided into good personal choices, helped to overcome misconceptions about the limits on their options, and taught that they can do anything. In these ways they can then become responsible for their future, lead and integrate their communities, and act as role models for others.

Ambassadress for the nation

Another version of the self-made girl as ideal citizen is the young woman who overcomes adversity and becomes a success through her own efforts alone. An example of this can be found in the representation and celebration of young migrant and refugee women through national awards, media features, and civics lessons. This is what feminist and critical race theorist Sonia Shah describes as "the celebrated immigrant." One illustration of this phenomenon is the Young Australian of the Year competition, won in 1998 by a young woman named Tan Le. The civics curriculum materials developed by Curriculum Corporation for the Department of Education, Science and Training describe her thus:

> She was so clever and hard working at school that she went to university when she was only 16. Since then, Le has worked very hard to help the Vietnamese people of Melbourne, Victoria. She became president of a group that works with immigrants and helps them find jobs.... She is now working to help people do business with Asian countries.[11]

Accompanying media reports detail her childhood experience of escape from Vietnam and arrival in Australia in a fishing boat. This narrative of triumph highlights how self-invention is possible in the most difficult circumstances. It also allays fears about social disintegration due to migration by demonstrating the power of the self-made (refugee) girl to create harmony and social connections (as well as economic growth). Tan Le is smart and disciplined; she is a helper, assisting other immigrants by integrating them into the workforce, and now encouraging "people" (presumably Anglo Australians) with profit-making pursuits in Asia. Not only does this image of the self-made girl citizen draw on a variety of cultural stereotypes about Vietnamese migrants, it also highlights how responsibilities of the state have been devolved onto individuals. Tan Le is rewarded for taking personal responsibility for the social rights of other citizens, for helping them develop business interests, for assisting migrants, and most importantly, for doing it herself.

Self-made citizenship is thus something that young women are idealized as excelling at, in that they are entrepreneurial, act as role models for others, are involved in their communities, and have been responsible for their own success. Significantly, good citizenship is constructed not just by agents of the state, as in the case of Tan Le, but also by private corporations, as we shall see. Young women are leading examples of DIY citizenship, but they are also invested in as key players in comforting narratives of national continuity in times of change, mass movements of people around the world, and the loosening of traditional social bonds within communities.

Girl soldiers

One of the more literal ways young women can perform a defense of the nation is through military activity. Military service in the contemporary context is frequently represented as an experience capturing the key elements of the new young citizen: self-sufficiency, leadership, confidence, responsibility, and fun civic engagement. The debate about young women's participation in the armed forces and acceptance at military academies has been framed primarily as a feminist one. Their integration into this last bastion of male separatism is imagined as the final victory for women's liberation. Indeed, it represents the reversal of some women's status from oppressed victim to empowered liberator in a very interesting manner. Military action has frequently been performed and justified in the name of liberation of an oppressed people, often represented by the status of women. For example, the American campaign in Afghanistan in 2002 and the war in Iraq in 2003 have both been sold in part as missions to liberate people from backward, particularly Muslim, extremism. The most commonly used symbol of this extremism is the burka. With the integration of young women into the armed forces, they are now being invited onto the side of the liberators. It is now their duty to free the women who are still oppressed, who do not have the advantages of personal freedom or the opportunities enjoyed by the can-do girls. In other words, it is the future girls who are best able to liberate those stuck in the past. [. . .]

The US Army slogan is "An army of one," and the Reserve-specific slogan is "Wear a uniform once a month. Be a soldier every day." On the website a head-and-shoulders photo of SPC Sarah Ahrens accompanies this script.[12] She wears a military uniform and gazes out confidently and unsmilingly past the viewer. Her demeanor is at once hopeful, determined, and self-assured. She conveys that she has a job to do and will do it, although her disposition seems fresh and sanguine rather than grim. Her name implies she is not Latina, and her picture suggests that she is not African American, although these populations are overrepresented in the armed forces compared with their percentage in the general population.[13] Beneath this image is the following message:

> When you join the Army Reserve, you're making a commitment not only to your country, but also to yourself. You'll be a stronger person. A better citizen. And the world will see your strength. You'll be an Army of One in the Army Reserve.[14]

This narrative underscores the self-making and self-sufficiency of the can-do girl, as well as appealing to an older American frontier/vigilante discourse. The defense of the nation is at the same time a defense of the individual. Against the common image of the military as an homogenizing and deindividualizing institution, the message here is that the Army Reserve enhances strength of self. Again, we see the devolution onto the individual of responsibility for the public good. By implication, all those who are not reservists are suspect or lesser citizens. The Army Reserve promises to remake the girl self, such that she will "be a soldier every day." In other words she will not be absorbed by the army and thereby lose her identity, but it will become part of her. [. . .]

Multicultural citizenship

Young women have also emerged recently as symbolic defenses against social change created by globalization, migration, civil conflict, and threats to human security. These conditions have triggered uncertainty about national identities, and, in many cases, xenophobic policies and attitudes have flourished as a consequence. As cultural sociologist Nira Yuval-Davis has argued, young women throughout history have been utilized symbolically as the spirit and honor of nations. A quite concrete example of this was the opening ceremony of the 2000 Olympic Games: a theatrical performance of the history and culture of Australia, led by a white, blonde, thirteen-year-old girl.

In recent times young migrant women have taken on a particular role in calming fears about social disintegration caused by war, poverty, and especially migration by personifying an unthreatening blended citizenship. Both Nira Yuval-Davis and psychologist Oliva Espin among others have discussed the ways in which women come to symbolize appropriate "acculturation" – those migrants who are best able to carry the hopes and traditions of their cultures of origin and blend these unproblematically with the values and lifestyle of their new nations. In her book *The Modern Girl* education sociologist Lesley Johnson notes that during the late 1950s a role emerged of the young migrant woman as "ambassadress" for the nation. She analyzes this phenomenon in terms of the meaning of beauty contests at the time. She argues that a young woman's success in these contests, a sign that she had accomplished the making of an appropriate young feminine self, became bound up in the making of nations. This was especially significant in countries such as Australia, which were seeking to manipulate and manage fears about the meaning of migrant populations in the defining of a new, modern social world. Attractive young women were picked out as "typical" representatives of the broader migrant population. Johnson writes that "images of innocent, youthful femininity (the migrant girl) served to defuse the sense of threat, the sense of the foreign as dangerous,"[15] and she shows how these images were circulated via public events such as debutante balls, beauty contests, and sporting meets. For example, the selection of Russian-Australian Tania Verstak as Miss Australia in 1961 and Miss International Beauty in 1962 served to reassure Australia and other "young" nations that migrants were an unthreatening asset who were keen to please. [. . .]

The promotion of certain kinds of young female migrants as ambassadresses captures the construction of good multicultural citizenship in action. The enthusiastic reception of Tania Verstak on the part of the media and social commentators in the early 1960s mirrors the promotion of the Russian-Australian pole vaulter Tatiana Grigorieva during the 2000 Sydney Olympics. In both instances the image of the attractive and charming young migrant woman is considered an excellent embodiment of the nation's values. Both Verstak and Grigorieva symbolized the migrant success story of determination and hard work resulting in internationally recognized achievements. Both were unequivocal about representing their new country, in spite of being first-generation migrants. And significantly, both achieved ambassadorial success through the display of the ideal feminine body, as constructed during each of these eras.

Verstak represented "glamour, poise, a figure correctly proportioned and a charming personality,"[16] and exhibited these qualities through passive display, as a beauty mannequin. Grigorieva, however, personifies contemporary, youthful femininity through active embodiment of a physical self that is not just "to be touched and looked at,"[17] but is powerful, strong and capable. Cultural studies scholar Susan Bordo notes that this change in ideal from a general, soft slenderness to taut slimness is peculiar to our times. Johanna Wyn suggests that today, "Young womes's bodies can also be seen as a form of compulsory performativity," and she notes in particular the importance of the display of a midriff that is toned and therefore controlled.[18] Tattoos and belly-button piercings are popular modes of decorating and highlighting this part of the young female body as a site which has been worked on. Grigorieva represents this shift to an ideal young female body that is toned and trim, with good, but not excessive, muscle definition and very little fat. Her midriff tattoo (a flower), peeking out form the top of her sports briefs, is also a sign of a more assertive female sexuality and is as much an ideal accoutrement for a successful contemporary young woman's body as Verstak's long white gloves were for a previous generation. And just as Verstak's heterosexuality was celebrated with her transformation into Mrs Peter Young,[19] Grigorieva's is assured by her marriage to a fellow Russian immigrant.

The celebration of Verstak and Grigorieva as embodiments of a blended Australianness and as ideal role models for young Australian women occurred within times of significant unrest and uncertainty about youth, gender, and nation. Both the late 1950s and late 1990s saw rising concern about the place of migrants in a "new" Australia. The construction of the good migrant, who worked hard and did not complain, became conflated with both a good femininity and an appropriate national identity. Through the 1990s and into the twenty-first century, more and more cultural groups were drawn into this picture. This is well illustrated by the treatment of migrants from Southeast and East Asia. As people from these regions, predominantly women, become more visible in their protests against labor exploitation – for example, in outsourced "sweat shops" – a new image of the good Asian girl emerged as a symbol for the nation. This also coincided with rising concern in the form of a moral panic about young Asian gangs, drug dealers and users, criminals, and dole (welfare) cheats. The emerging threat of young people of Southeast Asian origin, either first or second generation, who were not grateful, who did not assimilate, and who were becoming politically organized and active was counteracted by strong messages about "good young Asians." The construction of the quiet and studious Asian girl, which had circulated for some time previously,[20] was combined with the added qualities of civic spirit and entrepreneurship to create this image, as we saw earlier in the case of Tan Le. And in 2001 the young "Asian" girl as the ideal Australian citizen was reinforced by the selection of fifteen-year-old Hayley Eves, a young woman of South Korean origin, to make a keynote address, as the representative of Australian youth, at the centennial commemoration of the opening of the Australian Federation Parliament. Eves was described in the media as "young, gorgeous, feisty and political,"[21] her can-do, girl-power qualities clearly enhanced her role as civic representative. Le and Eves serve as powerful counterpoints to "troublesome" young Asian migrants. [. . .]

Young women have been drawn into the defense of national identity, citizenship, migrant assimilation, and human security at a time when all of these concepts appear to be under threat. The construction of the girl as the ideal citizen, ambassadress, or savior/leader of her nation suggests the ways in which new forms of young womanhood are invested in to counter the perceived threats of globalization and migration. Sport, entertainment, and glamor have become important modes by which young women are drawn into allaying fears about the loss of social bonds and homogeneous national identities. Events as benign as the Eurovision Song Contest are opportunities for the performance of comforting narratives about nation, and this is more and more likely to be achieved through such figures as young Swedish women of African origin or Russian-born Latvians. Global citizenship in the hands of girls is gentle entertainment. The World Association of Girls Guides and Girl Scouts recommends the promotion of world citizenship through slide shows about other countries, barbecues with international cuisine, and singing in another language. New toys for girls position them as global citizens; for example, the action figure dolls the Get Real Girls come with passports, travels stamps, postcards, and a digital video journal to record their international adventures. Fears about immigration, multiculturalism, and the disappearance of strong national and cultural borders are quelled by the images of young women as either the unthreatening face of the "other" who only seeks to be accepted and to entertain, or the ethical and caring future leader of a global citizenry. As we shall see next, another complication is that the construction of these self-made girls and ambassadresses blends national and commercial interests in defining contemporary youth citizenship.

Consumer citizens

The third way in which young women are configured as the new citizens is by their representation as smart consumers. As outlined earlier, civil rights have been reconstructed as choices, freedoms, and powers of consumption. Côté and Allahar suggest that "young people are encouraged to narrow their thinking and to focus on issues of personal materialism and consumerism, from which big business is the principal beneficiary."[22] Young women are apparently taking up these freedoms with great gusto. The Australian *Sun-Herald* newspaper article "Girls Just Wanna Shop" reports on market research demonstrating "the marketing power of Australia's latest spenders: self-aware, assertive and consumer-savvy teenage girls." The manager of the market research company who conducted the survey of girls' consumer habits connects self-confidence with consumer power. He is quoted as saying, "We have a teaching environment that has created the knowledge that girls can do it, girls should and they will achieve." This kind of girlpower translates into young women's increased capacity to wield power as consumers, to buy what they like, and to spend their discretionary income on carefully selected products that make a statement about who they are.

Interestingly, the market research company director suggests that this new kind of powerful girl consumer is fundamentally different from her mother's generation, and when she grows older

> there won't be that angst, that self-doubt, that wrestling with the sort of issues that their working or at-home mother are heavily and noticeably debating. It won't even be a factor, it will be "this is my choice, this is what I'm doing."[23]

Although he does not make clear what these issues are, the logical inference is the balance of work and family, with the implication that now that young women have been liberated from lack of confidence, money making and a consumer lifestyle will take precedence. These young women are seen to have effectively solved the problems of their mothers simply by being empowered and decisive, which they have learned about through consumption. Youthful consumption is a way to rehearse the guilt-free making of choices that can then be articulated on a larger scale later in life. Specifically, it helps young women choose to become different kinds of citizens, in fact, the kinds of highly valued citizen mothers discussed earlier.

McRobbie argues that this linking of neoliberal ideologies about individual choice with a distorted kind of feminism serves to reconfigure young women's political agendas "through the seductions of individual success, the lure of female empowerment and the love of money."[24] In short, real capacity to have a voice, to participate, and to make social change is reinvented as the ability to make personal choices about consumer products. Just as entrepreneurship has come to stand in for social rights, so too has consumption become bound up in one's capacity for citizenship in other ways. Hopkins argues that "the new 'power girl' is a role model, a savior and a market niche. Certainly, savvy marketers have recognized and catered to the power of girls and young women as economic agents."[25] [. . .]

Empowerment and consumption are thus closely linked through the associations made between products for young women and being confident, strong, assertive, a leader, a role model, and in charge. Consumption is a shortcut to power. As Jessica Taft argues, in these ways "girls' power is defined only as a power to buy, rather than a power to create, think and to act. As such, it promotes another barrier to girls' expression of social critique and their political and civic participation." This blending of the political aspects of citizenship with one's ability to consume has particular effects for those young women who are shut out of the consumption process due to lack of money. Being unable to participate in the right kinds of consumption processes means one is "at-risk" of engaging in disordered patterns of consumption, thereby being excluded from occupying powerful social positions. As Chris Griffin argues, "The subject position of the consuming girl is not of equivalent relevance for all girls and young women: it is profoundly shaped by class, ethnicity, sexuality and disability."[26] Power, visibility, and the occupation of public space are achieved through shopping, but shopping depends on disposable income and the cultural capital that enables one to engage successfully in consumer practices. This returns us to the new conditions for social rights: Young women are expected to be responsible for their economic independence in an extremely limited labor market and with no help from the state, and the evidence that they have accomplished this goal is in their consumption patterns. Therefore, those who cannot consume are doubly disengaged from citizenship.

It is interesting to note how the self-made girl, the ambassadress, and the consumer citizen all come together in a construction of ideal youthful femininity bound by discourses of self-invention, entrepreneurship, consumption, and success. [. . .] It is not simply that good citizenship and success are achieved for young women by their involvement in marketing consumer products. Rather, they are part of the production of a narrative about young feminine citizenship as a purchasable commodity, as made most real in the act of consumption. Being self-made and motivated, achieving financial success, and representing one's country become bound up in a story about girls' citizenship as product. Makeup, lingerie, sporting goods, fashion, and music are the accessories for citizenship.

The "positive qualities" that these role models represent can in fact be purchased. While consumer choice has become an important way for young women to express themselves, it is only a small minority of young women who have the disposable income to become consumer citizens. [. . .]

Conclusion

In this chapter we have seen how social, political, and civil rights have been reconfigured, such that young women are constructed as personally liable for their economic independence, as exemplars of civic responsibility and unthreatening multiculturalism, and most powerfully as consumers in the marketplace. Narratives of personal responsibility, economic success, and "being the best you can be" are drawn into contemporary modes of young citizenship for all youth, but for girls in particular. In these ways young women are imagined and constructed as the ideal new citizens for a changing world. They are representatives of their nations in times of uncertainty, and they lead the way for new modes of civic life that must manage reconfigured interactions between the state, the market, and communities. They are supposed to take personal responsibility for their social rights and manage the work/family nexus without state support in the form of welfare or policy change. Political engagement takes the form of making consumer choices and modeling self-starting leadership. The neoliberal model of youth citizenship thus merges well with a version of can-do girlhood that emphasizes self-invention, personal responsibility, and individual economic empowerment. This new citizenship delegitimizes other forms of enacting rights such as making demands on the state or participating in political protest. Some young women, such as young mothers, "disordered consumers," or antiracist activists, can thereby be split off from the mainstream of good girl citizens.

Notes

1 Bussemaker and Voet, 1998, p. 8.
2 McRobbie, 2001.
3 Fine, personal communication, 2003.
4 See Fine and Weis, 1998; Probert and MacDonald, 1999; Proweller, 2000.
5 See Phoenix, 1991.
6 Rose, 1990: 226.
7 McRobbie, 2000 (chapter 9 "Sweet Smell of Success? New Ways of Being Young Women"): 211, 213.
8 Hopkins, 2002, p. 94.
9 Cynthia Griffin, 2001.
10 www.worldywca.org/campaign/en/overview/ (Accessed May 2003).
11 Australian Commonwealth Government Department of Education, Science and Training www.curriculum.edu.au/democracy/biographies/tanle.htm (Accessed May 2003).
12 Following the end of the war in Iraq, this image was replaced by one of (a smiling) SPC Jessica Smothers.
13 For example, 39 percent of the U.S. defense forces is made up of minority ethnicities; see Defense Manpower Data Center, 2002.
14 www.goarmyreserve.com/index02.htm (Accessed May 2003).
15 Johnson, 1993, p. 143.
16 Johnson, 1993, p. 137–138.
17 Gilbert and Taylor, 1991, p. 13.
18 Wyn, 2001.

19 Johnson, 1993, p. 141.
20 Kelly, 1986; Matthews, 2002.
21 Schubert, 2001.
22 Côté and Allahar, 1996, p. 134.
23 Cox, 2000.
24 McRobbie, 2000, p. 21.
25 Hopkins, 2002, p. 23.
26 Christine Griffin, 2001.

References

Bordo, Susan (1995) Unbearable Weight: Feminism, *Western Culture and the Body*, Berkeley: University of Califronia Press.

Bussemaker, Jet, and Rian Voet (1998) "Introduction," in Jet Bussemaker and Rian Voet (eds) *Gender, Participation and Citizenship in the Netherlands*, Aldershot, U.K.: Ashgate.

Côté, James E. and Anton L. Allahar (1996) *Generation On Hold: Coming of Age in the Late Twentieth Century*, New York: New York University Press.

Cox, Kate (2000) "Girls Just Wanna Shop," *Sun-Herald* (Sydney), July 16, 14.

Fine, Michelle, personal communication, 2003.

Fine, Michelle, and Lois Weis (1998) *The Unknown City: Lives of Poor and Working-Class Young Adults*, Boston: Beacon Press.

Gilbert, Pam, and Sandra Taylor (1991) *Fashioning the Feminine: Girls, Popular Culture and Schooling*, Sydney: Allen and Unwin.

Griffin, Christine (2001) "Good Girls, Bad Girls: Anglo-Centrism and Diversity in the Constitution of Contemporary Girlhood," unpublished paper presented at *A New Girl Order?* conference, London, Nov. 14–16.

Griffin, Cynthia E. (2001) "Girl School," *Enterpreneur* (June): 32.

Hopkins, Susan (2002) *Girl Heroes: The New Force in Popular Culture*, Sydney: Pluto Press.

Johnson, Lesley (1993) *The Modern Girl: Girlhood and Growing Up*, St. Leonards, Australia: Allen and Unwin.

Kelly, Paula (1986) "The Double-Bind: The Educational Dilemmas of Young Women From Indo-China,' *Youth Studies Australia* 5, no. 2 (Aug.): 24–27.

Lister, Ruth (1997) *Citizenship: Feminist Perspectives*, London: Macmillan.

McRobbie, Angela (2000) *Feminism and Youth Culture*, rev. edn, London: Macmillan.

—— (2001) "Good Girls, Bad Girls? Gemale Success and the New Meritocracy," unpublished keynote address presented at *A New Girl Order?* conference, London, Nov. 14–16.

Matthews, Julie (2002), "Racialised Schooling, 'Ethnic Success' and Asian-Australian Students," *British Journal of Sociology of Education* 23, no. 2: 193–207.

Phoenix, Ann (1991) *Young Mothers?* Oxford: Polity Press.

Probert, Belinda, and Fiona Macdonald (1999) *Young Women: Poles of Experience in Work and Parenting*, Melbourne: Brotherhood of St. Laurence.

Proweller, Amira (2000) "Re-Writing/-Righting Lives: Voices of Pregnant and Parenting Teenagers in an Al-ternative School," in Weis and Fine (eds) Construction Site: *Excavating Race, Class and Gender amongst Urban Youth*, New York: Teachers College Press.

Rose, Nikolas (1990) *Governing the Soul: The Shaping of the Private Self*, London: Routledge.

Schubert, Misha (2001) "Teenager's Vision of a Grown-Up Republic," *The Australian*, May 10, 5.

Shah, Sonia (2001) "The Celebrated Immigrant," *Z Maganine*, April. www.zmag.org (Accessed May 2003).

Taft, Jessica (2001) "Girl Power Politics: Pop Culture Barriers and Organizational Resistance," unpublished paper presented at *A New Girl Order?* conference, London, Nov. 14–16.

Van Drenth, Annemieke (1998) "Citizenship, Participation and the Social Policy on Girls in the Netherlands," in Jet Bussemaker and Rian Voet (eds) *Gender, Participation and Citizenship in the Netherlands*, Aldershot, UK.: Ashgate.

Wyn, Johanna (2001) "What Are Young Women Getting Out of Education? A Perspective on Young Women's Outcomes Ten Years After Leaving School," unpublished paper presented at *New Directions in Feminist Youth Research* conference, Monash University, Clayton, Australia, May 17.

Yuval-Davis, Nira (1992) *Nationalism, Racism and Gender Relations*, The Hague: Institute of Social Studies.

INDEX